W9-DAN-253

HOLY SCRIPTURE

BOOKS BY G. C. BERKOUWER

MODERN UNCERTAINTY AND CHRISTIAN FAITH
RECENT DEVELOPMENTS IN ROMAN CATHOLIC THOUGHT
THE TRIUMPH OF GRACE IN THE THEOLOGY OF KARL BARTH
THE SECOND VATICAN COUNCIL AND THE NEW CATHOLICISM

STUDIES IN DOGMATICS SERIES —

THE PROVIDENCE OF GOD
FAITH AND SANCTIFICATION
FAITH AND JUSTIFICATION
FAITH AND PERSEVERANCE
THE PERSON OF CHRIST
GENERAL REVELATION
DIVINE ELECTION
MAN: THE IMAGE OF GOD
THE WORK OF CHRIST
THE SACRAMENTS
SIN
THE RETURN OF CHRIST
HOLY SCRIPTURE

Studies in Dogmatics

Holy Scripture

BY

G. C. BERKOUWER

PROFESSOR OF SYSTEMATIC THEOLOGY

FREE UNIVERSITY OF AMSTERDAM

WILLIAM B. EERDMANS PUBLISHING COMPANY

GRAND RAPIDS, MICHIGAN

Printed in the United States of America

Translated and edited by Jack B. Rogers
from
the Dutch edition, *De Heilige Schrift,* I and II
published by J. H. Kok N.V., Kampen, The Netherlands,
1966 and 1967

Library of Congress Cataloging in Publication Data

Berkouwer, Gerrit Cornelis, 1903-
Holy Scripture.

(His Studies in dogmatics)
Translation of De Heilige Schrift.
1. Bible — Criticism, interpretation, etc.
2. Bible — Evidences, authority, etc. I. Rogers,
Jack Bartlett, ed. II. Title.
BS518.D8B4713 220.6 74-32237
ISBN 0-8028-3394-2

CONTENTS

ABBREVIATIONS

AT	– Altes Testament, alttestamentliche, etc.
BC	– Belgic Confession
CD	– Barth, *Church Dogmatics*
Enc.	– Kuyper, *Encyclopedie der Heilige Godgeleerdheid*
ET	– English Translation
GD	– Bavinck, *Gereformeerde Dogmatiek*
HC	– Heidelberg Catechism
Inst.	– Calvin, *Institutes of the Christian Religion*
NT	– New Testament, Nieuwe Testament, etc.
OT	– Old Testament, Oude Testament, etc.
Princ.	– Kuyper, *Principles of Sacred Theology*
R.G.G.	– *Die Religion in Geschichte und Gegenwart* (3rd ed.; Tübingen, 1957-63)
TDNT	– Kittel-Friedrich (ed.), *Theological Dictionary of the New Testament*
Z.Th.K.	– *Zeitschrift für Theologie und Kirche*

TRANSLATOR'S INTRODUCTION

This volume represents the combined efforts of many people. Cornelius Lambregtse and John Veenstra had done basic translations of some of the chapters before I came to work on it. I would also like to make special note of the work of Dr. Karl Hanhart in assisting in the translation itself. Others have given me invaluable assistance in making the work more relevant to the English-speaking public, especially by searching out published English translations of material originally cited in other languages. Tom McGrath, Don McKim, Eric Behrens and Jim Richardson have been most helpful in this regard. I trust that this team approach has yielded a better translation; but the responsibility for the final product is entirely mine.

This work has not only been translated but edited. The material of the original two-volume work, *De Heilige Schrift,* has been decreased by approximately one-third. Such editing is always subject to question and the rationale for it needs to be made clear.

My chief concern has been to make Berkouwer's central message regarding the nature of Holy Scripture accessible to the largest English-speaking public. Accordingly, I have concentrated on the development of Berkouwer's own point of view and its immediate sources rather than detailing all of his interaction with persons holding other viewpoints. While this will deprive the scholar of some bibliography, it has hopefully made the main body of this important work more understandable to the non-specialist. Berkouwer has always been concerned that theology be relevant to those in the pulpit and the pew as well as to those in the study. It is my hope that this work will prove useful to members of all three groups in their work and in their daily interaction with Holy Scripture.

JACK B. ROGERS

CHAPTER ONE

HOLY SCRIPTURE AND CERTAINTY

IT WILL PROBABLY SURPRISE NO ONE, particularly in these days, that our reflection on Holy Scripture as the Word of God begins with an introductory chapter on Holy Scripture and the certainty of faith. The relationship between these two has become increasingly central among the many questions that have arisen regarding Holy Scripture and its authority, trustworthiness, and infallibility. Especially since the appearance of historical criticism, it has become an urgent question indeed whether we can still in good conscience confess Holy Scripture as the Word of God, as it was unquestionably confessed for a long time in church history.

Someone might ask, however — without thereby wishing to deny that Holy Scripture has become, in Claus Westermann's words, a "controversial Bible"[1] — whether it is wise in a discussion of the doctrine of Holy Scripture to introduce at the outset the problem of certainty as it is related to questions of the day. Would it not be much more reasonable first of all to deal with Scripture as such, with its inspiration and its attributes, and only afterwards to discuss faith in Scripture, the certainty of faith, and the crisis that can result and indeed has arisen? In fact, must not the latter approach be considered the only legitimate method? Does not a preceding discussion of belief in Scripture and certainty inevitably distort a person's view of the objectivity of Scripture? Can he not be influenced by the contemporary controversy to such an extent that he can hardly find the way to the true nature of Scripture?

In answer to such criticism, one might note that it may be prompted by an incorrect conception of theology, a conception which considers it possible to discuss Holy Scripture apart from a personal relationship of belief in it, as though that alone

1. Westermann, *Our Controversial Bible* (ET, 1969).

would constitute true "objectivity." Moreover, such critics are wrongly afraid that active participation in current discussions of Holy Scripture will inevitably lead to a subjectivism regarding Scripture, for they see involvement and correlation as subjectivism. On the contrary, the pure correlation of faith is decisively determined by the object of faith, namely, God and his Word (I Thess. 1:8: ". . . your faith in God").

To consider first the present controversy — the questions concerning Scripture and certainty — and afterwards the testimony of the Holy Spirit, does not, therefore, imply that Scripture somehow derives its authority from the believer's faith: this idea is already rendered untenable by the very nature of faith, which rests on and trusts in the Word of God. This is evident from the Belgic Confession, which speaks of God's Word in confessing terms.[2] The fact that this confession is now being severely questioned and contested is all the more reason for us to consider from the very beginning a few questions with which everyone who is abreast of his times inevitably comes into contact when reflecting on Scripture. Furthermore, it is impossible to consider the doctrine of Holy Scripture in the abstract, outside the context of the present day, for many current questions and problems face the church as well as individuals. The doctrine of Scripture is by no means shut up in the theologian's study. Its authority presents itself to us with the demand that we "always be prepared to make a defense to any one who calls you to account for the hope that is in you" (I Pet. 3:15). Our account of this hope cannot be separated from our confession that Scripture is the Word of God, a word that also has a future dimension (II Pet. 3:13: "But according to his promise we wait for . . ."). It is understandable that such accounting must be done with a clear conscience (I Pet. 3:16). This points to man's personal life, for there is a close connection between one's personal life and the account which he gives. When responsibly discussing Scripture in an attempt to arrive at the truth about it, we do well to remember that our account must be given "with gentleness and reverence," and that the believer "may not shorten or weaken the gospel, but must accept the entire doctrine."[3]

All this does not mean that the doctrine of Holy Scripture

2. E.g., *BC,* Art. III: "We confess . . ."; Art. V: "We receive . . ."; Art. VII: "We believe. . . ."

3. R. Schnackenburg, *Die Petrusbriefe* (1961), p. 101.

must be expounded as an apologetic;[4] yet it is becoming increasingly difficult to discuss Holy Scripture without considering all the burning questions about the authority of the Bible with which those inside the church are engaged. If Paul's admonition that "any one who thinks that he stands take heed lest he fall" (I Cor. 10:12) applies to one's confession of God's Word and his standing fast in that confession, then one must be on his guard against becoming alienated from that steadfast confession — a process that can set in before one realizes it. This would imply, by the nature of Holy Scripture, an estrangement from the gospel as well. Moreover, it cannot be denied that the church itself has long been occupied with many reorientations in the realm of theology, and finds itself compelled to account for the nature of inspiration, among other things. We are reminded, by way of background, of what is called — even in catechism books — the transition from a more "mechanical" to a more "organic" view of Scripture. It is clear that this too will determine the nature of one's account.

Recent confessional formulations show that we are not merely dealing with a theological interest in the doctrine of Scripture. Scripture has not been given to the church primarily as a study book for "theology" as such. Thus, when the church clearly is concerning itself increasingly with the meaning of its confession regarding Scripture, it indicates a readiness to give an account amidst the many questions concerning the authority of Holy Scripture.

There can be no doubt that for a long time during church history certainty of faith was specifically linked to the trustworthiness of Holy Scripture as the Word of God. Undoubtedly, Herman Bavinck is referring to this when he writes that there is no doctrine "on which there is more unanimity than on that of Holy Scripture."[5] From its earliest days the church held that Scripture is not an imperfect, humanly untrustworthy book of various religious experiences, but one with a peculiar mystery,[6]

4. We may concede an element of truth in Emil Brunner's analysis of "eristic" theology (from *eris*: discord), even though such "polemic" theology must abandon all self-assurance and not be solely directed against others, since it also concerns us, as we must "take every thought captive to obey Christ" (II Cor. 10:5). Cf. E. Brunner, "Die andere Aufgabe der Theologie," *Zwischen den Zeiten* (1929).
5. *Gereformeerde Dogmatiek* (1928), I, 372.
6. Cf. M. Barth, *Conversation with the Bible* (1964), and "The Mystery of the Scriptures" in J. D. Smart, *The Interpretation of Scripture* (1961), p. 17 ("this strange and mysterious quality").

even though the nature of that mystery was often a point of controversy. This position was clearly and decisively based on many statements of Scripture itself, among them the statements that Scripture is God-breathed (II Tim. 3:16), and that men moved by the Holy Spirit *spoke* from God (II Pet. 1:21), a statement that was always considered to have indirect significance for the *written* Word. We are also reminded in the discussion of Scripture of the function of the phrase "it is written" as the final and ultimate appeal of the Lord himself in his temptations (Mt. 4:4, 6, 10), and we are reminded of many statements, both warning and admonishing, "to live according to the scripture" (I Cor. 4:6). Such statements constituted the background of the discussion and the heeding of the Word in the church and of the conviction that Holy Scripture is the trustworthy Word of God. The church realized that these statements drew concrete lines of demarcation, and they remembered John's warning regarding the Apocalypse, that no one was to add to or take away from the words of that prophecy (Rev. 22:18-19).

Seen in this light, it is understandable that any questioning of the authority of Holy Scripture inevitably evoked questions concerning the inviolability of faith, certainty, and the confession of the church. If doubts regarding the *vox Dei* arose here, could not the situation then be compared with the silence of unanswered questions during the days of Israel, when "the word of the Lord was rare" (I Sam. 3:1)? Does uncertainty regarding the *vox Dei* that was heard in Scripture not immediately cripple the knowledge of which the Heidelberg Catechism speaks: we know about the salvation in Christ "from the holy gospel"[7] – a statement that was always viewed in inseparable relationship to Holy Scripture?

A crisis has arisen in the hearts and minds of many people concerning this knowledge and certainty. There is a very close connection between this crisis and the development of the so-called historical criticism of Scripture, which drew attention to the nature of these scriptures as *human* writings. To be sure, the church's confessions had never denied this human element, but with the rise of historical criticism the focus of attention was strongly directed toward the human aspect. It received specific significance for the understanding of Scripture. Often, Scripture was considered human in contrast to the earlier acceptance of its supernatural character: its unique and exceptional

7. *HC*, Q. 19.

origin and nature because of its divine inspiration. Many aspects of this criticism will be considered more extensively later, but at this point it should be indicated that this criticism found its basis in the irrefutable fact that the authors were human. It resulted from opposition to an earlier emphasis on the divine nature of Scripture, which, it was felt, did not do justice to its true nature. This historical criticism did not originate suddenly;[8] rather, it developed through an increasingly growing conviction that men could not continue to speak simply about a divine, extra-special side of Scripture. Further, men could only continue to protest against a gradual "historicizing" of Scripture out of dogmatic prejudice and loyalty.[9] An honest approach to Scripture through historical examination simply had to result in questioning the church's traditional confession that *Sacra Scriptura est Verbum Dei*. For various reasons students of Scripture began to wonder more and more whether Holy Scripture as God's Word was truly beyond all criticism as the indubitable *vox Dei,* as a book — however human — of indisputably divine signature.

It was inevitable that this radical question — and many others implied in it — should have a profound effect upon the life of the church, which until then had unquestioningly accepted the trustworthiness of Holy Scripture. Was it still possible, in view of this criticism in both its more and less radical[10] forms, to rely on the words of Scripture in life and death? Could it still be considered, proclaimed, and recommended as a lamp to our feet and as a light to our path? Was it still possible, not so much in view of a wholly rationalistic criticism of Scripture as in view of the implicating of many related areas (among them, the history of religions), to continue to speak of the uniqueness of Scripture because of its divine inspiration, identifying Scripture with the prophetic word that shines as a "lamp in a dark place until the day dawns and the morning star rises in your

8. A much discussed question is whether historical criticism may not have points of contact in the Reformation, specifically in Luther and Calvin. According to G. Ebeling, this is definitely the case: nineteenth-century Protestantism aligned itself with "the decision of the Reformers in the sixteenth century" (*Word and Faith* [1963], p. 55).
9. B. Lohse, *A Short History of Christian Doctrine* (ET, 1966), p. 225. Lohse speaks of "the problem of historical thinking with all its consequences for the faith and doctrine of the church."
10. Lohse, p. 226, where he speaks of a criticism that was sharper than any that had ever been launched against Scripture by any heresy prior to the eighteenth century.

hearts" (II Pet. 1:19)? In the times of the earlier unproblematical faith in Scripture, reference was made without this consciousness of tension to Paul's urgent statement that the saying about Christ's coming into the world is "worthy of full acceptance" (I Tim. 1:15). In this connection the question arises whether it is perhaps possible, and even legitimate, not to be disturbed by the many questions and criticisms of the historical critics but rather to turn away from them as if they were agents of total de-Christianization that more and more silenced the voice of God.

In answer to this last question, it is not possible to localize the criticism only among those who reject the message of the gospel. On the contrary, not all historical criticism proceeded from the assumption that only human reason had the right to judge the truth. The church was confronted with a concern for the human quality of Holy Scripture on the part of those for whom Scripture nevertheless was very important in preaching and theology, and who could not be accused of hostility toward God or of refusal to submit to his law (cf. Rom. 8:7). Thus, it was confronted with a complex phenomenon, and the questions multiplied, centering around what obedience Scripture implied and must imply. Gradually, all these questions took on an undeniable existential seriousness, for the true nature of listening to the voice of God was at stake.

When Abraham Kuyper came to grips with the criticism of Scripture in his day, he sharply formulated this existential character of the problem. He attacked the criticism of his day "in its questionable effect upon the church of the living God."[11] It is obvious that Kuyper had in mind all forms of radical criticism, for he used terms like "critical vandalism,"[12] "Scripture anatomists,"[13] "recklessness and vivisection."[14] These radical critics of Scripture create distrust and doubt by denying what formerly applied as the standard of faith: "When Scripture has spoken, all contradiction ceases; when it has testified, the last remnant of doubt vanishes."[15] But even though Kuyper is referring particularly to radical criticism, it is clear that the contrast between criticism and authority occupies his mind. The

11. Part of the title of one of his publications (1881).
12. *Ibid.*, p. 43. Kuyper mentions by name only Kuenen in the Netherlands, and elsewhere especially R. Rothe.
13. *Ibid.*
14. *Ibid.*, p. 13.
15. *Ibid.*, p. 15.

logic of criticism is contrasted with a non-critical, receptive listening to the voice of God, like Samuel's "Speak, Lord, for thy servant hears" (I Sam. 3:10). Behind his considerations is a recollection of the relationship between God's Word and the certainty of faith. Only God himself can give us definite and indubitable certainty and place us for time and eternity on an immovable foundation. Much strife and opposition in the church must be viewed in this light, as must the emphasis on the judging but unjudgeable Word of God. The Word must be praised and trusted (see Ps. 56:10-11), as Scripture informs us with its unique divinity and self-authentication.

From Kuyper's rejection of criticism we might conclude that he sees the entire course of historico-critical examination as a delusion that can bear no fruit. But after his sharp rejection of criticism, he says that "the gigantic work performed on Scripture by our present-day critics" is not lost. He is convinced that this work will increase our insight into "the origin of Holy Scripture and the process of its coming into being" and into the time and milieu in which an individual book of the Bible came into being.[16] We are confronted here with an examination of God's Word that inevitably compels a closer reflection. The act of listening and obeying apparently cannot be isolated from a certain examination that leads to understanding. This, however, raises the question of whether historical examination constitutes a threat to the church's faith or contains a possibility for a better understanding of Scripture and consequently better preaching by the church. These questions currently play an important role in theology. Everywhere we observe a desire to remove the dualism between simple faith and biblical science,[17] and the question is asked whether historico-critical study may possibly render the church of Jesus Christ a service. Attention is not demanded for the "humanization" of Scripture in contrast to its formerly accepted authority, but for the possibility of a deeper and clearer understanding of God's message that comes to us in Scripture.

It is of the utmost importance to know whether historico-

16. *Ibid.*, p. 29. Kuyper mentions the "introduction" to Scripture and the "vestibule" of the lower studies (p. 9). His objection is directed against *hypertrophy* (p. 9). According to him, the "historico-critical introductory studies must definitely be continued. . . . I objected only to the excessive proportions to which they are pursued." On the "vestibule," see K. Barth in a preface to *The Epistle to the Romans* (ET, 1968).
17. On this relationship, see H. Diem, *Dogmatics* (ET, 1959).

critical examination can render such a service, and if so, in what respect the result of the studies Kuyper mentions is not a threat but an aid to the acceptance of Scripture's authority in the correct understanding of the message of salvation. For the person who views the dualism between simple faith and biblical science as a real danger, there is the inevitable problem of the function of all questions that come up in the examination of Scripture. What meaning can they have in the light of the obedience that is demanded? Does the correlation of the Word of God and our hearing possibly have a timeless character, lying wholly outside historical development, so that there is no place for questions and problems? Obviously, this question must be answered negatively: we are not dealing with a miraculous voice of God that can be understood and obeyed only through an inner illumination, but with Holy Scripture, which we truly may and must examine.

The tendency to separate our relation to Scripture from every historical insight is understandable because of the fear that our faith may become dependent upon science, and the fear of a historicism that makes Scripture relative and dissolves its authority. But these fears should not cause us to brush aside the questions that arise from the timeless correlation between Scripture and faith. Furthermore, the history of the church would be wholly against such a procedure. An undeniable shifting and development is to be noticed in the understanding of Scripture. This understanding is inexplicable apart from historical development and the extension of the limits of our knowledge.[18] When R. Schippers speaks in this connection of a "technique of listening,"[19] he is not referring to a scientific construction by which the "wise and prudent" have an advantage over the "children." Instead, he means a manner of listening in changed times, times that have acquired much more knowledge regarding the origin and nature of Scripture. To remove all questions and new insights from the minds of the hearers proved impossible; consequently, they were confronted with the important question whether many concepts — listening, obedience, and acceptance — were not now beginning to lose some of their familiar and trusted connotations for many people. These hearers had not paid any attention whatsoever to "questions regarding Scripture" at first, but now, with the popularization of all sorts of results of biblical science, they were confronted with new

18. Bavinck, *GD,* I, 402 ("in recent years").
19. "Biblicisme en fundamentalisme," *Bezinning* (1959).

questions. Chief among these was the question concerning the meaning of *est* in the confession: *Sacra Scriptura est Verbum Dei*. Finally, we understand the significance of these questions when we realize that, amidst our reflection, Paul's warning sounds in our ears: that we ought "not to go beyond the things which are written" (I Cor. 4:6 [ASV]). We can call this limit — which structures one's listening — the focal point of the entire doctrine of Scripture.

When the radical critics concluded from the "human character" of Scripture that they had a right to criticize it — and many of them claimed that an honest historical examination left little or nothing of the nimbus of infallibility, supernaturalness, and uniqueness — their opponents were tempted to present the divine character of Scripture in such a manner that the human character could be of little significance. We can detect in this reaction a desire to depend on the *divine* as opposed to the *human* word. We recall the poet who cried out in his consternation: "All men are liars" (Ps. 116:11 [KJV]), and the words of Paul: "Let God be true, but every man a liar" (Rom. 3:4 [KJV], where Paul refers to Ps. 51:4, after quoting Ps. 116:11). This distinction between God and man plays an important role in many considerations. To be sure, those who used this defense did not do so in order to deny the human character of Scripture,[20] but rather so to cover over the human element by the divine that there was hardly anything relevant left of the human.

It is not surprising in this connection that the problem of Docetism entered rather frequently into the discussions of the doctrine of Scripture. Docetism played an important role in the Christological conflict of the early church, especially in its minimizing of the significance of Christ's being *vere homo*. As a result of this characteristic, the name Docetism was also applied to a doctrine of Scripture that held certain views about the human aspect of Scripture; but this did not explain what significance this human element could have for the correct understanding of the divine authority of Holy Scripture. Even though we must avoid drawing too quick and too easy a parallel between incarnation and inscripturation[21] (we hope to take up

20. R. Preus, in *The Inspiration of Scripture: A Study of the Theology of the Seventeenth-Century Lutheran Dogmaticians* (1955), p. 70, concerning the Lutheran dogmaticians: "They felt no need to emphasize this fact since it was accepted by everyone in their day."

21. M. Barth, *Conversation with the Bible,* Ch. 5, "A Christological Analogy for Two Natures." Barth refers to Origen as the first Christian thinker who concerned himself with this analogy (pp. 146-151).

this matter again in another context), we acknowledge that it is no wonder the participants in this argument were reminded of Docetism. Docetism wished to emphasize particularly Christ's *divinity* and his deliverance, and its emphasis on God's act in Christ wholly obscured his *humanity*. When the church realized the danger of Docetism and attacked the various forms of monophysitism, refusing to view Christ's incarnation as a "manifestation," which would rob the expression *vere homo* of all true meaning,[22] it entered upon a course the consequences of which it certainly could not calculate; nevertheless, it took this course intuitively and consciously on the basis of the biblical testimony.

Whatever we may think of the analogy between the doctrine of Scripture and Christology, a form of Docetism can enter the discussion of the former.[23] This becomes evident in the minimization of the human aspect of Scripture in order to emphasize fully its divine character. Even though it is true that the attack against Docetism can be construed as an effort to "humanize" Scripture — contrary to the Christological teaching of the early church — nevertheless the church's tendency to minimize the human aspect of Scripture must be clearly recognized. The human element of Scripture does not receive the attention it deserves if certainty of faith can only be grounded in the divine testimony, for then it can no longer be maintained that God's Word came to us in the form of human witness.

In this connection, the question frequently arose whether a kind of Docetism possibly lay behind the so-called theory of mechanical inspiration. One must deal carefully with the concept "mechanical." Often, however, it is obvious that mere recognition of a human element does not necessarily guarantee that full justice is done to many aspects of this human element. Sometimes the impression is given that the divine *suggestio verborum* virtually excludes the human side. It is not difficult to discover a concept of competition (between the divine and the human) in which the accent on the divine is subtracted from the fully human writings, and it seems as though where God works and is present the human necessarily begins to fade

22. The church's rejection of even partial Docetism is particularly manifest in the denunciation in A.D. 381 of Apollinarius, who was an outspoken opponent of Arius, and who with Athanasius wished to maintain the confession *vere deus*.

23. See, among others, B. Hägglund, *Die Heilige Schrift und ihre Deutung in der Theologie Joh. Gerhards* (1951), p. 115, on "a definite parallel" between Gerhard's doctrine of Scripture and "enhypostasis Christology."

and disappear. Recently, this idea of competition has diminished in the light of a better understanding that the divine Word does *not* eradicate the outlines of the human testimony but, on the contrary, leaves plenty of room for them.[24] This liberating insight, which can be clearly observed already in Bavinck,[25] shows that Docetism is not opposed by a negative but by a positive determination to do full justice to the Word of God. We may not risk tarnishing the mystery of Scripture by disqualifying the God-ordained way in which it came to us. Moreover, to think that the trustworthiness of Scripture is protected by means of a docetic view of it is to display a totally wrong concept of Scripture. Amidst many dangers, the conviction has gradually become stronger that the human character of Scripture is not an accidental or peripheral condition of the Word of God but something that legitimately deserves our full attention.

It is perfectly clear what Bavinck means by saying that the organic concept of Scripture is frequently applied as a tool to undermine belief in the Spirit's authorship.[26] However, instead of reacting negatively to this, he quite correctly shows that the Holy Spirit "despised nothing human."[27] Thus, he refutes at a decisive juncture the competition and rèciprocal limitation, and goes on to point out what he calls the historical and psychological "mediation" of revelation. Because of this, he says, only in recent years has full light been shed on this matter.[28] He does not see all this as a limitation of or a threat to certainty but, on the contrary, as of the utmost importance for a deeper understanding of Holy Scripture.

The fear that this aspect of the doctrine of Scripture implies a threat to and an historicizing of the authority of Scripture is really the result of an artificial view of revelation. Those who hold such a view deny that shifts and changes in the history of the church can originate from a better understanding of Holy Scripture. They forget that Scripture is written in human words

24. Ebeling, *Theology and Proclamation* (1966), p. 146, n. 9. He correctly says that by obscuring Christ's true humanity "we also undermine our statements about the real divinity, even when the diminution of the humanity occurs as the result of apparently laying too great a stress on the other side."

25. *GD,* I, 402, where he writes about not destroying but establishing and strengthening man's active part. According to him, what Scripture teaches concerning the relation between God and his creatures induces us to assume this regarding the inspiration of Holy Scripture.

26. *Ibid.,* p. 405.

27. *Ibid.,* p. 413.

28. *Ibid.,* p. 402.

and consequently offers men legitimate freedom to examine these words and try to understand them. Moreover, those who hold a docetic view of Scripture can never completely disregard the fact that God's Word has come to us by way of human translations, a fact that cannot be denied.[29] Examining Holy Scripture does not imply a testing of the *vox Dei* by human reason. It is clear that the understanding of Scripture is also determined, by virtue of its nature and substance, by the role that historical development begins to play in the understanding of it. Sometimes earlier "certainties" can gradually turn into uncertainties. This phenomenon can be seen in the trial of Galileo, whose examiners thought that his ideas were "clearly at variance with Holy Scripture."[30] When better insights into this matter later took hold, it did not mean that faith had capitulated to science; rather, it was the result of a changed insight into the nature of Holy Scripture regarding that point. Surely no one today would insist that this was jeopardizing the certainty of faith. Though this well-known example may no longer engage us in a similar tension, its historical seriousness and significance may not be underestimated. We must continue to be alert to the church's realization that its certainty is bound to certain norms and that a feeling of subjective certainty does not guarantee irrefutable certainty. For this reason the church may never refuse the testing of its certainty. It must realize that it is not the certainty, but the truth *in* the certainty that makes us free, and that there is a way of understanding Holy Scripture that does not estrange us from the gospel. Hence, there is every reason to remember the power of God's Word for all times, and the blessing of the Word that is not fettered (II Tim. 2:9).

It would be incorrect to suppose that the problem of the testing of all certainty occurred only in times past. On the contrary, such questions continue to arise even today, and frequent heated discussions on the subject reveal how concerned the

29. See Luther's well-known statement: "Thus if the gospel is dear to us, we must pay great attention to the languages in which it comes. For it was not without purpose that God let the scripture be written in two languages alone, the Old Testament in Hebrew and the New in Greek. . . . And let us realize that we shall scarcely be able to maintain the gospel without languages. Languages are the sheaths in which the knife of the Spirit is contained" (Ebeling, *Luther: An Introduction to His Thought* [ET, 1970], p. 30).

30. See A. Richardson, *The Bible in the Age of Science* (1961), pp. 16-17 on Galileo's battle, not against Scripture, but against the Aristotelian philosophy of nature; cf. Bavinck, *GD,* I, 417.

participants are that certainty is at stake. In our day the consideration of the question of authority has been concretely narrowed down in numerous discussions of fundamentalism, particularly of the fundamentalist view of Scripture and the apologetics implied therein. Fundamentalism, which originated in the United States, had from the beginning a very defensive character, since it considered its calling to be a defense against every liberal and modernistic criticism of Christian tenets (for example, those tenets regarding creation and evolution). Fundamentalists wished to defend the "fundamentals," the objectivity of faith and the central truths of Christianity based on the absolute infallibility and trustworthiness of Holy Scripture.[31] They were motivated by the biblical admonition to "hold fast what you have, so that no one may seize your crown" (Rev. 3:11), and to "guard what has been entrusted to you" (I Tim. 6:20).

Upon closer scrutiny, however, fundamentalism proves to be far from a simple phenomenon. The use of the word "fundamentalism" becomes unclear if it is intended to indicate the necessary preservation of the foundation that results, according to Scripture, in a blessing (I Cor. 3:10-12; Mt. 7:24ff.). Such a use of the term implies that fundamentalism is no more than an echo of the biblical testimony that speaks of the foundation that is laid (I Cor. 3:11), of the value of an anchor of the soul that is sure and steadfast (Heb. 6:19; II Pet. 1:10-21), and that speaks of faith as a substance which also expresses an inviolable certainty (Heb. 11:1 – "the assurance of things hoped for"). This foundation as such, therefore, cannot explain the nature of fundamentalism. To be sure, many expressions from the fundamentalist camp frequently give the impression that the acceptance of a fundamental truth and a certainty that cannot be subjectified are at stake, especially when its members gladly accept the name "fundamentalist" to set them apart from those who have fallen victim to the influence of subjectivism. This, however, terminates the discussion at the point where it actually should begin. Especially concerning the doctrine of Holy Scripture, the fundamentalists' call to a simple and childlike acceptance of Scripture – no matter how seriously they mean

31. For analyses of fundamentalism, see, for instance, *R.G.G.*, II, 3 (Ahlström); cf. *Christlijke Encyclopedie* (N. B. Stonehouse); A. Cole, "Gabriel Hebert on 'Fundamentalism and the Church of God,'" *The Reformed Theological Review* (1958), pp. 11ff.; J. I. Packer, *"Fundamentalism" and the Word of God* (1958); R. J. Jaberg, "Is There Room for Fundamentalists?" *Christianity Today* (1960); E. Walhout, "The Liberal-Fundamentalist Debate," *ibid.* (1963).

this — is not unique to them, because in this respect they are not any different from many others who are equally convinced that God's Word is a lamp to our feet and a light upon our path. The issue is undoubtedly far more complicated, as is already evident from the many analyses of this phenomenon.

Ahlström described fundamentalism as "a fervent but poorly informed protest movement against extreme and militant liberalism."[32] Stonehouse mentions that fundamentalism evidences a lack of sound biblical knowledge and historical perspective and has "certain emphases and peculiarities" that make it impossible to identify it with orthodoxy.[33] This and similar criticism is by no means intended to deny the good intentions of fundamentalism: no good cause is served by making it the butt of "professional gossip." It would be incorrect to ignore its legitimate "wholeness of dedication" in the discussion.[34] The person who concurs in the lamentation of Psalm 11:3 ("If the foundations are destroyed, what can the righteous do?") cannot avoid trying to analyze fundamentalism's apologetics, especially its view of Holy Scripture and its authority.

I believe that I am judging no one unfairly when I say that fundamentalism, in its eagerness to maintain Holy Scripture's divinity, does not fully realize the significance of Holy Scripture as a prophetic-apostolic, and consequently human, testimony. It is true that fundamentalists do not deny the human element in Scripture, but they allow their apologetics to be determined by the fear that emphasis on the human witness may threaten and overshadow Scripture's divinity. From an historical and psychological point of view, this reactionary position is quite understandable in the light of much "humanizing" of Holy Scripture that has taken place. Yet that does not prevent other, more serious, problems from presenting themselves; for it is God's way with and in Scripture that is at stake. Fundamentalism has hardly come to grips with the problem of whether attention for the human character of Holy Scripture might be of great importance for its correct understanding. Fundamentalists often give the impression that the point at issue is the acceptance or rejection of the *vox Dei,* of Scripture's infallibility. They suggest that, in spite of many divergences within fundamentalist circles in understanding Scripture, an *a priori* acceptance of

32. *Op. cit.,* p. 1179.
33. *Op. cit.,* p. 93.
34. Thus, correctly, Jaberg, *op. cit.* What is referred to here is using the word loosely and flippantly, which easily degenerates into name-calling.

Scripture's infallibility precludes all dangers. Thus, they manifest great tolerance for all who maintain the fundamentalist view of Holy Scripture. They tend to relativize concrete obedience in understanding Scripture. The result is that their apologetic, which is meant to safeguard Scripture's divine aspect, threatens in many respects to block the road to a correct understanding of Scripture, which is normative, by ignoring and neglecting its human aspect.

There are indications that some fundamentalists sense this danger; we could, to a certain extent, speak of "the uneasy conscience of modern fundamentalism."[35] Generally speaking, however, their rejection is reactionary because of their fear that the divine nature of revelation will suffer in an overemphasis on its human nature. They feel that reflection on the nature of authority is not without its dangers (we must keep in mind how emphatically Bavinck speaks of this "nature"), for they remember that in human relationships reflection on the nature of authority can be a form of rejection of authority. So, to avoid this pitfall, must they not insist on obedient submission in childlike faith? This seeming appeal to the biblical injunction to obedience, to an undivided attention for the *vox Dei,* is probably the explanation of the hold fundamentalism has had on many who want to follow the path of simple faith amid much criticism. The dilemma suddenly seems very simple: "The Bible is none other than the voice of Him that sitteth upon the Throne."[36]

In answer to Richardson's criticism of J. W. Burgon in the *Chambers Encyclopaedia,* J. I. Packer points out that Burgon (in 1860) rejected the theory of mechanical inspiration, adding that "the method of inspiration is one of the many things I cannot understand." But it is obvious that this does not resolve the real issue; in fact, it does not even approach it. By speaking as he does, Burgon is simply forced to give an explanation of "the method of inspiration" regarding the testimony of Scripture: "Every book of it, every chapter of it, every word of it, every syllable of it, every letter of it, is the direct utterance of the Most High."[37] This statement of his disregards all nuances of Scripture (consider the Psalms, Job, Ecclesiastes), as though

35. The title of a book by Carl F. H. Henry, which, however, does not deal with Scripture but with social concepts.
36. A statement by J. W. Burgon, quoted by J. I. Packer, *Fundamentalism,* p. 180.
37. *Ibid.*

it were a string of divine or supernaturally revealed statements, ignoring the fact that God's Word has passed through humanity and has incorporated its service. The rejection of the theory of dictation as such sheds no light whatsoever on the meaning of the human aspect of Holy Scripture, because just at the crucial moment this aspect is barred from consideration. This results in an isolation of Holy Scripture and a bringing of all parts of it down to the same level.[38] The rejection of this theory is no doubt partly determined by fundamentalism's reaction to all kinds of theories of revelation that deny the presence of any element of "truth-communication" in Scripture,[39] and so substitute an existential "encounter" in which there is no room for "objectification."[40] And in the face of the many evolutions in recent theology, fundamentalists feel the more justified in their convictions.

Fundamentalists allowed themselves, however, to be guided by the "wholly divine or wholly human" dilemma, and thus they allowed the camp they opposed to force a problem on them.[41] As a result, it became impossible for them to do full justice to the rich variation of the biblical witness that speaks of law and gospel, of promise and fulfillment, and that re-echoes God's voice to us through all the tensions of human life. They incorporated the words of Scripture in their process of leveling to such a degree that a consideration of interpreting Scripture seemed practically superfluous to them, since they hold that what is revealed is to be accepted solely on the basis of its revelational quality. Thus, to them the human aspect of Holy Scripture lost all constitutive meaning and became blurred through the overwhelming divine reality of God's speaking. Fundamentalism's failure to be impressed by the criticism raised against its isolation and leveling of Scripture goes hand in hand with the fact that it considers itself bound to the content of the

38. Stonehouse, *op. cit.,* speaks of "the reduction of the organism of the revealed truths to isolated fragments."
39. H. Daniel Friberg, "The Word of God and 'Propositional Truth,'" *Christianity Today,* VII (1963), pp. 19ff., tries to give an analysis. Cf. the sharp formulation by D. B. Knox, "Propositional Revelation — the Only Revelation," *The Reformed Theological Review* (1960), pp. 1-9.
40. The problems that arise in connection with the creeds may be seen in H. Ott, *Theology and Preaching: A programme of work in dogmatics, arranged with reference to Questions 1-11 of the Heidelberg Cathechism* (ET, 1965).
41. Cf. R. Schippers, *op. cit.,* p. 70, on allowing one's opponents to determine one's methods (regarding doctrines).

biblical witness. Consequently, fundamentalists are not conscious of having parted with the position of the Reformation.

This, however, may not induce us to view fundamentalism as an innocent theory. On the contrary, fundamentalism greatly obscures the contexts in which God himself gave us Scripture. Back of fundamentalism lies something of an unconscious wish not to have God's Word enter the creaturely realm — or, to use Bavinck's words, "into the humanly weak and despised and base" — and the wish that Scripture should not subject itself "as writing to the fate of all writings."[42] This background, as a matter of course, determines fundamentalist apologetics. That becomes the more obvious when we see Bavinck struggle to conquer the "either divine or human" dilemma in order to discover the meaning of our receiving this Scripture, "in order that the excellency of the power of Scripture be of God and not from us."[43] We notice, therefore, that Bavinck concerns himself with Scripture on a wholly different level than does fundamentalism. His reflection is not in competition with his obedience but is part of it and oriented towards it. Thus, Bavinck need not concern himself with negative apologetics but can consider numerous new questions and "many and very serious objections" to the inspiration of Scripture.[44] Bavinck points to the self-witness of Scripture, which is unalterable, and he acknowledges moreover that the examination of Scripture in recent years comes up with "phenomena and facts that can hardly be reconciled with this self-witness."[45]

The difference between fundamentalism and Bavinck is not that his confession regarding Scripture is less positive than fundamentalism's, but that he gives much more attention to the manner in which Scripture came to us as *human* witness. Because of the divine nature of Scripture, the human witness does not become less important to Bavinck; rather, it receives special significance. This does not result from a relativizing of Scripture, but from his great respect for the manner of revelation that itself compels us to reflect on the nature of Scripture's authority. This is why he could warn against subscribing to a theory of inspiration that emphasizes "the new, the supernatural element present in inspiration,"[46] and remember that the truth

42. *GD,* I, 405.
43. *Ibid.* "Scripture is wholly the product of the Spirit of God, and at the same time wholly the product of the activity of the writers."
44. *Ibid.,* p. 410.
45. *Ibid.,* p. 389.
46. *Ibid.,* p. 401.

in numerous parts of Scripture constantly has a different nature.[47] His statement that by no means everything "that is included in Scripture has normative authority for our faith and life"[48] is an attack upon the leveling process desired by those who view Scripture as "a law book of articles."[49] Here there is no evidence of rebellion against God's speaking, but rather a refusal to maintain the divinity of Scripture by minimizing its human character. By rejecting false dilemmas, Bavinck could keep an eye on the many questions of his day, and he was kept from a course of action that could not have contributed anything to a better understanding of Holy Scripture.

When various new insights are advanced in a changed theological climate, a sense of crisis often arises in the minds of conservatives. In such a case, it is very important that their apologetics not take on a negative character, and that they follow no course from which they must later retreat. If they were to claim that all new questions are motivated by the scholars' desire to do away with the authority of Scripture, they would be misrepresenting scholarship. One result of the new biblical research has been the demand for an "organic" view of Scripture. The "contemporaneity of the new light," of which Bavinck speaks, is not meant to turn our attention away from Scripture but to concentrate our attention on a better understanding of it. As a result, Bavinck did not capitulate in any way to the criticism of Scripture of his day. Instead, he analyzed this criticism and arrived at the conclusion that the critics had totally lost sight of the purpose of Holy Scripture.[50] This does not mean that Bavinck considered this criticism to be nothing more than the result of a misunderstanding, but that he calls attention to what the *intent* — the specific and emphatic objective — of Scripture is. The important thing to notice is that Bavinck's rejection of biblical criticism takes the form of a positive contribution to the understanding of the nature of Scripture. It goes without saying that here many new questions could be raised. For example, what exactly is this "goal" *(scopus)* of Scripture?[51] Is it

47. *Ibid.*, p. 419. Earlier theology concerned itself with the problem regarding the nature of the authority in the terminologically unclear differentiation between historical and normative authority of Scripture. We hope to return to this later.
48. *Ibid.*, p. 428.
49. *Ibid.*, p. 429.
50. *Ibid.*, p. 415.
51. We are referring to the historically important article by E. Bizer, "Die reformatorische Orthodoxie und der Cartesianismus," *Z.Th.K.* (1958),

not possible to misuse this idea by drawing many subjectivistic conclusions from it? It is obvious, however, that no apologetics may ignore the questions concerning the nature of the authority of Holy Scripture that increasingly occupied the mind of Bavinck. In spite of the many changes and questions around him, he concluded his chapter on "the God-breathed character of Scripture" with these words:

> In a human manner it always speaks of the highest and most holy, of the eternal and invisible things. Like Christ, it considers nothing that is human strange. But that is why it is a book for mankind and lasts until the end of the ages. It is old, without ever aging. It always remains young and flourishing; it is the language of life. *Verbum Dei manet in aeternum.*[52]

In connection with the discussion of criticism, the authority of Scripture, and the certainty of faith, a remarkable element in negative apologetics should be noted. The opponents of criticism of Scripture, in spite of their rejection of criticism and its accompanying scientific approach to Holy Scripture, have occasionally shown a sudden interest in science, that is, when its results can be incorporated into their own apologetics. Whenever science arrives at certain conclusions that appear to confirm the concrete historical information of Scripture, they seize upon these results and point to them as proof that the Bible was right after all.[53] Thus, they make it look, to believers and unbelievers alike, that the battle against criticism is virtually decided. Their desire is to put the church at ease with the demonstration that criticism has been evidently rash and prejudiced in many respects. But this contact with science is wholly incidental and for the purpose of strengthening their own viewpoint, and they show no further interest in historical criticism.

This is not to say, however, that every reference to the untenability of earlier criticism is to be disregarded. The warning against rashly absolute pronouncements is especially legitimate when the critics themselves follow a course that is too easy and fixed *a priori*. We must even insist on the right and the necessity to ask whether the historical approach to Holy Scripture is

pp. 308ff., which shows that the question concerning the *scopus* of Scripture played an important role long ago.

52. *GD*, I, 420.

53. See, e.g., W. Keller, *The Bible as History: A Confirmation of the Book of Books* (ET, 1956).

truly scientific or whether it proceeds from *a priori* assumptions. Today there is definitely a consensus of opinion that immanental and evolutionistic considerations have played a role in many forms of criticism.[54] On the other hand, we may not allow the sterility of a negative approach to close our eyes to the fact that often a profound problem was involved with the meaning of history in God's revelational activity. This consideration also plays a role in fundamentalism and in the frequently heated theological discussions of today, especially where the dualism between "the realm of faith" and historico-critical examination of the Bible is rejected.

God's revelation must not be seen as a timeless and supra-historical event but as a manifestation in history, and interest in this history and its relation to revelation is therefore perfectly legitimate.[55] The many discussions in our day – regarding both the Old and the New Testaments – on the relation between kerygma and history are an illustration in point. Central in this is the so-called historical relatedness *(Geschichtsbezogenheit)* of the Christian faith, which makes it impossible for us to take refuge in a timeless kerygma that has not a single point of contact with real history. It is in this way that we are to understand the discussion that centers around von Rad's position that the object of historico-critical investigation is "a critically assured minimum" in contrast to the kerygmatic view that is after a theological maximum.[56] Here we see no separation between history and kerygma, and therefore the questions concerning the basis of the kerygma and the nature of its relation to historical reality become extremely relevant. How can the kerygma have any meaning at all when the critical method limits the historical to a minimum or wholly eliminates it? What is the relation between kerygma and history with regard to the message concerning God's activity in history?

Long before this discussion erupted in regard to the Old

54. See, e.g., Th. C. Vriezen, *An Outline of OT Theology* (ET, 1970), pp. 18-19. The problem concerning the background of historical criticism already in the 19th century played a role in connection with the OT, especially in relation to Hegel's philosophy. Abraham Kuyper, *De Hedendaagse Schriftkritiek* (1881), discusses particularly R. Rothe, then mentions Schleiermacher's influence, and warns generally against deism (p. 37). He mentions further the philosophical principle of evolution, from which the current study of Scripture has derived its impetus (p. 11). See also G. von Rad, *OT Theology* (1962), I, 109.

55. Cf.; N. H. Ridderbos, "Reversals of Old Testament Criticism," *Revelation and the Bible,* ed. C. F. H. Henry (1958), pp. 346ff.

56. Von Rad, I, 108.

Testament, it was concentrated on the New Testament and the nature of its kerygma. Many theologians concerned themselves with the limits of historical criticism, especially in connection with the relationship between the kerygma and the historical Jesus. Already W. Herrmann discussed the "historical-relatedness" of the Christian faith in relation to historical examination and the ground of faith, which he felt could not be dependent upon this.[57] E. Brunner also felt that faith, because of its dependence upon history, could not go together "with every kind of criticism," for instance, the denial of the existence of Christ.[58] This inevitably brought into view the nature and structure of historical study — except on the part of those who uncritically accepted such study — until the core of faith seemed to disappear from history.

In the reflection on the nature and limits of historical criticism, the question regarding faith and its certainty plays an important role. We notice an inclination to oppose a view of the truth regarding the kerygma that differs very little structurally from that of idealism, which for reasons of principle rejected any significance of history for the grounding of faith. Today we see a shifting from the erstwhile skepticism to a more or less tolerant view regarding the historical Jesus. We mention the so-called post-Bultmannian phase in New Testament theology, which has been called a "surprising change of front," since it attempts to determine the limits of criticism; it is now no longer primarily interested in what is untrue in the Gospels, for example, but in what is true.[59] Against this changed background emerges the nature of historical knowledge and an

57. See Berkouwer, *Geloof en Openbaring in de Nieuwere Duitse Theologie* (1932), pp. 401ff.
58. *The Mediator* (1947), p. 168; cf. W. Pannenberg, "Redemptive Event and History," *Basic Questions in Theology,* I (1970), p. 56. "The reference of the Christian faith to history unavoidably carries with it the demand that the believer must not try to save himself from historical-critical questions by means of some 'invulnerable area' — otherwise it will lose its historical basis." Pannenberg, however, is not pessimistic, and he refers to the "famous prediction" by E. Troeltsch in 1911: "The sensational disavowals will disappear when one works objectively with these things." Pannenberg tries to conquer the dualism without resorting to pure apologetics. For various complications, see his *Jesus — God and Man* (1968), pp. 66ff.
59. E. Käsemann, "The Problem of the Historical Jesus," *Essays on New Testament Themes* (1964), pp. 18-19 (the article appeared first in 1954). See also p. 34. Käsemann sees the change of front as a reaction against Bultmann's "radicalism" (p. 16). Cf. R. H. Fuller, *The New Testament in Current Study* (1962), pp. 25f.; A. Richardson, *History,*

attempt to replace the dehistoricizing kerygma theology by — or at least create room for — a reflection on the problem of certainty, for which existentialism had offered a simplistic solution.

Theology is still struggling with the question raised by Lessing in *Der Beweis des Geistes und der Kraft* (1777), which touched on the relation between historic factuality and faith. Although his eighteenth-century terminology may sound rather peculiar — that "accidental historical truths cannot be the basis for 'necessary truths of reason' " — we can say that this problem, lifted out of the context of its time, exerts suggestive power concerning the relativity of the "historical examination." Currently, many attempts are being made to overcome the dualism accompanying it. And when we observe the motives behind the opposition to total "dehistoricization" of the gospel, we can realize that any view of Scripture that considers irrelevant Bavinck's attention for the nature of Holy Scripture, its authority, and its description of history, offers no solution. For those who hold such a view run the risk, in their rejection of the kerygma theology, of ending up with a different separation between kerygma and history — the kerygma-less history — which also blocks the way to a correct understanding of the gospel.

At this juncture it is important to point out that the discussion of Holy Scripture and certainty must not be seen only in the light of historical criticism; there is another aspect of the conflict to be observed. Consideration has frequently been given to the nature of various kinds of certainties, especially the confession of the trustworthiness of Scripture. Many have pointed out the real danger that an incorrect connection between Scripture and certainty of faith can be made by proceeding *a priori* from the premise that for our certainty of faith we need an immovable basis to the conclusion that we can find this only in an infallible Scripture. It is especially the so-called orthodox view of Scripture that came to the fore in this analysis. M. Kähler accuses the orthodox theologians of adhering to a position that evidences a purely artificial character, since they do not deduce the authority of Holy Scripture from "the actual data of the Bible," but from those requirements that they, according to their viewpoint, believe they must, and consequently may insist on for "a trustworthy transmission of revelation."[60] Hence,

Sacred and Profane (1964), pp. 139-153; J. D. Smart, *The Interpretation of Scripture* (1961), pp. 229ff.

60. M. Kähler, *The So-Called Historical Jesus and the Historic, Biblical Christ* (1964), p. 113.

this accusation is directed against the tendency to link certainty to a factual condition that can be pointed out and concretely seized upon in "their need for a visible and juridically factual final authority."[61] This authority could offer the ultimate defense against doubt and uncertainty.

Such critics believed they were especially justified in giving this psychological explanation of the theory of verbal inspiration, particularly as it was developed in post-Reformation theology.[62] They considered the theory of verbal inspiration an attempt to make the basis of certainty of faith immovable by an *a priori* preclusion of every element of uncertainty because of the unique, supernatural, divine quality of Holy Scripture. Thus, they asserted, faith in Scripture actually manifested the character of a religious postulate.[63] They found confirmation for this religio-psychological explanation by showing that such a doctrine of verbal inspiration and its absolute certainties had remarkable parallels in non-Christian religions' evaluation of their holy books, particularly in Islam's evaluation of the Koran. From Bavinck's observation that the teaching of the Koran "shows remarkable parallels with that of the Christian Church regarding Scripture,"[64] the critics concluded that this was a matter of parallel constructions that could be explained as a longing for certainty in religion – a need to be removed from all problems by a reliance on "holy documents." Besides the religio-historic parallels, some have mentioned the parallel between the doctrines of the infallibility of Scripture and that of the pope – a parallel no less revealing and significant. Thus, Korff said that Protestantism had fallen into the same error as had Rome, since it attached the seal of "infallibility" to Scripture in order to avoid every risk regarding certainty.[65] And in this connection

61. P. C. van Leeuwen, "De vraag naar de laatste autoriteit," *Vox Theologica* (1936), p. 26.
62. Often the question has been asked whether this theory is already present in Luther and Calvin. Regarding Calvin, this is denied by W. Krusche, *Das Wirken des Heiligen Geistes nach Calvin* (1957), p. 161; and regarding Luther, it is denied by L. Pinomaa, *Faith Victorious: An Introduction to Luther's Theology* (ET, 1963), p. 104, who calls this supposition "foreign to Luther."
63. We mention only H. G. Fritzsche, *Lehrbuch der Dogmatik* (1964), I, 114: "... there was a search for certainty and completeness"; W. Trillhaas, *Dogmatik* (1962), pp. 75f.
64. Bavinck, *GD*, I, 348.
65. F. W. Korff, "Schrift en Traditie," *Onder Eigen Vaandel* (1937), p. 295.

the question was raised whether it would not be preferable to subject oneself to a living pope than to a paper pope.[66]

This many-sided argument confronts us with an analysis that is clearly of the utmost significance for the entire doctrine of Scripture. Those who arrived at it intended thereby to point out an incorrect view of the certainty of faith. This faulty view was based on a rationally developed infallibility of Scripture that was supposed to preclude all doubts. Their intention was not to attack the authority of Scripture in any way, but rather to criticize a certain theory of inspiration. In our time, the central point at issue has again become the post-Reformation theology in connection with the emerging Aristotelianism in theology, which has also begun to influence the doctrine of Scripture. This faulty view has occurred as theologians, in immediate relation to affirmation and certainty, began to interpret the word *est* in the expression *Sacra Scriptura est Verbum Dei* in such a manner that Scripture's divinity was thought to be found in its inner substantial form and had become an essential predicate of Holy Scripture as an inspired book that was elevated to the level of a source of supernatural truths.[67] Critics of this view considered the manner in which inspiration was described and developed as a dissolution of the witnessing character of Holy Scripture, for, they said, in this view "not the witnesses but the dictating Spirit guarantees the truth of the written word."[68] They saw this whole system of philosophical concepts and theoretical objectification as the result of an establishing of a basis of certainty whereby the inspiration already guaranteed certainty quite apart from the witness – the message – of Scripture, whose certainty could rest only on a preceding certainty regarding the source of this witness – Holy Scripture.

It is not now our intention to examine whether this analysis of the post-Reformation theology does full justice to it.[69] Due

66. See Berkouwer, *Het Probleem der Schriftkritiek* (1938), pp. 215f.
67. Much has been written on the post-Reformation theology, both Lutheran and Reformed. Among the older works are K. Heim, *Das Gewissheitsproblem in der systematischen Theologie bis Schleiermacher* (1911); P. Althaus, *Die Prinzipien der deutschen reformierten Dogmatik im Zeitalter der aristotelischen Scholastik* (1914), especially pp. 214ff. More recent works include E. Bizer, "Die reformatorische Orthodoxie und der Cartesianismus," *Z.Th.K.* (1958), pp. 308f.; G. Wehrung, "Reformatorisch und orthodox," *Zeitschrift für systematische Theologie* (1953); Hägglund, *op. cit.*, pp. 77ff.; Preus, *op. cit.*, pp. 14ff.
68. See Trillhaas, p. 79.
69. We mention specifically the meaning of the distinction between the

to unmistakable philosophical infiltration, it presents such a complex phenomenon that it is impossible to give an evaluation of it without a broader analysis. We mention this dogmatic-historical reflection, however, because it is very evidently related to the present reflection on Holy Scripture and certainty. In this connection we must emphasize that certainty may never be approached by way of a postulate. Faith is not and cannot be based on a theoretical reflection on what, according to our insight, must be the nature of the divine revelation and on which ways and forms it must have come to us in order to be the guarantee of certainty.[70] The way of Christian faith is not one of a possibility becoming more clear on its way to the reality of certainty, but a subjection to the gospel, to the Christ of the Scriptures; and from this alone can a reflection on Holy Scripture proceed.[71] Most certainly this must be our point of departure when examining the question whether certain theories of inspiration were based on a postulate or whether many poor formulations merely tried to express the overwhelming power of the message of Scripture through the Holy Spirit. The repeated doxology on the words of the Lord as being pure words, purified seven times (Ps. 12:6), as truth (Ps. 119:160), as righteous (Ps. 119:144), as a lamp and light (Ps. 119:105), and as a joy of the heart, simply cannot be the result of a postulate nor guaranteed by one. They can be sung only in faith, experience, and heartfelt love (Ps. 119:111, 113). The trustworthiness of the Word does not subject itself to an *a priori* testing, but can only be understood in the all-pervasive power of the Word itself as

forma and the *materia* (especially the *forma* of Scripture). On this, see Preus, p. 14, and Hägglund, pp. 105ff.

70. After writing this chapter, I was impressed by H. N. Ridderbos' rejection of the postulate idea in these words: "The truth is that the infallibility of Scripture is in many respects different from what a theoretical concept of inspiration or infallibility wholly disconnected from the empirical would like to 'demand' it to be." See also his warning to be careful "with the argument of what, under the God-breathed character of the Spirit, is or is not possible." "De Speelruimte van de Geest," *Gereformeerd Weekblad* (March 26, 1965).

71. We will return later to the discussion of post-Reformation theology. The question is important because the opinion has often been expressed that this theology formed the occasion for the beginning of historical criticism which intended to "investigate" the supernatural quality of Scripture. See Ebeling, "The Significance of the Critical Historical Method for Church and Theology in Protestantism," Ch. I, *Word and Faith.*

the sword of the Spirit.[72] The genesis of faith in its subjection to Holy Scripture — the attentive listening to God's voice — can never be explained on the basis of a preceding guarantee regarding the power of certainty that God's Word commands. This also explains how certain shifts in the doctrine of Holy Scripture may temporarily cause a certain sense of crisis, but by no means cause an estrangement (by way of logical inference) from the richness of the biblical testimony. The reason for this is that no *a priori* theory can be the basis of certainty.[73] The way to certainty and faith in Scripture is the way of which Jeremiah in his encounter with God testifies: "O Lord, thou hast deceived me, and I was deceived; thou art stronger than I, and thou hast prevailed" (Jer. 20:7).

This by no means implies that the authority of Scripture is relativized. Rather, we are reminded that the way is pointed out to us, and that only by walking this way can we confess that Holy Scripture is the Word of God. Thus, we can also understand why Bavinck, in his chapter "The God-breathed Character of Holy Scripture," deals with the continual struggle of believers to make every thought captive to Christ (II Cor. 10:5).[74] This struggle, which is aimed at removing any resistance to faith and obedience (Heb. 12:3; Lk. 2:34; 12:10), does not imply that reflection on Holy Scripture is harmful or even unnecessary; rather, we must remember that while reflecting on Scripture we are to be aware of the dangers surrounding the confession concerning Scripture and its true and authentic character. In a time when there were great excitement and tense feelings regarding Holy Scripture, Bavinck reminded us of the dangers surrounding our own position, dangers that are never precluded, even when we consciously accept the doctrine of inspiration. Without ever closing his eyes to what was really at stake in the many forms of criticism of Scripture, he nevertheless spoke of the possibility that even without openly criticizing Scripture we can be far removed from a truly believing subjection to its testimony. A certain view of the inspiration and authority of Scripture does not necessarily imply a believing acceptance. There are different kinds of opposition to the real authority of Scrip-

72. Ephesians 6:17. We frequently meet in the NT the trustworthiness of the Word: I Tim. 1:15; 4:9; II Tim. 2:11; Titus 3:8. Here the Word appears to be the foundation for the certainty of faith. See C. F. D. Moule, *The Birth of the NT* (1962), p. 222.

73. Cf. Bavinck, *GD,* I, 407.

74. *Ibid.,* p. 412.

ture that are not precluded or conquered by any kind of theory. When Bavinck reflects on the attack upon Holy Scripture, he sees this attack first of all as enmity of the human heart, which can manifest itself in various ways:

> It is by no means only, and maybe not even most, prominent in the criticism to which Scripture is subjected in our day. Scripture as the Word of God meets with opposition and unbelief from every psychic human being. In the period of dead orthodoxy unbelief in Scripture was in principle just as powerful as in our historico-critical age.[75]

With this remarkable statement Bavinck does not intend to minimize the dangers of criticism of Scripture, which would be wholly contrary to his theology. What he does wish to point out is that subjection to the authority of Scripture is not threatened only by the critic of Scripture; it is also threatened by those who, within a formal and traditional scriptural confession, really do not subject themselves to this authority and do not manifest the reality of their confession in daily life. Dead orthodoxy is not usually included among the forms of scriptural criticism, enmity, and unbelief. But Bavinck's concern renders more than an effective protest against dead orthodoxy. Further, he wants to emphasize that scriptural authority and belief may not be formalized, for faith and its certainty cannot exist for a moment if they are not related to the content and the message of Scripture. Just as we are convinced of the truth and believe and accept it only when we walk in it (see II Jn. 4; III Jn. 3, 4; II Jn. 6), so our belief in Scripture is true only when our confession of its authority is accompanied by a response to its testimony in faith. Bavinck's warning is so serious and meaningful because it is possible for the confession of Scripture's authority and inspiration to be maintained for a long time as an apparent part of the church's heritage of faith without there being any evidence of a real living faith anymore. It is possible never to question the authority of Scripture without walking in the truth. And to call such a thing "belief" in Scripture, only because this particular confession has not been rejected, is to give an entirely different meaning to the word "belief" than what the church means by true Christian belief (see Chapter Two).

It is, therefore, necessary to consider this aspect of alienation

75. *Ibid.*, p. 411.

fully. We are not merely dealing here with a "practical" supplement to theology, but with something essential that inevitably arises out of reflection on the power and riches of Holy Scripture. We cannot speak of an unchanged "belief in Scripture" where, in a diminished contact with Scripture, it has petrified — without certainty. It is not surprising that Bavinck, in his warning against dead orthodoxy because of its lack of belief in Scripture, sees such a close connection between faith in Scripture and the certainty of salvation. That gives him the opportunity to place criticism of Scripture in a broad perspective and to remind us of the lasting struggle that believers on earth can never hope to escape.

With this recognition, discussion of the criticism of Scripture receives full significance and becomes fruitful. There is in the human heart a contradiction of God's truth and wisdom that can manifest itself in many different forms. This danger must compel us to that care which the mystery of Scripture itself — God's chosen way of revelation — calls forth, an attentiveness that by no means confines the truth that must guide us when we attempt to understand the way in which Scripture itself speaks to us. Thus, the confession of Holy Scripture is never a finished business but a continuous evangelical mandate. This emphasis by no means implies a subjectivizing of Holy Scripture and its authority. Rather, the connection between the authority of Scripture and faith is the opposite of such subjectivizing, just as correlation is the opposite of projection. Therefore, to make the authority of Scripture a projection or a postulate is impossible. The church can continue to put its trust in the living Word of God and to seek certainty only where it can truly be found. This is of great importance in a time when the authority of Scripture is so much questioned. The questioning of the divine authority can be resisted only by a respect for the contexts in which Scripture comes to us. Thus the church can rest in the purity of God's testimony. We must realize that, in a preoccupation with the human testimony and in a legitimate changing from a mechanical to an organic inspiration, it is possible that we gradually remove ourselves from the divine authority by tarnishing the biblical mystery. We can also remove ourselves from the true authority of Scripture, even while recognizing its divine aspect, by not truly following Christ, who comes to us in the cloak of Holy Scripture. And finally we can, individualistically and through personal preference, limit and violate the normative nature of Holy Scripture, and on the basis of these selections remove ourselves far from the fellowship of the church.[76]

Alongside and contrary to these ways there is another way. That way is not from the possibility to the reality of certainty, but the way we must take on the basis of the command not to stumble over the *skandalon* character of the gospel, in which the biblical testimony participates. In that way, further examination of the mystery of Scripture is legitimate. And this need not result in a contradiction of the heart, as long as the form — the cloak — of Scripture is seen and understood, "that by steadfastness and by the encouragement of the Scriptures we might have hope" (Rom. 14:4). Thus, the church has formulated its confession regarding Holy Scripture in the urgent appeal *tolle, lege* — "Come and hear!" (cf. "Come and see" in Jn. 1:47). This appeal played such an important role in Augustine's conversion and led him to heed the concrete admonition of Scripture to "put on Christ."[77]

When the church in its confession and preaching — its *apologia* — continues to advocate this way in its witness, the impression may be given that listening now has become much more difficult and complicated than in earlier days. So we may ask whether a faith that avoids all problems is possibly closer to God's intentions with Holy Scripture. The answer to these suggestions can only be found when we are convinced that the interest in Holy Scripture as prophetic-apostolic testimony need not run contrary to a true attentiveness to God's voice, but can be a way to a deeper believing understanding of what the Spirit says to the church. When the Reformation theologians reflected on ultimate certainty, the result was a hitherto unknown interest in the concrete words of Holy Scripture as evidenced by countless commentaries. That this did not result in a biblical "scientism" significant only to "the wise and prudent" is especially evident from the fact that in this new situation the name of the Holy Spirit was reverently mentioned. In spite of many sectarian appeals to the Spirit, at the center of the Reformers' confessing they pointed to the witness of the Holy Spirit.

What is — and what can be — the meaning and significance of this remarkable confession, which has been interpreted in so

76. Cf. K. Aland, *The Problem of the New Testament Canon* (1962) on "a narrowing and shortening" of the canon, "even in churches where the canon is determined with absolute rigidity" (p. 28). For more on this, see Ch. 3.

77. *Confessions,* VIII, 12 (xxx) (Rom. 13:14).

many different ways and has evoked so much controversy? What does the reference to *this great witness* mean amidst all these problems concerning Scripture in the ever-threatening crisis regarding certainty?

CHAPTER TWO

THE TESTIMONY OF THE SPIRIT

THERE HAS ALWAYS BEEN GREAT INTEREST in our confession of the testimony of the Holy Spirit regarding belief in Scripture. This shows that belief in Scripture was not considered an irrational, isolated response, but rather a commitment that had a connection with the Holy Spirit and with a divine witness. On the other hand, it points out that this belief was not viewed as a rational insight — an intellectual acceptance of the trustworthiness of Scripture within an impersonal relationship to it — which in a true Christian faith was merely accompanied by a trust in a personal God. On the contrary, this kind of dualism was emphatically rejected. It was realized that faith in the sense of "faith *in*" was a personal relationship of trust in another person;[1] but the intent was never to see belief in Scripture as something impersonal or objective.

Remarkably, during the Reformation, theologians did not merely relate the witness of the Spirit to man's filial relationship to God, but they also related it to his belief in Scripture. This happened in a time when frequent isolated and fragmentary references to the Spirit were being made — a fact the Reformers (Luther as well as Calvin) always viewed as the danger of what has usually been called "spiritualism."[2] Despite running the risk of being associated with this movement, which in some ways minimized the written Word as something "external," the Reformers did not hesitate to mention the name of the Holy Spirit at the decisive juncture of faith and its certainty. Later theologians pointed out the problems inherent in this confession,

1. See Bavinck, *GD,* I, 539, on belief *in* Christ and "believing Scripture."
2. We cannot justly speak of Luther's "spiritualism" (because of his extensive discussion of the essence and the work of the Spirit) as does K. G. Steck, *Luther und die Schwärmer* (1955), p. 12. To use this word to contradict R. Prenter, *Spiritus Creator* (ET, 1953), who speaks of Luther's "antispiritualism," is confusing the issue.

accusing the Reformers of intending to point out the objectivity of the witness of Scripture as the witness of the Spirit and then still accepting a witness of the Spirit in the heart. Did not such a "doubling" of the witness indicate the Reformers' inability to solve the problem of certainty? Was not this "objectivity" (trustworthiness and self-authentication) unsatisfactory to them, so that they felt the need for a *testimonium internum?* On this basis, Strauss considered this confession "the Achilles' heel of the Protestant system."[3] Obviously his meaning is that for Protestantism the ultimate authority no longer resided in the "objective" revelation itself, but in the human heart, feeling, or experience, or at least in the subjectivity of an "internal" revelation.

It is, of course, very important to determine whether this pneumatological confession of the Reformers does indeed contain a possible unconscious opening that can admit the subjectivism of the doctrine that the inner light is the true light of revelation. These are the problems that arise repeatedly in the many discussions of the witness of the Holy Spirit. The Reformed churches have never issued a further declaration concerning the *testimonium Spiritus Sancti,* but theologians have asked whether this confession evidences an inner contradiction or rather a deep and responsible perspective.

The Reformation confession of the *testimonium Spiritus Sancti* must be considered against the background of the controversial situation at that time: Rome's very strong emphasis upon the authority of the church, in which the *testimonium ecclesiae* played an important part in the attainment of certainty. Were not the believers after all taken by the hand and safely guided by the church in their personal lives as well as in their contact with the gospel? A reflection upon this question is found in Article V of the Belgic Confession, which says that we accept without any doubt all that is written in the holy and canonical books, "not so much because the Church receives and approves them as such, but more especially because the Holy Ghost witnesses in our hearts that they are from God." There is something striking about the wording here. The contrast is not one of "not . . . but" (as might have been expected on the basis of the controversy with Rome), but rather one of "not so much . . . but more especially." No doubt the reason for this

3. D. F. Strauss, *Die christliche Glaubenslehre* (1840), I, 136. Cf. O. Weber, *Grundlagen der Dogmatik* (1955), I, 268; Bavinck, *GD,* I, 554, 569; K. Barth, *Church Dogmatics* (ET, 1956), I, 2, 598.

is that the composers of the confession did not wish to give the impression that the church and its testimony in the life of faith and subjection to Holy Scripture are entirely without significance. What the confession does say is that the authority of the church can never be the ultimate and final ground of belief in Scripture. This echoes Calvin, who calls the belief that Scripture is important only to the extent conceded to it by the suffrage of the church a pernicious error. Furthermore, according to Calvin, to say that the amount of reverence due Holy Scripture depends on the determination of the church is an insult to the Holy Spirit (*Inst.*, I, vii, 1).

Yet Calvin does not wish to deny the importance of the church, and in this connection he cites Augustine's often quoted statement: "I would not believe the gospel, except as moved by the authority of the Catholic Church" (*Inst.*, I, vii, 3). Calvin's interpretation of this statement is that a person who does not yet have faith can embrace the gospel only through the authority of the church,[4] but not that faith in Scripture finds its ultimate explanation in the authority of the church. The real and ultimate explanation is, according to Augustine, that our spirit is not enlightened by men but by the Spirit of God himself. For Calvin, too, the authority of the church is the introduction "through which we are prepared for belief in the gospel"; but we are fully convinced only in a higher way—by the hidden witness of the Spirit (*Inst.*, I, vii, 5).

Only God himself is a sufficient witness to himself. The Word of God finds no acceptance until it is sealed by the inward witness of the Spirit, and the heart finds its rest in Scripture only through this inward teaching. Scripture is not subject to human argumentation and proof, and Scripture's own assuring power is higher and stronger than all human judgment. No matter how large a role the church may play in the genetic process[5] of ascertaining, ultimately no one can accept Scripture *because* the church testifies that it is God's Word. The moving of the church as *praedicatrix evangelii*[6] is not the ultimate

4. A. Kuyper, *Principles of Sacred Theology* (ET, 1898), p. 555, where he discusses this statement of Augustine and speaks of "the link of the Church." Moreover, according to Kuyper, the word "gospel" in this statement *(evangelio non crederem)* has been incorrectly understood as the *Sacra Scriptura inspirata*.
5. Obviously, this genetic aspect, this *coming* to certainty, cannot be separated from the question regarding the foundation of faith, but the differentiation does not therefore lose its significance.
6. Kuyper, *loc. cit.*

explanation of faith in Scripture. This conviction is also expressed in other Reformed confessions, which always speak of the convincing power of the Holy Spirit in connection with belief in Scripture.[7] The inevitable question of what is meant by the *testimonium Spiritus Sancti* arises at this point. It is a separate, mystical, and supernatural witness of the Spirit, and therefore called a hidden operation? Is this witness the voice of God — the real revelation — in contrast to the revelation of Scripture, which in itself is insufficient? Were this so, it would be justifiable to speak of a separate pneumatic characteristic that assures us of the divine origin and quality of Holy Scripture and contains a confirmation of Scripture as a book. This pneumatic aspect could explain why one person accepts Scripture and another does not. If one were to take the words of Article V *(BC)* — "the Spirit testifies in our hearts that they come from God" — out of context, he might indeed arrive at such a conclusion and interpret the confession to mean that there is a separate witness of the Spirit — in the sense of some form of spiritualism. But it has been constantly, and correctly, pointed out that in the context of the Reformation this simply could not have been the intention of Article V, since the confession of the *testimonium* is never contrasted with that of Holy Scripture or its authority and self-authentication. In any case, there is no formal confirmation or voice that whispers something to us about the origin or quality of Scripture. Preiss points out that only later did theologians begin to speak more and more formally and abstractly about the convincing *testimonium*, "as if there were such a thing as a formal authority of an abstract Word of God apart from its content." By speaking thus, the *testimonium* was reduced to an "abstract and artificial matter."[8]

Whenever the words "abstract" and "formal" appear frequently in the discussion, what is meant is that Scripture is

7. Cf. The French Confession of Faith (1559), Art. IV (in P. Schaff, *The Creeds of Christendom* [1877], III, 361); Scots Confession (1560), Art. XIX (Schaff, p. 464); Helvetic Confession (1562), which says that it is not *ex hominibus* (Schaff, p. 237); Westminster Confession (1647), which says, "... our full persuasion ... is from the inward work of the Holy Spirit" (Schaff, p. 603); Waldensian Confession (1655), which says, "... not only from the testimony of the Church, but more especially ..." and then lists the truth of the teaching contained in Scripture and "the operation of the Holy Spirit" (Schaff, pp. 759f.). The Waldensian also states that the Spirit makes us "receive with reverence the testimony which the Church on that point renders us" (p. 760).
8. Th. Preiss, *Das innere Zeugnis des Heiligen Geistes* (1947), pp. 14-15.

received as writing, as a book of divine quality, while its content and message as such are thereby not taken into account from the outset. We are touching here on a very important point of the doctrine of Scripture, which also forms the background of many discussions. Bavinck's criticism that Calvin and other Reformed theologians "related the *testimonium Spiritus Sancti* much too one-sidedly to the authority of Scripture,"[9] is itself a dogmatic-historical assertion; but, whether his criticism is historically correct or not, he is undoubtedly dealing with the same central problem. His own view concerning the *testimonium* becomes apparent here: "It seemed that this doctrine had no other context than the subjective assurance that Scripture was the Word of God." As a result, the *testimonium* became something separate: "It was isolated from the life of faith and seemed to imply an extraordinary revelation, about which Michaelis was honest enough to declare that he had never experienced it."[10]

After criticizing this "one-sidedness," Bavinck goes on to say that Scripture itself speaks quite differently, and that the testimony of the Spirit is not a dream or a vision or "a voice from heaven." What does Bavinck mean by his rather strong objection to isolating the *testimonium* from the life of faith?[11] Obviously, it is inevitable that such an isolation will determine the nature of the *testimonium*. Bavinck points out that the witness of the Spirit "gives no assurance regarding the objective truths of salvation apart from connection with the condition of the religious subject," because it first of all has a bearing on a person's sonship.[12] It is only thus that the Spirit brings us to a believing subjection to Holy Scripture, uniting us "in the same measure and power to it as to the person of Christ."[13] Seen in this way, the correlation between Scripture and faith loses all its foreboding formality. Thus, Bavinck obviously wished to answer Strauss's charge that the doctrine regarding the *testimonium* was Protestantism's great weakness, for to Bavinck it is the very cornerstone of the Christian confession, the crown and victory of the truth.[14]

9. *GD*, I, 563.
10. *Ibid.*, pp. 563ff. Michaelis' statement also appears on p. 554.
11. R. Preus, *The Inspiration of Scripture*, p. 115. Preus accuses the Lutherans of the same thing. They viewed the *testimonium* "almost exclusively in reference to the authority of Scripture." Cf. also "a one-sided emphasis on the witness of the Spirit in respect to Scripture."
12. *GD*, I, 564.
13. *Ibid.*, p. 567.
14. *Ibid.*, pp. 554, 569-70. Bavinck mentions Strauss's criticism twice.

Bavinck places the *testimonium* fully in the dynamic context of the entire life of faith. It is so intertwined with that life that, according to him, "our belief in Scripture decreases and increases together with our trust in Christ."[15] He adds that the *testimonium* is not always equally strong, and hence it is no *a priori* confirmation that always remains the same because of its origin in the Holy Spirit. This also implies, concerning the nature of the testimony, that it does not supply direct certainty regarding the authenticity, canonicity, or even the inspiration of Holy Scripture; nor regarding the historical, chronological, and geographical data "as such"; nor regarding the facts of salvation as *nuda facta;*[16] nor, finally, regarding the closedness of the canon, as if it were possible to solve the problems regarding canonicity with an appeal to the witness of the Spirit.[17] Instead, it is inseparably connected with faith and salvation in Christ. In this way Bavinck tried to avoid any formalization and isolation of the doctrine, as well as every form of dualism between belief in Scripture and faith in Christ. The *testimonium* does not supply an *a priori* certainty regarding Scripture, which afterwards is supplemented with and through its message.

The problem of the doctrine of the *testimonium* is also especially illuminated by the way in which Kuyper has handled it. He proceeds from the assumption that the *testimonium* directly addresses itself to us personally, but that it is no magical event or supernatural message from God that says, "This Scripture is My Word."[18] According to him, such a notion is definitely "uninformed" and inevitably leads to a false mysticism that ultimately minimizes the authority of Scripture. Rather, the inseparable connection between belief in Scripture and certainty of faith must be emphasized. Referring to Article IX of the Belgic Confession ("All this we know as well from the testimonies of Holy Writ as from their operations, and chiefly by those we feel in ourselves"), Kuyper speaks of the "melody of redemption." Belief in the divine nature of Holy Scripture "rests upon the experience of spiritual life." Hence the *testimonium* usually works "gradually and unobserved."[19] The Spirit's witness begins by binding us to the center of Scripture, namely, Jesus Christ. The extent of this authority is of no

15. *Ibid.,* p. 569.
16. *Ibid.,* pp. 565-69.
17. Regarding the witness and canonicity, see H. N. Ridderbos, *The Authority of the New Testament Scriptures* (1963), pp. 10ff., 39-40.
18. *Princ.,* p. 557.
19. *Ibid.,* pp. 558-559.

significance at first. Only by degrees does Scripture begin to fascinate us by its organic composition in a gradual assimilation process regarding its content and its message. Hence, Kuyper rejects what Heim later called an *a priori,* formal "assurance," for with faith in Scripture the only thing that counts is faith in the promise. Experiencing the *divinitas* of Scripture takes place through experiencing God's *benevolentia.* In spite of the many complicating factors in Kuyper's theology, there are clear similarities between his and Bavinck's, because both reject isolation of the *testimonium.* Kuyper insists that the connection between the *testimonium Spiritus Sancti* and faith in Christ[20] is so close that the *testimonium* is a part of every conversion.[21] Hence his strong rejection of a "magical" *testimonium* separate from the Christian life, which can easily lead to religious fanaticism.[22] When one is in contact with Holy Scripture, the testimony of the Spirit shows him as the sinner and shows the marvelous way of deliverance. It is in this way that the Spirit witnesses concerning the Word, as "Holy Scripture in divine splendor commences to scintillate before our eyes."[23]

It is important that both Bavinck and Kuyper reject the idea that Scripture is the object of the *testimonium* apart from its message, for as Kuyper points out, such a view is contrary to the way in which faith works, which excludes such a formalization. Furthermore, this separation fails to do full justice to the fact that there is the closest connection between the words of Holy Scripture and that about which they speak and witness. To formalize Holy Scripture in this way is as nonsensical as to praise a book without reading it; to do so violates the word-character of Holy Scripture. Whoever envisions the Spirit's testimony as an independent, isolated witness affording *a priori* certainty about the quality of Scripture, cannot escape voiding the words of Holy Scripture itself. For on such a view the way of faith splits into two parts: first, the way to certainty regarding Scripture, and then the way to the message. Such an abstract division does not coincide with the correct understanding of the way expressed in the church's confession that the "Holy Scriptures fully contain the will of God and that whatsoever man ought to believe unto salvation is sufficiently taught therein"

20. Cf. Bavinck, *GD,* I, 569, on the increase and decrease of faith in Scripture, and the cited part in Kuyper's *Locus de Sacra Scriptura,* p. 197, on the differences in rapidity and clarity of the process of the *testimonium.*
21. Kuyper, *Locus,* p. 199.
22. Kuyper, *The Work of the Holy Spirit* (1900), p. 192.
23. *Ibid.,* p. 193.

(*BC,* Art. VII). Whoever makes a distinction regarding certainty at this point must inevitably view the *testimonium* as a mysterious event, as "a supernatural factor of an incomprehensible nature that is added to the Word and its impotence."[24] No added recognition of the self-authentication of Scripture can change this, for the mystery of the witness has already preceded the message of Holy Scripture; and thus it becomes impossible to recognize how Scripture itself speaks concerning the words that come to us. Scripture deals with "words" in their relation to the message of salvation, as Peter says to Christ: "Lord, to whom shall we go? You have the words of eternal life; and we have believed, and have come to know, that you are the Holy One of God" (Jn. 6:68-69).[25] In spite of its seemingly greater objectivity, all formalizing of the *testimonium* and certainty violates the true meaning and intent of Holy Scripture.

The crucial nature of the subject under discussion makes it important to examine whether Bavinck's opinion that Calvin was too one-sided is indeed justified, especially since Calvin's influence on the confession is unmistakable. This, in turn, is important for a correct understanding of Article V, which states that the Holy Spirit witnesses in our hearts that these books are from God. Did Calvin have in mind a separate and precedent assurance by the witness of the Spirit regarding Holy Scripture in its capacity as writing? Is he concerned with the *divinitas* of Scripture "without thereby bringing the soteriological aspect of faith to the fore?"[26] Krusche is of the opinion that this kind of conclusion might be drawn from the *Institutes,* but that Calvin's commentaries offer an entirely different picture,[27] in which the *testimonium Spiritus Sancti* is not seen as giving prior certainty about the special divine quality of Holy Scripture. However, it is not easy to get a clear picture.

Calvin mentions the testimony of the Spirit in connection with his discussion of Holy Scripture, but later, in his chapter on faith, he does not mention it (*Inst.,* III, ii, 41). This may give the impression that he teaches that faith in Scripture precedes saving faith. However, according to the *Institutes* (I, vi, 2), faith in Scripture and saving faith coincide. Krusche refers to

24. P. Althaus, *Die Prinzipien,* p. 209. See "a wholly incomprehensible operation of the Spirit" (pp. 211, 234, 264).
25. See Jn. 6:63: ". . . the words that I have spoken to you are spirit and life."
26. W. Krusche, *Das Wirken,* p. 216. Krusche answers this question in the negative.
27. *Ibid.,* p. 217.

Calvin's exegesis of Ephesians 1:13: "The true conviction which believers have of the Word of God, of their own salvation, and of all religion [springs] . . . from the sealing of the Spirit," who makes their consciences more certain and removes all doubt.[28] At crucial points it is clear that Krusche is justified in his conclusion that "Calvin has not torn asunder certainty of Scripture and certainty of faith." [29] Calvin does speak emphatically of the *testimonium* and Holy Scripture, but the manner in which he does so does not warrant the charge of formalizing. Rather, Calvin sees Scripture as the clothes in which Christ comes to us (*Inst.,* III, ii, 6; cf. his commentary on I Pet. 2:8); whereas faith is the knowledge of God's will for us, which is learned from his Word (*Inst.,* III, ii, 6). For this reason there is no isolated objectification in Calvin, nor a mere interest in showing that there is a God, but a concern that we learn to know what his will concerning us is.[30]

In Bavinck's short survey of the history of this confession, he points out that in the course of time it began to lose its place of honor in Reformed theology and to yield to an "enlightenment" that credited the mind with insight into the divine nature of Scripture.[31] This "enlightenment" had no room for a direct correlation between the Word of God and faith, since it interposed between the two all kinds of reasonings and arguments to prove the truth of Holy Scripture. Later, rationalism secularized this position.

According to Bavinck, the doctrine of the *testimonium* was somehow revived again when it was realized that rationalism was untrustworthy and apologetics unfruitful. In this connection he mentions Kant's criticism of the proofs for the existence of God. Once again there was room for the conviction that it is meaningful to speak of a testimony of the Spirit, because it was seen that the ultimate basis of faith cannot lie outside of us in proofs and arguments, the church, or tradition, "but can be found only in man himself, in the religious subject."[32] Bavinck here expresses his appreciation for any insight into the uniqueness of *religious* certainty.

Only the Holy Spirit himself can give certainty and con-

28. *Ibid.* See "firm and steady conviction" and the testimony of his adoption in his commentary on Eph. 1:13.
29. *Ibid.*
30. "For it is not so much our concern to know who he is in himself, as what he wills to be toward us" (*Inst.,* III, ii, 6).
31. *GD,* I, 553.
32. *Ibid.,* p. 555.

quer all doubts; even though man himself is directly involved in every aspect of his life, the *auctoritas divina* is all-pervasive.[33] Hence, by saying that the "ultimate basis of faith is in the religious subject," Bavinck does not mean that it is not God but man who creates certainty: on the contrary, "the subject does not create the truth; it only recognizes and acknowledges it."[34] That is why he can say in one breath that the ultimate basis of faith lies in the religious subject and that Holy Scripture is self-authenticating, the final ground of faith,[35] and add to it that "carefully speaking," the testimony of the Spirit is not the ultimate ground.[36] Thus, it is not the testimony of man's own spirit but the testimony of God that causes man to rest in his salvation. In this way Bavinck maintains the correlative connection between faith and revelation, and refuses to proceed from an alleged continuity between man's own spirit and judgment and the testimony of the Spirit. Bavinck's rejection of the isolation and supernaturalization of the *testimonium* does not lead him to deny the testimony of the Spirit to and in man over against man's autonomous judgment.

It is not difficult to see why, in connection with salvation and certainty, the church's reflection and discussion always centered on the Holy Spirit. From the Word of God it increasingly learned to understand better that certainty of faith was by no means a self-evident human correlate of revelation by natural rational insight. The biblical-pneumatological aspect of faith, knowledge, trust, and certainty is clearly seen in the fact that faith and knowledge do not come from "flesh and blood" (see Mt. 16:17), and in the radical and revealing statement that "no one comprehends the thoughts of God except the Spirit of God" (I Cor. 2:11). According to the New Testament, certainty can never be explained in terms of the receptivity of the human heart or its capacity to reassure itself and convince itself of the truth. In the words of Paul, it is God himself who has revealed it to us through the Spirit, who "searches everything, even the depths of God" (I Cor. 2:10). The Spirit is given "that we might understand the gifts bestowed on us by God" (v. 12). We need to be "taught by the Spirit" (v. 13), since "the unspiritual man does not receive

33. *Ibid.,* p. 432.
34. *Ibid.,* p. 557.
35. *Ibid.,* p. 559.
36. *Ibid.,* p. 569.

the gifts of the Spirit of God," and is thus unable to understand them (vv. 14, 15).

The consideration of the mystery of the knowledge of God, of faith, and of complete, limitless trust, is not a general epistemological problem concerning the various ways in which man arrives at certain knowledge, but a confrontation with the marvel of the gift of being taught and led. Realizing this, the church was prompted to proceed with care in its own life and in its witness and exhortation, avoiding the use of force or coercion. At the same time, it is clear that a realization of the necessity of the decisive and exclusive significance of the Spirit's work for true knowledge and understanding does not mean an esoteric acceptance of an uncontrollable and irrational event that surprises a person in the darkness and isolation of his uncomprehending life, but instead points to the operation of the Spirit in its convincing nature. The wonder of faith and certainty may not be described as an irrational event or fact unapproachable except through individual experiences like that of the healed man born blind: "... one thing I know, that though I was blind, now I see" (Jn. 9:25). Rather, the New Testament depicts the wonder of faith in a wealth of essential contexts. Christ promises that the Holy Spirit "will guide you into all the truth" (Jn. 16:13). As the Spirit of truth, he bears witness to Christ (Jn. 15:26), and in direct relationship with him he "convinces the world of sin, of righteousness, and of judgment" (Jn. 16:8).

The powerful operation of the testimony of the Spirit centers in the salvation that has appeared in Christ. It is impressive how the New Testament speaks of the way that leads to faith and certainty as a testimony of Christ bearing witness to himself, and of the Father bearing witness to him (Jn. 8:18-19).[37]

37. Note the reference that the witness of two persons is true (v. 17; cf. Deut. 17:6; 19:15). When the legitimacy of Christ's statements are at stake, he also says that his witness would not be true if he would bear witness to himself. Someone else bears witness to him, and that testimony is true (Jn. 5:32). Cf. the Pharisees' accusation: "You are bearing witness to yourself; your testimony is not true" (Jn. 8:13), and Christ's answer: "Even if I do bear witness to myself, my testimony is true." It is obvious that the variation is determined by the different situations and is not contradictory (Jn. 5:31; 8:14-18), because in the one instance where he does not bear witness to himself, he takes into account "the people and their manner of thinking" regarding a profound testimony of oneself (N. Brox, *Zeuge und Märtyrer. Untersuchungen zur frühchristlicher Zeugnis-terminologie* [1961], p. 73). Cf. also Jn. 7:18 on speaking on one's own authority and seeking glory by doing so, and on

This legitimating is taken up and secured by the Holy Spirit and carried out into the world. The Spirit speaks, proclaims, and bears witness to this truth in spite of all opposition, and his testimony is trustworthy. The New Testament presents a unique connection between the Holy Spirit and the truth: "And the Spirit is the witness, because the Spirit is the truth" (I Jn. 5:7).

The New Testament does not, however, envision an isolated and supernatural testimony of the Spirit present in the human world of lies as a fact that cannot be further described. Rather, his testimony is the foundation and ferment of the witness of the apostles, who received the promise that the Spirit of the Father would speak through them at the time that they were called to bear witness to the Gentiles (Mt. 10:18; cf. Acts 1:8). Their witness came into being under the authorization and blessing of the Spirit to the extent that it could be said that it was not they who spoke, but the Spirit of the Father in them, who engaged their witness in his service (Acts 5:32; Jn. 15:27; Acts 22:20). From the world of men – amidst all its uncertainty – the testimony of God resounds as a true and trustworthy word of man, as the human witness concerning Christ. Because of this concrete content of the testimony of the Spirit and of eyewitnesses, this testimony cannot be understood as an errant, mysterious, irrational event.[38] Rather, its structure is thus so that it is recognizable; and because this testimony can be recognized, the church warns the believers not to believe every spirit, but to "test the spirits whether they are of God" (I Jn. 4:1; cf. I Cor. 12:10). This warning does not imply any sort of higher criterion by which the Spirit himself can be tested, but it is meant to criticize arbitrary appeals to the Spirit. The definitive criterion is the coming of Jesus Christ in the flesh (I Jn. 4:6). Only thereby can the Holy Spirit's testimony in the correlation between man's confession and man's witness be recognized.[39]

being true in seeking the glory of one's sender. See also C. H. Dodd, *The Interpretation of the Fourth Gospel* (1953), p. 329 and Bultmann's commentary on John (ET, 1971), pp. 263-64, 280-81.

38. Cf. Preiss, p. 28.
39. The application of this criterion is clearly evident in I Cor. 12:3 in the contrast of "Jesus be cursed!" and "Jesus is Lord." Cf. W. Schmithals, *Gnosticism in Corinth* (ET, 1971), pp. 124ff. Schmithals specifically answers the question how anyone in the church could say *anathema Iesous,* considering this a Gnostic separation between the heavenly pneuma-Christ and the man Jesus (pp. 127-28). He says that he finds

The testimony of the Spirit does not exclude man, but wins his inner consent. This is evident above all in Romans, where the Spirit's witness is directly related to man's being a child of God: "... it is the Spirit himself bearing witness with our spirit that we are children of God" (8:16). Because Paul's statement is so specific, it is obvious how necessary it is to give further explanation whenever we describe the Spirit's testimony by the term "formal." For the concrete content of this testimony is the *adoptio* in direct relation to the receiving of the Spirit "by whom we cry, 'Abba! Father!' " (v. 15). It is by means of a testimony that this unassailable certainty, with all its concomitant eschatological perspective, grows (v. 17). This testimony of the Spirit is called "a bearing witness with" our spirit (Rom. 8:16). This description of it points out how much this testimony touches man, without being in immediate continuity with the natural heart or explicable on the basis of anything in man himself. One could speak of being filled with words by the mystery, citing a great variety of references (Rom. 8:15; Gal. 4:6; Rom. 8:26-27). Such Scripture passages are an urgent exhortation to carefulness in theological formulation and a warning against simplistic biblicism.

All this shows a concentration on the believer's filial relationship to God. It is no wonder that Paul's statement on the Spirit's witness to the believer's sonship has played an important role in many discussions of the *testimonium* and Holy Scripture. Theologians have always sensed intuitively that one cannot dualistically place the confession of the Reformation alongside the certainty concerning one's sonship. Bavinck declares emphatically that, regarding the Spirit's testimony, one must first of all think of this filial relationship, calling it "the central truth, the core and focus of this testimony."[40] Furthermore, realizing the necessity for this doctrine to be based on the pronouncements of the Bible, theologians had to continually take into account its explicit statement regarding man's sonship, particularly when they discussed the *testimonium* in connection with Holy Scripture. The Reformed confession can be correctly understood and function only in connection with this testimony regarding the believer's sonship.

this exegesis already with Godet. For a different opinion, see F. W. Grosheide, *Commentary on the First Epistle to the Corinthians* (1953), p. 281, who does not think that this text has reference to an actual event in the church. Schmithals especially points out the connection between I Cor. 12 and I Jn. (p. 126).

40. *GD,* I, 564.

There can be no splitting of the *testimonium* into two separate *testimonia,* namely, one regarding our sonship, and another concerning the truth of Scripture. In the light of the New Testament we clearly see the victorious nature of the Spirit's witness. It is a witness concerning Christ and his salvation that reaches to the depths of the heart in the face of all former estrangement, bondage, doubt, and uncertainty. Although Bavinck does not examine the New Testament witness terminology exclusively, he nevertheless clearly reflects its tenor when he calls the *testimonium* "the triumph of the Holy Spirit in the world," "the victory of the foolishness of the cross over the wisdom of the world," and "the triumph of the thoughts of God over the deliberations of men."[41] This triumph does not manifest an independent illumination of the Spirit. Whenever the doctrine of the *testimonium* went in that direction, the Word of God was devaluated. But neither is the confession of the *testimonium* a theoretical explanation of certainty on the basis of an established cause. Rather, it is a confessing declaration, an account of the way that leads from the Word to faith and its certainty.[42]

This has often been expressed in a way that seems to be a subtle differentiation at first glance, but which nevertheless has something essential in view: that the witness of the Spirit is not the ultimate basis of faith, and that we believe Scripture "not *because* of but *through* the Spirit's testimony."[43] These formulations can be understood correctly only if they are not regarded as theoretical constructs but rather as part of a believing understanding of the miracle of certainty, which does not originate in man himself amid all his uncertainty and doubt. The Reformed confession is the discovery, already reflected in Jeremiah: "O Lord, thou hast deceived[44] me, and I was deceived; thou art stronger than I, and thou hast prevailed" (Jer. 20:7). This prevailing power of God has nothing to do with coercion; nevertheless, in faith it is understood as divine force and triumph, with the attendant subjective correlate of capitulation, which in turn becomes the source of the greatest freedom and certainty.

On the basis of the New Testament, the confession of the

41. *Ibid.,* p. 570.
42. Cf. G. W. Locher, *Testimonium internum: Calvins Lehre vom Heiligen Geist und das hermeneutische Problem* (1964), p. 6.
43. Bavinck, *GD,* I, 568; cf. Krusche, p. 208.
44. The Dutch Nieuwe Vertaling, which Berkouwer uses, has the word "overwhelmed" or "liberally overridden" here (tr. note).

Spirit is first of all related to salvation in Christ; and *then* the Word of God is discussed. It has often been noted that Scripture itself speaks of a testimony of the Spirit, but not in direct relation to Holy Scripture. This argument seemed to be quite powerful, especially over against the Reformation's emphasis on *sola Scriptura* in the foundation of its dogma. It is obvious, however, that precisely because of the *sola Scriptura* principle Reformed theology was not confronted with the dilemma of a dualism between authoritative Scripture and the message it brings, because Reformed theology hears the message of salvation precisely in the witness of Scripture. Hence, there can be no objection to the expression "faith in Scripture" (except for the possible misunderstanding of it), and it is incorrect to say that this is the same as a trivial faith in a book. To deduce a contradiction from this is nothing but an abstraction in which one no longer understands the power and the miracle of the testimony. This miracle is the miracle of the burning heart about which the disciples on the road to Emmaus speak in inescapable connection with Christ's testimony: "Did not our hearts burn within us while he talked to us on the road, while he opened to us the scriptures?" (Lk. 24:32). This is no irrational fact that as an immediate and direct event is disconnected from the message of Scripture.[45] On the contrary, just when we speak about the Spirit's testimony and the heart, we are warned against devaluating the written and spoken Word. The question is not whether faith in Scripture can be joined with true Christian faith, but only in what way there can be such a combination or harmony.

This question is of decisive significance for understanding the confession of the *testimonium Spiritus Sancti.* Central to this question is the meaning of "faith" in the expression "faith in Scripture," especially as it comes to a head in Question 21 of the Heidelberg Catechism: "What is true faith?" The Catechism then speaks of holding for truth all that God has revealed in his Word — which is a "sure knowledge" — and it speaks of a "firm confidence which the Holy Spirit works in my heart by the gospel." The wording strongly emphasizes the "for me" aspect.

Theologians have long discussed the relationship between "knowledge" and "firm confidence." Many have preferred to solve the problem by resorting to a less dualistic terminology such as found in Calvin's definition of faith as "a firm and

45. Cf. Heidegger's opposition to the "irrational movement of the heart" in H. Heppe, *Reformed Dogmatics* (ET, 1950), p. 25.

certain knowledge of God's benevolence toward us" (*Inst.*, III, ii, 7). We need not go further into this matter of wording, since it is generally agreed that Calvin on the one hand does not mean by *cognitio* a purely intellectual knowledge, and that the Catechism on the other is not referring to a combination of intellectual *fides historica* and trusting *fides salvifica*. Common to all attempts at formulating the essence of Christian faith was the conviction that Christian faith is not — as it has been expressed — an act of the mind as *cum assensu cogitare*, as assent to all those things that God sets forth to be believed.[46] Neither in Calvin ("toward us" and "God's benevolence") nor in the Catechism is there an isolation or autonomizing of belief in Scripture. True belief in Scripture is possible and real only in relation to the message of Scripture. According to Bavinck, the Reformation theologians presented "an idea of the object and essence of faith" totally different from an intellectual "assent."[47] In fact, they opposed the notion that soon became predominant in the church of "an intellectual assent to revealed truth,"[48] a notion that "had very negative results" in practical life.[49] The Reformation theologians discovered the religious nature of faith. They did not merely add the *fides historica* and the *fides salvifica* to a mechanical total, for even though they spoke of knowledge and trust, nevertheless the knowledge they had in mind was "totally different from that of historical faith."[50] It is good to recall all these things when reflecting on the nature of belief in Scripture. When the "acceptance" of Holy Scripture as the Word of God is separated from a living faith in Christ, it is meaningless and confusing to call this acceptance belief in Scripture or an "element" of the Christian faith.[51] This does not imply an underestimation of Scripture or of belief in it, but rather a great respect for Scripture, which in its testimony addresses itself to our faith. Hence, it is of great importance that the Reformed confessions definitely do not

46. *GD*, IV, 85.
47. *Ibid.*, p. 87.
48. *Ibid.*, I, 540.
49. *Ibid.*, IV, 85. According to Bavinck, no justice was done to the grand teaching of Scripture "because theologians proceeded from the everyday meaning of the word and lost sight of the religious meaning which it had in Scripture."
50. *Ibid.*, I, 541.
51. Cf. Calvin's critical reminder that if someone believes that God exists, and that the recorded history of Christ is true, such belief is worth nothing and does not deserve the name of faith (*ita indigna est fidei appellatione*), with reference to Jas. 2:19 (*Opera Selecta*, I, 68, 69).

view faith in Scripture as a preparation for true faith, or as a component of it which, if so desired, can be considered independent of it; but they connect faith in Scripture with the testimony of the Holy Spirit. They thereby do full justice to the profoundness of the biblical concept of faith, because this implies that faith in Scripture is possible and real only in connection with the witness of the Spirit to Christ and his salvation. Calvin's "toward us" and the catechism's "firm confidence" are not an anthropocentric departure from the "objective" truth of Scripture, but instead point to the purpose of Scripture: "... these [signs] are written that you may believe that Jesus is the Christ, the Son of God, and that believing you may have life in his name" (Jn. 20:31). The true meaning of faith in Scripture can be understood only in the full stature of the one true and living faith, as this is described in various words, such as: accepting, holding for truth, knowing and trusting, embracing and relying. The confession of the *testimonium Spiritus Sancti* once and for all precludes every separation of faith in Christ from faith in Scripture. Faith in Scripture is not a separate belief that must be complemented by trust.[52] The Reformation, by its confession of the testimony of the Holy Spirit, has freed faith in Scripture from its isolation and impoverishment and thus pointed out the way to a true acceptance of the prophetic-apostolic witness.

If the true confession of the testimony of the Spirit precludes the method of supplementing one kind of faith with another, neither can later critics be correct in saying that this confession leads its defenders into a vicious circle because they simultaneously confess the self-authentication of Holy Scripture.[53]

The Reformers linked the confession of the Spirit's testimony harmoniously with a great concentration on the witness of Holy Scripture. They did so because they were fully convinced that the testimony of Scripture, which addressed itself to faith, did not automatically evoke faith by way of a natural self-evidence

52. Cf. Bavinck's objection to the concept that the *fides informis* must be complemented until it becomes *fides formata* (*GD*, I, 541). Cf. also Kuyper, *E Voto*, I, 129.

53. Bavinck discusses the critics who claim that their opponents appeal to the testimony of the Spirit while at the same time insisting on the self-authentication of Scripture and then believe in revelation because there is a revelation (the *testimonium*) *concerning* revelation (I, 550, 568). Bavinck says that this is a misinterpretation of the confession because its intent is not to point out a final basis for testing and justifying Holy Scripture.

of the written Word. In this connection Calvin writes that the Word can at best touch the ears but not the heart (*Inst.*, III, i, 4). With this anthropological presentation he means to point out that there is not a single thing that can convince man, in his estrangement and isolation, of the truth of this message except God himself.[54] That is why the Reformers never devaluated the message on the basis of a misunderstood testimony of the Spirit that in essence is no more than a mystical and immediate revelation; on the contrary, it is exactly by means of this confession that they evoke and stimulate attention for this message. This confession is not a theoretical, causal explanation, but one that at the same time comprises confession of guilt and confidence in the Word. Calvin is concerned with the reality of faith and its inviolable certainty through the spirit of Christ,[55] and it is in this connection that he speaks of the blindness of our eyes which prevents us from seeing the riches of Christ that the gospel offers us.

Calvin can then approach the marvel of faith on the basis of the "secret efficacy of the Spirit" and his illumination and renovation,[56] in order to express, in an halting anthropological distinction, that the decision does not fall in the mind but in the heart (*Inst.*, III, ii, 33). By thus pointing to the heart, the confession of the testimony of the Spirit does not devaluate the Word of God; neither does it allow the inward witness to prevail over the outward, since the *testimonium* certifies the words of none other than human witnesses.[57]

We are not dealing with an isolated testimony that can afford

54. Besides many similar statements by Calvin, we refer to Luther's: "One can preach the Word to me, but to put it in my heart nobody can but God only; He must speak in my heart, otherwise nothing will come of it" (quoted in P. Althaus, *Die Christliche Wahrheit* [1947], I, 221).
55. Cf. Calvin on I Cor. 2:10, where he refers to the Spirit, and adds "for the encouragement of believers" as if we were told: "Let it be enough for us that we have the Spirit of God as witness." Cf. also *posse comprehendi Evangelii doctrinam* through the testimony of the Spirit (Locher, *op. cit.*, p. 19).
56. Locher, p. 19.
57. "Let this point therefore stand: that those whom the Holy Spirit has inwardly taught truly rest upon Scripture" (*Inst.*, I, vii, 5). See also what follows in connection with Scripture's self-authentication. It is not fair to lift Calvin's statements on the outward preaching as being "useless and vain unless the teaching of the Spirit is added to it" (in his commentary on Jn. 14:26) out of their context, because it is exactly his opposition to abstraction that governs his polemical thinking. Cf. his commentary on Rom. 10:17, on the voice of man being his virtue.

certainty concerning the authority of Scripture apart from trust, but with one that binds us to the message, to the testimony of Scripture itself. Krusche has pointed out many places in Calvin's commentaries where he relates the testimony of the Spirit and the sealing by the Spirit to the resurrection of Christ, the gospel, the promise, and the adoption as being the contents of the prophetic-apostolic witness.[58] Wholly in line with this is Calvin's rejection of a spiritualism that makes great display of the superiority of the Spirit, but rejects all reading of Scripture itself, and derides the simplicity of "those who, as they express it, still follow the dead and killing letter" (*Inst.,* I, ix, 1). These men tear asunder what is indissolubly joined in union.[59] For the Spirit does not give new and hitherto unheard revelations,[60] but confirms the teaching of the gospel in our hearts. Within the concrete situation at the time of the Reformation, this meant the rejection of the appeal to the Spirit which inevitably and always must lead to the triumph of subjectivism, and hence it would be incorrect to view Calvin's doctrine of the *testimonium* and the self-authentication of Scripture as a one-sided reaction against spiritualism.[61] He is concerned with the meaning of Old Testament prophecy — the Spirit and the Word — and with the connection between the witnessing Spirit of Christ and the apostolic witness which he himself has called forth. For that reason Calvin rejects the contextless contrasts between *pneuma* and *gramma,* between spirit and letter, since Scripture is not merely outward and hence unreal *gramma* — worthless and insufficient. Calvin does not abstract the letters and words of Holy Scripture from the context and relatedness in which they serve and function; and he calls attention to the "living oracles" that Moses received to give to the people (Acts 7:38). To speak of Scripture as, and to reduce it to, mere *gramma* is nothing else than an abstraction of the letters of a book as such, because then the phrase "as such" points up the illegitimacy of the abstraction. On the basis of the context of the written and spoken word,

58. Cf. Krusche, p. 212, and Calvin's commentary on Rom. 1:4; I Cor. 1:6; Eph. 1:4; and I Cor. 2:12.
59. *Inst.,* I, ix, 1. Calvin quotes here (as in I, vii, 4) Isa. 59:21: "My Spirit which is upon you, and my words which I have put in your mouth."
60. Cf. Calvin's commentary on Jn. 14:26: the Spirit is not "a constructor of new revelations." Cf. also on Jn. 16:12: against blasphemy.
61. Cf. Peter Brunner, *Vom Glauben bei Calvin* (1925), p. 98, against Karl Heim. Prenter's *Spiritus Creator,* pp. 105ff., points out that Luther's position is already noticeable before his attack on spiritualism. It only increases to greater polemic intensity.

Calvin can answer the question why Stephen calls the law "living oracles": Christ himself is contained therein.[62]

When it is thus clear from the nature and the contents of the scriptural witness that the work of the Spirit by no means relativizes it, then it is also obvious that there are not two separate kinds of witness, one that must be called the outer and the other the inner testimony. Only robbing the written words of their meaning can lead to such dualism and in the end to a spiritualism that always thrives on dualism and exerts its suggestive power.[63] For that reason Calvin calls faith "the principal work of the Holy Spirit" and the Spirit "the inner teacher," and thus he conquers the contrast between figurative and real (*Inst.*, III, i, 4). The action of the Spirit of Christ, the Paraclete himself, calls forth the human testimony. Hence, the Spirit does not minimize this testimony but only man's reasoning, which he exposes to the light of the ultimate proof of the truth of Scripture, which is derived from the person of God himself.[64] So the *testimonium Spiritus Sancti* does not oppose the self-authentication of Scripture, but forms a unity with it when it is received as directed towards Christ and his salvation.

From all the aspects of the confession of the *testimonium Spiritus Sancti,* it is evident that the problem of ultimate cer-

62. Cf. Calvin's commentary on Acts 7:38: "But it is asked, 'Why does he call the Law a living word?'" This does not contradict II Cor. 3, Calvin correctly says, because Paul does not view the word and preaching as a dead letter and sound, and is not speaking of a dead letter, but of a letter that works death, of an active *gramma,* for example, when the law is divorced from the gospel and presented as the way to salvation (II Cor. 3:6). Cf. Calvin's commentary on II Cor. and *Inst.*, I, ix, 3, with reference to the disciples on the way to Emmaus and to I Thess. 5:19-20 (the warning against quenching the Spirit and despising prophesying). Calvin's views are still very valuable, especially over against the interpretation of II Cor. 3:6 (the killing written code) which has become tradition. On the *pneuma-gramma* antithesis, cf. *TDNT,* I, 765-768.
63. Cf. Prenter, *op. cit.,* p. 104, who describes the background of the problem with which the Reformation wrestled as follows: "On the one side there is such a strong emphasis on the sovereignty of the Spirit that the outward Word seems to be reduced to a comparatively insignificant accompanying phenomenon of the free work of the Spirit. On the other side there is so strong an emphasis on the connection of the Spirit to the outward Word, on its being a necessary consequence of the Word, that the Spirit seems to become a mere attribute to the Word."
64. *Inst.,* I, vii, 4: "Thus, the highest proof of Scripture derives in general from the fact that God in person speaks in it." Cf. I, vii, 1: ". . . the Scriptures obtain full authority among believers only when men regard them as having sprung from heaven, as if there the living words of God were heard."

tainty is at stake here. The Reformers, surrounded as they were by Roman Catholicism and spiritualism, fully realized that what was at stake was "the hearing of God's very own Word,"[65] with certainty and comfort as the goal of that which was written (cf. Rom. 15:4).

This confession of the testimony of the Spirit was not intended to give a rational and theoretical solution or explanation to the relationship between Word and Spirit. The Reformers realized that it is impossible to ascribe all kinds of human experiences to the Spirit's operation. For those who do so, the function of Scripture and of preaching is to illustrate what is experienced in the depths of subjectivity and not the confrontation of man with the authoritative testimony of God. But even subsequent to the rejection of such an exclusion of the Word, the mystery of Word and Spirit remains unfathomable. When confronted with the Word, we cannot by means of a solution or technique trace or circumscribe the way from the Word to faith. Every attempt to somehow clarify the mystery remains revealingly unsatisfactory. This becomes evident as soon as we try to express this mystery in all kinds of exclusive terminology, and to express the operation, power, and conviction of the Spirit as *with* the Word or as *through* the Word. We can observe that in the history of the Reformed churches, theologians were of the opinion that the mystery could be expressed both as *with* and as *through* without doing injustice to it by emphasizing both the significance and power of the Word, which deals with this "absolutely incomparable matter,"[66] and the witnessing and convincing Spirit who wins the hearts over to Christ.

The mystery cuts across every exclusive formulation[67] and itself points out the way from the Word to faith, a way in which we can walk only in fear and trembling. It is remarkable that all kinds of seemingly logical arguments and conclusions may

65. Holl, "Luther und die Schwärmer," *Luther* (1923), p. 431, in connection with the Holy Spirit. See also Calvin, *Inst.*, I, vii, 4: "... God alone is a fit witness of himself in his Word...." Cf. W. Niesel, *The Theology of Calvin* (ET, 1956), p. 33.
66. Weber, *Grundlagen*, I, 269.
67. No doubt that is what the Augsburg Confession is referring to when it says, "For by the Word and Sacraments, as by instruments, the Holy Spirit is given: who worketh faith, where and when it pleaseth God, in those that hear the gospel ..." (Schaff, *Confessions*, III, 10). Cf. Berkouwer, *Sin* (ET, 1971), pp. 214ff., where I have extensively discussed the matter that it is incorrect to say that the Reformed position exclusively sees it as "with the Word."

lead to an impasse that leaves no more room for the ministry and man's responsibility. To sense and emphasize this is not a flight into an irrationalism that prefers vagueness rather than clarity of insight and confession, but directly results from the nature of the witness of God and the mystery of the Spirit which can be understood only by faith. Rationalization of this mystery always leads to conclusions which in the preaching reveal themselves as illegitimate foreign elements. Men have given rational explanations of the relation between the Word and the Spirit such that the testimony of Scripture and of preaching were suddenly placed in a vacuum and reduced to powerless and hence meaningless "outward" things. By misinterpreting the striving of the Spirit that calls the human witness into his service, they finally ended up in the direction of spiritualism. Thus, Holy Scripture became merely a "revelation" that was confirmed by an added testimony of the Holy Spirit, and thus the connection with the human testimony regarding salvation in history became obscured. This opened the way to an appeal to the Spirit as *privatus Spiritus,* and he was used as a criterion that cast its shadow of doubt on the trustworthiness and persuasiveness of the prophetic-apostolic testimony. The relation between faith and revelation took on more and more formal traits, and men became ignorant of the way in which Scripture itself speaks of the claim of the gospel as the power of God (I Cor. 1:18 – the word of the cross) and the sword of the Spirit (Eph. 6:17). The protest (which in itself is justifiable) against externalization and literalism could thus develop into a denial of the meaningful language of Scripture by abstracting the testimony that comes to us in words into mere "word" and "letters."[68] Individualism and subjectivism misinterpreted the meaning and intent of the Spirit's words, with the result that the emphasis on "for us" (and "for me") narrowed down and reduced the divine to one's own existential experiences. A more serious caricature of the Spirit's witness is hardly imaginable, and the Reformers, although in groping and halting language, clearly saw and proclaimed this. Exactly in view of these errors, the Reformed confession of the

68. Remarkably revealing is Paul's statement that his gospel preaching had come to the church "not only in word, but also in power and in the Holy Spirit" (I Thess. 1:5). This has nothing to do with spiritualism. Cf. the antithesis in I Cor. 1:17 (the wisdom of words) and I Cor. 4:20 (power versus words) – a clear *polemic.* Cf. further many expressions in I Thess., such as receiving the Word with joy in the Holy Spirit (1:6), the sounding forth of the Word (1:8), the active Word (2:13), speaking to save (2:16), and the glorification of the Word (II Thess. 3:1).

testimony of the Spirit is the definitive defense,[69] because in the controversy regarding certainty – in the midst of many and varied kinds of "spirits" – it points to the way of faith that removes all autonomy, both theoretical and practical, from every reflection on the criteria. To those traveling the way of faith, the testimony of the Spirit does not merely "compensate" for the Word that "as such" (the "as such" of an abstraction) is inoperative and powerless, but binds them increasingly to the witness concerning Christ. Hence, we are confronted with the fact that, by precluding every mechanical "certification," all dogmatic reflection of its own nature must remind us of the prayer, "Come, Creator Spirit!" We are not concerned here with an edifying and practical application of the doctrine, but with its own structure and contents. This also implies a serious warning against the idea that a traditional belief in Scripture can be retained when a living subjection to the message of Scripture no longer governs life to the depths of the heart. For belief in Scripture conforms to the will of God only when it is the response to the preaching of the mystery which "now is disclosed and through the prophetic writings is made known . . . according to the command of the eternal God, to bring about the obedience of faith" (Rom. 16:26). Belief in Scripture is inseparably connected with this testimony – with the gospel. Without this gospel it is doomed to rigidity.

In a cultural surrounding which engulfs the "controversial Bible" with disquietude and various attacks, the preaching of the gospel is itself the only way in which we can speak about Scripture, not in whispers but with thankfulness and songs of praise. In this we follow the Israelite when he spoke of God's Word as his lamp and light and testified to his love for the law (Ps. 119:105, 113). In this way we come to understand the witness of the Paraclete and through this in turn the secret of true piety – the divine command to pay attention to the witness of Scripture (Rom. 16:26). These then become "spotlights illuminating the magnificent drama of God's saving acts."[70]

In a noteworthy formulation appended to the confession regarding the *testimonium,* the Belgic Confession expressly states

69. According to Weber (p. 268), this confession is "the only really new development which Reformed theology has contributed regarding the basis of the authority of Scripture, i.e., this discovery in connection with "a new encounter with Scripture" which is so characteristic of the Reformation.

70. H. N. Ridderbos, *Aan De Romeinen* (1959), p. 354.

that a recognition of the witness of the Spirit does not endanger or belittle the testimony of Scripture: ". . . whereof they carry the evidence in themselves. For the very blind are able to perceive that the things foretold in them are fulfilling" (Art. V; Schaff, III, 387). It can readily be understood that these words occasioned much debate. This becomes evident when we take note of the manner in which Calvin spoke of the testimony of the Holy Spirit. He separated it from all proofs or rational arguments for the trustworthiness of Scripture. Questions have been raised whether these words of the Belgic Confession agreed with the real intention of the confession regarding the testimony of the Spirit. For does not this confession speak of the mysterious nature of faith in Scripture in the sense that Scripture is not matter-of-fact and not readily apparent to human understanding? Is this decisive perspective not contradicted by adducing "evidence," and by giving it a function parallel to the internal witness in establishing certainty? The striking assertion that even the blind are able to perceive[71] appeared to support such objections, especially in the light of later attempts to posit various "proofs" for the trustworthiness of Scripture alongside the testimony of the Spirit. Was it not the real intention of the confession of the testimony of the Spirit to point out that the heart was blind and closed to this very witness of God and through this to posit the need for prayer for continuing illumination so that man might receive the miracle of vision and understanding?

It is not easy in this discussion to arrive at a conclusion by means of the words which really stand out — the "evidence" and the "very blind" being able to perceive. He who recognizes the human side and the incomplete nature of confessional statements and wishes to guard himself against mere harmonization must confront the distinct fact that the "evidence" adduced here differs from the proofs and arguments which were later coordinated with the *testimonium Spiritus Sancti*. For, while Article V does not mention the varied qualities of Scripture itself, it distinctly approaches the Word of God on the basis of its contents. The writers clearly did not wish to isolate the *testimonium Spiritus Sancti* from the message of Scripture, and in the same breath they mentioned the self-authenticating nature of Scripture's witness. They did so by relating this self-authenticating element to the content and message of Scripture. The fact that the "evidence" of this authority and trustworthi-

71. The Dutch version, which Berkouwer cites, has an even stronger expression. It states that the blind can "touch" the evidence (tr. note).

ness are inherent in Scripture was pointed out by a reference to the fulfillment of God's Word in history. Polman's heavy emphasis on this aspect is quite correct. A merely natural recognition of Scripture as a supernatural phenomenon with the consequent "rational" proofs is not possible. Scripture authenticates itself, especially where its message is concerned. This then is Polman's intention when he forbids us to look upon Scripture as a "precious document with a certain quantity of truths" in separation from the continuing mighty acts of God.[72] We must rather focus our attention on the fulfillment of that Word. We must see the promises of God as words which do not fall to the ground nor return to him empty (I Sam. 3:19 and Isa. 55:11). It is my opinion that such a view does not proceed from an outlook on history that circumvents faith. The formulation, "even the very blind are able to perceive," does not intend to replace the uniqueness of the *testimonium Spiritus Sancti* by mere rational insight and intrinsically convincing evidence. It rather seeks to manifest the confidence of a faith that knows that the acts of God are not esoteric mysteries. The problem that Article V wishes to comment on is not the completion of the testimony of the Holy Spirit; it gives us a perspective on that testimony and the acts of God. This is in itself an important indication that, although the confession is diametrically opposed to every attempt to formalize the Word, it yet refers to Scripture as the mighty oracles and the acts of God himself. Its reference to the fact that even the blind can touch reminds us of Paul's retort to Festus' criticism of his defense. When accused of madness, he did not fall back on being privy to an esoteric mystery open only to initiates, but rather affirms that he is speaking the "sober truth" and accurately indicates that what happened "was not done in a corner" (Acts 26:25-27). Speaking about the "evidence" inherent in Scripture, evidence which culminates in a reference to the truth and the power of God's Word, adds no "arguments" to the witness of the Spirit, but rather proffers a perspective on a nonreactionary confession of this testimony, a confession which does not alienate us from the message of Scripture but rather allows us to rest in it.

We have noted in passing that Bavinck answered Strauss's contention that the confession of the *testimonium Spiritus*

72. A. D. R. Polman, *Woord en Belijdenis,* I, 111. See also his *Nederlandse Geloofsbelijdenis,* I, 226ff. Polman's emphasis is on Scripture's focus on God's mighty deeds and on the redemptive-historical character of God's Word.

Sancti is "the Achilles' heel of the Protestant system."[73] Bavinck countered by asserting that what here seems to be weakness or indefensibility is in reality a sign of power, indeed the cornerstone of the Christian confession of the Spirit's triumph in the world. Besides evincing a remarkable parallel to Barth on this point,[74] this answer, at first glance, seems to be not much more than a rather easy piece of apologetic one-upmanship which does not really do justice to Strauss's objection. Only recently was such a transposition – moving from weakness to strength – brought sharply to the fore in H. A. Smit's critique of Kierkegaard. Smit sees this turning of what has always been considered Christianity's weakest point into its point of strength as "the key to his defense of Christianity," and describes this method as "this judo-like ability to turn weakness into strength."[75] Without examining the structure of Kierkegaard's apologetics any further, we can readily see that a similar parallel is conspicuously present in Bavinck's answer to Strauss. He formulates it in the context of his apologetic for the Christian faith and the testimony of the Holy Spirit. It is exactly this testimony which is for him "the crown and seal of all Christian truth, the triumph of the Spirit in the world."[76] By transposing in his answer from the weak to the strong, he is not indulging in mere rhetorical technique which reveals its own weakness in a meaningless shift of words. He instead draws attention to the depth of certainty, a depth which does not and cannot find its origin in human reason, but which can only come about through the testimony of the Spirit. Bavinck sees such a formulation as clearly and essentially related to the manner in which Paul discusses strength

73. Strauss, *op. cit.,* I, 136. In his opinion this weakness becomes apparent in two possible perversions. It can lead to fanaticism (which treats the Spirit as a source of new revelation and opposes it to Scripture) and to rationalism. For he asks, "Who then assures me that my experience derives from the working of the Holy Spirit in me?" It does not help, according to Strauss, to "posit between the Scripture and the human spirit a 'divine something' testifying in my spirit to the former, for who then witnesses to me of the divinity of such a testimony?"
74. Compare Barth's answer to Strauss: "Indeed who does attest the divinity of this witness? What Strauss failed to see is that there is no Protestant 'system,' but that the Protestant church and Protestant doctrine has necessarily and gladly to leave this question unanswered; because at its weakest point, where it can only acknowledge and confess, it has all its indestructible strength" (*CD,* I/2, 537). Cf. also Weber, I, 268.
75. *Kierkegaard's Pilgrimage of Man. The Road of Self-positing and Self-abdication* (1965), pp. 37ff.
76. *GD,* I, 570.

and weakness: the foolish and the weak things of God which are stronger and wiser than men (I Cor. 1:25). Human reason holds them to be madness because they are spiritually discerned (I Cor. 2:14). Bavinck does not by mere technique transpose them into strength and glory; for they are *in reality* "the essence and glory of Christianity."[77] This power is the reverse side of the secret, which is revealed not to the wise and understanding but to babes (Mt. 11:25; cf. 16:17), a secret for which Christ thanked the Father. Bavinck's argument versus Strauss[78] reminds one of the deepest motifs of Luther's *theologia crucis,* when it denies to rational and autonomous man a way to God outside the cross. This apologetic does not therefore glorify a weakness into an ode to uncertainty or a protest against assurance. In a pastoral-theological examination it rather seeks to point out the only way in which an answer is found to the deepest quest for certainty.

The strong language which Bavinck uses to express the confession of the testimony of the Spirit could lead to the understanding that this confession provides us with one simple and sufficient answer to the manifold questions which are so often denoted as "problems regarding Scripture." This is not at all the case. We can instead see that many important questions concerning this confession will continue to engage our attention. For instance, if we take this Reformation confession to definitively exclude every attempt at formalizing and mechanizing the testimony while we focus our attention on the message of Scripture in its peculiar authority, we are directly confronted with the question regarding the subjection of our faith to the entire Bible. How must we consider the testimony of the Spirit when it confronts us with God's message as the message of Holy Scripture? Keeping the concrete Scripture in mind, the holy and canonical books listed in the Belgic Confession, does not our confession of the *testimonium Spiritus Sancti,* despite its focus

77. Cf. Smit's characterization of Kierkegaard: "Here is an apologetic which need not be ashamed. It does not betray the Christian faith by subjecting it to Reason; instead Reason is brought into subjection and becomes the servant of faith" (p. 39). This certainly cannot be labeled a "technique."

78. One could question whether Bavinck's answer meets Strauss's criticism *precisely*. The latter saw in this confession an untenable antinomy. Yet it must be granted that Bavinck met it in its very core. By saying that the "preceding demonstration" is not necessary when one is in communion with God, he robs Strauss's contention of its basis. Cf. R. Rothe's *Zur Dogmatik* (1869), pp. 151ff.

on the message of Scripture, ultimately lead to an interpretation of this *testimonium* as an autonomous witness to the canonicity of the several books? We are faced with the fact that precisely this question, even though the answer is negative, in turn raises numerous new queries, which have always played a large part in the reflection upon Scripture as the Word of God. How do we go from Article V, in speaking of concrete canonical books "for the regulation, foundation, and confirmation of our faith," to a believing study of God's Word as a prophetic-apostolic witness?

These questions bring us to a new and important aspect of the doctrine of Holy Scripture. It has been the starting point of many discussions and has occupied, especially in our time, a dominant place. We refer to the specific and determined manner in which the church has confessed Holy Scripture as *canon*.

CHAPTER THREE

HOLY SCRIPTURE AS CANON

WE HAVE NOTED that the Reformed confession of the testimony of the Spirit regarding Holy Scripture automatically leads to a consideration of this Scripture as canon. This is especially true since this confession is not merely an escape into spiritualism but is inseparably joined to the confession of the self-authentication of Scripture. We must, therefore, pay attention to the central place which the canonical, normative aspect of Scripture has historically been given in the church.

In the daily existence of the church, it would be absurd to speak of the "problem" of the canon. The church's proclamation of the Word and the comfort and admonition it draws from the gospel are based on and limited to these writings; and this limitation does not bother it at all. Yet it would be incorrect to deem a consideration of the canonical question superfluous on the basis of this concrete situation. For this very unproblematical situation is the matrix for a conscious perspective on the power and the authority of preaching this Word alone. Even where this question is not explicitly raised, such circumscription and delimitation still subconsciously rule the life of the church. The result is that preaching and sermons not based on canonical Scripture are immediately felt to be illegitimate.

The canon and its authority have been especially prominent topics of discussion since historical criticism began to examine the Bible. It began to look at the Bible as canon and pointed to the fact that it had come about as the result of a lengthy process consisting of many factors and circumstances. Out of the prevailing atmosphere of historical relativity it was asked whether or not the traditional view of Scripture as canon could be maintained. And thus men were led to speak of a crisis.[1] This crisis

1. Cf. G. Hornig, *Die Anfänge der historisch-kritischen Theologie* (1961), pp. 60ff.; H. E. Weber, *Reformation, Orthodoxie und Rationalismus* (1940), I, 2, 260ff.; H. J. Kraus, *Geschichte der historisch-kritischen*

affected not only theological reflection but also the church itself, inasmuch as the latter never spoke of Scripture as relative and historically determined, but as authoritative, as the complete guide for faith and life.

Did this crisis regarding the conception of the canon have to lead to a suspension of all real authority? Or was there a possibility that one could still speak legitimately and meaningfully about the canon of sacred Scripture even while paying complete attention to its historical aspect? That was the question which began to engage more and more scholars and which has dominated the discussions until now.

Behind it all lies the church's acceptance of the canon — albeit in many variations. It was a recognition which was extended to the Old as well as to the New Testament; for from its very beginning the church accepted the Old Testament as a trustworthy testimony regarding the acts of God in history, as his Word and deeds in Israel. The Old Testament was viewed as a testimony which, in accordance with its own promissory nature, had been fulfilled in the messianic era. Therefore, the church did not merely mechanically connect the New Testament to the Old Testament. For the New Testament itself cannot be understood apart from the Old; it continually points to the Old Testament, to the trustworthy *graphē,* to that which has been written. Essential to this tie of the church to the Old Testament has been the word of Christ that Scripture testifies to him (Jn. 5:39). His words to the travelers to Emmaus and his interpretation of the Old Testament are also important. Beginning with Moses and the prophets, Christ pointed out "in all the scriptures the things concerning himself" (Lk. 24:27). The acceptance of the New Testament did not in any way mean disregarding its warning that we should not "go beyond the things which are written" (I Cor. 4:6, ASV).

Marcion's criticism of the Old Testament did not shake the church's conscious dependence on it; rather, it served to strengthen this dependence. In no way was the newness of the New Testament minimized: it was instead seen as that very newness for which the Old Testament itself had been aiming, as the fulfillment in Jesus Christ of the testimony regarding God's acts in Israel, as the end of a continuum.[2] Despite the

Erforschung des Alten Testaments (1956); N. Appel, *Kanon und Krise. Die Kanonskrise im heutigen Protestantismus* (1964).

2. Marcion especially placed a heavy emphasis on the completely *new* in the NT. Cf. E. C. Blackman, *Marcion and his Influence* (1948), pp. 113ff.

many questions and problems which this issue has raised in church history, the church's bond to the Old Testament has determined her life. It is understandable then that many of the questions regarding the extent of the Christian canon were focused on the New Testament, for the canon was generally considered to be closed — even though it is now evident that we can hardly speak of an official synagogical closing.[3]

In a discussion of the origin of the New Testament, the next question to be raised was naturally that of the marks of canonicity. It was a question which could also be asked regarding the Old Testament. J. L. Koole, in his discussion of the canonization of the Old Testament, does not see much value in the theory that canonization was a defense against diverging points of view. He instead asks whether or not a connection can be established between the experience of the Scripture's power, the confession of forgiveness of sins, and the experience of the joy and the responsibility of a congregation as a community.[4] For Koole it is incorrect to operate with a conception of canonicity "which accents juridical validity,"[5] or with a conception which is merely formal, a characteristic which is absolutely foreign to the Old Testament.

Here we touch upon incisive questions. These questions in turn are often closely connected with the distinction between a *formal* and a *material* concept of canonicity. The term "formal" is here meant to describe the impossibility of coming to a clear conception of canonicity apart from both the content and the power of the Old Testament witness itself. The result is that when the actual worth or authority of the Old Testament as canon for the New Testament congregation was discussed, this worth was not attributed to an irrational or contingent factuality any more than it had been by the Old Testament congregation. Rather, the stress was laid on subjugation in faith to this witness. Later, when the Old Testament became increasingly subjected to scientific investigation, such an acceptance of the Old Testament in its totality and the casualness with which it was accepted were increasingly criticized. In this context we also find

3. Consider the uncertainty regarding the so-called Synod of Jamnia (approx. 90-100 A.D.). Cf. J. L. Koole, *Het probleem van de canonisatie van het OT* (1955), p. 10. According to Koole, no one can point to "a single authority or any specific point in time by which and when this 'canonization' took place."
4. *Ibid.*, p. 14.
5. *Ibid.*, p. 19.

the problem which is so prominent in our age, the "canon within the canon" of the New Testament, and, along with that, the "Auswahl," the selection or conscious reduction of the factual canon to the real canon of the Old Testament.

It is this aspect, the centering of attention on a particular point, that begins to assume a greater role in the reflection on the "traditional" canon. The result is that many parallels come to the fore in a consideration of the New Testament canon. For example, the Old Testament also can be subjected to the test of Luther's "was Christum treibt" (that which sets forth Christ). Thus, the whole problem of the *notae canonicitatis* is posited in principle. Alongside that is the problem of the significance of a divine canon within the human prophetic witness of the Old Testament. What sorts of motives exerted influence on the formation of the canon?[6] Church history's consideration of this question, which is so intimately tied to the one regarding the Christological nature of the Old Testament, has been shaped by both an historical and a theological aspect. The latter concerns the respect which was accorded this canon in history; thus, the aspect of faith was especially central in New Testament canonics. There is here a discernible – and to a degree traceable – process of growth leading to the official ecclesiastical closing and fixation at the synods of Hippo (393 A.D.) and Carthage (397 A.D.); but it is clear that even before such a fixation, at the end of the fourth century, the New Testament canon was factually authoritative.[7]

The relationship between the canon as both norm and authority and the human considerations that can be discerned in the history of the canon soon assumed center stage. He who approaches the canon from a perspective which sharply differentiates between the divine and the human, will not even recognize the validity of speaking about a canonical "problem"; for in such a view the divine definitely rules out the possibility of a problem. The result is the apparent failure to appreciate the fact that human considerations did play a large role in the formation of the canon. This is indisputably proved by the fact that the New Testament canon that we possess was not rigidly fixed from its beginning. We find uncertainty and hesitance. Thus, it is certainly legitimate to consider the question of whether there were certain discernible motives which influenced

6. Cf. Vriezen, *OT Theology*, pp. 98-99.
7. As is apparent from the well-known Easter Festal Letter (No. 39) of Athanasius, 367 A.D.

the fixation and the extent of the New Testament canon. Could there have been one definite and objective criterion by which the canon might have been elevated beyond all doubt and by which a *numerus clausus,* an unexceedable and definite number of books, was established? Men have often wanted to infer such certainty and definiteness from an emphatic revelation concerning the inspiration of the canonical writings: their canonicity would surely then be guaranteed. Such a point of view, historically not uncommon in Roman Catholic circles, aroused much opposition. It was seen — and not unjustly so — as a way out, taken because of the insufficiency of other explanations. It provided a postulate by which the uncertainty that could arise from an historical process would be eliminated *a priori.* Moreover, it was argued that, if one supposed such a "revelation," then the real way in which the canon arose, with all its incumbent hesitance, defied explanation.[8] The problem of canonicity cannot be made clear by giving it a foundation that stands completely by itself. When this is realized, one naturally returns to face the question of the human-ecclesiastical considerations and the principle of differentiation by which the choice, the fixation, and the closing of the canon were influenced and determined.

Dealing with this question forces us to face a peculiar problem. In any process of differentiation there is sifting; there is a critical element. Because of this — and more especially so since Scripture is the Word of God — it has often been thought that the idea of a normative canon excluded any human criteria. The very idea of a canon clashed with any attempt to adduce merely human judgments as criteria and standards. For, the argument goes, is not the idea of the canon closely related to Paul's admonition to take every thought into captivity to Christ (II Cor. 10:5), and by doing this, into obedience unto this unique canon which testifies to him?[9] If the canon is canon indeed, how then can anyone suppose that it can confront us as formed, as the result of a process in which human judgments actually participated? Does not every *nota canonicitatis* lead to a distortion, if not a suspension, of the canon?

The word *kanōn* is generally defined as meaning measuring

8. Cf. K. Rahner, *Inspiration in the Bible* (ET, 1961), pp. 28ff. about the inexplicability which would have resulted if an "explicit statement" had been available.

9. Consider also Acts 17:11 and the testing which takes place in the examination of the Scriptures "to see *if* these things were so." Cf. Calvin's commentary on this text.

rod or line, a trustworthy norm immune to criticism. To be sure, the word was later also used to signify ecclesiastical dogmas as seen in Trent and in the "canons" of Dort. The ancient church often spoke of *ho kanōn tēs alētheias;* but even though the danger of identification exists,[10] it is wise to say that here a more "relational canonicity" was intended,[11] one which was sought in the conformity of *the* canon.[12] In the New Testament, "canon" signifies a standard of judgment, a norm to which every believer is subjected. Paul writes about the rule *(kanōn)* by which one must walk[13] so that by it one can determine if a man belongs to the "Israel of God" and consequently shares in its peace and mercy (Gal. 6:16). It is clear that here no human criterion is meant, but rather a canon normative for human life. And from this vantage point one can begin to see the problem of the marks of canonicity.

When one reflects upon the marks of canonicity, questions automatically arise as to the nature of the human activity which can be denoted as the "accepting," the *recipere* of the canon. What does the "we receive" of Article V of the Belgic Confession mean?[14] Is it a reception without any motives and therefore unable to sustain any further comment? Or is it indeed possible to more closely examine its nature? It is apparent that the church did not intend this activity to be one by which the canon should in reality be established. But to realize this does not as yet clarify the reception of the canon as it exists concretely. For the rejection of every possibility of a creation of the canon at the least precludes giving the canon an integral part in the course of human history and admitting that in this process various human considerations played a part.

The so-called human factor in the historical process of the

10. For a treatment of the *regula fidei* and the way it functions, see J. N. D. Kelly, *Early Christian Doctrines* (1958), pp. 35ff.; Aland, *The Problem of the NT Canon,* p. 17; *TDNT,* III, 596-602 for *kanōn.*
11. Confessionalism appreciates this relationship theoretically, but it does not really function fully in ecclesiastical practice. For a position which opposes all blurring of distinctions, see *BC,* Art. VII concerning the truth which "is above all."
12. Cf. *TDNT,* III, 600: "that which is valid and binding in the Church."
13. *Ibid.,* III, 598; the Vulgate uses "regula." Cf. also II Cor. 10:13-16 about the rule by which Paul labors.
14. Already in the Canon Muratori the term *recipere* is found (Grosheide, *Canoniek van het NT,* p. 105). It also occurs in much patristic writing in the sense of "accepting that which is canonical" (p. 107). The Latin verb *recipere* will be used throughout to denote this accepting activity of the church.

canon has been dealt with in diverse ways.[15] The awareness of the fact that "the canon in its concrete form is the result of an historical development,"[16] can only be credited to another fact: in sacred Scripture we never confront God speaking outside of human media, outside of the horizontal perspective and history. We meet the Word of God as canon precisely in the witness of the prophets and the apostles. When God speaks to the boy Samuel, his Word resounding in the sphere of human reality, the lad fails three times to differentiate between God's call and Eli's voice. Only Eli's insight brings him to the awareness, which results in heedful listening: "Speak, Lord, for thy servant hears" (I Sam. 3:2-10).[17] We focus on this incident because true listening to the voice of God always involves an evaluation and differentiation. When the Word of the Lord comes to a man, it comes into his own life on his own level. It does not come in a strange extraterrestrial or supratemporal manner, consequently making it unnecessary to distinguish it from other voices because it is incomparably and therefore irresistibly unique. Instead, it confronts man in his own creaturely existence. This also happens in preaching with human speech and even more so when the Word comes to us in writing, in a human attestation. Through this medium it is absorbed into the flow of history and thus continues to reach out to man.

Ours is a world of speech, of many words, of many written presentations of views. It is necessary to distinguish and discern.[18] It was therefore entirely correct for men, when confronted with criticism of the "external letter," to point back continuously to the meaning of "that which was written," thus not enclosing the truth of God within the moment of divine revelation but allowing it to disclose perspectives into every age. The basis of such criticism — which misjudges Scripture by appealing to the Spirit — is invariably an individualistic experi-

15. Kuyper, *Enc.*, III, 39, regarding "the human factor in establishing the canon" and the deliberation and evaluation which this human struggle and uncertainty entailed.
16. H. N. Ridderbos, *Authority*, pp. 37, 47.
17. Cf. the confusion in Jn. 12:29: the voice, an angel, or a thunderclap.
18. Paul gives thanks to God in I Thess. 2:13 that the Thessalonians received the Word of God which was preached to them, "not as the word of men but as what it really is, the word of God." In this "not-but" there is certainly no denial of the human character of preaching, but there is instead a reference to its nature, which was acknowledged and recognized. We will consider the phrase "what it really is" in another place.

ence of salvation. It neglects the universal implication of salvation and misses the meaning of Bavinck's dictum, that God's revelation entered the realm of the creaturely, became Scripture, and "as writing subjected itself to the fate of all writing."[19] In the many forms of supernaturalism there hides the ardent desire for such a revelation, which by its "purity" would free us from all the complications of the creaturely, the human, and the historical. This sort of "supernaturalism" does not understand that God is indeed the God of history and that Scripture speaks about his acts in every age, and precisely for that reason demands our full attention.

Yet others have taken this last thought as their basis for arguing that in the period of revelation there was as yet no future perspective inherent in the gospel. They claim that only the "delay of the parousia" can explain the "delegation" of the apostolic preaching. In essence they say that "the problem of the canon is that of the absence of the parousia."[20] But this point of view also has acute problems with the canon. Marxsen must speak of a "potential" canon — one which was not really intended for the future. The canon was accepted by the church only as it became aware of an historical progression which it had not expected. The church bridged the gap between itself and time as it stretched out "with the help of links connecting it to a later era."[21] Even those who think that "consistent" eschatology unjustly views the canon as a solution by which a virtue is created out of a necessity, must nevertheless admit that the meaning of the canon is intrinsically connected with the progression of history.[22] Both the progress of preaching and the

19. *GD,* I, 405, 351. Consider the dictum of J. G. Hamann, a man who paid so much attention to language: "God reveals himself — the Creator of the world is an author!" (in O. Rodenberg, *Das unvergleichliche Wort* [1964], p. 32).
20. W. Marxsen, "Das Problem des NT Kanons aus der Sicht des Exegeten," *Neue Zeitschrift für Systematische Theologie* (1960), p. 144. See also M. Werner, *The Formation of Christian Dogma* (ET, 1957), pp. 64ff. According to Werner, the development led to a tradition in which a "de-eschatologizing" took place and in which the form of this world, "which is passing away" (I Cor. 7:31), is transformed from a present into a future in which the canon is given a place with the new tradition as its content (pp. 68-69). See Cullmann's criticism of "consistent" eschatology in connection with the canon as the norm for the church "in the time thereafter" (*Salvation in History* [ET, 1967], pp. 298-99).
21. Marxsen, p. 144.
22. In this connection Cullmann has repeatedly called attention to Jn. 17:20. See *Peter, Disciple, Apostle, Martyr* (ET, 1962), p. 215; and concerning a related passage (Jn. 10:16) see *Salvation in History,* p. 282.

founding of the church are resolutely based in history and likewise in the inscripturation of the apostolic testimony. Rahner has said of this that the church "addresses herself . . . towards her own Future," with the canon becoming "the norm for the later church."[23] It is then not merely a coincidence that while we are considering the problem of the canon we will continue to encounter the historical aspect.

While reflecting upon this historical process of growth, men have followed many paths. These paths could have led to the realization that this process, even though it was channeled through human intermediaries, did not have to lead to a canon burdened with problems. The chief of these problems seems to be the concrete closing of the canon as the capstone of the process. Reformed theology generally repudiates the notion that one can appeal to the testimony of the Spirit in order to accept a canon which is actually closed. It is clear that such an appeal seeks so to connect faith and canon that the historical process can in no way cast shadows of doubt across our certainty.[24] This, however, places that very historical process which led to the fact of the canon in the foreground. The next attempted solution tried to connect the process with a specific guiding of the Holy Spirit, a "special providence," usually designated as the "acts of God with respect to the canon." The intent of this was to point out that in the last analysis it was not the human factors that led to the formation and closing of the canon, but rather God's care over the latter. Abraham Kuyper, for example, took this position.[25]

In this appeal to the providence of God as the key to the process of the canon, one motive stands out. It is the desire to see Scripture as canon from the perspective of its root in God — "to see it as guaranteed in a special way to its very borders. The uncertain elements are thus eliminated from the process, because the result of the process is forecast by providence. The net re-

23. Rahner, pp. 49-50. Cf. also C. H. Ratschow, "Zur Frage der Begründung des NT Kanons aus der Sicht der Syst. Theol.," *N.Z.S.Th.* (1960), p. 155. Here he points out that we are dependent on "tradition in the form of attestation," since revelation in Jesus Christ took place only once in "space and time."

24. See Ridderbos, *Authority*, pp. 11ff. and 39ff. against the view which holds that the testimony is an *authority* that in cases of doubt and uncertainty hands down a final decision; cf. Bavinck, *GD*, I, 567, who holds that "neither authenticity, nor canonicity, nor even inspiration," is the true object of the testimony.

25. *Enc.*, III, 28-41; cf. *Princ.*, pp. 478-481, 553ff.

sult is that such a claim as this acquires a peculiarly incidental and fragmentary aspect: it cannot but raise incisive questions regarding the connection of the providence of God with the everyday course of events.[26] On the one hand, this approach to the canon is understandable. The canon in its normativity is directly related to the founding of the church and points to that relationship;[27] but this cannot really legitimize the attempt to explain the history of the canonical process during the first centuries by calling in a "special providence." Hence, it is understandable that Ridderbos, without limiting our confession of the providence of God, denies such an attempt the right to be an explanatory principle. For here – as well as in other solutions – there is an attempt, after the fact, to point out another authority "to justify the canon."[28] And this while the historical course of the canon-forming process proves how very careful one must be in borrowing a ground for the recognition of canonicity from the providence of God. Ridderbos is of the opinion that one's grounds for recognizing the canon may not be found above or outside the canon, but only in the *a priori* of the canon itself.[29]

In all the attempts to remove the uncertainty and relativity that surround the canon by appealing to some outside and isolated authority, one basic motive can be discerned. It is the desire to withdraw the canon – and to see it always as with-

26. This sort of appeal finds a remarkable parallel in the Roman Catholic conception of the Spirit's guidance in the church. By means of it the history of the church – at least as far as her *magisterium* is concerned – is given an *a priori* position. The Reformation has rejected this appeal, not because the leading of the Spirit is held to be insignificant and the promise of the Spirit (Jn. 16:13) is not taken seriously, but because here the nature of the faith-promise correlation is at stake. This correlation makes it impossible to explain *a priori* the history of the church in the past, present, and future, all on the basis of the promise. See Berkouwer, *The Second Vatican Council and the New Catholicism* (ET, 1965), Ch. 7.
27. This can always serve as a basis for the reference to the *providentia*. Cf. Aland, who also accords a role to the *a posteriori* element: "It remains inexplicable, if, behind the human activity and the questionable standards of men, one does not presuppose the control of the *providentia Dei,* the working of the Holy Spirit" (*Problem of NT Canon,* p. 25). As far as the usage of the *notae canonicitatis* is concerned, one can speak of repeatedly "inadequate external standards of discrimination" and of a *confusio hominum*. Yet this does not exclude the fact that the canon, "at least in its decisive component parts," is the result of Providence (p. 33). This formulation of Aland focuses the problem even more sharply than before.
28. *Authority,* p. 39. Cf. an "*a posteriori* divine sanction."
29. *Ibid.,* p. 40.

drawn — from the realm of human creative processes. Men want to express explicitly that the church did not critically, by means of its own sifting and weighing, create its own canon, but that it was instead subjected to the canon in all its priority. There can be no inkling of any "arbitrary and authoritative action"[30] whereby the church itself determined what the norm of its existence was to contain. Especially in reference to the synods of the latter half of the fourth century, stress is laid on the fact that already before that era the canon wielded a very definite authority. Hence, all that took place was the "codification and registration of that authority which had already for quite some time been recognized by the church."[31]

Yet the real point of the debate does not lie in these ecclesiastical functions, but rather in the entire canonical process. The problem is being raised in every discussion, since there is the increasing awareness that no honor is being paid to the canon by neglecting its mode of coming into being. In reaction to such oversight, some have placed the accent on precisely the exclusively human side of the process, or at least on the human sifting and evaluation that was involved. Some have desired to honor this human factor, this historical process, by speaking of the canon as a "creation" of the church. Harnack praised the canon as "a new creation" and deeply appreciated this "great and meritorious act" of the church.[32] In it he saw a defense against heresy and the other permutations of the original gospel. By means of the canon, the church, surrounded by confusion, pointed firmly to "the supreme and completely independent tribunal."[33] The description of the canon as a creation of the church is not in the least a uniquely Roman Catholic one. For others besides Harnack have used the term to express the church's part in the formation of the canon.[34] For that reason alone one may not place the frequent Roman Catholic usage of the term in the framework of the "autonomy" of a church that, by means of an ecclesiology in the form of a monologue, seeks

30. Bavinck, *GD,* I, 369.
31. *Ibid.,* p. 370. Cf. Aland, p. 18, about the canon growing "among the believers" and "only later... officially legitimatized from the top."
32. *History of Dogma* (ET, 1896), II, 62. Cf. also "conscious creation" in Harnack, *NT Studies,* Vol. VI: *The Origin of the NT and the Most Important Consequences of the New Creation* (1925), pp. 92ff.
33. Harnack, *History of Dogma,* II, 66. The struggle forced the "formation of a new Bible" (p. 46).
34. W. G. Kümmel calls the *closing* of the canon a creation of the church ("Notwendigkeit und Grenze des NT Kanons," *Z.Th.K.* [1950], p. 293).

to proclaim her own norm and direction. This is even more evident when one notes that the Roman Catholics emphatically reject the view that the church posits her own canon. They claim only that, when the canonical process has come to a close, the magisterial church provides certainty. Attention is especially focused on this closing[35] and on the authority of the church, which performs a decisive role in this closing. Behind this we find the well-known distinction between the canonical essence of Holy Scripture *(quoad se)*, as it is grounded in divine inspiration, and the confirmation of these books as canonical by the church *(quoad nos)*.[36]

Hence, we have to understand the term "creation" in a *noetic* rather than in an *ontic* sense, and then only in relation to the recognition of the canon by means of an authoritative decree of the church. The church can, however, only point to and name that canonical which is in itself already truly canonical.[37] Yet, found amid the relativity of the varied historical considerations and judgments of the first few centuries, this authority is of great importance.[38] Along with this, recent emphases have not only posited the authority of the church as especially visible in the closing of the canon, but have also attempted to elucidate the intent and the legitimacy of this authoritative decision. For this authority must be seen in the perspective of the being of

35. The "final and actual fixing" of the canon does not play a large role with Cullmann. He focuses on "the conception of the *idea* of a canon," i.e., the feeling that it was necessary for it to subject itself to a norm "in the awareness that the transmission of a tradition faithful to the truth could no longer be automatically guaranteed" (*Salvation*, p. 294). Cf. also *Die Tradition*, pp. 45, 47.
36. Cf. B. Bartmann, *Lehrbuch der Dogmatik*, I, 14.
37. Cf. P. Lengsfeld, *Überlieferung* (1958), p. 84: "On the catholic side the only thing that counts is that the church establishes and registers what *is* canonical, but it does not make a book canonical (and thus inspired) through its own decision and its own authority." Cf. the word "registers" used by Bavinck and Barth. Even bold statements like that of J. R. Geisselmann, that the canon "is purely a product of the Church" (*The Meaning of Tradition* [ET, 1966], p. 36), must be seen in this light. The fixation of the canon is distinguished from actual divine revelation since the former was "established solely by the Church" (p. 37). The Church did not *create* "the normative value of Scripture: it can only recognize it" (Y. Congar, *Tradition and Traditions* [ET, 1966], p. 419).
38. Cf. Bartmann, I, 14: "In Protestantism the canon from its inception is merely suspended in the air." Whoever will not accept the infallibility of the church's authority surrenders his faith in the church as "the pillar and foundation of the truth" (I Tim. 3:15). Thus H. Kruse, *Die H. Schr. in der theol. Erkenntnislehre* (1964), p. 46.

the church. Out of such a perspective one can speak of the "delimitation of herself" of the "primitive church" *(Urkirche)*.[39] Precisely because the church is truly the body of Christ, God's creation according to his unchangeable saving purpose, the church is thus ruling and norm-giving, rather than a church looking for the norm and adapting itself to that norm. This proceeds directly out of the definitive constitution of the church, which, as the body of Christ, possesses this capacity for judgment by means of the charisma given to it. An authoritative act and decision was, according to Rahner, not possible in the old covenant. In Old Testament times, "such a closed, authoritative formulation of a canon" did not take place and indeed could not have taken place. The synagogue was "capable of apostatizing" and thus lacked the capabilities to distinguish, which the church did have, since "it can never more be released from the truth."[40] Thus, for Rahner there exists a close correlation between ecclesiastical authority as exercised in the closing of the canon and the definitive eschatological reality of the church in its indefectibility.[41] That is why the church has the authority; and hence the *quoad nos* can provide a basis for surety regarding the extent of the canon. This is not a usurped authority but rather an authority that rests in "a constitutive element . . . of the primitive church."[42] Appel follows this line exactly when he speaks of the church's "self-authentication" as the only criterion of canonicity, able to remove all the uncertainty entailed by the historicity of the process of the canon.[43]

In this approach the problem of the historical process, with all its attendant hesitation and uncertainty, is really made irrelevant by the appeal to the being and the reality of the church. Thus, according to Rahner, the awareness of canonicity

39. Rahner, p. 47.
40. Rahner and Cullmann touch each other here. Cullmann has written that before the coming of Christ there could be no canon because "that whole period was not yet concluded" (*Salvation,* p. 301). Cf. the statement, "For *us,* thanks to the canon, the OT events have authoritative worth . . ." (p. 300). In spite of thoroughgoing discussions, one can say that from the Roman Catholic quarter — and that despite Cullmann's book on Peter — there is more real understanding of the salvation-historical point of view than in Bultmann's circle. Bultmann's reaction to Cullmann's *Salvation in History* is not as yet known to me, but can be surmised.
41. Cf. Berkouwer, *Second Vatican Council,* Ch. 7.
42. Rahner, p. 55.
43. *Kanon und Kirche* (1964), pp. 375ff. Appel speaks about "a period in which the self-authentication grew under the leading of the Holy Spirit."

does not follow from "an explicit and direct testimony by an apostle" — for then all hesitation would remain inexplicable — but rather out of the concrete origin of Holy Scripture itself as the "self-expression of the primitive church."[44] This takes time and the flow of history; thus, a phase of hesitation and uncertainty is explicable.

When one compares this Roman Catholic approach to church and canon with the one that refers to providence, the two views differ. Compared to the untraceable "leading" of the Spirit in divine providence, Rome's conception holds out a tangible and visible guarantee. Yet a strong formal similarity can be discerned: both conceptions focus on the extent of the boundaries of the canon without allowing the content, the message of the scriptural witness, to play a part from the beginning in the problem of the canon. It is not the case that the content of this witness is considered unimportant. What does become clear is that the problem of the fixation of the bounds is deemed to have a level of meaning all its own. This standard is then approached from a merely formal structure. This can be clearly seen in the way in which the concept of the self-authentication of Scripture is dealt with. In the framework of this conception it is of a much more *formal* character than is the case with the Reformed confession of the *autopistis* of Holy Scripture. When the latter deals with the self-authentication of Holy Scripture, the content and the message of Scripture play a decisive role from the very beginning. But when the church, on the basis of its own definite and qualified existence, can guarantee the canonicity of Scripture, then a merely formal conception of the canon is inescapable. Nor can there then be an answer to the question of which grounds and in what way the choice of the contents and the closing of the canon was determined. The problem of the "connaturality" in the initial acknowledgment and the later recognition of the canonical books as apostolic testimony and part of the very life of the church, is not resolved. The real problem of the canon is thus not solved by explaining authority in this sense — especially not since the canon embodies the norm for the church. The essence of the church does not imply that it is a measuring and a norm-giving church. The whole being of the church in her subjection to the canon is and can be truly revealed only under the normativity of the canon. Therefore, it remains impossible to speak of the "self-

44. Rahner, p. 67.

authentication" of the church. It is not our intention at all to suggest that besides this self-authentication (in the church-canon relationship) Rome does not acknowledge the confrontation of the church by the canon. But the ecclesiastical question par excellence that remains is this: Can the confrontation arising out of this *autopistis* still retain its complete and intrinsic meaning?[45] For the essence of the church cannot for a moment be freed from the one, only, and decisive structure of that which is truly canonical.

The dissatisfied feeling with which each of these attempted solutions leaves us (i.e., the providence of God, the testimony of the Spirit, or the authority of the church) is continuing evidence for one conclusion: there is no solitary, isolated authority which can, outside of the content and the depth of the canon itself, shed an illuminating light on the formation and the validation of the canon. Furthermore, one cannot escape the suspicion that in each of these attempts the canon itself is devaluated. For the relationship between faith and canon is continually approached by a predominantly theoretical explanation, by which it is meant to elucidate the authority of the canon. Here it is wise to remember that no one ever has been or will be induced to believe by such assurances of certainty. The road of faith is one of encounter and confrontation with the Word of God. This Word as the message of salvation cannot for a moment be left outside anyone's reflections as he deliberates about the canon. That is clearly seen in the New Testament when the preaching properly concerns itself with those matters concerning salvation that had been handed down and had to be guarded and kept (II Thess. 2:15, 3:6; Rom. 6:17; II Tim. 1:13-14; I Tim. 6:20).

Marcion's reduced and uniform "canon" sharpened the church's awareness of the apostolic foundation on which it had been built. On the basis of this foundation the church became aware of the meaning of a canon. In this process of becoming canon-conscious, the church's attention was focused on the salvation of God, which in the apostolic testimony comforted and admonished it. The testing of the spirits and of the writings had that salvation in mind. Thus, one finds already in the second century an emergent core of certainty: the "canon" composed of the Gospels and the Pauline corpus. But alongside this there is also evidence of uncertainties. Confronted with many testimonies, the church saw varied attempts to achieve purity in the

45. For more on this "confrontation" *(Gegenüber)*, see F. Holböck-Th. Sartory, *Mysterium Kirche* (1962), I, 13ff.

acknowledgment and recognition of what was canonical.[46] Here the question of apostolicity comes to the foreground, especially in the battle about the antilegomena. Thus the church's awareness of being bound to the apostolic testimony was expressed.

The Muratorian Canon lacks the Epistle to the Hebrews because its apostolicity (having an apostle as author) was doubted. Yet later, when the conviction that Paul was its author gained support, the book was accepted as canonical.[47] However, more than apostolicity was dealt with; the question of content was also considered. The ecclesiastical reaction against Montanism, for example, makes this clear. This movement appealed especially to Hebrews in reference to the problem of the so-called second repentance.[48] There is a similar reaction in the particularly Eastern movement which opposed the Apocalypse. It did so because the chiliasts went overboard in interpreting Chapter 20 of the Revelation to John. This opposition had not yet disappeared in the third and fourth centuries.[49] Thus, once one takes notice of these movements, it is very hard to deny the relative nature of many of the considerations which exercised a function in the canonical process, especially in determining the certainty of the central apostolic witness.

Those who move on a direct line from the canon in Christ, that is, from his blessing and redemptive authority as such, to the canon of the church as closed, no doubt intend to maintain the absolute nature of the canon. Yet such a move is not justifiable for those who consider unsatisfactory the *a priori* solutions with which we have dealt so far. The historical aspect of the canon disallows any unqualified speaking about the canonical process. One should rather follow Ridderbos, who notes that we must talk about the boundaries of the canon in a more "differentiating and perhaps a bit more relative manner."[50] He also notes

46. Cf. R. Schippers, *Het Evangelie van Thomas* (1960), p. 134. Also concerning Gnosticism as a rival to Christendom, see W. C. van Unnik, *Newly Discovered Gnostic Writings* (ET, 1960), pp. 38ff.
47. Cf. C. F. D. Moule, *The Birth of the New Testament,* p. 189 about the imprimatur; Aland, *op. cit.,* p. 22. Regarding II and III Jn. being antilegomena, see Schnackenburg, *Kommentar,* p. 265.
48. Cf. Ridderbos, *Authority,* p. 41, about Heb. 6:4; cf. also C. Spicq, *L'épître aux Hebreux* (1953), II, 167 concerning Heb. 6:4-6 as "a support to the Montanists and Novatians."
49. Ridderbos, p. 48. In the Festal Letter of Athanasius (367), the Apocalypse is given a place. It is generally accepted that Athanasius is here reflecting the influence the West had on him during his stay there. See N. B. Stonehouse, *The Apocalypse in the Ancient Church* (1929).
50. "De canon van het NT," *Kerk en Theologie* (1958), p. 94.

that the evidence given to the church "regarding the *final* boundaries is not as complete as that of the corpus of the canon which was commonly accepted from the beginning."[51]

It is clear that speaking which does take into account these nuances is not possible when one operates from a formalistic conception of the canon. One who critically uses the word "formalistic" in the discussion of canonicity may not do this as it has often been done in the past – by arranging the "formal" and the "material" antithetically. "Formal" was often taken to denote the *written* word in a derogatory way, whereas "material" was taken to describe the message. Such a contrast would devaluate the meaning or intent of the written word. Thus, when we speak of "formalistic," we mean to denote that position which accepts such a separation between "formal" and "material" as a starting point, and which isolates the word "written." Only when this distinction is destroyed will it be possible to understand the canon as the prophetic-apostolic testimony in all its normative structure.[52]

Opposition to a formalistic conception of canon is evident in Ridderbos. He takes the nature of the canonical authority into consideration in all his reflections. In order to correctly understand the canon, he wants to go behind Scripture in order to focus on the history of salvation out of which the canon has sprung, and thus on the "*why* and the *how* of the canon."[53] This searching behind Scripture does not wish to pit the material against the formal. It seeks rather to create more room for the meaning and the aim of that which is written, especially as it regards the message of Scripture. This message comes to us out of the history of salvation and thus must structure our reflection about the canon. When we must speak of a valid and authoritative tradition within the scriptural fixation,[54] and in which neither apostolicity[55] nor the testimony of the Holy Spirit[56] can be taken to guarantee canonicity, then only one way of reflecting properly on the canon remains: out of the authority given to the apostles. The question then arises whether a way

51. *Ibid.*
52. Kuyper stressed the "mystical" fact of the bond to Scripture very much and warned against the abstraction of tearing Scripture loose from its context (*Enc.*, III, 25).
53. *Authority*, pp. 13ff.
54. "De canon," p. 85.
55. *Authority*, pp. 35, 39.
56. *Authority*, passim; "De canon," p. 85.

can be found that leads from this authority to the canon as we have it. Furthermore, if there is a way, which one will it be?

It is not possible to identify this canon of the apostolic *a priori* with a list of the twenty-seven New Testament books.[57] "All the relativities, all the zig-zag movements, all the proofs for the church's fallibility" that one can find in the history of the canon make such identification impossible.[58] Nor does the Scripture itself testify to its boundaries. Thus, the only view of the canon which Ridderbos will hold as correct is what he calls the "redemptive-historical concept of the canon, or its redemptive-historical foundation."[59] Only then can it be determined "with what justification the church accepted the twenty-seven books of the New Testament in their delimited unity as canon."[60]

It is clear that here we find ourselves on a level completely distinct from that of a formalistic conception of the canon. For here we do not approach the canon in its structure out of merely formal criteria,[61] but rather out of its basis, its foundation in the history of salvation. In the canon the church, in faith, found its redemptive-historical foundations. This can only be understood when we pay attention to the kerygma, *martyria*, or *didache*, that is, the content of the New Testament witness.[62] Confronted by this testimony as the apostolic witness regarding God's one complete act of salvation, the church did not create the canon, but, indubitably assured regarding the content of this witness, subjected herself to it.[63]

This connection between church and canon has occupied the center of attention for some time. In decisive areas Ridderbos follows Cullmann, who has greatly elaborated on this redemptive-historical connection.[64] The relationship as seen in the church's subjection is based in her faith, a faith that knows

57. "De canon," p. 91.
58. *Ibid.*
59. *Authority*, p. 27; "De canon," p. 86.
60. "De canon," pp. 32-33.
61. Although Ridderbos (correctly) repudiates the antithesis of formal and material (*Authority*, p. 5), can he still, without contradicting this move, criticize the "mechanical isolation of the revelatory character of the Scripture" which some abstract from "formal statements regarding its authority" (p. xi)? Cf. pp. 44 and 51 regarding formal decisions and formal criteria of canonicity.
62. *Authority*, p. 53.
63. *Ibid.*, pp. 11, 13.
64. *Ibid.*, pp. 27 and 28; cf. "De Canon," p. 86, where he mentions Cullmann. For Cullmann's views, see *Christ and Time* (ET, 1950), pp. 144ff.; *Die Tradition*, p. 44; and *Salvation in History*, pp. 293ff.

it is dependent on the apostolic authority founded in Christ.[65] And it is thus that the closedness of the canon, in principle, takes on decisive significance. The canon is so closely tied to the history of salvation that it participates in a way in salvation's eternal nature.[66]

This in turn is connected with what Cullmann formulated. The church itself, he stated, had posited "a clear line of demarcation" between "the period of the Apostles and the period of the Church."[67] Only in this way can the deep meaning of the canon be understood. The promise of Christ "to establish his church upon the testimony of the apostles" is effected through the apostolic authority.[68]

The distinction between the time of the apostles and the time of the church is thus intrinsically dependent on a close connection between the canon and the history of salvation. In this way the perspective on its *a priori* nature and its founding significance is kept open.[69] Yet naturally the question arises of what must be understood by the word "canon" in this context. What precisely does it mean to say that Scripture itself "belongs rather to that very process of revelation which occurred in the fulness of time,"[70] and that the kerygma in Scripture is "itself taken up into and qualified by the absoluteness and uniqueness of the historical-redemptive event"?[71] It is clear that these fundamental reflections about the redemptive-historical canon may not lead us to think of the canon in its ultimately closed form, because the formation of that canon "belongs to the history of the church and not to the history of redemption."[72] Ridderbos thus distinguishes between a *qualitative* and a *quantitative* canon.[73] Like Cullmann,[74] his redemptive-historical elaboration

65. *Authority*, p. 33.
66. *Ibid.*, p. 28, where he states that the canon "bears an unrepeatable and exclusive character."
67. Cullmann, *Tradition*, p. 44; also cited by Ridderbos, *Authority*, p. 28, n. 104.
68. *Authority*, p. 41.
69. *Ibid.*, p. 28: "The boundary between church history and the history of redemption lies precisely, for the church, in the written canon."
70. *Ibid.*, p. 33.
71. *Ibid.*, p. 60.
72. *Ibid.*, p. 14.
73. *Ibid.*, pp. 44, 14. When Ridderbos writes that "the essence of the canon, not only in a qualitative but also in a quantitative sense," belongs to the presuppositions of the church (p. 44), he is not negating this distinction.
74. *Salvation in History*, p. 295: "When I speak of the canon, I mean, of

refers first of all to the qualitative one. With this in mind, we can then say that the question about the canon is not of an ecclesiastical but rather of a Christological nature.[75] This does not again mean a positing of the material over against the formal. It rather means that the written canon in its "externity"[76] is understandable only out of and by means of this redemptive-historical foundation, and therefore, as the qualitative canon, must be considered part of the history of salvation, the process of revelation.

Ridderbos has explicitly stated that he does not want to find any ground for our faith other than Scripture. His intent is rather "to delineate more sharply the essence of Scripture and the nature of its authority," that is, to clarify the relationship between the history of redemption and Holy Scripture.[77] It is not his intention to raise another criterion similar to the many others which have been proposed and used in the course of history, even though he uses terminology used previously (e.g., when he states that in Christ are based both salvation and its trustworthy communication, and further adds that "here lies to the present day the *principium canonicitatis*").[78] He wants to invigorate our reflection about the fact that in the canon the church both hears Christ speaking and knows itself to be bound to him.[79] One can, in my opinion, ask if it is not misleading to speak of a ground for recognition,[80] when it is openly Ridderbos' intention to manifest the canon in its immediate relation to the history of redemption. If this misunderstanding were removed, the real question regarding the canon could engage our attention more clearly. For it would then be concerned with the communication of salvation and the content of that communication as it determines the canon's authority and validity. Then the way from the apostolic kerygma to the church as it stands on this foundation becomes visible. It is the way of the kerygma, of the

course, here as in my earlier work, the conception of the *idea* of a canon, not its final and actual fixing, which extends over centuries." See also pp. 297 and 301.

75. *Authority*, p. 40. Cf. p. 47, and "De canon," p. 91. We saw that Rahner approached the canon ecclesiologically. It is plain, however, that he would not accept Ridderbos' dilemma.
76. "De canon," p. 85.
77. *Authority*, p. xii.
78. *Ibid.*, p. 47.
79. "De canon," p. 95.
80. Especially when the distinction between a ground of recognition and a ground of being is made. Cf. "De canon," p. 91.

proclamation of salvation through the witness of the apostles. This kerygma does not merely intend to further our knowledge, but desires to focus the establishing of the church upon this redemptive-historical foundation. Thus the canon becomes the foundation and the rule for the arising church.[81] The whole intent of this redemptive-historical aspect of the canon is then to point out the *why* and the *how* of the canon,[82] instead of holding up a criterion that would neglect or circumvent Scripture in order to establish the canonicity of the canon. The redemptive-historical conception of the canon does not intend to prove canonicity; instead, it wishes to set forth relationships which make impossible any attempt to abstract the canon from Christ, through any formalistic conceptions of the canon. By using such conceptions in the past, men have always sought various solutions to a problem which was formally insoluble, since the authority which issues out of the Word of God itself was not recognized to be that by which "believers are bound"[83] — a link which no theoretical insight into the possibility and the meaning of the canon can establish.

This clarification of a conception of canon, which does not contain a new criterion in the old sense of that term, also does not pretend to solve all the questions regarding the canon as a "quantitative" canon. The vision of the canon described above especially intends to honor the historical element in "the period of the church." This implies that there can be no self-evident identification of the canon and the books of the New Testament. It is true that early there was no doubt about most of the New Testament books,[84] but this does not say that there are no historical aspects connected with the fundamental relationship of the canon to Christ. For in this historical process, when the oral tradition began to fade away, the church fell back upon the fixed inscripturation.[85] Then it began to be more clearly aware of the canon in its quantitative meaning.

When one deals with the quantitative canon, he encounters

81. *Authority,* p. 59. Cf. his remarks about the remarkable "about-face" which took place in NT studies regarding the kerygmatic character of the contents of the NT Scripture (p. 55), and about this as a better awareness for the true nature of the NT (p. 59). Many contemporary remarks about the so-called kerygma-theology tend to ignore the nuances and thus stand to lose the gains about which Ridderbos is speaking.
82. "De canon," p. 58.
83. *Authority,* p. 11.
84. "De canon," p. 93.
85. *Ibid.,* pp. 93, 95.

the problem of its delineation or, to put it another way, the problem of certainty regarding the core and uncertainty regarding the periphery. Viewing the evidence concerning that which the church received in the canon, we can say that "regarding the boundaries of the canon, this evidence was not as complete as it was about the corpus of the canon which had been accepted from the beginning."[86] In the period of the church, the relative aspect becomes apparent. Regarding the boundaries of the canon, Ridderbos speaks about the church's accounting to itself regarding its origin and foundation, and thus establishing what it in essence had already known.[87] Considering these boundaries, especially when dealing with the canon in the historical form of its closing, one encounters terms such as "more relative" and "less evident." Here the church, the *ecclesia audiens,* was directly and actively involved. And here one sees the church's activity in the "reception" of the canon outlined much more sharply than when it confronted the clarity and the self-evident nature of the central message of salvation. The latter, with inherent authority and power, clearly put the church in a receptive position. If one approaches this union of an absolute and a relative from an *a priori* theoretical perspective, he may be led to conclude that this in essence amounts to a suspension of the canon. Yet, if one does not want to rest on the absolute authority of the church, an authority which ends all uncertainty, and if one will not acknowledge that it is the testimony of the Spirit that persuades us of canonicity – since the very nature of this testimony conflicts with such persuasion – then no other way remains open than the way which the church actually took: the one in which the content of Scripture and its message played a role which cannot be ignored.

One is naturally led to focus on two phenomena. The first one is the central canon, recognized early by the church, albeit not yet by official decree. The second is that body of writings in which the evidences of apostolicity did not immediately address the church in such a way that all opposition to them was silenced. Thus, Ridderbos draws a conclusion (to the discussion of the boundaries) that is related to a process of comparison. He says that "the decisions made with regard to the limits of the canon conformed to the very nature of the existing canon."[88]

86. *Ibid.,* p. 94; cf. *Authority,* pp. 42-47.
87. "De canon," pp. 94-95.
88. *Authority,* p. 51. About this "canon," as it was already accepted at the end of the second century, see E. Hennecke and W. Schneemelcher,

Such a formulation can only be understood when the message of salvation is held to be the central core of the canon. Here the point of view is that the antilegomena accepted in the closing had to be in conformity to the canon already accepted. This point of view is decisive. One sees it also in Calvin: when he was dealing with several disputed books, he was persuaded about them because they did not contain anything which conflicted with the writings already beyond debate.[89]

The formulations which point to a comparison with those works already accepted with certainty are in many ways negative ones: they usually speak of "nothing that conflicts with. . . ." This evidently does not endanger the certainty. The nature of the canon does not demand that in order for the canon to be authoritative, its boundaries must be readily provable and perspicuous. Nor does it warrant such a state of finality that the outlines of the historical and the relative are erased. One is involuntarily led to picture the church in the period when the battle over the antilegomena had not yet been decided as a church whose certainty and joy of faith were not yet threatened. This is additional evidence for the fact that we cannot and may not view the canon formalistically. No doubt one can see in the closing of the canon the church's giving account "regarding her origin and foundation,"[90] but our being united to Christ through the canon is not grounded in any such authoritative decision of

New Testament Apocrypha (ET, 1963), I, 39. Cf. also "wide-ranging agreement" and the "Muratori Canon" (pp. 43-45).

89. Ridderbos speaks about Calvin's statements, "which are so frequently criticized, but which are not so easily improved upon" (*Authority,* p. 51). Note here Calvin's introduction to his commentary on II Peter. We not only see here some hesitancy about the author but also the conclusion that there is nothing there which is unworthy of Peter *(nihil habet Petro indignum),* but that it "shows throughout the power and grace of the apostolic spirit" and that "it extols in high terms the grace of God" (*Commentary on the Second Epistle of Peter* [ET, 1963], p. 325). Hence he cannot "repudiate" it. Cf. his introduction to the Epistle of James. He finds no "just cause for rejecting it" after analyzing the content. He adds, "It is enough to make men receive this Epistle, that it contains nothing unworthy of an Apostle of Christ" (*Commentary on the Catholic Epistles,* Owen ed. [1948], p. 276).

90. "De canon," p. 95. By the very nature of the case, the nature of the *recipere* has always been important. Regarding the Muratorian Canon and the motives for the *recipere,* see K. Stendahl, "The Formation of the Canon," *Current Issues in New Testament Interpretation,* Klassen and Snyder, eds. (1962), pp. 239ff. Here he speaks of this canon as "a most intriguing witness to the process of canonization," especially in connection with Paul's epistles (p. 242).

the church. Nor can it be explained by the testimony of the Holy Spirit, if the latter is taken to mean a sure removal of all doubt regarding the canonicity of all these books in order thus to clear the way to faith in Christ. It is surely not easy, especially with the boundaries of the canon in mind, to give a precise description of the *recipere* in all of its aspects. Ridderbos speaks of the church's "accounting for herself" regarding the boundaries of the canon in the same way he speaks of the "self-determination" of the qualitative canon. Certainty can only be based on the message of salvation, and on that basis alone does the church confess that she hears and comprehends the Word of God. This confession does not entail an irrational faith in Scripture, which could only be spiritually explained. Rather, this confession points to that Word which met us in the church's *recipere* and which moved on with us into history.

Hence, one must not start to make distinctions between "center" and "periphery" in the canon in a manner which presupposes that the periphery is unimportant. We should instead see how the history of the canon indicates that the church was led, in the matter of the boundaries of the canon, by a basic commitment centered in the gospel. Thus, the original hesitations about the boundaries and the resulting negative formulations did not injure the canon in the church's own eyes. Notwithstanding the recognition of an historical aspect and the distinction between the apostolic period and the period of the church, the church has confessed that it was, via the canon, united in a saving way to its Lord. Bavinck writes that that recognition – with a few exceptions – came about of itself.[91] The canonicity is rooted in the "existence" of the canonical books. They have their authority *jure suo,* by the fact that they exist.

It is the union of "that which had been given"[92] and the *recipere* of the church that is the real mystery of the canon. Now the use of the word "mystery" can mean that we are avoiding an unsolved problem, or it can mean that we are dodging the difficulties of a problem we have raised ourselves. But here the word is used meaningfully and responsibly: the reality of the apostolic authority justifies its use. For that authority did not bring about a merely passive subjection of the church to this witness, nor did it raise up the church on this foundation against its own will. Rather, the church consciously

91. *GD,* I, 371. Cf. also *Magnalia Dei* (1909), p. 118.
92. Cf. Ratschow, p. 158.

focuses on this *recipere*. The correlation of faith and the Word of God does not presuppose a creative functioning of faith itself, but rather recognizes that an active faith entrusts itself to and yields to the Word. In the same way, the *recipere* is related to the foundation on which the church is built, and in that reliance on the apostolic witness the historical form of the canon represents no threat to certainty. This certainty arises from the message itself and therefore is never an isolated or closed affair, but is continually aimed at the increasing understanding of Scripture, which testifies to Christ.

It is important to remember that the whole process of selection and preferred choices has been an important question by itself — completely apart from the contemporary discussions of the unity of the New Testament. Aland has pointed out that even when the actual canon is not at all at stake, "a narrowing and a shortening" of the canon still often occurs.[93] This is, for instance, precisely the case in the varied ways in which Scripture functions, often called the problem of the "functional Bible." It would be unfair to localize such selection and reduction in various sects, even though among them this phenomenon often occurs in spectacular ways. It is shown by their preferences for certain texts to the exclusion of others. The latter are pushed into the background and no longer function in reality, having been stripped of their power by a peculiar *a priori* hermeneutic of Scripture.[94] One can accordingly typify the problem of the "canon-in-the-canon" as a genuinely ecumenical one and the greatest source of unrest in the present state of confessional differences. The fact remains, however, that this sort of reductionary approach to the canon, while it is a general danger confronting every reader of Scripture, is in several contemporary theological conceptions being made the only legitimate approach to the New Testament.

Käsemann is very much aware of the sectarian problem of the "canon-in-the-canon." He holds the hermeneutical question to be "completely unsolved."[95] He goes on to say that "the sects provide evidence that God is also capable of blinding us and

93. Aland, pp. 28ff.
94. Cf. *CD*, I/2, p. 478: "Holy Scripture has always been defined in the church with varying degrees of emphasis on the constituent parts." He then recalls Luther's dictum, "was Christum treibt" (that which sets forth Christ).
95. "Thoughts on the Present Controversy about Scriptural Interpretation," *New Testament Questions of Today* (ET, 1969), p. 269.

hardening us by means of the Bible, although, and precisely because, we boast of observing the letter of the Bible."[96]

One can ask whether such a rigorous judgment is called for, especially if one considers the problems which surface in Käsemann's own views of the canon. His harsh question whether the devout alone possess the key to Holy Scripture cannot hide that problem; nor can his sharp reaction against biblicism and those who merely see Scripture as "a reliquary, or a book of oracles."[97] His problem is revealed in the variations of the canon which are discovered within the canon. Take, for example, Braun's and Käsemann's own divergent versions of what is really central to the New Testament. In no way do I here wish to adduce the divergence of others as evidence for the unity of Scripture. I do want to show, however, that the manner in which the discerning of the spirits is often applied to the New Testament is itself an indication of a definite problem. This problem reaches into the very depths of the interpretation of Scripture as canon and there creates a crisis in the *recipere* itself.

It should be realized that many reactionary factors are at work here, especially reactions to the various forms of exegetical harmonism. Such harmonism fails to appreciate the reliefs which stand out in Scripture; nor is it aware of Scripture's many divergent strains. It could be called docetism of Scripture. As such it can hardly admit, and thus shows very little interest in, the different perspectives and openly polemical parts of Scripture. Nor can it honor the various ways in which Scripture thinks and talks about the same Lord.

To thus be faced with a choice between harmonism and an ever regressing search for the canon-behind-the-canon as the only legitimate approach to sacred Scripture, is to be confronted with a dreary dilemma. Yet it is often my impression that such a choice is being forced upon us. This is all the more reason that the discussion of the canon should force us to reflect on the meaning of the unity of Scripture. Until now, dogmatics usually taught that there were four attributes of Scripture: its necessity, authority, sufficiency and perspicuity. This part of the doctrine of Scripture was usually approached out of a polemical context. The result was that, since the unity of Scripture was hardly ever assailed, this attribute was more or less neglected. Now the modern problem of a "canon in and behind the canon" clearly

96. *Ibid.,* p. 272.
97. *Ibid.*

posits the question whether or not any other confession of the unity of Scripture as canon than that of harmonization is possible. It is imperative that in our dealing with this attribute of Scripture we make some unmistakable decisions regarding our way of looking at the normativity of the Word of God.

The search for a canon in the scriptural canon of the New Testament has often been connected directly with Luther's much discussed dictum: only "was Christum treibt" (that which sets forth Christ) is canonical. It would be incorrect to say *a priori,* on the basis of Luther's strong adherence to the gospel, that such a connection could not exist. For it cannot be denied that Luther did not merely state that Scripture testifies to Christ, but that the way in which he used this criterion had an indubitably critical aspect to it.[98] His statements regarding James's epistle are an eloquent example of that. An extensive investigation of Luther's view of Scripture is not possible here. Yet the problem itself is sufficiently important to be looked at in connection with the search being described here. It can be asked whether, in the thought of the Reformation — with its explicit emphasis on *sola Scriptura* — we find a critique which posits itself over Scripture. Is there a critique which subjects Scripture, as it is authoritative for and normative in the church, to a critical judgment?[99] What can be the background of Luther's statement that the Epistle of James "has no evangelical nature to it"? What about his other statements which create the impression that "was Christum treibt" provides us with a usable standard in the differentiation between what is and what is not canonical?[100]

It is clear that Luther did not arrive at these critical expressions by means of merely formal criteria. He was instead concerned with the apostolic, evangelical content of Scripture. Starting from the central message of salvation, he arrived at a certain classification. In this scheme he attributed special value to the Gospel of John, to the Pauline corpus, and to I Peter and I John, while he assumed a very critical stance towards James,

98. Luther's dictum was not only used regarding the NT but also the OT. Cf. G. Bornkamm, *Luther and the OT* (ET, 1969).
99. Regarding Luther's "was Christum treibt," see W. J. Kooiman, *Luther and the Bible* (ET, 1961), pp. 225ff. (note the bibliography).
100. The much cited dictum of Luther that over against those who appealed to Scripture against Christ, he would appeal to Christ against Scripture (Kooiman, p. 227), is without doubt highly influenced by polemical considerations.

Jude, Hebrews and the Apocalypse.[101] Given the fact that Luther so very heavily emphasized the normativity of Holy Scripture and the concept that the Word must be allowed to stand to its very letters,[102] it is understandable that many have refused to accept the notion that Luther, by means of his dictum, had suddenly jumped into the maelstrom of subjectivism. On the other hand, he provided a criterion for canonicity to which many would later appeal for support of modern interpretations of a canon-within-the-canon.[103] Luther's view can thus be described as a Christological conception of the canon, or as a redemptive-historical concept of canonicity. Starting from the biblical premise that Scripture testifies to Christ, Luther is continually concerned with the relationship of the entire apostolic testimony to Christ.[104] Although at first, in his commentary on Romans,[105] he saw no contradiction between Paul and James, he later arrived at his critical position regarding the latter. No doubt this was also influenced by the Roman Catholic opposition: they confronted him with the letter of James and emphasized the words about being justified "not by faith alone."[106] Confronted with such scriptural evidence,[107] Luther concluded that the *sola fide* and the quotation "not by faith alone" could not be harmonized. As a result, his position was often represented as a definitely disobedient one of "biblical criticism."[108]

101. Cf. W. Maurer, "Luthers Verständnis des NT Kanons," *Die Verbindlichkeit des Kanons* (1960), p. 73.
102. Cf. Kooiman, p. 229.
103. Ridderbos, *Authority,* p. 4. He states that for Luther this did not signify a subjectivizing of the content of revelation. Yet Ridderbos asserts that Luther also introduced the idea of a "canon-within-the-canon," which not only focused attention on the subject but introduced a critical aspect.
104. Cf. Maurer, p. 77. Luther says: "Take Christ out of the Scriptures and what greater will you discover in them?" (O. Ritschl, *Dogmengeschichte des Protestantismus* [1908], I, p. 87).
105. Cf. Maurer and M. Dibelius, *Der Brief des Jacobus* (1956), p. 56, concerning the distinction between the *opera legis* (Paul) and the *opera fidei* (James).
106. Jas. 2:24. One of the times this happened was at the Leipzig Disputation by Eck. Cf. P. Bergauer, *Der Jacobusbrief bei Augustinus* (1962), p. 88.
107. The caustic nature of the conflict roots in the fact that here the appeal against Luther was not based on tradition but on Scripture *(ouk monon).*
108. Bergauer, p. 92. Notice especially his comment on Luther's "subjective position, beset with dogmatic presuppositions," with reference to Jas. 4:6, where we read that God opposes the proud.

This is certainly an understandable critique, beginning from a concept of the complete authority of the church as an institution which has defined the bounds of the canon once and for all. But a position such as this is not possible for those who stand in the line of the Reformation — not even for those who are convinced that the charge that James wrote an unevangelical and "strawy" epistle is unjust.[109]

It must be realized that Luther indissolubly connected faith in Scripture with the joyful acceptance of the message of Scripture. Here lies the very root of his problem: from the obvious center of the message of salvation[110] he began to make critical remarks about the Epistle of James.[111] A comparison can be made between his position and that of the early church in its battle over the antilegomena, especially Hebrews and the Apocalypse. The very explicit appeals which others (i.e., the Montanists and chiliasts) made to these writings created temporary reactionary movements in the church regarding their canonicity. In Luther's similar case, conformity to what had been and what was considered to be the incontrovertible and central message of salvation was at stake. The same conformity looms large in Calvin's thought. Calvin concluded about James that there is no *justa causa* to plead against him, while Luther, starting from the clarity of the Word of God, the perspicuity of the gospel,[112]

109. The conflict regarding James continues until the present time, especially in the study of his relation to Paul. Cf. Berkouwer, *Faith and Justification* (ET, 1954), pp. 129ff.; G. Eichholz, *Jakobus und Paulus* (1953) and *Glaube und Werk bei Paulus und Jacobus* (1961), pp. 54ff.; P. Stuhlmacher, *Gerechtigkeit Gottes bei Paulus* (1965), pp. 191-194, concerning James and Paul as "theological alternatives and never as complementary" (p. 194). Nor does the criticism concern the faith-works problem alone. See N. Alexander, "The United Character of the NT Witness of the Christ-Event," *The NT in Historical and Contemporary Perspective* (1965), p. 11.

110. Later I hope to touch on this again in connection with the perspicuity of Scripture.

111. It is incorrect to say that Luther later retracted his criticisms. Cf. Kooiman, pp. 226 and 229, about critical comments of Luther made even after 1540.

112. Cf. R. Herrmann, *Von der Klarheit der H. Schrift* (1958), pp. 63ff.; K. Holl, "Luthers Bedeutung für den Fortschritt der Auslegungskunst," *Gesammelte Aufsätze zur Kirchengeschichte* (1948), pp. 551ff. This perspicuity was not for Luther a merely simplistic and superficial perspicuity. Cf. Holl, p. 559: "I indeed acknowledge that there are many obscure and abstruse passages in the Scriptures, not because the matter is so lofty, but because of our ignorance of grammar and vocabulary. The passages themselves do not obscure our knowledge of the totality of Scripture."

could not discover the conformity and coherence of James to that gospel. Luther's commitment to the indissoluble connection between belief in Scripture and the assurance of faith, as well as to the unity and harmony of the message of Scripture,[113] does not allow him to withhold judgment on James; thus his criticism. Related as it was to the historical growth of the canon and based on the same core which had been decisive for the early church when it fixed bounds, it was for him entirely possible and legitimate.

One might ask whether it would not have been possible in Luther's situation to practice reticence and caution within the community of the church, especially when in concrete situations such as this the connection with "was Christum treibt" could not be discovered with sufficient clarity. I do not think that such caution should be branded as a legalistic submission to the canon. It is rather an enduring necessity and one that recognizes the danger that attends any exegetical "principle," a principle which does not recognize the limitations and the continuing growth of our insight. Even the "perspicuity" of Scripture, or the very central biblical truth that Scripture does testify to Christ, may never become an authority which could — within the church — change our temporary insight into a permanently closed case.

Yet it would be unwarranted to approach Luther's conception of Scripture exclusively from this incidental problem. After all, it did not lead to the destruction of the gospel professed by the canon.[114] Luther's subjection to Scripture would deny any position wishing to view his criticism as a surrender to subjectivism. This comes out more clearly when later men began to use his adage as a principle designed to open the way for relativizing the gospel. Two things stand out then. First of all, the intertwining of the absolute and the relative, a process which Ridderbos mentions regarding the bounds of the canon, must be kept in mind when Luther's hesitancy and criticism are dealt with.[115] And on the other hand, account must be given of the

113. Holl, pp. 559ff.

114. Bergauer claims that this does happen (*Der Jakobusbrief*, pp. 88ff.). This conclusion must be seen as an adjunct of his view of the "forensic" theory of justification.

115. Cf. Kooiman, p. 226, regarding the fact that not one Lutheran creed contains a list of the canonical books. This difference from the Reformed churches (cf. *BC*, Art. VI), as far as I can see, is not a difference of principle in their appreciation of the canon but must be

lurking danger of every "hermeneutical" principle that is used regarding the canon and the exposition of Scripture. Furthermore, the methodology of every "canon-in-the-canon" is dangerous, especially when it manifestly contradicts the church's — and Luther's — *recipere* of the gospel.

One final point remains regarding the conception of the canon, the *tota Scriptura* and the *recipere* of the church. This is the well-known distinction between the canonical and the apocryphal books. The congregations, in their dependence on sacred Scripture, are not often aware of this controversy. In the Belgic Confession we find a special article devoted to it. Article VI posits that the apocryphal books do not have the kind of power and authority needed either to serve as the basis for any article of faith or to contest or diminish the authority of the canonical books. But after that the distinction appears to be relativized. For the article goes on to state that the church may read the books and derive instruction from them "insofar as they agree with the canonical books."[116] A great deal of controversy has raged about this formulation, for we see that the distinction does allow the apocryphal books some sort of function in the church. This in turn led to their inclusion in many editions of the Bible.

Since this distinction of relative values does not change the basic thrust of Article VI (apocryphal equals non-canonical), the problem of the bounds of the canon remains a very real one. It is especially important to remember that this distinction must be seen as a part of the Rome-Reformation controversy. Rome included the apocryphal books in the canon, and it saw in the canon of the Reformation a reduction of the canon of the church.[117] Trent considered the Apocrypha, which had already been included in the lists of Hippo and Carthage, as part of the definitive canon.

Behind these divergent assessments, which center on the canon's *boundaries*, we can see that the *content* of the Apocrypha plays a larger role. The distinction between canonical and apocryphal was not intended to be an irrational one. It is vitally

seen as a result of certain nuances of interpretation regarding the problem of the boundaries of the canon in its historical form.

116. It is clear that this could not be said of the NT Apocrypha, e.g., certain of the gnostic writings which were excluded by the canon in an entirely different manner.

117. Already in 1520, Karlstadt rejected the Apocrypha. For Luther on this, see Polman, *Onze Nederlandse Geloofsbelijdenis*, I, 243.

dependent on the content on which the church's *recipere* is focused. Thus, while Polman speaks of the faith-judgment, he points to the trivial contents of the Apocrypha and the diverse errors which clearly show that these books are not canonical.[118] This brings us back to the most basic aspect of the whole canonical problem, that is, the nature and the basis of the *recipere* — a posture which is not an autonomous choice but a subjection to normativity.

The Reformation, unwilling and unable to rest on a formal ecclesiastical and authoritative decision, also distinguished between canonical and apocryphal books. It was aware that one can only talk about the canon while being continually bound to the witness of the content of sacred Scripture. Thus, the distinction which Article VI makes is not an *a priori* and merely formal one by which the content of these writings was omitted from consideration.[119] The *recipere* took place in intimate union with the power and clear presence of the apostolic testimony present in the hearing of God's Word. The *a priori* of the canon does not conflict with that.

We see the historical aspect surface whenever the Word of God becomes human writing and thus subjects itself to the possibility of translation. Many of the faithful in the early church held that their relation to the message of salvation was inextricably bound to the Septuagint — itself a translation. Neither the church nor the apostles had any apparent problems with that. They did not doubt that they were really being confronted with the message, because the church did not see herself as dealing with a "secondary" Old Testament.[120] At a later time the historical questions about the relation between the Palestinian and the Alexandrian canons arose. Yet, whereas this is not considered an urgent problem, it is clear how much the message of Scripture, as it comes in the accepted canon, has guided and ruled the life of the church. It is impossible to understand all

118. *Ibid.*, p. 246. Cf. Polman, *Woord en Belijdenis,* I, 220.

119. The Reformation also appealed to the *content* of the Apocrypha in its opposition to the Roman Catholic appeal to these books. Here the Roman Catholic Church found teachings and practices, e.g., purgatory and intercessions for the dead, which the Reformation rejected as non-evangelical (B. M. Metzger, *An Introduction to the Apocrypha* [1957], p. 181).

120. Cf. E. Würthwein, *The Text of the OT: An Introduction to Kittel-Kahle's Biblia Hebraica* (ET, 1957), p. 34, concerning the influence of the OT in this translation "for centuries" and "for the early church ... the only normative form of the OT."

the varied facets of faith and its commitment to Scripture from the perspective of a formalistic conception of the canon. Such a conception holds that faith and its assurance can only be deemed surely founded when they are dependent on a canon that has been relieved of historicity, of both a process of growth and the discernment of the church. That this is an altogether erroneous approach to the problem of the canon is evident from the many real questions to which the Septuagint translation has given birth. Some have dealt with this translation as it was used by the New Testament to quote from the Old, others with the "authority" which it enjoyed in the church as *the* form of the Old Testament Word of God.

This is a subject which has usually been dealt with in theological reflections on the nature of inspiration, especially since there are in the Septuagint elements of diverse interpretations of the Old Testament.[121] But within the framework of this chapter it is important to note that via this translation the Apocrypha was placed in the canon of the early church. At the time of the Reformation decision, the historical and material factors were important. These factors were closely tied to the written nature of God's Word, which came *into* history. Those who wish to ignore these historical factors and only recognize certainty as possible on the basis of a demonstrable and perspicuous (i.e., a sort of suprahistorical) canonicity, erroneously presuppose that the way of faith starts from *a priori* certainty. We have seen earlier how intensely Kuyper fought this presupposition. He pointed to the fact that the testimony of the Spirit ties us to the core of Scripture, and that the authority which then begins to address us out of this center ends "as *Scripture* by imposing sacred obligations upon us," until finally "in form and content both, the Scripture comes to stand before us as an authority from God."[122]

In such a manner the church arrived at its confession regarding the Bible. It testified that here it had heard God's Word and that here it continued to hear it. While thus referring to the canon, the church spoke of the "sufficiency" of Scripture. This took place in the belief that every request for more illumi-

121. Cf. Würthwein, pp. 47ff.; S. Kistemaker, *The Psalm Citations in the Epistle to the Hebrews* (1961), pp. 89-90; R. Nicole, "New Testament Use of the Old Testament," *Revelation and the Bible,* pp. 142ff.

122. *Princ.,* pp. 568ff. Cf. also regarding the testimony of the Spirit, Polman, who asserts: "The *testimonium Spiritus Sancti* does not solve any canonical questions" (*De Theologie van Augustinus,* I, 206).

nation (outside of this "lamp unto our feet") would necessarily relativize that which had been received and heard in the Word. It should caution us to note that Philip, who asked for "more," because only then would the first revelation be sufficient, was admonished to return to that which already had been given in Christ (Jn. 14:8-9).

There is really more to the confession of the sufficiency of Scripture than a reference to the Reformed polemic with Rome about the supplemental or interpretive role of tradition. It is of much more central importance to our confession of faith in Holy Scripture. In a later chapter this sufficiency of sacred Scripture will be dealt with as one of the attributes of Scripture. Here, however, it again alerts us to the struggle about the canon as "open" or "closed." When an "open" canon is advocated, it is usually done from the canon's historical aspect, that is, the *recipere* as one of the actions of the church. The possibility of such a new *recipere* on the church's part is then raised, especially regarding those materials which were not allotted a place during the historical growth of the canon.

The acknowledgment in principle of such an open canon over against the "absolutizing of the canonical bounds" is, however, usually tied to a relativizing of this "openness."[123] This is done on the basis of its actually being closed and its existence as authoritative for the church. A warning is thus given to all those who might think that one of the implications of an open canon is the "insufficiency" of the given and accepted canon. One often gets the impression that the recognition of such an open canon is only barely practical. It is highly theoretical and abstract because it concerns historical and ecclesiastical possibilities — in an analogy to the earlier *recipere* — but only as possibilities surrounded by many reservations.[124] These reservations are closely coupled with the recognition of those who see that, as the canon served to found the church on the apostolic foundation, it did so in the course of the history of salvation. With these reservations they intend to point out that the crux of the matter is not some new revelation, but rather the possibility of

123. Weber, *Grundlagen,* I, p. 283. According to W. Elert (*Der Christliche Glaube* [1941], p. 222), the dividing line between an evangelical and a non-evangelical conception of the canon can be found here, i.e., whether it is or is not dependent on "the authorities of the fourth and fifth centuries." Cf. Barth, *CD,* I/2, pp. 597ff.; Althaus, *Die Christliche Wahrheit,* I, 185ff.; W. Trillhaas, *Dogmatik,* pp. 72ff.; H. G. Fritzsche, *Lehrbuch der Dogmatik,* I, 111ff.

124. See esp. *CD,* I/2, 599-601.

a new, incidental *recipere* of writings which could become known in their harmony with and conformity to the canon already accepted — thus in fact a new recognition of the canonical gospel.[125]

Even here we shall have to admit that an appeal to the providence of God in and above the formation of the canon can bring us to a satisfactory solution no more than it could in the problem of the antilegomena. But we should ask whether or not our reflection about these future "possibilities" does give us some light on the church's *recipere* of the canon, which serves to found the church and to point out its faith.

To posit this question is not *ipso facto* a formal sanctioning of the past. It does not say that the past is superior to the present life of the church as it hears God's Word today. It is even less an incarceration of the Spirit in the church.[126] It is instead a demand that attention be paid to that concrete sufficiency of Holy Scripture which was accepted by the church as the decisive guide to its origin and as the scepter extended over it.[127] Men will continue to be aware that the disjunction between the time of the apostles and that of the church (with an eye to the growth of the canon) does not solve or even clarify all questions. Because of the decisive structure of the canon — in its historical growth — we can understand why the "open" canon displays such theoretical, barely functional characteristics. These in turn conjure up another set of reservations and doubts.[128] Indeed, one often gets the impression that the theory of the open canon provides not so much an account of the real possibilities which exist, as it does a warning against treating the Word of God as an objective thing. It should be concluded that this function of the open canon does not at all shed new light on the church. The pure understanding of the canon (also in its actually closed nature) already contains this warning against

125. Cf. Aland, pp. 24ff., concerning the decision by the church regarding an eventual "extension." Aland denies that the latter will happen. Cf. the "re-discovery" of the Didache in the 19th century (p. 26), which failed to raise the issue.
126. Cf. Harnack about the "Spirit being actually chased into a book" (*The Origin of the NT*, p. 36).
127. Cf. Ridderbos, *Authority*, p. 33.
128. See Althaus, I, 193. He is "in principle" for keeping the canon open. However, he does "not take seriously" the correction of "the boundaries as the Ancient Church drew them." On the other hand he would not object to including any lost letter of Paul, "or any other important testimony from the apostolic era" in the canon, should they be found.

objectifying the Word by consideration of the intent of the canon itself.[129] The road that the church has walked, in a continual process of stumbling and rising again, has been the road of confrontation with the canon. This canon it accepted by faith and, obeying the call to hear the voice of its Lord, confessed to all who follow.

The present state of theology makes clear that reflection on the open canon in the light of future "possibilities" is completely overshadowed by the vision of the canon that does not so much envision an *extension* of the canon as it does a *reduction* to the "canon-within-the-canon."[130] It thus remains necessary to give an account of the nature and the dynamics of the church's confession as it recognizes and acknowledges its apostolic foundation. This confession, by which the church subjects itself, however active it may be, to the Word of its Lord, and in which the church speaks of the God-breathed and authoritative character of the witness of Scripture, cannot be taken as an independent explanation of the phenomenon of Holy Scripture.[131] This confession is completely suffused with the call to the church and others to listen to the voice of the Lord like sheep who know the voice of the shepherd and who do not acknowledge the voice of a stranger (Jn. 10:5).

A true confession of Holy Scripture is possible only when one has yielded himself to the testimony of Scripture. Only on the path of faith does our certainty grow regarding Scripture as the cloak in which Christ comes to us.[132] Such walking on the

129. For the "function" of the open canon, see Althaus, p. 193. He holds that it is precisely the "unhedged openness" and the "perennially open question of its boundaries" that guarantees "the true evangelical meaning and intent" of the canon against "all attempts to make the Scripture formally the servant of the Canon."

130. Cf. Aland, p. 27. He thinks it "characteristic" that "when demands are made today for a revision of the Canon, they are always in the direction of its reduction, not of its enlargement."

131. Cf. Bavinck, *GD,* I, 407, concerning interpretation, theory and confession. One can ask if here is where one finds the connection with the remarkable dictum of Bavinck that there exists no dogma "about which there is more unity than that of the Holy Scripture" (p. 372). Later he repeated it: "There is no dogma about which so many are so completely agreed" (p. 561).

132. "This, then, is the true knowledge of Christ, if we receive him as he is offered by the Father: namely, clothed with his gospel. For just as he has been appointed as the goal of our faith, so we cannot take the right road to him unless the gospel goes before us" (*Inst.,* III, ii, 6 [McNeill ed., I, 548]). See also the example of Scripture as the mirror (p. 549).

path of faith will also completely reveal the meaning of the *recipere* as an acceptance of Christ; this acceptance comes in the unity and indissolubility (Col. 2:6; I Thess. 2:13) in which the New Testament presents a faith which hears, accepts, and guards the Word of God. Therefore, one can never legitimately devaluate Scripture while intending to pay attention to the content of the message. One must speak of the Christ *of Scripture.* Whoever dissolves this unity and thus divides the one true faith not only attacks the certainty of faith, but does so by suspending and secularizing the intent and meaning of faith in Scripture. Hence Calvin, when defining faith, can say about the conviction of the truth of God: "As for its certainty, so long as your mind is at war with itself, the Word will be of doubtful and weak authority, or rather of none."[133] It would be a perversion of Calvin's correlative meaning concerning faith and the Word, if anyone would, on the basis of this statement, conclude that God's Word derives its authority from faith. He is instead vividly pointing out the way — the only way — whereby we can truly come to Christ through the Word.[134] Every reflection on Scripture and on the canon must terminate in the reminder of the danger of this canon's fading away. The danger is that we then, whether aware of it or not, would replace it with a canon of our own creation. And thus we would replace the *recipere* by a projection of our own minds — regardless of the hermeneutical wrappings in which we would cover it.

When we understand this warning, the seemingly technical and historical problem of the canon is seen in its full meaning and scope. When we see that the biblical text about Scripture's witnessing to Christ is brought to the fore, showing that a search of Scripture does not necessarily lead to a coming to Christ (Jn. 5:39-40), then this message tests every consideration of the canon and every confession of Holy Scripture by the touchstone of this coming to him. In that way the reception is connected to the Word, the Word which is *kritikos* and "discerns the thoughts and intentions of the heart" (Heb. 4:12). The history of the *recipere* might for a moment make us think that we ourselves are called to the function of being "critical," and

133. "Now, therefore, we hold faith to be a knowledge of God's will towards us, perceived from his Word" (*ibid.*, p. 549).

134. Cf. Calvin on Col. 2:6. Because the *prophecy* regarding Christ has been fulfilled, they must all the more cling to the doctrine "as delivered to them by Epaphras." He follows this by saying: "As Isaiah said, 'This is the way, walk ye in it.' "

that the whole battle over the marks of canonicity is clearly centered on this problem. But the unique nature of the *recipere* instead points to the contrary. Our attention to the canon, to the scriptural testimony of the Old and New Testaments, to Scripture's unique origin and inspiration, can only serve a believing search of Scripture. This search must have its origin in the prophetic-apostolic testimony concerning Christ. Such a search may provoke many questions and may be attended by many dangers — that is, the danger that the key of knowledge may be taken away (Lk. 11:52). But it is absolutely necessary and legitimate (I Pet. 1:10-11; I Cor. 2:10).

If we consider the manner in which the Word of God comes to us, our listening to God's voice does not need to be threatened by scientific research into Holy Scripture. Man's listening is only threatened when he stumbles over the *skandalon,* which in the Bible reaches, limits, and blesses us as the "scandal" of Christ. That is why the most insistent warning regarding the canon concerns man's continual standing on the foundation: "Therefore let anyone who thinks that he stands take heed lest he fall" (I Cor. 10:12). This warning does not oppose the consolation which Scripture affords (Rom. 15:4). It rather focuses on it. It is very much like the warning not to go beyond that which is written (I Cor. 4:6). And it is inseparably joined to the beatitude, "Blessed are those who hear the Word of God and keep it" (Lk. 11:28).

CHAPTER FOUR

AUTHORITY AND INTERPRETATION

WHEN THE CHURCH CONFESSES THE BIBLE as its canon, that is, the norm and rule for its entire existence in this world, as it moves into the future, then every reflection on this canon directly leads one to this question: How is Holy Scripture revered concretely, and what form does this confession, this faith in Scripture, take? This recognition has been expressed in many ways and formulations. Some have spoken of obedience, some of careful listening, others of subjecting themselves; but all of these words (concentrated in the *recipere,* which we discussed above) only become fully and deeply known when they afford some perspective on the reality of faith in Scripture as it continually confronts the message of Scripture itself. The seriousness and responsibility of such a confession of faith in Scripture is revealed in this, that regarding it the word of John also obtains: "Little children, let us not love in word or speech, but in deed and in truth" (I Jn. 3:18). For when the canon of Holy Scripture is confessed, such a confession not only accepts a limitation enjoining it "not to go beyond the things which are written" (I Cor. 4:6; cf. Rev. 22:18-19); it also acknowledges a concrete subjection, a readiness to focus attentively on the testimony of the Bible.

This faith in Scripture can thus be described as the attention of the "understanding heart" for which Solomon prayed when he ascended the throne (I Kgs. 3:9-11). For the confession that "we receive" the "holy and canonical books" (*BC,* Art. V) takes form in the attention we pay to the words — to all the diverse words of Holy Scripture. Only in these is the confession tested and does it find its touchstone. Only in this way is it manifested whether the confession was one "in deed and truth." Faith in Scripture — as we noted earlier — is never to be understood formalistically, but is seen as clearly connected with the testimony of the Holy Spirit. It follows that for such a true faith in Scripture to be meaningful, the interpretation of Scripture is of the essence. Such faith is not a mysterious or irrational experience locked within the human heart. It is instead an experience that is continually cast back upon the Word of God in its multiformity and the inexhaustible richness of its words. It is then not surprising that precisely in this context the authority of Scripture and the recognition of it come to play such a prominent role, and that the question of the interpretation of Scripure is also central. On the basis of a formalized conception of the Bible, this would be inexplicable. But when one confesses that faith is intrinsically related to and dependent on the message of Scripture, concentrated attention for a correct understanding of Scripture follows naturally. Even one who discerns the danger that the hermeneutical problem may force a subsumption of all of theology under hermeneutics should not in reaction misjudge the significance of a correct understanding of Scripture. For not in separation from, but rather in connection with, the understanding of Holy Scripture does it become evident whether its authority is really honored.

The fact that hermeneutics is continually busy with rules for the exposition of Scripture shows a desire to oppose the arbitrariness which, despite the recognition of Scripture as God's Word, neglects its concrete authority. It is impossible for any theological study to bypass these questions. For in every hermeneutical question lies an aspect which is intrinsically tied to the confession of scriptural authority. In the same way the Reformation hermeneutical rule *Sacra Scriptura sui ipsius interpres*[1] sought to provide a direct view of the distinctive and unique authority of Scripture.[2] This authority opposed all forms of subjectivism which do not openly conform to it.

So great is the danger of such subjectivism and its recurrence that many have lost heart. Such a variety of differing and mutually exclusive "interpretations" arose — all appealing to the same Scripture — that serious people began to wonder whether an all-pervasive and seemingly indestructible influence of subjectivism in the understanding of Scripture is not the cause of the plurality of confessions in the church. Do not all people

1. Hereafter translated either in whole or in part as "Sacred Scripture is its own interpreter," or on occasion, "interprets itself" (tr. note).
2. The Reformation never deluded itself with the thought that correct hermeneutical rules guaranteed true obedience to Scripture. It took the rules as "warnings." Calvin speaks of a way "to lead us with straight firm steps to the will of God" (*Inst.*, II, viii, 8).

read Scripture from their own current perspectives and presuppositions? Do they not cast it in the form of their own organizing systems, with all kinds of conscious or subconscious preferences, ways of selection which force the understanding of Scripture into one particular direction? Earlier we referred to Aland's comments on "a narrowing and a shortening" of the canon, not as a conscious reduction of Scripture but as a practical use of it in "teaching, exegesis and preaching," with varying emphases on specific aspects of its witness.[3]

Is it indeed possible for us to read Scripture with free, unbiased, and listening attention? Or do we hear in God's Word that which we already know, that is, the images, feelings, and presuppositions of our own hearts? Is there still a real encounter with the Word of God when we speak about the ecclesiastically accepted canon? Can we come to Scripture with our subjectivity without allowing that subjectivity to have a creative and projective power?

We should never minimize the seriousness of these questions, especially since here both the authority of Scripture and faith in Scripture are at stake. It is evident that arbitrariness threatens and suspends obedience and that it can serve the deep forces of resistance to the authority of the gospel, which is not "a man's gospel" (Gal. 1:11). This becomes apparent in diverse interpretations of the gospel. Take, for instance, the crude way in which the national-socialistic era (Nazism) perverted the gospel. In 1933, a motion contained the call to take seriously the heroic Jesus-figure as the basis for a relevant Christendom in which the proud man supplanted the timid and broken slave. Nietzsche was being proclaimed instead of the gospel (cf. Mt. 21 and Jn. 6). There are also more finely honed possibilities for "interpretation" — harder to recognize and therefore deadlier. There is no more incisive question concerning our relation to Scripture than the one regarding the shaping of our listening and obedience to that Scripture. For Scripture can be interpreted in a manner which pays little or no attention to the intent or mind of the Spirit.[4]

3. *Problem of the NT Canon*, pp. 28-29.
4. In Rom. 8:27, one finds the words "the mind of the Spirit" [Berkouwer's translation uses the "intention" of the Spirit]. Although the context gives a broader perspective than just the idea of "intention," there is yet a basic connection due to the saving will of God and the searching of the heart. Cf. H. N. Ridderbos, *Aan De Romeinen*, p. 193; O. Michel, *Der Brief an die Römer* (1955), p. 179 concerning the end after which the Spirit seeks.

We must contend with varied opposition toward a correct interpretation of Scripture. Even though it is clear that no single theory or technique concerning rules of interpretation *ipso facto* guarantees such a correct understanding, it is still necessary to warn ourselves and others against mere arbitrariness. It is exactly that arbitrariness which is so ironically described in Werenfels' aphorism: "Here is the book in which each one seeks his dogmas."[5] The question whether there is true obedience in active and true listening (as in Ps. 85:8: "Let me hear what God the Lord will speak") deserves our attention. Only when we pay strict attention can we expect to see the day dawn and the arising of the morning star (II Pet. 1:19). And only in traveling this road is our confession of the canon truly faith in Scripture.

The word "hermeneutic" derives from *hermeneuein,* a word found in the New Testament. There it means to transpose into another language, to translate — also in the sense of interpreting or explaining. The latter sense is always found in the context of bridging a gap, for example, when Scripture was explained by Christ to the travelers to Emmaus. Beginning with Moses and all the prophets, "he interpreted to them in all the scriptures the things concerning himself" (Lk. 24:27). Such explanation is focused directly on the understanding of Scripture together with faith. Christ reproaches them for their foolishness and slowness "to believe all that the prophets have spoken." For this was not some intellectual deficiency but a lack of understanding due to the state of their hearts. In the exposition — the interpretation — is a pointing to the meaning of the words. In Philip's instruction of the Ethiopian eunuch, the *interpretation* of Isaiah 53 becomes the proclamation of Jesus (Acts 8:35). The glossolalia in I Corinthians likewise needed interpretation, a bridging of the gap. Diverse *charismata* are given by the Spirit, and among them are both tongues and the interpretation of tongues (I Cor. 12:10; 14:26), so that the word which is spoken may be clear and the congregation may be edified (I Cor. 14:5, 26, 27; cf. 14:13). It is not edified by mysterious utterings but by interpretation, by being led into the meaning in order to see the clarity of the words.

5. *Hic liber est, in quo quaerit dogmata quisque.* Often in the 16th century, Rome accused the Reformation of such arbitrariness. Cf. Calvin, "Articles Agreed Upon by the Faculty of Sacred Theology of Paris . . . with the Antidote," *Tracts and Treatises* (ET, 1958), I, 104. The Roman Catholic accusation is recorded that "Scripture is like a nose of wax because it can be bent hither and thither." See Ebeling, *Luther,* p. 97: "A proverbial saying with which Luther was acquainted."

The interpretation of Scripture is so important because there we hear the message of salvation. The bridging of the gap aims straight for that salvation. It seeks to eliminate the strangeness and mysteriousness of the message.[6] For even when the latter comes to us in our own language (Acts 2:6), just hearing or reading it does not necessarily entail a clear understanding of it. Chasms may open when Scripture is handled in a way which does not do justice to the meaning and intent of its words. It is even possible to stand within the bounds of Scripture itself and yet to twist it. This is what is meant in II Peter 3:16, where the unstable and ignorant are seen to be twisting Scripture on a rack. The result is a darkening of the mind, a closing of the heart, something which boils down to a turning "away from listening to the truth" (II Tim. 4:4); a ceasing to be "sound in faith" (I Tim. 1:13-14). The resultant "misunderstanding" may then not just be blamed on the "difficulty" of Paul's language (II Pet. 3:16); similar "misunderstanding" is applied to the rest of Scripture.

One can speak of a conflict between the stance of the reader and of the meaning of the words confronting him. It is not warranted to speak of a natural harmony between hearing or reading and understanding. When Christ accuses the Pharisees of not knowing Scripture (Mt. 22:29), he is not saying that they are strangers to it. For he asks, "Have you not read?" (Mt. 22:31), and they in turn appeal to Moses. But they do not know or understand Scripture and do not discern its deep intent. They err (Mt. 22:29) and miss the message of Scripture. Even though the law occupied such a central focus in their life, it appeared that they had "taken away the key of knowledge" (Lk. 11:52) and thus had left the gate to the treasury of Scripture closed. Reading does not necessarily lead to understanding. When the eunuch is reading Isaiah 53, Philip asks him, "Do you understand what you are reading?" (Acts 8:30). Scripture is then explained to him by preaching about Jesus (Acts 8:35). Regarding the parables, Christ states that to the disciples it has been given to know the secret of the kingdom of God. But then there are those who can "see but not perceive, and may indeed hear but not understand" (Mk. 4:12). This is why it is mandatory that a man both read and understand (Mk. 13:14). There-

6. *Translation* of Scripture already clearly shows the bridging of a distance. Concerning the problematics of translation and interpretation, see W. Schwarz, *Principles and Problems of Biblical Translation* (1955), especially regarding the LXX, pp. 17ff.

fore, one must take heed as to how he hears (Lk. 8:18); he must both hear and understand (Mt. 15:10). For a man can read the Torah and be continually engrossed in it and yet not be able to give it its due (Rom. 9:31). There can be some initial understanding; something which can and must be deepened, as was the case with Apollos. He was "well versed in the scriptures" (Acts 18:24ff.), instructed in the way of the Lord, and even fervent in the Spirit, teaching accurately the things concerning Jesus, "though he knew only the baptism of John" (Acts 18:25).

Despite such initial understanding, it was possible that the way of God could be expounded to him more accurately (Acts 18:26). At stake is a continually deeper intrusion into the mystery of the written message, into the *meaning* of the words. One can hear only "madness," as Agrippa did, in the words of salvation, while for Paul these words were the "sober truth" (Acts 26:24-25). It is possible for the meaning of Scripture to be misread and misunderstood. The reason does not lie in the obscurity and impenetrability of the words, but in the missing willingness to truly and sincerely listen, to be susceptible to guidance and instruction (Acts 8:31-39) — the very opposite of the picture of the eunuch who, after the scriptural exposition, went on his way rejoicing.

In many varied ways we are reminded of the state of our hearts when we read Scripture. Various more or less impressive presuppositions can block our path to understanding it. The approaches to the written words containing the message of salvation are open; the attitude of the heart is the determining factor. Thus, Paul can speak of a "veiled" reading of the old covenant, something which is also termed a veil over the mind (II Cor. 3:14-15).[7] Only when a man turns to the Lord, when in Christ the intent of the words is highlighted and understood, is that veil removed (II Cor. 3:16). The Lord is depicted as the one who removes the veil and bestows freedom so that his glory is seen with unveiled face (II Cor. 3:17-18).

When the Spirit and repentance are thus so heavily emphasized, the question arises whether all understanding of Scripture is not of a purely charismatic nature, as mysterious as the blowing of the wind and a new birth in the Spirit (Jn. 3:8). Scripture emphasizes a correct state of receptivity, the necessary enlightenment of the eyes (Eph. 1:18), the illumined understanding (Ps. 119:125, 135, 136). We need insight (Eph. 3:18) as opposed to

7. Berkouwer's version uses "heart" here (tr. note).

futile minds, darkened understanding, and ignorance due to hardness of heart (Eph. 4:17ff.). There is a call not to be foolish but rather to understand what the will of the Lord is (Eph. 5:17). The Old Testament often describes such understanding not as a natural capacity but as a gift of wisdom and insight (I Kgs. 3:9; Dan. 2:21).[8]

In this context one can well ask whether or not the true understanding of the meaning of Scripture is at all concerned with the problems comprising the subject of hermeneutics. For it deals with rules, with a certain normativity, with laws that must manifest themselves in any interpretation, lest it be arbitrary instead of correct.[9] Is it true that in the understanding of Scripture we meet a mysterious, charismatic, and insoluble mystery? Does something break through and subvert all hermeneutical "logic" and every rule? On a path like this, one could hold that the letter does not count anymore. Then it is chiefly the Spirit who, free from every method and technique, guides into all truth (Jn. 16:13).

Questions like these have continually drawn attention in any discussion of the interpretation of Scripture. When one reads the warning, "He who has an ear, let him hear what the Spirit says to the churches" (Rev. 2:7), one cannot pass them by. For such a statement regarding concentrated listening is diametrically opposed to the adamant heart which does not hear "the law and the words which the Lord of hosts had sent by his Spirit through the former prophets" (Zech. 7:12). Putting true understanding in this light, we can find only one form of pure understanding and exposition. It has been discussed as a particular type of exegesis, namely, pneumatic or "spiritual" exegesis. The plea for such an exegesis has arisen out of dissatisfaction with historical-critical research. In the latter the message of Holy Scripture and our hearing of the *vox Dei* seemed to be lost within a maze of historical, psychological, sociological, and religious details. In reaction to historical-critical research, some laid emphasis on the biblical text that "no one comprehends the thoughts of God except the Spirit of God," and that only where the Spirit has been bestowed can one speak of understanding (I Cor. 2:11-12). Being taught by the Spirit is thus posited over against all human wisdom (I Cor. 2:13; 1:20; 2:5). Must this not lead to an exclusively pneumatic exegesis?[10]

8. Cf. von Rad, *Old Testament Theology*, I, 442ff. concerning the *charismata*.
9. Cf. Kuyper on hermeneutics as "the logic of exegesis" (*Enc.*, III, 90ff.).
10. Take Daniel's exposition of dreams as an analogy (Dan. 2:4ff.; 4:9ff.;

For some time pneumatic exegesis has been influential in certain places. The reactionary element was recognized, however, and it signaled the danger that, following this course, it was difficult to evade spiritualism. It was pointed out that injustice was done to the meaning of the witness of Scripture itself. For it is worth noting that when the eunuch is unsure about the meaning of Isaiah 53, Philip, who was sent to him by the Spirit (Acts 8:29), instructs him "beginning with this scripture" (Acts 8:35), and thus causes him to go on his way rejoicing. Christ himself, in his instruction of the travelers to Emmaus, also begins with the scriptural testimony (Lk. 24:27) and thus fully honors its significance.[11] Understanding is not achieved by putting Scripture aside. All pneumatic exegesis contains a misunderstanding of the fact that the message of salvation does not come to us in a mysterious, cryptic, and unintelligible language of the Spirit, which can only be understood charismatically and pneumatically. The message of salvation comes instead in meaningful human language. Pneumatic exegesis turns Scripture into a mysterious entity, completely inaccessible to everyone lacking the charisma of the Spirit. In opposition to pneumatic exegesis, men again began to focus attention on the literary-historical approach. Since understanding is concerned with the concrete words of Scripture, a special *hermeneutica sacra* was not deemed necessary. It would suggest that there was a special sacred, or at least peculiar, approach to the text of Scripture. This was seen as a misrepresentation of the text itself. The biblical text, which comes to us as all other human writings do, can therefore only be understood by the general hermeneutical rules applicable to all of human literature.

It is interesting, especially in this context, that even those who speak of a special theological hermeneutic, still do not want to flee from an interpretation of the words in some pneumatological mysticism which follows a path far removed from that of hermeneutics. When Kuyper states that in the exposition of Scripture a certain factor is dealt with, "which regular hermeneutics cannot deal with since it is not found in any other document," he immediately qualifies his statement. By referring to such a "special factor" he is not talking about a "mystical"

7:15-16). Also see Eccl. 8:1: "Who is like the wise man and who knows the interpretation of a thing?" Concerning this *pesher,* which surmounts human possibilities, see F. F. Bruce, *Biblical Exegesis in the Qumran Texts* (1959), pp. 7ff.

11. See the image of "hearts burning" within them as a result of Christ's opening of the Scripture (Lk. 24:32).

element in the sense of a *deus ex machina*.[12] This would be immune to all control and make any definite theory of investigation impossible. He seeks to avoid the dualism by seeing theological hermeneutics rooted in the "logical train of thought of general hermeneutics," so that, "in so far as it adopts the latter's rules, it does not bear any special character."[13] Even though it must consider that exceptional factor which distinguishes Scripture from all other writings, it may not "for one moment relinquish the general principles of hermeneutics,"[14] but may only allow a theological factor to dominate them. That is why Kuyper calls hermeneutics a mixed science. On the one hand, it cannot be separated from faith in Scripture, and on the other hand, it cannot be based on a source totally independent of and outside the norms of regular hermeneutics.

Kuyper then conceived of the following solution: regular hermeneutics ceases when one understands the intent of the author;[15] but at that point the duty of biblical exegesis is not yet finished, since we are basically concerned with what God himself has to say to us. And thus the discussion of such a special hermeneutics led Kuyper to the problem of the "sense" of Scripture, that of the intention of the secondary authors *and* of the primary author. Such a dual solution does not seek to show a way in which, on the basis of a pneumatic exegesis, the exposition of the words themselves is made irrelevant.[16] The way to understand the intent of the hidden meaning must be pointed out, and thus, in order not to fall into every sort of arbitrariness, one will always have to start out from the basis of Scripture itself.[17] In opposition to pneumatic exegesis, stress is increasingly laid on remaining bound to the text in order

12. *Enc.*, III, 95.
13. *Ibid.*, p. 107.
14. *Ibid.*
15. *Ibid.*, p. 96.
16. Kuyper uses "mysticism" in two ways. On p. 95 he speaks of it in the sense of a *deus ex machina*. Later he mentions the recognition of the "mystical" factor in the interpretation of Scripture (p. 101). On the basis of Gal. 4:24, he sees the deeper meaning of the OT as the hermeneutical rule of Paul. Although he recognizes the fact that various "allegorists" walk in a maze, he chooses the recognition of a higher "sense" of Scripture above the narrow view of those cautious interpreters who "cannot see anything mystical in and behind the written word" (p. 101). Concerning Paul's use of the hermeneutical principle, see I Cor. 9:9 (as it relates to Deut. 25:4); cf. I Tim. 5:18.
17. *Enc.*, III, 105.

that the understanding may truly remain an understanding of the *text*.

For a considerable time questions such as these have played an important role in the scientific approach to Scripture. Already at the end of the nineteenth century it was questioned whether a university graduate versed in the historical-critical investigation of Scripture could still truly preach the Word of God. The same question was asked concerning Barth's attempt to approach the hermeneutical problem pragmatically. He did not choose the pneumatological approach, free of the use of the texts themselves, but spoke of dissatisfaction with the diverse types of exegesis and their results. Especially because of his book *Epistle to the Romans,*[18] he was accused of doing injustice to the historical-critical approach to Scripture. In the preface to the second edition he answered that he had only wished to combat the tendency of recent commentators to "confine themselves to an interpretation of the text which seems to me to be no commentary at all, but merely the first step to a commentary. Recent commentaries contain no more than a reconstruction of the text, a rendering of the Greek words and phrases by their precise equivalents. . . ."[19] As far as he is concerned, pressing beyond this preliminary work to "an understanding of Paul" is at stake, that is, an understanding of what he could have intended, so that "the actual meaning" of that which is set out in the epistle is disclosed. We must literally rethink the text so that it becomes transparent to us,[20] and all our attention is focused completely on the subject matter at hand. For the text deals with a specific matter,[21] is engrossed with it and directed towards it. Only in this way is there again a visible and a viable connection between exegesis and preaching. Barth points to the fact that written words may not be isolated but that they require our attention to that which is spoken. The point of departure is and continues to be the text itself, and no possibility for escape from the text to the Spirit or from literary-historical methods to a pneumatic one is open.

The philological approach remains for Barth "the first step

18. (ET, 6th ed., 1963). See therein the preface to the second edition, p. 6.
19. *Ibid.*
20. *Ibid.,* p. 7; cf. p. 9: "It was this miserable situation that compelled me as a pastor to undertake a more precise understanding and interpretation of the Bible."
21. See Koole, *Hermeneutische Oriëntatie,* p. 24: "The understanding of a text does not just seek the elucidation of the words used but that of the intended matter."

on the way from text to sermon." Decisive for this labor is that which is at its heart, the subject matter, the *content* of the documents, "the note-worthy matter which concerned the writers of the sources, the biblical object."[22] Hence one cannot call Barth's approach pneumatic.[23] It is theological exegesis.[24] Pneumatic exegesis ultimately devalues the meaning of the written word because it is dissatisfied with grammatical and literary-historical exegesis. Theological exegesis seeks attention for the fact that the text cannot be understood apart from a full recognition of the text's relationship to and focus on the matter which is discussed in it.[25] When the unsatisfactory nature of pneumatic exegesis has been accentuated, and when understanding is not viewed as derived from a charisma rendering immersion in the text superfluous, another question arises. In which way will understanding no longer bear the character of dogmatic exegesis, a dangerous self-projecting activity? In what way can a pure interpretation be attained? The other side of the same issue is: How is Scripture's own authority truly honored?

This question about authority and interpretation and their relationship has always centered around the well-known reminder of II Peter 1:20: "No prophecy of scripture is a matter of one's own interpretation." To the present day there has been much difference of opinion regarding this incisive claim. Roman Catholic exegesis sees it as containing a contrast between independent and ecclesiastical exegesis. It is taken to be a prime source of justification for the decree of Trent that it is the church's right "to judge regarding the true sense and interpretation of holy Scriptures."[26] There are also non-Catholic exegetes

22. Cf. extensively F. Schmid, *Verkündigung und Dogmatik in der Theol. K. Barths* (1964), pp. 41ff.; G. Eichholz, "Der Ansatz Barths in der Hermeneutik," *Antwort 1956,* also in *Tradition and Interpretation* (1965).
23. In the preface to *The Epistle to the Philippians* (ET, 1962), he describes pneumatic exegesis as "this unpleasant catch-word." Cf. Barth, *Grundfragen* (1935), p. 15.
24. *Grundfragen,* pp. 14ff.
25. Cf. Miskotte, *When the Gods are Silent,* pp. 143ff. He therefore wants no special hermeneutical method. He views liberal scriptural criticism as particularly fatal since it refuses to understand the biblical writers on the grounds of the matter which moves them. Also see *CD,* I/2, p. 464 on the taking seriously of the text, but the text says "something specific." This applies to every human word and therefore no special hermeneutic is needed (pp. 468ff.). To neither Barth nor Miskotte does this signify a misunderstanding of the uniqueness of Scripture.
26. Denzinger, *The Sources of Catholic Dogma* (ET, 1957), section 786.

who take the same approach as part of their views on II Peter. Thus, Käsemann, for example, sees very clear signs of the so-called primitive Catholicism in the epistle, and consequently sees in II Peter 1:20 an "ecclesiastically authoritative interpretation."[27] The ecclesiastical teaching position here delineates itself over against enthusiasm leading to arbitrariness. II Peter offers a remedy against it: "A personal exegesis, undertaken by the individual, not authorized or previously prescribed by the official teaching ministry, is not permitted."[28] Although interpretation of Scripture was open to everyone in the early church by means of the Spirit, now the Spirit is bound to the offices, and interpretation is no longer entrusted to individual believers, to the "laity."

This position, which envisions the church as the hermeneutical point of departure, certainly does not receive any direct and open support in Peter's epistle. The rejection of the "own interpretation" can more reasonably be seen as a protest against a self-imposed arbitrary position, since it explicitly warns against a "twisting" of Scripture based on individual preference (II Pet. 3:16). Not a word in the text suggests any antithesis between "individual" and "ecclesiastical."[29] Thus, the impression is inescapable that Käsemann's views that the whole epistle of II Peter is an expression of primitive Catholicism have strongly influenced the interpretation of the text.

When one has been warned against arbitrary interpretation, the integral union of the recognition of scriptural authority and the correct interpretation of Scripture takes on an even greater significance. In this area scholars have often tried to use the concept of a key. The image already occurs in the New Testament in a specific way: it is the key of knowledge. Christ accuses the scribes of having taken away "the key of knowledge" (Lk. 11:52). They are thus standing before the closed gates of the kingdom; they themselves did not enter and they hindered others who tried (cf. Mt. 23:13; Rom. 2:20). Their dogmatic exegesis is an interpretation of the Torah on the basis of which they have rejected Christ. Hence they lack any vision of his being the Messiah. The key was not lost; in their prejudice they removed it.

27. *Essays on New Testament Themes,* pp. 189ff.
28. *Ibid.,* p. 190. See also W. Marxsen, *Der "Frühkatholizismus" im NT* (1958), pp. 8ff.
29. Calvin, in his commentary on II Peter, attacks the "ecclesiastical" exposition. Let me also point out that *idia* occurs several times in II Peter without the individual-communal (churchly) dilemma. Cf. 1:3; 2:16, 22; 3:3; 3:16, 17.

It should not surprise us that this image of the key has often been used as a hermeneutical tool. The question then posed was whether it is possible to point out any such key as a legitimate way into Holy Scripture.[30] A way to attain correct knowledge of Scripture was hoped for so that Scripture would no longer remain closed because a key was lacking. Hermeneutically speaking, this key was not intended to be a theory or technique which would as such disclose the correct entrance to the edifice of Holy Scripture. The true understanding of Scripture is not automatically guaranteed by pure theories and clear hermeneutical rules. Even though hermeneutics is to warn against arbitrary expositions, and even though it is "methodical," this does not yet mean that the way of understanding will be free of dangers and the possibilities of getting lost. It does not mean that reflecting on this way while confronting dogmatic exegesis loses its importance. The distinction between conscious and unconscious dogmatic exegesis has often been made. The former denoted a conscious acceptance of a second source alongside Scripture. More often than not people pointed to the Roman Catholic view of Scripture *and* tradition.

This aspect will not be discussed here. Recent developments in Roman Catholic theology have strongly protested against the so-called two-source theory.[31] But we must especially realize that the problem of dogmatic exegesis most often assumes an unconscious form which does not even endanger the *sola Scriptura*. The danger of an unconscious dogmatic exegesis is not one which can be casually attributed only to others. It conceals itself in many forms. Since it continually appeals to Holy Scripture, it is difficult to spot, and thus the hermeneutical problem in all of this is sharply delineated.

Dogmatic exegesis has especially been discussed in the context of the question whether or not it was possible to approach Scripture and to listen to its message without prejudices. For a long time the "presuppositionless" exegesis had been seen as an ideal, posited over against "reading into" Scripture the views of a position already held. It held that to do justice to Scripture one had to approach and explore it without starting from an *a priori* theory regarding its origin and quality as compared to other religious writings. In this context warnings are even now

30. Cf. *TDNT*, III, 744-753 regarding the key.
31. Cf. Berkouwer, *The Second Vatican Council and the New Catholicism*, Ch. 4.

hurled against presuppositions, out of a fear that they can produce results — such as attempted harmonizations — which dictate that the actual Scripture is allowed to speak only in conformity to the presuppositions. At the same time, our age has witnessed the surrender of the "blank sheet of paper" *(tabula rasa)* approach to Scripture. This is not primarily because it is an impossible demand, but rather because this ideal is based on an incorrect notion of the process of knowing.

The new problem has become especially relevant because of the influence of Bultmann. He holds that every historical understanding presupposes a relationship between the interpreter and the matter which must be interpreted and understood.[32] It is not permissible to proceed on the basis of fixed presuppositions in order to get definite exegetical results. But there is always a "pre-understanding" in the sense that we are never merely neutral observers. Neutral observation might be conceivable if Scripture had been intended to inform us about various neutral tidbits of information. Real understanding acknowledges a necessary *relationship* between our life and the text. This relationship is based on the quest after God, which motivates human life.[33] The text speaks within human existence and thus comes to us with a claim *(Anspruch)*. This does not call for a type of pneumatic exegesis, as though something mysterious could take place during hearing and understanding. But neutral and general truths, objects which we could grasp, are not at the heart of it either. The proclamation "addresses" us: it calls for our attention.[34] It calls for decision in an unmistakable *tua res agitur;*[35] it wants "engagement."[36] This relation to human existence is of essential importance for the hermeneutical problem. For, according to Bultmann, when we "interrogate" *(befragen)* the New Testament, we must not look for objective depictions which can enrich us intellectually. We should rather note the

32. "Is Exegesis without Presuppositions Possible?" *Existence and Faith* (ET, 1969), pp. 289ff. The exegete is "no *tabula rasa.*" This is thus a different rejection of "presuppositionless" exegesis than that of Barth. For Barth the argument is determined by the character of Holy Scripture (cf. *Grundfragen,* pp. 14ff.).

33. *Existence and Faith,* p. 295. He sees this relationship as the "direction of the inquiry," and so as the hermeneutical principle applying at any given time ("The Problem of Hermeneutics," *Essays Philosophical and Theological* [ET, 1955], p. 252).

34. Bultmann, *Glauben und Verstehen,* III (1960), pp. 166ff.

35. "The matter concerns you."

36. K. Frör, *Biblische Hermeneutik* (1961), p. 36.

relevance and the implications of the kerygma and heed the understanding of human existence which is expressed.[37]

One can call Bultmann's position a very special correlation between proclamation and human existence. The question which becomes real with every dogmatic exegesis arises here also. Does not the "pre-understanding" of human existence function in such a manner that it structures and delimits the message of Scripture? Bultmann is well aware of this problem, and he holds that in no way is it true that human existence is only confirmed by the kerygma. For theology would thus become anthropology, and human existence the canon for understanding. The acts of God are rather the "given data" and can never be deduced from human existence. But there is indeed that relevance of the kerygma for our existence, already visible in God's "turning toward us" in his *pro nobis*. Anyone reflecting on understanding may thus not discard the structure of our humanity as irrelevant.

This leads us to what is now commonly called the "hermeneutical circle." The term usually describes the relationship of the understanding of the whole of Scripture to its parts and vice versa.[38] It is understandable that the circle has also been invoked in opposition to the "pre-understanding" (i.e., the interpreter is no *tabula rasa*). The idea is that understanding, though it focuses on the text, is yet not the sum total of variously understood parts, since the "pre-understanding" cannot be eliminated. The part which subjectivity plays in the process of understanding must be recognized.[39] In all of this the circle itself is not at stake, inasmuch as it demands attention to the particular involvement of the interpreter, who does not approach the text of Scripture with a clean slate. The critical question in regard to this is whether or not the "encounter," the positing of the *a priori* of the text over against all of the interpreter's baggage and presuppositions, is completely recognized. Only then does the circle avoid being a necessarily vicious one. Only when the aim is a correlation between kerygma and existence, in which existence itself, despite every accent on the text, is made the final "canon" for its understanding, will such a peculiarly vicious

37. "New Testament and Mythology," *Kerygma and Myth* (ET, 1961), pp. 1-44.
38. Cf. H. G. Gadamer, *Wahrheit und Methode, Grundzüge einer philosophischen Hermeneutik* (1965), pp. 275ff. For the "circular relationship" see Frör, p. 55; O. Rodenberg, *Um die Wahrheit der Heiligen Schrift* (1963), pp. 41ff.
39. Cf. Ebeling, "The Part of Subjectivity in Understanding" (*R.G.G.*, III [3], Col. 257).

circle be created. It is evident that the correlation concept, which intends to point out a relationship that is unique, cannot function as a magical formula. For by the very nature of the case, everything depends on the question, In what way does one talk about man's relation to revelation?

The word "correlation" was already used during the Reformation.[40] It also plays a decisive role in the theological and philosophical thought of Paul Tillich.[41] The meaning and intent of such correlation can only be derived from the total context. For, in every consideration of relationship or correlation, various forms of subjectivism can begin to dominate its structure.[42] The correlation found in the "question and answer" method of both Tillich and Bultmann has an altogether different aim than that which the Reformation intended. At that time the priority of revelation for the path of faith was expressed, and the answer of faith was manifested as one heavily emphasizing its directedness to that revelation. This was done on the basis that the acting of God transcends man's subjectivity and faith, something which does not compete with the *tua res agitur,* but rather supposes it.[43]

I hold it to be in conflict with the Reformation correlation to posit the existential "meaning" of dogma over against "actuality," and thus to proclaim it as "canon." But it is something altogether different when men of the Reformation, out of the

40. Think of the statements in Melanchthon's *Apology*: "the promise and faith are to be correlated," and "the promise of mercy must be correlated with faith, for it cannot be apprehended without it" (J. T. Müller, *Die Symbol. Bücher der evang. Luth. Kirche* [1928], p. 142).
41. *Systematic Theology* (1957), II, 13 concerning correlation as *method,* "the correlation between existential questions and theological answers." On the one hand he states that "the existential question . . . is not the source for the revelatory answer formulated by theology," and on the other that it is "impossible" and "wrong . . . to derive the question implied in existence from the revelatory answer, because the revelatory answer is meaningless if there is no question to which it is the answer. Man cannot receive an answer to a question he has not asked."
42. I already pointed to this in *Geloof en Openbaring in de nieuwere Duitse Theol.,* p. 222, when I used the word "correlation" entirely free from the "interdependence" problem of Tillich and in the sense of the mutual involvement of faith and revelation on the way of faith.
43. In this connection I have always spoken about the correlative relationships, e.g., concerning the non-meritorial character of faith (faith as instrument). See *Faith and Justification* (ET, 1954); regarding the continuity of the church and her indefectibility, see *The Second Vatican Council;* the perseverance of the saints (concerning *perseverance* and *preservation*), *Faith and Perseverance* (ET, 1958).

depth and breadth of the correlation — and often in sharp reply to scholasticism — clearly expressed the saving significance of that actuality and the *tua res agitur* which it contains.[44]

Bultmann's attention to the "addressee" of the kerygma in hermeneutics and the hermeneutical circle is inseparably connected with what he sees as the essence of interpretation, that is, the search for and discovery of the real "intention" of Scripture. This can only be approached by the analysis of existentialist philosophy and understood as the "intention of the Biblical statements."[45] This concept of "intention" is one of the manifestations of a serious problem which continually recurs in hermeneutics. It is basic to Bultmann: it can be said that in Bultmann's thought the problem of dogmatic exegesis confronts us in a hermeneutical form. Already in 1925, his attention to the structure of human existence was strictly bound up with the horizon of understanding.[46] He tied the exegesis of the New Testament to the "self-interpretation of man" and has since branded as illegitimate every attack on the function of this "self-interpretation," considering these attacks irrelevant. Indeed, he would not be very receptive to Calvin's view of the relationship between the knowledge of God and the self-knowledge of man: "It is certain that man never achieves a clear knowledge of himself unless he has first looked on God's face, and then descends from contemplating him to scrutinize himself."[47] Since this is a very close relationship, Bultmann would point out that the existential hermeneutic is concerned with something quite different from Calvin's insight. It is not pure religious self-knowledge; it is rather the neutral existential analysis. For interpretation it is decisive, since it is the key, the possibility of understanding in the deepest sense of the word.[48] But it is precisely in this way that the consequences of this hermeneutical *a priori* — increasingly of a self-evident character as far as Bultmann is concerned — become clear.

44. Think of *HC,* Lord's Day 14: the "purpose" of the holy conception and birth of Jesus Christ. Cf. also the "profit" for us of his resurrection (Q. 45), his ascension (Q. 49), and the "comfort" of the parousia. These statements have nothing to do with polarity, interdependence, subjectivism and existentialism.

45. *Kerygma und Mythos,* II, 188. Cf. E. Fuchs, *Zum hermeneutischen Problem in der Theologie* (1959), p. 87.

46. Bultmann, "Das Problem einer theol. Exegese des NT," *Zwischen den Zeiten* (1925), p. 354.

47. *Inst.,* I, i, 2.

48. *Inst.,* I, i, 1-3.

Before we consider the "intention" idea more closely, I want to further illustrate the problem of interpretation by mentioning that Melanchthon is often appealed to here: "This is to know Christ, to wit, to know his benefits and not as they [the scholastics] teach, to perceive his natures and the mode of his incarnation."[49] Bultmann especially has cited Melanchthon to show that demythologization wishes to act in accordance with this dictum. Beside it he places a statement by W. Herrmann: "We can say nothing about God and who He is for Himself: but only consider what He does to us."[50] Melanchthon's statement is thus incorporated into the methodology of the existentialist philosophical founding of hermeneutics. There is every reason to question whether Melanchthon is done justice in this way. This question is also important since it implies another question concerning this new vision of "kerygma and existence": whether or not the Reformation frame of thought indeed does contain a point of contact here, as far as correlation is concerned. It must be admitted that Melanchthon's maxim is found in a concrete and clearly anti-speculative context. He speaks of the true knowledge of Christ, as approached from the Pauline contrast between wisdom and foolishness. He thus intends to oppose the scholastics and their gospel-eclipsing disputations. The much cited warning is intrinsically related to another statement: "The mysteries of divinity we have the more rightly adored than investigated."[51]

It is evident that what Melanchthon says about knowing Christ is not directed against any objectification which would cause our vision of his saving intent, and hence his "benefits for us," to be lost. Therefore, this dictum cannot be used toward a method of correlation which does not allow any room for the salvation which has come to us from the past; it instead rejects this as an "objectification." When Melanchthon speaks of the aim of Christ's coming, his warning is undeniably of existential import. However, it finds itself in a context radically different from that in which Bultmann places it.[52] The question has been asked whether, already in Melanchthon's wording, the significance of Christ (the "for us" of his "benefits") is sepa-

49. Melanchthon, *The Loci Communes of Philip Melanchthon* (ET, 1944), p. 68.
50. *Kerygma und Mythos,* II, 184.
51. Melanchthon, p. 67.
52. In order to correctly understand the statement of Melanchthon, see his protest against turning "our minds from Christ unto the frigid disputations of others" (pp. 7-8).

rated from the reality of the person of Christ. Is there a point of contact here for the modern emphasis on "significance" *(Bedeutsamkeit)*?[53] In my opinion, this dilemma was not a real one for Melanchthon and the Reformation. The "significance" can never be isolated from the redemptive-historical *work* of Christ — the work which includes all of his benefits.[54]

When we consider the appeal to Melanchthon's statement incorrect and somewhat anachronistic and thus not usable for the new hermeneutics, we do not thereby deny that within the Reformation there existed a strong awareness of the kerygmatic intent of the gospel, and the related "for me" and "for us."[55] It is an aspect continually visible in the Reformation, as it is in the polemical statement of Melanchthon. Moreover, it gives a direct link to Scripture itself and to the Nicene Creed that Christ came down "for our salvation" and was crucified. Here one finds the echo of Paul's statement explicitly directed to the acts of God in Christ "for us": ". . . who was put to death for our trespasses and raised for our justification" (Rom. 4:25). The actual dispute lies in the manner in which the Reformation's "for me" is used and incorporated into the correlation of kerygma and existence and thus transformed to a hermeneutical key.

Just as Feuerbach cannot appeal to Luther,[56] the modern hermeneutic of the "for me" of human existence cannot be seen as in line with the Reformation *pro me*. For the Reformation correlation, which completely honors the kerygma and the *pro nobis*, is thus broken into an ultimately inescapable subjective-objective polarity. The fact that here we are dealing with a hermeneutical approach does not in principle change things, since this hermeneutical "canon" loses its perspective on the central directedness of the gospel. This directedness of the gospel is and remains focused on man, but cannot in its structure and horizon be hermeneutically approached from human existence

53. Cf. J. M. de Jong, *Kerugma* (1958), p. 139 concerning positing "significance" and the being of God-in-Christ against each other. He does not judge Melanchthon's statement.
54. Cf. R. Prenter, *Creation and Redemption*, p. 343.
55. Cf. Calvin, *Inst.*, II, ix, 3, p. 426: "We enjoy Christ only as we embrace Christ clad in his own promises."
56. Ebeling, *Luther*, pp. 250ff. in connection with the often quoted words of Luther: "For the two belong together, faith and God. So that to which you give up and hand over your heart is truly your God" (Ebeling: "One could almost imagine that one was listening to Ludwig Feuerbach," p. 250). Ebeling approaches this all from the hermeneutical perspective (pp. 253-54) in an interpretation which, in my opinion, does not do justice to the meaning of Luther's correlation.

itself — through a neutral analysis — but only from the content and direction of the evangel itself. This evangel does not make questions of interpretation meaningless, but it does freely and sovereignly withdraw itself from a hermeneutic which wishes to mark the kerygma as a matter of logical consequence only, and to fix it as the "answer" to a "question," thus acknowledging this question to be of constitutive importance in the determination of the central focus of Holy Scripture.

Yet this may not lead us in reaction to posit the purposefulness of Scripture against the "intention" idea or against the concentrated attention to its "goal" *(scopus)*. It cannot be denied that the attempts to find out the goal of Scripture were focused on this intention. It is this intentionality which is given with the witness of Holy Scripture itself, since Scripture is directed by means of human words with unmistakable clarity to man himself. Thus, it does not allow us to be in the dark even for a moment regarding its goal-directedness. That is why reflection on the goal of Scripture is completely legitimate and indeed of essential importance for the understanding of Scripture.

This hermeneutical problem of the goal of Scripture is a very real one in our time, especially in regard to the confession of the church as it was formulated in ages gone by. Due to further investigation of Scripture and new questions, later periods witnessed new reflection on the bond to the confessional past of the church with concomitant discussion about what the church intended in its formulations. By doing this, men do not intend to posit the goal of our confessing against the text of the confession. Rather, by means of an historical interpretation of the confession, they seek to point out the deepest intention in the speaking of the church.[57] This hermeneutical point of view is very significant today, though it was not altogether unknown in the past.[58] It goes without saying that, in regard to its goal, one must continually guard against the danger of making the intention of Holy Scripture the product of a projection — the problem of dogmatic exegesis. Yet that does not relieve anyone of the duty to closely watch for the directedness of Scripture as he listens to it.

Seen from the perspective of *sola Scriptura,* this will not be an abstract and empty confession. The concreteness of the goal idea is of great importance. One cannot here speak of an

57. In Catholic circles the so-called new theology has brought this problem to focus. Cf. Berkouwer, *Second Vatican Council,* Ch. 4.
58. Bizer, *loc. cit.*

arbitrary approach to Holy Scripture, since the fact remains that Scripture itself in a very explicit way speaks about its intention and directedness. Think of the description of the signs of Jesus focused on a concrete goal: "But these are written that you may believe that Jesus is the Christ, the Son of God, and that believing you may have life in his name" (Jn. 20:31). That which is written is like an arrow shot to hit man's heart. In Romans 15:4 we again read that "whatever was written in former days was written for our instruction, that by steadfastness and by the encouragement of the scriptures we might have hope." Regarding Abraham it is said that his faith was reckoned to him as righteousness; Paul speaks about it as having a goal: "But the words, 'it was reckoned to him,' were written not for his sake alone, but for ours also. It will be reckoned to us..." (Rom. 4:23-24).[59] One cannot understand the written word when this direction is not kept in mind and one reads only "old stories." Thus, Paul saw that what had happened to Israel in the wilderness was important far beyond its time. For what happened to them there was to us "as a warning," and that is why it was *written down* "for our instruction, upon whom the end of the ages has come" (I Cor. 10:11). The directedness of history itself is mirrored in the recorded words. Thus, on the basis of the goal of the *graphē*, Paul can write that it is useful for many things, "for teaching, for reproof, for correction, and for training in righteousness, that the man of God may be complete, equipped for every good work" (II Tim. 3:16).

The intent and the significance of that which is written are continually expressed in a broad final horizon of God's intentions. Thus, mention is made of "prophetic utterances which pointed to you, that inspired by them you may wage the good warfare, holding faith and a good conscience" (I Tim. 1:18-19).[60]

The directedness of Scripture is also mentioned by Bavinck, who sees great truth in Baronius' statement that Scripture does not tell us what things are like in heaven but rather how we get there. He sees no delimitation of scriptural authority in reflec-

59. Cf. Ridderbos, *Aan De Romeinen,* p. 103 concerning Paul's conception of Scripture: "The meaning and the power of Scripture does not only consist of the description of God's saving work in history but also in the application and the realization of that work in the present."

60. Cf. the directedness of the story of Abraham and his two sons and its final application, which is identical to a "speaking" of Scripture in a new situation (Gal. 4:21-31, esp. 30). Also the directedness, the "indication" of the Spirit in the prediction of the suffering of Christ (I Pet. 1:11).

tion on its goal, but does see it as compelling our attention to what he termed the theological purpose of Scripture — "that we might know God unto salvation."[61] In this connection he calls the Word of God "religious," a word *unto* salvation,[62] and no scientific book in the narrow sense of the word. According to Bavinck, Scripture never concerns itself purposely with science as such and "does not concern itself with the scientifically precise language of astronomy, physiology, and psychology, etc."[63]

The historiography of Scripture "follows its own direction and aims for its own goal,"[64] while the prophets of the Old Testament delineate the future in such a way that we — asking after the intention — repeatedly must confront the question "whether that which they wrote is intended realistically or symbolically."[65] All of this does not just mean that Holy Scripture is totally focused on man, seeking to reach him. It is also related to a correct understanding of Scripture and its actual authority. That is what Bavinck had in mind when he wrote that the truth of Scripture is "absolutely not in all its components part of the same nature."[66] This does not imply a relativizing of Scripture's authority, but rather seeks to understand that authority completely as functional and real. All of this will later occupy us in greater detail. I now want to point out that the incisive questions are connected with the correct understanding of the authority of Scripture. It is understandable that concerning the question of the purpose of Scripture, the question whether the attention to such a goal opens the way to subjectivism and arbitrariness is also raised. Repulsing this danger, one can be drawn again to a leveling vision — one which allows place for neither the question of goal nor Bavinck's question about the nature of scriptural authority. A leveling view places the "words" of Scripture alongside each other without any differentiation, and the one purpose of Scripture seems to be that we should subject ourselves to its authority.

61. *GD,* I, 416, 417. The "religious" concept is for Bavinck something quite different from Bonhoeffer's idea expressed in the plea for "a nonreligious interpretation" of biblical concepts. Cf. Ebeling, "The nonreligious interpretation of biblical concepts" (*Word and Faith,* pp. 98ff.).
62. *GD,* I, p. 447. See Bavinck's exposition here of the "perspicuity" of Scripture as related to what is necessary "unto salvation" and the "reader desirous of salvation."
63. *Ibid.,* p. 417.
64. *Ibid.,* p. 419.
65. *Ibid.,* p. 420.
66. *Ibid.,* p. 419.

The church, however, has never quite come to clarity about this. Diverse experiences taught it that such leveling did indeed seek to honor scriptural authority, but at the same time seemed to undercut that authority. One cannot and may not withdraw from the question of intent or goal, but he must always be aware of the present and threatening danger of mere arbitrariness. This danger arises when the intent of Scripture is interpreted in such a way that it is difficult to discover whether it is truly Scripture's own and not our purpose. It would be deceptive to think that hermeneutics automatically shields us from such dangers. Discussing authority together with interpretation cannot signify that Scripture derives its authority in some way from our interpretation. It means that this authority is only honored in a correct interpretation according to God's purpose, when hearing and understanding lead to heeding and doing.

Nowhere was the relationship between authority and interpretation so clearly expressed as in the Reformation confession of Scripture, which, based on *sola Scriptura,* offered a perspective on the real relationship between authority and interpretation, and expressed it in its hermeneutical rule: *Sacra Scriptura sui ipsius interpres* (Sacred Scripture is its own interpreter).

On hearing this rule, one can react that it is polemically understandable but really not a concrete and fruitful notion for the present interpretation of Scripture. The formula is indeed a polemical focusing of the *sola Scriptura* on interpretation. This already excludes the possibility of speaking of a purely formal rule without diverse perspectives. It contains a concrete rejection of other interpretations which are foreign to the nature of Scripture. By so doing it naturally reminds us of the scriptural message that no prophecy of Scripture is a matter of one's own interpretation (II Pet. 1:20).

The personification of Scripture as interpreter (Gal. 3:8, 22; Rom. 9:17) intends more than a half-serious attempt which was not to be taken as a piece of actual and living interpretation. Rather, it includes the awareness that here no dead letter is at stake, but Scripture in its witness by the hand of the Spirit. Thus conceived, the phrase "is its own interpreter" draws a clear boundary which has been very important for the Reformation. Luther discussed it in the same context when he wrote, "The interpretation of Holy Scripture is not a matter of one's own spirit."[67] Calvin spoke of the Holy Spirit as "a unique self-

67. Cf. Ritschl, *Dogmengeschichte des Protestantismus,* I, 83ff.; Ebeling, *Word and Faith,* p. 306, where he quotes Luther: "Scripture is of itself

interpreter," since he spoke by the prophets.[68] It would be incorrect to see any real difference between them. The statement "Sacred Scripture is its own interpreter" does not for Luther exclude the fact that the Spirit causes us to understand the mysteries of God that we as yet do not grasp, if we, without his light, force our way into Scripture. At the same time, the reference to the Spirit as "a unique interpreter" is not a detour around Scripture. The Reformation rule was not intended to be something which as a matter of course holds for all of Scripture to a certain degree, but as a reference to the sovereign Word and to the Spirit ("is its own interpreter" is mostly seen as concerning the intention of the author whom one seeks to know in every text). For the testimony of God has an origin and a mystery and thus demands that it be validated and understood on its own authority.[69]

In this conjunction of Scripture and Spirit,[70] Scripture itself has a very real place. This reference does not seek to eliminate human interpretation, as is decisively shown by the Reformation's attention to Scripture. Luther, for one, often pointed to the significance of language study for a better understanding of Scripture.[71] It can even be said that it was precisely that concept ("interprets itself") which led to concern for the meaning of Scripture itself and its interpretation by human activity — some-

most certain, most easy, most open, its own interpreter, proving all things of all, judging and illuminating (Ps. 119:130)."

68. Calvin's comm. on II Pet. 1:20 (also in a polemical context): "But he is saying that whatever men bring to it of their own is profane." Prophecy is read "with advantage" when "we put aside our carnal understanding and subject ourselves to the teaching of the Holy Spirit," as contrasted to the "profanation of Scripture," which occurs when we "presumptuously" force our way into it.
69. That emphasis explains many confessional formulations, e.g., The Scots Confession of Faith (1560) (Schaff, *op. cit.*, p. 463), which simultaneously speaks about Scripture and the Spirit; The Westminster Confession, pp. 605-606, which speaks of "the Scripture itself" and "the Supreme Judge," i.e., the Spirit. Concerning Scripture as interpreter and the Spirit, see M. Chemnitz, *Examination of the Decrees of the Council of Trent* (ET, 1933-63 [microfilm, Concordia Theological Seminary]), p. 176, Section VIII. Many of the formulations echo II Pet. 1:20.
70. Luther has written in the same context about the correct hearing of the proclamation of the Word of God on the basis of Ps. 40:7 (opened ears) and Heb. 10:5 in his commentary. Luther already transcended the antithesis between pneumatic exegesis and textual analysis since reference to the Spirit does not exclude Scripture.
71. See Holl, *Luther*, p. 569 for Luther's statement about Hebrew and Greek. Cf. Ebeling, *Luther*, pp. 29ff.

thing in which Scripture itself as interpreter plays a decisive role.[72] This is evident from the Reformation's resistance to allegorical exegesis, in which Scripture was explained in such a way that its own "sense" was lost in a multiplicity of meanings.[73] Opposing a powerful tradition marked by attempts to search out different "senses" of Holy Scripture and attempts to seek more what the "literal sense" had to offer, the Reformation returned to the text itself, to its own words and significance, and to the literal sense as the "true sense." Motivating this resistance to allegorical exegesis was a protest against the arbitrariness of intriguing and spellbinding parallels and analogies, which frequently had obscured both the meaning of Scripture and the vision of the history of the acts of God. This resistance also contained a protest against the attack on the "is its own interpreter." This was not only the case with Luther's struggle to escape from allegorical exegesis. Calvin also saw in allegorical exegesis a rape of the real sense of Holy Scripture — a search for mysteries deeper than those which confront us in the text itself. He writes about a *commentum Satanae* which seeks to remove the authority of Scripture, and he denies that the fruitfulness of Scripture is rooted in a "variety of senses."[74] This is not a level literalism devoid of all reliefs, designed to rob Scripture of its depth and riches. The questions regarding the deep meaning of Scripture continually engaged the Reformers.[75]

Rejection of allegorical exegesis wishes to refer to the necessity of always returning to the words of Scripture in their perspicuity and sufficiency. And these properties of Scripture, especially the perspicuity, naturally raise other questions. But the plea for "interpreting itself" implies a deep respect for the

72. Luther defended himself against the reproach of highhanded exposition in connection with the *allein* of his exposition of Rom. 3:28.
73. Cf. Berkouwer, *The Person of Christ*, p. 121.
74. "It seems to me far too frivolous to search for allegories" (*Comm.*, Dan. 8:25); cf. *Comm.*, Gal. 4:22 (against Origen). Here he talks about the "natural and simple meaning of Scripture"; cf. *Comm.*, II Cor. 3:6: concerning allegorical exegesis as a "most disastrous error" and the "source of many evils."
75. Regarding "this is an allegory" of Gal. 4:24, see Calvin on *"hatina estin allēgoroumena"* as an "occasion" for Origen. He contests allegorical exegesis and wants to maintain the "true sense," yet does not disavow the relationships and perspectives offered by it (the figure of Abraham and his two sons prefigures the "image of the Church"). "An *anagoge* of this kind is not foreign to the genuine and literal meaning," and I acknowledge "that Scripture is the most rich and inexhaustible fount of all wisdom."

text, for the Word *written*. This rule cannot function as a magical tool to effect a solution to all questions of interpretation. But it does contain a warning that serves as a guide giving directions at the very beginning of the road.

The question *how* we can do justice to the "is its own interpreter" comes up next. One can refer to our calling to attentive listening to the words of Scripture, to the quietness of receptive attention (in all activity), in which the voice of God is not lost in the clamor of voices around and within us. But such a correct typification of our initial and further work with Scripture does not deny that all this must receive concrete form and content in the actual interpretation of Holy Scripture. The history of the church shows that such attention is not at all a self-apparent and unthreatened attitude.

We now confront the noteworthy fact that, during the rise of historical criticism, concentrated attention to the text of Scripture was considered vital and necessary. Criticism protested against every form of Scripture exposition which went to work with *a priori* and external standards. It wanted to proceed from Scripture as it actually existed; it sought to understand Scripture in the way in which it came to us in order thus to honor the "interprets itself." This is what it claimed in its historical exposition of Scripture: something supposedly free of all the *a prioris* of dogmatic systems or ecclesiastical symbolics. In that way justice could be done to Scripture itself.

The possibility of abstracting the phrase "interprets itself" from the Reformation confession and incorporating it into a method stressing precision regarding the "literal sense" as well as the background and the motives behind "that which is written," does not in any way mean that the concept "is its own interpreter" should lose its significance for the Reformation understanding of Scripture. We can instead say that Luther's rule indeed shared in opening the way for and served as a strong stimulus to the scientific study of Holy Scripture. The phrase "interprets itself" and the reference to the Spirit as a "unique interpreter" may, for the Reformation at least, have contained a religious depth and significance regarding the view of the message of Scripture. This does not exclude, but rather includes, concentrated attention on "Scripture itself," along with the accompanying questions of interpretation.

One of the questions which demanded more and more attention in the churches of the Reformation was that of the so-called literary genre. This was not an attempt to find a mysterious, critically selective rule of thumb by which Scripture could be measured, but rather an attempt to do justice to the specifics of Scripture's testimony in all its varying parts. In one sense it was a problem that already occupied Bavinck. He wrote that the God-breathed character *(theopneustia)* of Scripture "caused every genre of literature to serve its purpose" and that "in all these portions of Scripture, truth continually assumes another character."[76] In exegetical activity the problem of the different genres is seen in dealing with the apocalyptic genre. Here was the ever-present awareness that different "rules" of interpretation were called for than the ones used in the understanding of the historical sections. This is a distinction that has played an important part in the exegesis of the Revelation to John, since there were many eschatological expectations based on a literal interpretation of the apocalyptic predictions.

All of this shows that such a serious attempt to do justice to literary types was motivated by the desire to deal correctly with the *sui ipsius interpres.* Furthermore, this was done in opposition to a leveling and reliefless exegesis. Naturally, strife and controversy arose when tension with earlier confessions of the church became visible, especially when presuppositions used in the formulation of these confessions clearly showed the background of a certain interpretation of Scripture. That is where one sees that Scripture is not interpreted in a vacuum outside the life of the church, in contrast to the view that the scientific study of Scripture in our time has completely failed to affect the life of the church. Such a separation of Scripture from science would misrepresent the relationship which both have to the true meaning of Scripture. Tensions may arise over the question whether and to what extent the church's confession is concretely touched by this new research. The church is therefore never free of its own responsibility and can never blindly subject itself to the "dictates of science." This holds true even when the dictates are those of theology taking the form of scientific biblical studies. But new questions which force renewed reflection can arise.

Since any decision on new matters can only be accepted as clear and legitimate on the basis of scriptural witness, there is always a real possibility that in Reformation churches new developments may arise because of the concept "is its own interpreter." One can only describe this as freedom of exegesis — an inseparable concomitant of this Reformation confession. It is a

76. *GD,* I, 419; cf. Kuyper about "the peculiar character of the several distinguishable segments of Scripture."

freedom that has nothing to do with a neutral "presuppositionlessness," which is only theoretically interested in the results of biblical research, whatever they may be. Anyone who in this way, outside of the implications of ecclesiastical confession, seeks to exult in such freedom would forget one thing. In its confession the church did not seek to exhibit all the intellectual knowledge of Scripture that it had attained, with the inherent note that it was prepared to correct incorrect exegesis. Rather, the church sought to confess its faith.

This is radically different from a knowledge that must always be seen as in principle open to correction by new insight and acquisition. The living confession of the church — the commonly accepted and undoubted Christian faith — very clearly carries in itself the hallmark of irrevocability. It is found on a different plane than a formalism that might, theoretically at least, be ready to accept the total destruction of the faith as plausible. According to the original and self-evident intention of this confession, this irrevocability manifests itself in the choice and submission of faith, which opposes every approach to this "confessing" from outside faith.

Yet this irrevocability did not lead the church to desert Scripture once it had confessed its faith on the basis of the gospel. In all its speaking and confessing, the church did not wish to withdraw from being tested by the gospel. And thus it was that the church — in a Reformation manner — spoke of its readiness to bow again and again to the scepter of the gospel. Freedom of exegesis is intrinsically involved in this and honors the dictum "is its own interpreter," an activity which posits limits and thus opens the view to unlimited perspectives. The confession of the church fully honors this freedom, since it consciously placed the authority of Scripture above "customs, or the great multitude, or antiquity, or succession of times and persons, or councils, decrees or statutes."[77] This confession does not arise from a revolutionary sentiment. Rather, the reference to the normative mystery of the gospel and the polemical character of the quoted article of faith (against Rome) does not preclude its lasting and universal validity.

When we view the matter in this way, we can understand Kuyper's expression that freedom of exegesis is a *duty* "to the confessional life of the Church."[78] He wants to maintain that freedom, since "this provides the constant stimulus to turn back

77. *BC,* Art. VII; cf. Schaff, *Creeds,* III, 388.
78. *Princ.,* p. 596.

from the confession to the Word of God, and so prevents the Church from living on the water in the pitcher, and allowing itself to be cut off from the Fountain whence that water was drawn."[79] Finding this critical view within the Reformation confessions does not testify to an internal antinomy. It rather points to a continual awareness and a repeated acceptance of the responsibility critically to reflect on the basis of the confession "is its own interpreter." Such freedom of exegesis, bound up as it is with a warning against arbitrariness, sheds a unique light on all discussions about the interpretation of Scripture. Equipped with growing insights, the church could not and would not withdraw from new questions.

It has been repeatedly pointed out that behind many of the questions presently related to the interpretation of Holy Scripture looms the important presence of science.[80] It is often asked whether the questions we face are truly related to the *sui ipsius interpres* or whether they have arisen from the scientific process of disclosure. Is it not noteworthy that many of the newer questions are inseparably connected with the "increased light," which everyone, including those in orthodox circles, talks about? Does this not, as far as the interpretation of Scripture is concerned, raise the question of the relationship between God's Word as a lamp and such "new light"? The words "lamp" and "light" themselves are so intrinsically related (Ps. 119:105) that the question whether or not one can speak of a "dual light" in scriptural interpretation is a natural one. The way in which this relationship is usually discussed is by maintaining that certain results of science, be it natural science or historical research, can provide the "occasion" for understanding various aspects of Scripture in a different way than before.[81] If this is indeed the case, then what is the relationship between such an "occasion" and the authoritative power of "Sacred Scripture is its own interpreter"? Does it mean that science has become a fellow

79. *Ibid.*, p. 597. Kuyper relates this freedom to the fact that Scripture is given to us in human language and that human activity regarding Scripture receives the highest stimulation.
80. The word "science" is used throughout this book in a much broader sense than is usual in the U.S.A. Berkouwer's concept of a science is equivalent to our notion of an academic discipline. Thus, studies done in the humanities and social sciences as well as the natural sciences are included. Theology is also a science, since it proceeds by orderly, academic research and reflection (tr. note).
81. Cf. N. H. Ridderbos, *Is There a Conflict Between Genesis 1 and Natural Science?* (ET, 1957), pp. 20-21 concerning this different understanding.

interpreter, or is it impossible to state the problem in such a way?

The contemporary situation clearly shows that, despite the awareness of the occasion which can be found in science, some are still persuaded that this in no way injures the *sui ipsius interpres*. It is not true that, as far as the Reformation was concerned, Scripture alone was its own interpreter and that now we see a second interpreter being added. If that were the case, it might be better to recognize that the Reformation scriptural principle now appears insufficient and out of date. Instead, the whole "occasion" problem, in the course of an historical process of disclosure, has led to a deeper realization of that which already became significant in an earlier age — even though in a scattered and fragmentary form — that is, the specific purpose of Scripture and Scripture's nature which concurred with that purpose. This allows one to conclude that those things that through science became an "occasion" for further reflection did not weaken or relativize the study of Holy Scripture, but strengthened and stimulated to a new concentration on the *sui ipsius interpres*. This has gone hand in hand with an increasing revulsion against "harmonism" and "concordism,"[82] phenomena which all too often advance a view of Scripture that demands too much of it. Thus, they set themselves the task of resolving various "conflicts." When, however, the *sui ipsius interpres* receives increasingly concrete attention, it also becomes apparent that science cannot become an "interpreter" alongside Scripture itself. This is one pretension not found in the circles of science itself, except for odd cases of vain scientific idealism which are convinced that the light of Scripture has been permanently extinguished by that of science. Not just to spite science, but rather because of its totally different nature and of the secret of Scripture — the secret of the gospel — we will have to continue on the basis of the "is its own interpreter" and thus continue to honor Scripture as canon.

No one will be able to contend that the relationship between science as "occasion" and the changing interpretation of Scripture is a simple and readily perspicuous one. Neither will it always be possible to determine precisely how science, as but one facet of our multiple way of life, began to function as the

82. Cf. Bavinck's warning against "exegetical bungling," *Kennis en Leven*, (1922), p. 199. Cf. also *GD*, II, 485 concerning St. Augustine's warning not to take something as in conflict with Scripture too quickly, i.e., without serious study or through sheer ignorance. Bavinck sees this as a warning not always heeded by theologians.

occasion for a new reflection.[83] And certainly we cannot accept, without testing, the results of every exegesis which claims to allow the final decision to rest in Scripture itself. To determine whether the relationship is valid, we must ask the question whether or not attention was diverted from Scripture rather than focused on it. Those who see the *lamp* of the Word of God on a continuum with the new and increased *light* of science, lit before all the world, inevitably arrive at a dangerous crossroads. They will either follow a course condescending to Scripture and its message, or they will tend to abandon every new question about interpretation because of the danger involved. Both paths must be avoided. There is a path whereon it can be understood that the development of problems like those now facing the church is not merely fortuitous in the course of history. Such a path would be inconceivable to a mentality whose trust in Scripture is built on its "supernaturalness," its suspension above all time and humanness. This mentality would not really allow any interpretation — exactly what is called for in many of Scripture's admonitions — on the grounds that the immediate voice of God is miraculously direct. But when this testimony comes to us through the prism of humanity traveling the Spirit's paths, it is clear that only in actual communion with Scripture can the power and blessing of this unique Word be understood in the form in which it comes to us.

Those who, because of the complicated questions of interpretation, the dangers of projection and twisting, of subjectivism and objectivism, want to give up trying to understand Scripture in accordance with its divine intent, have been seized by irresolute doubt. This doubt thinks that the risks of Scripture, subjected as it is to the fate of all human writings, are too great and too disturbing to guarantee unweakened knowledge. To overcome doubt of this kind, we must not allow any questions of interpretation, including those arising from newly disclosed knowledge, to hinder new essays into scriptural understanding from the vantage point of the *sui ipsius interpres.* On these voyages we will be aware that no single postulate that circumvents this dictum can in fact block our way. There is no single technique able to provide the key to the secret of Scripture, not even a perfected hermeneutics.

Such a recognition does not signal an escape into a charisma that would be able to lift us beyond every bothersome question

83. In this context, think of the meaningful question of N. H. Ridderbos, "Who knows his heart?" (*Is There a Conflict,* p. 67).

of interpretation. Indeed, such questions at times threaten all certainty. But the history of the church confirms that only by way of continuing attention and concentration can the depth of the gospel of Scripture be increasingly understood. The Word of God has not abruptly overwhelmed us in a way designed to neutralize all human activity; it has come in a way that opens before us a vista of joy and surprise. There is a gladness because of the understanding provided by the enormous labors to which this Scripture has given rise in token of its depth and inexhaustibility. It is good to focus our attention on the fact that church history confirms the significance of hermeneutical questions. It affords examples of the church defending the authority of Holy Scripture against incorrect presuppositions concerning the nature of its authority. The methods of defense later forced the church to change "earlier interpretations." It is not necessary to deny the concern of such appeals to Scripture in order to see the hermeneutical problems which surfaced. It is a question of what can be termed "asking too much" of Scripture.

The well-known Galileo case bothers nobody anymore, but it is still hermeneutically instructive as an illustration of the manner in which the authority of Scripture was called upon. There was, for instance, the so-called *Mosaica physica,* in which, both as a whole and in various points, the reliability of Scripture was at stake, and during which certain interpretations were charged with being an insult to the Holy Spirit, who cannot lie.[84] This happened at a time when Cartesianism was launching many new ideas, including some connecting Scripture with conceptions no longer accepted. New hermeneutical questions and problems were therefore quickly suspected of having affinities with Cartesianism. In this complicated historical situation, real questions regarding scriptural interpretation were raised. Already there we can sense a growing awareness in the church that it was not justifiable to allow itself to be led by a reaction against all kinds of dangers; men began to realize that hermeneutically a lesson lay in the much too strongly stated ecclesiastical claims that had to be reconsidered later.

Even though the discussion concentrated on questions of the biblical view of the world, the problem took shape by means of the undeniable sharpness with which the discussion of the au-

84. Information can be found in Bizer, "Die reformatorische Orthodoxie und der Cartesianismus," *Z.Th.K.,* pp. 360ff.; *idem, Früh-orthodoxie und Rationalismus* (1963), esp. pp. 32ff.; J. Baur, *Die Vernunft zwischen Ontologie und Evangelium* (1962).

thority of Scripture was waged. When Christoph Wittich began to talk emphatically about the "goal" *(scopus)* of Scripture, he had to give an account of himself before the 1660 Synod of Gelderland. The Synod affirmed his orthodoxy. But the questions later recurred more intensely. One finds them, for instance, in Bavinck, when he so emphatically points to the goal and purpose of Scripture. These questions become more complicated as they become deeply involved with history; but such complications do not set aside the real problems. One can indeed say that those who, because of hesitancy and wariness, abandon new hermeneutical questions contribute to the relativizing of scriptural authority.[85] The possibility of making "is its own interpreter" a formal interpretative rule, and as such an opening for use by rationalistic and haughty criticism, reminds us that twisting Scripture is and remains a palpable danger. But this can never remove the depth of the Reformation insight in which, without making the letter of Scripture irrelevant, "is its own interpreter" has been viewed as united to the Spirit as the Paraclete, in order thus to testify to the critical and liberating power of the Word of God.

To confess Holy Scripture and its authority is to be aware of the command to understand and to interpret it. It always places us at the beginning of a road that we can only travel in "fear and trepidation." This beginning is not a biblicist misinterpretation of the church's dealing with Scripture and its confession, but an awareness of the abiding power and reality of its authority. Even when one consistently rejects all spiritualism, which relativizes the meaning and function of the written words, and when one also puts aside "pneumatic" exegesis, which sets charisma in opposition to patient and precise interpretation, he must remind himself that the Israelite, who knew the commandments, was yet compelled to pray, "Hide not thy commandments from me!" (Ps. 119:19). Such remembrance, joined as it is with our obedience and expectation, also serves to remind us of the confession of the "small beginning" of our obedience.[86] This does not relativize our confession of faith in Scripture; it establishes it. Such a confession will only be deeper when the forces that threaten the attentiveness of the heart are recognized. And the truthfulness of this confession is revealed

85. In the history of the church it is evident that unrest can never be removed by ecclesiastical inattention to real questions.
86. *HC,* Q and A. 114; also the relationship between hearing (Rom. 10:16; Gal. 3:2) and obedience (I Pet. 1:22).

in the ever-present readiness to accept a new commission regarding the more powerful comprehension of the breadth and length and height and depth of Christ's love (Eph. 3:18). Only the acceptance of this commission shows that Scripture is truly honored.

In our time of many unsolved questions, speaking about Holy Scripture threatens to be transposed into a whisper expressing the fear that we find ourselves in an unavoidable transition from living with a reliable — in many ways — to an unreliable Scripture. It is extremely important to be aware that in this way an unavoidable crisis in the confession of Holy Scripture is created. For then one says simply that he would rather not connect Scripture and the Comforter — either in church or in witness. The discussion about Scripture, its God-breathed character and authority, cannot take place via a coerced concession to a new hermeneutical method and the "occasion" of science. It can only take place in the perspective of that trustworthiness of Scripture which enables us to abandon ourselves in complete trust to its authority and to preach its message. Only in this way can the church continue to remind itself of the seriousness and the clarity with which the prophetic witness speaks about both nonlistening and the staying of the dawn (Isa. 8:20), and promises the rising of the morning star within our hearts (II Pet. 1:19). In every dealing we have with Scripture and in all our reflection on its God-breathed character, we are tested — by all the questions and problems — concerning whether we have lapsed into the paradox of a relativized authority, or if we can with increasing certainty agree with Luther's statement, so basic to the interpretation of Holy Scripture: *Spiritus Sanctus non est scepticus.*[87]

87. *De servo arbitrio* (1525); O. Clemen, *Luthers Werke* (1913), III, 100. The complete citation runs as follows: "The Holy Spirit is *no* skeptic; nor has he written dubious opinions in our hearts but assertions concerning life itself and experience more certain and firmly established in all."

CHAPTER FIVE

THE GOD-BREATHED CHARACTER OF HOLY SCRIPTURE

MANY QUESTIONS CONCERNING HOLY SCRIPTURE have been discussed through the centuries. All are inseparably linked to the confession that Scripture is "God-breathed."[1] In the church this term is better known as "inspired." The word "God-breathed" *(theopneustos)* comes directly from the Pauline words: *pasa graphē theopneustos,* usually translated "all scripture is inspired" (II Tim. 3:16). One need not be inclined to limit dogmatic reflection only to scriptural terms. Yet one may not simply presuppose that *theopneustos* and "inspiration" are completely identical and can serve equally to denote the mystery of Holy Scripture. It is noteworthy first of all that *theopneustos* entails a positive description and relates Scripture directly to God.[2] In the second place, it ought to be remembered that a number of ideas are associated with the concept of inspiration that color it in a certain way, for example, being inspired aesthetically, which is not included in the notion "God-breathed." In this respect inspiration does not quite agree with *theopneustos.* The term "God-breathed" does more justice to the unique work of the Holy Spirit in Scripture than does the word "inspiration." II Timothy 3:16 speaks literally of Scripture's having been given by breathing, not by inspiring. Those who wish to continue to use the word "inspiration" ought to keep this in mind. Warfield points to this fact: "The preposition 'in' is wholly lacking in the term and is not demanded for the sense in any of its implications."[3] Since *theopneustos* means God-breathed, one must say: "The traditional translation of the word by the Latin

1. Greek: *theopneustos.*
2. The word "inspiration" is admittedly also used in the sense of the Vulgate: *Omnis scriptura divinitus inspirata.*
3. B. B. Warfield, *The Inspiration and Authority of the Bible* (1948), p. 284.

inspiratus a Deo is no doubt also discredited, if we are to take it at the foot of the letter."[4] In discussing these terms we are not simply playing a subtle and useless word game. It is of great importance to know what the *theopneustos* of Scripture really means. One who hesitates to substitute the word "inspiration" for *theopneustos* can, however, acknowledge that *divinitus* indeed agrees with Paul's word and points to a unique origin and to a unique relation of Holy Scripture to God.

The statement that the human word of the *graphē* (writing, or scripture) is God-breathed undoubtedly points to the mystery of its being filled with truth and trustworthiness. The meaning of this God-breathed writing is evident; it is aimed at a concrete and great goal: for teaching, for reproof, for correction, and all this is summarized into one goal, "that the man of God may be complete, equipped for every good work" (II Tim. 3:16-17). In Paul's statement, the dimension of "in the name of God" is visible, just as the "by God" is of decisive significance in other expressions, such as *theodidaktos*: "You yourselves have been taught by God to love one another" (I Thess. 4:9). John speaks of those who have heard and learned from the Father, with reference to the prophecy: "And they shall all be taught by God" (Jn. 6:45).[5] Thus, *theopneustos* points to an essential relationship between the breath of the Spirit and the *graphē*. This is the mystery of Scripture which the church desired to express in its confession. This mystery is the uniqueness through which Holy Scripture in all its humanity was distinguished from all other human writing. Men clearly realized that II Timothy 3:16 did not offer us a theory of the "mode" of the God-breathed character of Scripture.[6] The varied theories concerning the mode of inspiration had many unhealthy consequences. Nevertheless, one hears in this passage that the written Scripture cannot be understood in a correct way without the breath of the Spirit.

At once we are confronted with the various differences of opinion concerning this statement by Paul. A discussion has arisen concerning the meaning of the word *theopneustos*. Should one understand it passively (God-breathed) or actively (God-breathing)? In my opinion, a growing consensus coming from

4. *Ibid.*, p. 296.
5. Cf. Jer. 31:34; Isa. 54:13; II Pet. 1:21.
6. Cf. *TDNT*, VI, 454f.; Bavinck, *GD*, I, 407: "no explanation of Scripture and thus really also no theory."

this discussion has led toward a passive meaning.[7] However, there is yet another difference expressed in the translations. We read in the Revised Standard Version: "All scripture is inspired by God," while The New English Bible has it: "Every inspired scripture has its use for teaching." The first translation offers a kind of definition: it is stated of the *graphē* that it is *theopneustos*. In The New English Bible translation Paul's statement is less definitive; it is said of each inspired scripture that it is useful. The God-breathed nature is presupposed rather than emphasized; it is not used in an expressly descriptive and predicative sense.

The difference in translation has left a question whether this statement of Paul has in each translation the same ability to serve as a prooftext as it has done throughout the history of the church. Generally, the cue was taken from this "definition" character of Paul's word to indicate the God-breathed nature of Scripture. Does the translation "every inspired scripture" have the same power as proof?

One ought not build far-reaching conclusions on the basis of differences in translations. Even if the version "every inspired scripture" is the correct one, it certainly is not vague. This is clear from the context. In his exhortation to Timothy, Paul wrote concretely concerning "the sacred writings" which Timothy knew from childhood (II Tim. 3:15). These sacred writings point in a specific direction and are therefore profitable because they are able to instruct man for salvation through faith in Christ Jesus. Paul writes, therefore, of "all scripture" against a background of this God-breathed Holy Scripture. Thus, every word belonging to Holy Scripture is profitable and purposeful (II Tim. 3:16, 17). The relationship between the concrete writing and its God-breathed nature is beyond doubt in both translations. The New English Bible translation therefore cannot be used in an attempt to escape the force of *theopneustos* as definitive. The mystery of the written Scripture fills the entire passage. The written Scripture is destined for a great purpose and thus daily proves its concrete significance. At any rate, preference for The New English Bible translation does not diminish the confession of the God-breathed character of Scripture. Even though Paul may not have intended specifically to propound the God-breathed character of the written Scripture, it is nevertheless

7. The discussion is most often concentrated on the views of inspiration of H. Cremer in *Realencyclopädie für protestantische Theologie und Kirche*, IX. Cf. Warfield, pp. 245f.; Bavinck, *GD*, I, 395.

presupposed in his reference to the usefulness of Scripture. One may well speak of the "functional character" of the God-breathed writing in both translations of Paul's words.[8] However, the functional character should not be isolated and put in opposition to the mystery of the God-breathed character of Scripture. In this connection the church has spoken in its confession that "Holy Scripture *is* the Word of God." The scriptures of the Old Testament which Paul had in mind are holy and thus "functional" and of utmost importance.

Paul does not give a more accurate description of the word *theopneustos,* but he does underscore the great significance of the *graphē.* The functional character of Scripture is most closely related to salvation and to the future; it is aimed at concrete wisdom and salvation.[9] One cannot bypass or surpass the knowledge of Scripture "from childhood"; it is meaningful and necessary for the fulfillment of one's high calling. The *graphē* of which Paul speaks is directly related to the secret entrusted to us, and we should continue therein (II Tim. 3:14).

That another biblical passage is always discussed alongside II Timothy 3:16 in considering Holy Scripture is certainly not a coincidence. It states that prophecy has not come by the impulse of man, "but men moved by the Holy Spirit spoke from God" (II Pet. 1:21). True, this passage deals with prophecy, with the speaking of prophets *(elalēsan).* Yet, this statement has always been related to the God-breathed character of Scripture. For also in this passage the fact that the Word of God comes to us is referred to the origin of prophecy. The *apo theou* is made the dimension of authority, trustworthiness, and immutability. This origin does not exclude the human character of it (men have spoken); but this "from God" gives a unique quality of trustworthiness to these human words, which is essential for the God-breathed Scripture.[10] Confronting a rising of God's Word out of the human heart is the impulse of the Spirit. The firmness of these human words is the mystery of Spirit.[11]

II Peter 1:21 clearly does not speak of the God-breathed writing in explicit terms, for the attention is focused on men

8. Cf. *TDNT,* VI, 454.
9. It is good to remember the unconcerned way in which the NT writers speak of the Scripture as "profitable" without anxiety about pragmatism and functionalism. Cf. *HC,* Qs. 49, 59.
10. Concerning a "most remarkable comparative," cf. *CD,* I/2, 504; *TDNT,* I, 602.
11. Cf. II Pet. 1:21; Ex. 35:21f.; Acts 2:2; see *TDNT,* VI, 346.

and their being moved by the Spirit. It should not surprise us that also in the light of this passage the church confessed that in Scripture we do not have to do with the unmysterious human opinions and convictions of ancient days but with the inescapability and the authority of *Deus dixit* (God has spoken) in the human words of Scripture. This expresses the deepest dimension of scriptural faith. The biblical reference to this "from God" has occupied the mind of the church in its reflection on Scripture.

The explanation for this concentrated attention is not an interest in one miracle or another. It grew in the church in and through its involvement with this writing. The confession of the church is not one which preceded preaching and this involvement as an empty and formal commitment to Holy Scripture. This attention can be explained only as a coming to know, a living into and growing into this amazing human writing with its unique witness to the living God. It is evident also that the so-called self-witness of Holy Scripture played a role in this involvement. This self-witness of Scripture is not an independent "proof" for the divinity of the truth that seems to precede faith in the message of Holy Scripture.[12] It has always been of import for scriptural faith that Holy Scripture came to us with this self-witness of the "from God." The witness did not play a role in the life of the church and in its reflection concerning the mystery of the Scripture apart from faith, but in a believing involvement with Scripture and its message. Thus, we touch on a deep relationship between *origin* and *authority*.

This relationship plays an important role in many connections in Scripture itself. The dispute between Jesus and the chief priests and elders is a clear example. Here the authority *(exousia)* by which Jesus does all sorts of things is at stake (Mt. 21:23). In this controversy concerning legality Jesus questions his opponents concerning the baptism of John: was his baptism "from heaven or from men" (Mt. 21:25)? Here the question of origin is immediately connected with the question of authority, which is evident from the reaction to this question. If the answer were "from men," they would have to fear the multitude, which held that John was a prophet. If the answer were "from heaven,"

12. Kuyper, *Princ.*, pp. 428-29: "The naive catechetical method of proving the inspiration of the Holy Scripture from II Tim. 3:16 or II Pet. 1:21 cannot be laid to the charge of our Reformed theologians. They did not hesitate to expose the inconclusiveness of such circle-reasoning. They appeal indeed to this and similar utterances, when it concerned the question of what interpretation of inspiration the Holy Scripture itself gives us." Cf. Bavinck, *GD*, I, 424.

they would be asked why they had not believed John. The view of the prophetic depth-perspective in the man John is decisive for the dimension of the words "from above." The words "from heaven" are linked to authority and thus call for faith. The origin constitutes the decisive authority that has a defining and challenging power which is intended to exclude all doubt. The authority is "the possibility granted by a higher norm or court."[13] We discover the same relationship between origin and authority in the controversy between true and false prophecy. Some prophets, soothsayers, and dreamers led the people astray and lacked any authority, because they had not been sent, even though they pretended to speak in the name of Yahweh (Jer. 29:8, 9). They spoke their own word, "for it is a lie which they are prophesying to you in my name." The origin of their words is dark and illegitimate: "they speak visions of their own minds" (Jer. 23:16; Deut. 18:20), and the people should not listen to them (Jer. 29:8).

The question of what criteria to use to distinguish between true and false prophecy understandably caused anguish and fear in Israel, for false prophets also said, "Thus says the Lord." Yet there was no doubt concerning the matter of the origin itself as the foundation of its legitimacy. The question of the criteria of recognition arose in all kinds of situations in the life of Israel. Various phenomena, events, and deeds were seen under the critical light of the origin.[14] This also appears from the admonition in the New Testament that one is to test the spirits "to see whether they are of God" (I Jn. 4:1). Here true and false prophecy are as opposite as the fatherhood of God and that of the devil (Jn. 8:41-44). The legitimacy of being a child of God is embraced in the words "of God" (Acts 26:19; Gal. 1:12). Thus, the question of the origin has played an important role in the reflection concerning Scripture. It formed the background (positively or negatively) of much anxiety about Scripture, especially when criticism attempted to expose its human character and relativity. The attention given to the origin was not merely a matter of theoretical interest; it was a religious question related to stability, certainty, and trustworthiness. At the same time, this question could not be answered outside of

13. *TDNT*, II, 562.
14. G. Quell, *Wahre und falsche Propheten* (1952), pp. 105f.; W. Zimmerli, "Der Wahrheitserweis Jahwes nach der Botschaft der beiden Exilspropheten," *Tradition und Situation. Festschrift für A. Weiser* (1963), pp. 133f.; von Rad, *OT Theology*, II, 209ff.

involvement with Scripture but only by listening to this writing, which led to the church's confession: *Sacra Scriptura est Verbum Dei* (Holy Scripture *is* the Word of God). This answer of the confession is actually a witness pointing to the origin and the mystery, to the contrast between true and false, to the true authority which asks for faith and obedience. This dimension is of decisive importance for all reflection about Holy Scripture.

Specifically, this reflection deals with the fact that in Scripture we encounter real human words. The "is" has to be considered in order to avoid the impression of a mysterious and miraculous identity which could not be investigated further.[15] Referring to Scripture as the Word of God, the church was convinced, in agreement with the text from II Peter, that the gospel is the opposite of cleverly devised myths of men (II Pet. 1:16). But the way of the Word did not exclude the ministry of man. Throughout Scripture we see that man comes to the fore in his ministry and witness. The fact that Scripture and the prophets are *from God* (II Pet. 1:21; Ezek. 2-6) does not rule out the human witness in a divine monergism, but includes this witness in a unique manner. God's Word has not come to us as a stupendous supernatural miracle that shies away from every link with the human in order thus to be truly divine. Rather, when God speaks, human voices ring in our ears. Many attempts have been made to describe this relationship. For instance, this relationship has been expressed as the *taking into service* of men by the Holy Spirit. Repeatedly we are referred to the many examples of the taking into service of a prophet, a human child, and words. Obviously, the connection between God's speaking and the human word is very close and real. One can describe this relationship without exaggeration as *identity*. So it is said that the Spirit speaks by the prophets (II Sam. 23:2; Heb. 1:1) and that God speaks "by the mouth of his holy prophets" (Acts 3:21). What they say to the people they proclaim with an emphatic "thus says the Lord God" (Ezek. 2:4; 3:11), as they speak with God's word (Ezek. 3:4).

The divine dimension of his Word by men is paralleled by the divine raising of a prophet "from your brethren" (Deut.

15. The word "is" played an important role in the 16th century discussion of the sacraments. See Berkouwer, *The Sacraments* (ET, 1969), pp. 259ff. Also see I Thess. 2:13 and Phil. 3:19. The Second Helvetic Confession (Art. I) confesses that the *preaching* of the Word of God *is* the Word of God (Arthur C. Cochrane, ed., *Reformed Confessions of the 16th Century* [1966], p. 225).

18:15). At once his authority is indicated: "You shall listen to him in whatever he tells you" (Acts 3:22). And if Israel no longer wishes to hear the voice of God nor see the great fire, the Word of God comes to them by a prophet from their midst ("like you"): "And I will put my words in his mouth, and he shall speak to them all that I command him" (Deut. 18:16-18). The trustworthiness and the authority as well as the call to faith and obedience is indicated by this employment, this delegation.

Yahweh sends words by his Spirit through the former prophets (Zech. 7:7, 12), and God's own calling is manifested in them. When men refuse to listen and their heart is turned to adamant, his wrath is kindled because he called and they did not give heed (Zech. 7:11-13; Ezek. 3:7-9). Thus, in a variety of ways it is expressed that God's authority becomes present in and through this ministry of men. It really reaches men, so that no one can ignore God's speaking via the humanness of the prophetic words. One might speak here of "identification" not as a mixture of the divine and the human, but in the sense of this "sending," this employing whereby the Word of God indeed comes to us just as it is upon the tongue of the prophets (II Sam. 23:2; Dan. 4:8-9; Gen. 21:38). Thus it addresses men with authority, and those who hear the prophetic human word perceive the voice of God. The prophetic word is truly God's Word, not because human words are transubstantiated into something divine, but because the word of the prophets is truly God's Word addressed to men. We see this as clearly in the authoritative apostolic witness as we saw it in the prophetic word. In that apostolic word salvation is found for those who believe (I Cor. 1:21). Paul brings "the testimony of God" to the Corinthians (I Cor. 2:1). When they believe, faith is not based on the wisdom of men but on the power of God (I Cor. 2:5). Paul called the apostles "ambassadors of Christ," and he adds: "God making his appeal through us" (II Cor. 5:20).[16] It is a real admonition of God "through us." This mediation is expressed in many ways in the New Testament, and every time the authority — the supremacy — is at stake. When the apostles bring the Word of God to the congregation, they do this "in the sight of God," and their word is trustworthy just as God himself is

16. Cf. *TDNT,* VI, 681. We think of the well-known comment by Calvin that Scripture has authority for believers when they "regard them as having sprung from heaven, as if there the living words of God were heard" (*Inst.,* I, vii, 1). Cf. M. A. Chevalier, *Esprit de Dieu, paroles d'hommes* (1966), pp. 65ff.

trustworthy (II Cor. 12:19). Every consideration of the Word of God must be seen against the decisive background of that which is expressed in this terminology of identity. It may be included in the urgent admonition: "whoever speaks," be "as one who utters oracles of God" (I Pet. 4:11; cf. Eph. 3:7; Col. 1:23; Lk. 1:2; Acts 6:4). This identity comes into sharp focus in Christ's word to his disciples: "He who hears you hears me, and he who rejects you rejects me" (Lk. 10:16).[17] The speech of men in prophecy is the way of the reliable testimony of God.

The church has also confessed that Holy Scripture *is* the Word of God against the background of this identity in prophecy and apostolate. The speaking of God through men is not a substitution of God's Word for that of man. It remains man's own speech through the Holy Spirit in the mission to speak words (Jer. 26:5): the authorization of this human speech is found in this mission. Thus, in obedience to the Word itself, the church speaks of Holy Scripture when reference is made to the books of the Bible, the gospel promised by the prophets in Holy Scripture (Rom. 1:2). The word "holy" does not imply a mysterious sacredness of a book, nor does it make human words into something divine.[18] The confession concerning Scripture — with its emphatic "is" — does not imply the worship of a book. At issue is whether and in what way faith is related to the "*gospel* promised *in* Holy Scripture."[19] Scripture is central because of its nature and intent. For this Scripture is only referred to because its sense and intent is the divine message of salvation.[20] The words testify to it and all attention is drawn to it as the testimony "concerning his Son" (Rom. 1:3). Thus, they are "sacred writings" (II Tim. 3:15)[21] having their origin in the command of God (Rom. 16:26). Scripture is not severed

17. Cf. Mt. 10:40 and Jn. 13:20. Barth writes correctly: "We must not weaken this. It does not say: 'also heareth me' or 'also receiveth me'" (*CD,* I/2, 487). See also I Sam. 8:7 and Ezek. 3:7.
18. Cf. *TDNT,* I, 751.
19. Cf. K. Runia, *Karl Barth's Doctrine of Holy Scripture* (1962), pp. 25f.
20. See Kuyper, *Princ.,* pp. 413-414: "This inspiration is no isolated fact, which stands by itself. He who takes it in this sense arrives at some sort of Koran, but not at Holy Scripture. In that case the principle of knowing *(cognoscendi)* is taken entirely apart from the principle of being *(essendi)* and causes the appearance of an exclusively intellectual product which is outside of reality. We then would have an inspiration which dictated intellectually, and could not communicate to us anything but a doctrine and law." Kuyper here is dealing with the relationship of the witness of Scripture to salvation history.
21. *TDNT,* I, 51.

from that which is real and truly human because of this "sacredness," but it comes to us in this human form. Of the humanly written *(Scriptura)* it is confessed: *est Verbum Dei.*

Scripture itself speaks clearly and simply concerning this human character. Moses said: "Honor your father and your mother" (Mk. 7:10; cf. Lk. 20:37) and Isaiah prophesied of Israel's alienation (Mt. 15:7-9; Mk. 7:6). However, the authority does not reside in one's own human word and with one's own initiative. Sometimes an author is referred to vaguely (Heb. 2:6; cf. 4:4) or merely as the Spirit, who speaks in Psalm 95, for example (Heb. 3:7). So Scripture is personified: it can say or do something. This points to a unique authority because of the testimony of God (Gal. 3:8, 22).[22] The Spirit can speak through David (Mt. 22:43) and in the prophets (I Pet. 1:11). He indicates (Heb. 9:8) and bears witness (Heb. 10:15); a quotation from Ezekiel in II Corinthians is introduced with "as God said" (II Cor. 6:16), and there is reference to "God's reply" (Rom. 11:4). The testimony of the Spirit is the end of all contradiction. God's speaking is so emphatically in human words that believing the Scripture is placed alongside believing the word that Jesus had spoken (Jn. 2:22). The rebuke of Christ to the Emmaus travelers is likewise focused on their slowness to believe "all that the prophets have spoken" (Lk. 24:25).

The authority of Scripture is particularly evident in Christ's words, "It is written" (Mt. 4:4), spoken during his temptation in the wilderness. There and elsewhere (Mt. 4:7, 10; Mk. 1:2; Lk. 2:23; Acts 7:42) they functioned prominently as a last appeal and as a redeeming and blessed limitation of all human meditation and speculation (I Cor. 4:6).[23] "It is written" points to the source with decisive authority: the written word which comes to us with authority and with the intent to awaken faith in the heart. There is no trace of a contrast between Scripture and the Spirit. In Jesus' thoughts and actions it functions at the very moment when he is led by the Spirit into the desert (Mt. 4:1). All his teaching is filled with listening and referring to Scripture: it cannot be broken (Jn. 10:35), it must be fulfilled (Mt. 26:54), and indeed was fulfilled (Lk. 4:21; Mk. 14:49; Lk. 22:37). When he asked, "Have you never read?" (Mt. 21:42), his reference is to God's authoritative instruction in Scripture (cf. Lk. 24:27). Failure to know Scripture is considered "wrong"

22. *TDNT*, I, 754.
23. Furthermore, Paul uses it fourteen times, sometimes as an argument (e.g., Gal. 3:12). Cf. *TDNT*, I, 746.

by Christ (Mt. 22:29). All this arises out of a life with Scripture, to which all his followers are called because the written Word comes to them with final saving authority. One must learn "to live according to Scripture" lest he fall in his pride (I Cor. 4:6). Man must live by it, be guided by it, be limited by it, and he must appeal to it.

By its nature, the written Word can never be formally isolated, because precisely that written Scripture testifies of salvation and is directed toward that salvation. And in that context words can become living words (Acts 7:38), full of authority. In "it is written" lies the perspective of God's speaking and the power and blessings of the written Word. It is possible, of course, to lapse into formalism and legalism with regard to the written Word, just as it is with the law, which in itself is holy and good (Rom. 7:12). But that does not deprive the written Word of its deep meaning and authority, its opening of vistas to the promise (cf. Rev. 22:18-19). Thus, one can also fully understand that the self-witness of Scripture has always had its place in the doctrine of Scripture. The doctrine does not limit its scope to a few texts about inspiration; it clearly points to the authoritative function of the written Word throughout, written by men and coming to us with divine authority.

In its listening to the purely human testimony, the church confessed its faith in Scripture against the background of this authoritative function of the written Word. It would have been a mistake to seek a foundation for this faith in a *theory* of inspiration.[24] Even at a time when deliberate reflection on inspiration had scarcely begun,[25] men put themselves under the authority of the written Word in faith. In hearing the human words of Scripture as the Word of God they emphasized especially the "from God" *(apo theou)* of II Peter 1:21 in the face of all doubt and denial; they scarcely felt the need for further reflection. The identification was apparently sufficient for the religious use of Holy Scripture. The God-breathed character of Scripture was clarified by means of various illustrations. For example, the apologist Athenagoras compared the God-breathed aspect to a lyre or a flute, or other musical instruments.[26] Men also used the term "dictation" by the Holy Spirit.[27] It would be a mistake to

24. Bavinck, *GD,* I, 407.
25. *Ibid.,* p. 375.
26. *Ibid.,* p. 374.
27. We encounter "dictation" not only in the decrees of Trent but in Calvin. See *Inst.,* IV, viii, 8, where with reference to "ancient Scrip-

formulate a supernaturalistic and mechanical theory of inspiration merely in view of such illustrations. By illustrations such as these the authors wish only to indicate the compulsion of the Spirit and therewith the dimension of the origin of the written Word. They wished to remain in agreement with all those indications in Scripture which deal with a prophetic and apostolic testimony "not by the impulse of men, but men moved by the Holy Spirit . . ." (II Pet. 1:21). They also sought harmony with Paul's words of praise for the Thessalonians, who received the proclaimed Word of God (the human word: "heard from us") "not as the word of men but as what it really is, the word of God . . ." (I Thess. 2:13).

For a long time there was livelier interest in the God-breathed character of God's Word, in the "is" of the confession (the reliable Word), than there was concentrated attention to that peculiar but very real functionality of the human side. Thus, the impression was given that the *mode* of the God-breathed character would be hardly relevant because the real nature of Holy Scripture was apparently found in "God's reply" (Rom. 11:4) and not in human utterance, in the Word of God and not in the word of man. Was it not enough to focus on God's Word without specific attention to the human instrument? Does not the function of that someone, who "somewhere" speaks, dwindle to nothing beside what is said as God's reliable testimony?

Later in the development of the doctrine of Holy Scripture, men began to distinguish between primary and secondary authors.[28] Of course, this easily led to a view of inspiration in which the function of man was relegated to a "secondary" position. Thus Bavinck, fully admitting the religious motif in the ancient church, referred to all sorts of expressions as betraying a "mechanical conception,"[29] adding that only in more recent times does one become fully conscious of the meaning of the so-called organic aspect.

In this historical judgment we touch on an incisive and still relevant aspect of the doctrine of Scripture. The question must be asked: has this development, in which a shift of emphasis has

ture," Calvin says: "With Christ's Spirit as precursor in a certain measure dictating the words." Cf. *Inst.,* IV, viii, 6: "composed under the Holy Spirit's dictation." For further examples see Krusche, *Das Wirken des Heiligen Geistes nach Calvin,* pp. 163-168.

28. *GD,* I, 402.
29. *Ibid.*

become evident, been meaningful and valuable, or has it indicated a defamation and humanization of Scripture — relativizing if not denying the significance of the biblical "from God." This question cannot be dismissed lightly; reflection is necessary on how far this alarming shift has gone in more recent times. Does man still trust the Word of God and use Scripture as in ancient times, when the images of the lyre, flute, and dictation illustrated the undoubted utterance of God. It can also be asked whether in more recent times the "is" of the Reformation's scriptural confession is still a true confession of faith and can continue to be amid so many questions concerning Scripture that increasingly occupy the church. Indeed, this question is of decisive significance for the continuance of the church and for the totality of the Christian life, which can only be truly Christian if it rests in the Word of God.[30] All these questions are inseparably related to the "God has spoken" as a testimony of one who never lies (Titus 1:2; cf. Num. 23:19; I Sam. 15:29; Heb. 6:18) — to which only the amen of faith can correspond.

It is not easy to give a complete analysis of the transition to the recent development of which Bavinck speaks. Many factors have influenced it. It can be stated in general that the growing attention to the "horizontality" of the genuinely human, to man's initiative and activity, can be explained in part by a growing aversion to so-called supernaturalism, which naively implied incidental and fragmentary "supernatural" acts of God in "nature," taking its cue from a supposed opposition of the supernatural to the natural. This supernaturalism prevailed in many discussions about the providence of God, specifically about miracles. The mystery of Scripture, of the "God has spoken," was also seen in the light of supernaturalism. It presupposed and stressed the supernatural origin of Scripture, and thus little attention was given to the actual historical origin of Scripture, or to the fact that men had written it.

Some time ago a sharp reaction against this supernaturalism set in. Kuyper emphasized the "mediate" activity of God, which is no less majestic than his immediate activity. In his effort to conquer dualism with a more "organic" view, he warned against the *deus ex machina* notion, against magic, and the miraculous.[31]

30. Cf. Calvin's commentary on II Cor. 5:7: "We do indeed see, but in a glass darkly, which means that we rest on the Word in place of the reality."
31. Kuyper rejects, e.g., "every interpretation of the miracle as a magical incident" (*Princ.*, p. 414). For a detailed treatment, see Berkouwer, *The Providence of God* (ET, 1952).

Bavinck criticized the "abstract-supernatural" for preventing man from truly becoming an "organ" of the divine.[32] Thus a transition, a shift in Bavinck's viewpoint, can be observed. This, of course, opens the possibility of a fall into horizontalism in such a way that in reality hardly any room is left for the "from God" of the Word.

There is every reason not to regard the use of "mechanical" and "organic" as a technically skillful solution which was apparently inevitable and by which all problems could be solved. We see rather that an "organic" conception of inspiration can also quickly lead to a competing field of problems. Now the human aspect is not threatened by the divine (from God: "God has spoken"), but the reverse is true: the perspective of the "is" which the church had in view can fade before an emphasis on the full and truly human aspect of Scripture. In the complicated defense of anti-supernaturalism, no one is likely to find a safe guarantee for a true Scripture faith in an "organic" view per se. And even one who does not see any future whatsoever in a repristination of supernaturalism is forced to acknowledge the legitimacy of the question of what influence anti-supernaturalism has had, and how it functions in the use of the Scripture — specifically in recent times. We note, however, in the midst of these questions, that generally the dangers of this derogation are clearly seen, while at the same time the legitimacy of the attention for the genuinely human in Scripture can continue to be upheld and respected without an implied threat to the Word of God.

It became more and more clear that it was no longer sufficient to recall the radical opposition between the truthfulness of God and the falseness of men, specifically with regard to the God-breathed character of Scripture (Rom. 3:4). Even when one ponders the words "not taught by human wisdom but taught by the Spirit" (I Cor. 2:13), it is indisputable that these are *Paul's* words (I Cor. 2:13a). One cannot place the speech of God in opposition to all human speech. Besides, the confession concerning God's Word is related to the "is" of the Scripture. This acknowledgment need not coincide in any respect with a humanization and derogation of the mystery of Holy Scripture. One should say rather that relativizing or neglecting the human aspect of Scripture is in conflict with the confession of the church. For it does not name the Word of God a miraculous phenomenon, but points to it in the prophetic-apostolic testi-

32. *GD,* I, 414.

mony of Holy Scripture. Only with this acknowledgment will it be possible finally to overcome this dilemma of a competition between divine and human.

In the course of historical research — which the very nature of Scripture as human word demanded — and with the discovery of interconnecting themes in Scripture, it was noted with increasing clarity that the term *theopneustos* (God-breathed) was something quite different from ecstatic inspiration. Bavinck, pointing out the change of view particularly in more recent times, mentions specifically the historical and psychological mediation of revelation in the transition from *mechanical* to *organic* inspiration.[33] The word "mediation" is especially arresting. The origin of Scripture (the "from God") is not in the least marred by the concept of mediation; on the other hand, this concept is included in inspiration. We have therefore good reason to consider *organic* inspiration, as it is usually called today.

For a considerable time the contrast between mechanical and organic has been received with a certain self-evidence. Strikingly, no one deliberately takes the side of a mechanical idea of inspiration in the discussion about organic inspiration. It is generally agreed that in God-breathed Scripture we are not involved with passive or unconscious holy writers. One generally calls attention to various kinds of activity of the authors as "organs" of God-breathed Scripture. Taken by itself, the word "organ" does not offer clear insight. We meet this term already in the ancient church, where Moses is called an "organ" of God's Word and the prophets "organs of the divine voice." Augustine discusses the Holy Spirit, who testifies "as if by means of an organ."[34] The word "organ" always indicates a definite relationship in which an event occurs; it was therefore often used to indicate the human functionality in the God-breathed Scripture. So we meet this relationship in the distinction between God as principal author of Scripture and the Bible writers as "instrumental authors."[35] It was thought that in this manner the double aspect of Scripture could be clarified, and the word "organ" or "instrument" could serve to indicate the relationship. However, these terms can be used in many varied ways. In Isaiah 10:15, Asshur is described as an "instrument" in God's hand— against

33. *Ibid.*, pp. 402, 409.
34. For these and older images, see Feiner-Löhrer, *Mysterium Salutis* (1965), p. 342; P. Grelot, *The Bible, Word of God* (ET, 1968).
35. Rahner, *Inspiration in the Bible*, pp. 9f.

Jerusalem. Indeed, we also hear of the arrogance of Asshur's motivations and activities (Isa. 10:10-15), but he is described from the viewpoint of God's supreme acts, which cut across every motivation of Asshur. Mechanical instruments illustrate the point: "Shall the axe vaunt itself over him who hews with it, or the saw magnify itself against him who wields it?" (Isa. 10:15). Similarly, there was the supremacy of Yahweh's acting through Cyrus, who is called a "servant" of the Lord and whose right hand is grasped by Yahweh (Isa. 45:1-6). God's actions can manifest themselves in an instrumental way by cutting across all kinds of human motives. The terminology "organic" or "instrumental" per se do not take us any further than the idea that a person is taken into God's service in one way or another.

It is clear from the above that the use of the term "organic" by itself, that is, by means of an organ or an instrument, throws little light on the discussion. The idea of organ even receives a place in what is usually called "mechanical" inspiration. The idea of human "mediation," of man's own activity and cooperation, is intuitively linked today with the word "organic" in contrast to a monergistic inspiration. Every aspect of the organic was certainly not meant to apply by analogy to inspiration, as the term functions in biology, for instance. True, the word is often used in a wider connection, as when Bavinck deals with an "organic" world view or with an "organic" interdependence of the human race, and when Kuyper places the "inspired organism" of Scripture over against any atomism. However, the real intention in the doctrine of Scripture is the interest in the peculiar and conscious functionality of man in the revelation of God.

For that reason, it is misleading to disqualify the term "organic inspiration" by linking it to all sorts of nineteenth-century views concerning organisms.[36] As far as the doctrine of the God-breathed character of Scripture is concerned, this word is used so concretely and characteristically that it cannot be discredited as mere terminology. Though it is not at all new, it serves today to avoid a magical and supernaturalistic view of Scripture and calls attention to the manner in which the biblical authors were taken into service. It is noteworthy that the problem is often expressed in terms of a union of the divine and the human

36. Cf. W. Maurer, "Das Prinzip des Organischen in der evangelischen Kirchengeschichtsschreibung des 19. Jahrhunderts," *Kerygma und Dogma* (1962), pp. 265f.

factors. All sorts of images are used to illustrate this union.[37] Though most of these illustrations are insufficient and sometimes even confusing and threatening to the "is" of the confession, in every instance the aim appears to be to respect the fact that Scripture comes to us in words as they are spoken by men. There is concern for the *human* reality. We encounter here a thought that is certainly not limited to Reformed theology. We also see, notably in Roman Catholic biblical scholarship, a parallel word usage to indicate the transition from the mechanical to the organic doctrine of inspiration.[38]

The ready acceptance of the term "organic inspiration" and the frequent discussion of it not only in the scholarly realm of theology but also in the church can be explained by the fact that men were impressed with the clear indication in Scripture itself that the peculiarities and activities of the biblical authors were not ignored in the God-breathed character of Scripture. In many ways mechanical inspiration is being rejected by reference to the difference in language and style of the evangelists, and to the initiative and deliberation of the evangelist Luke, as indicated in his prologue. Organic inspiration is accepted more and more as self-evident.

It has usually been felt that the newly chosen direction was needed, but at the same time questions about organic inspiration appeared to be more complicated than first thought, from the affirmation "not mechanical, but organic." This new road, moreover, did not appear to be without dangers and uncertainties. Bavinck already noted that the organic view was often used to attenuate the authorship of the Holy Spirit.[39] It shows that the mere wording of the "mechanical-organic" contrast does not offer a solution. Nevertheless, the beginning and direction of the road were indicated, and the endeavor was made to clarify its legitimacy without losing the perspective of the "God has spoken" in the attempt. What Scripture generally teaches us concerning the relationship between God and his creature suggests "that even the guidance of God's Spirit will not destroy man's own activity and inspiration but will precisely confirm and strengthen it."[40] Bavinck also rejects the idea that "God and

37. Kuyper, *Princ.,* pp. 473-481.
38. In the Dutch edition, Berkouwer frequently makes comparisons with Roman Catholic thought on Scripture. For a full treatment of this subject, see Berkouwer, *The Second Vatican Council,* especially Chs. 3, 4 and 5 (tr. note).
39. *GD,* I, 405.
40. *Ibid.,* p. 402.

his creature cannot be considered only as competitors,"[41] and he states conversely that God "does not destroy the independence and freedom of his creatures, but rather creates and maintains them."[42] Later Roman Catholic development has taken the same direction. All kinds of motifs and their background, especially concerning the formation of Scripture, are being explored and appreciated, so that the genuinely human character of Holy Scripture clearly comes to light. The desire on the side of the Protestants as well as the Roman Catholics has been to maintain and ponder the organic character of inspiration even though it might be accompanied by many dangers. Attention is focused on God's speaking "in the manner of men." The attempt to approach and describe the mystery of Scripture has been made through a reflection on this "in the manner of men,"[43] using the distinction between the primary author and secondary authors.

During the Reformation, the God-breathed character of Scripture was hardly a subject of theoretical reflection; the confession "the sacred Scripture is the Word of God" was the point of departure. But especially in post-Reformation theology, further descriptions and distinctions have been made. The God-breathed character of Scripture has been rather frequently described as "the impulse to write" and as "the suggestion of matters and words." Attention is sharply focused on a theoretical elaboration of the "from God," by way of an investigation not merely regarding the origin in the Spirit but also regarding the question of how this "cause" and "causing" must be conceived. Of course, the use of Scripture is not in the least neglected, but the cause behind this use is decisive, the cause which gave birth to Scripture in a *definite* way.[44] In a later period, this description focused in a consideration of how one must interpret this "suggestion of words." It is not surprising that a good deal of discussion arose concerning this very point. For the question was raised whether this kind of suggestion, usually called "verbal inspiration," still left room for the instrumentality of men, which theologians generally wished to honor. The "impulse to write" and the "suggestion of matters" was evidently not understood in

41. *GD,* II, 338.
42. *Ibid.* We find the same thought in H. Cremer, *Realencyclopädie für protestantische Theologie und Kirche,* IX. I have the impression that Bavinck often referred to this extensive article by Cremer.
43. *GD,* I, 420: Scripture speaks of the highest, holiest, eternal and invisible things "in a human way."
44. See, for example, the theologies of M. Chemnitz and J. Gerhard.

terms of an ecstatic inspiration.[45] The difficulty centered on the suggestion of *words*. Could anything other than an actual dictation be visualized under the suggestion that all the overwhelmingly suggested words were written down? The "mechanical dictation" concept was avoided by the notion of organic inspiration. For a long time theology was concerned with this problem of whether or not organic inspiration and verbal inspiration could be related. At the same time it was impossible, as many pointed out, to distinguish thoughts from words.[46]

Maintaining the inspiration of "each thought and each word,"[47] Kuyper added that this should not be understood as a "mechanical whispering" of words into the physical ear, but as "organically calling into being of words from men's own consciousness, that is, by using all those words that were present in the spiritual sensorium of the author."[48]

It can be asked not only whether this formulation results in clarity, but also whether it does not imply a certain shift in the impression which the phrase *"suggestion* of words" has on the hearer. Referring to I Corinthians 2:13 ("words not taught by human wisdom but taught by the Spirit"), Kuyper speaks of a "content pressed into me by the Spirit, given back in words which were forced out of me by the Spirit."[49] It is difficult to call this a fortunate description of the "suggestion of words." And it is evident that the possibility must be taken into account time and again of distinguishing verbal from mechanical. This is confirmed by the fact that even conservative theologians have often had difficulty with the term "verbal inspiration." J. Orr writes: "The phrase 'verbal inspiration' is one to which so great ambiguity attaches that it is now very commonly avoided by careful writers."[50] The term "verbal," according to Orr, makes one think of a dictation, in his opinion an indefensible position. According to Orr, "the reports of the Lord's own sayings in the gospel" clearly show "that absolute literality is not the essence of inspiration."[51] At stake is whether "the meaning of the saying is preserved, though the precise form of words

45. Cremer, p. 197.
46. See Charles Hodge, *Systematic Theology,* I (1873), 164; W. G. T. Shedd, *Dogmatic Theology,* I (1889), 89; cf. J. Packer, *Fundamentalism,* pp. 89f. ("words signify and safeguard meaning").
47. *Hedendaagse Schriftkritiek,* p. 21.
48. *Ibid.*
49. *Ibid.*
50. *Revelation and Inspiration* (1910), p. 209.
51. *Ibid.,* p. 210. Here he also points to the citations of the OT in the NT.

varies."[52] We note a similar hesitation by those who substitute *plenary* inspiration for *verbal* inspiration.[53] For here they have the whole Scripture in view, but want to escape the mechanical idea of inspiration. With this, one avoids the real question that arose concerning the meaning of verbal inspiration.[54] This question is all the more urgent since in theological discussions the doctrine of verbal inspiration is simply (without further thought) being equated with mechanical inspiration.[55] It cannot be denied that this objection is reasonable, especially in view of the "suggestion of words." Is it possible to understand verbal inspiration in any other way than as "mechanical dictation"? And why do some continue to use the term "verbal inspiration" while nonetheless sharply opposing any mechanical view?

There must be a definite reason for this tenacity, especially when this term is also used in discussions about organic inspiration. Often it appears to be motivated by a desire to maintain the connection between the God-breathed character of Scripture and the *words,* in the sense that the Word of God comes to us verbally. The expression "verbal inspiration" contains a protest against the personalization of inspiration, which we meet in the so-called theories of personal or dynamic inspiration. These theories do not deal as much with a God-breathed Scripture as with inspired *persons.* Obviously, there was no desire by those opposing this personal theory to deny that living persons were taken into service for revelation — as in the "being moved" of the prophets (II Pet. 1:21) — but rather to pay special attention to the *words* of Scripture. The explanation for the continued use of verbal inspiration has therefore been that "interest was centered not on the method, but the result. The idea was that the Holy Spirit so bore along the writers of the Holy Scripture, that their words are to be regarded as in every real sense His Words."[56] The God-breathed character of Scripture cannot be deduced from the piety of the biblical authors living in fellow-

52. *Ibid.*
53. Cf. W. Lee, *The Inspiration of Holy Scripture, Its Nature and Its Proof* (1864); L. Gaussen, *Theopneusty, or The Plenary Inspiration of Holy Scripture* (ET, 1842).
54. Bavinck, *GD,* I, 385: the "impulse to write" and the "suggestion of words" *historically* led to a mechanical doctrine of inspiration.
55. Fritzsche, *Lehrbuch der Dogmatik,* I, 112f.; A. Richardson speaks of "the theory of verbal inspiration or fundamentalism" (cited in H. D. McDonald, *Theories of Revelation: An Historical Study, 1860-1960* [1963], p. 261).
56. McDonald, p. 261.

ship with God. It is related to concrete words, to the written scriptures which are called "God-breathed." Barth, among others, recognized this motivation for verbal inspiration and gave it credit. The text and the words are decisively at stake in the God-breathed character of Scripture. "If God speaks to man, he really speaks the language of this concretely human word of man. That is the right and necessary truth in the concept of verbal inspiration."[57] The inspiration of the Scripture does not end in "our faith in it,"[58] for the church lives from and is confronted with the concrete words of Scripture. Otto Weber also refers to this motif of verbal inspiration, to the conviction that the Word of God comes to us in these words and that therefore the attention may not be called away from the words of the inspired authors.[59] Such an idea was frequently expressed when, with the arrival of historical criticism, opposition arose against the inspiration of "the specific words of Scripture," and some began to think of "inspired men, whose profound spirituality we must respect."[60] Smart sees in this shift an "escape" from the difficulties of the text – in the direction of an "inspired personality" behind the text. He states in contrast: "The revelation is in the text itself, in the words that confront us there in all their strangeness."[61] We meet the same criticism against "personal" inspiration in Bavinck, who mentions specifically Schleiermacher. With the latter, inspiration becomes an habitual quality of the authors. According to Bavinck, this view almost completely suppresses the ancient doctrine of inspiration.[62] If this criticism indeed plays an important role in maintaining the term "verbal," then it is to be understood that this range of problems also ought to be discussed by those who are opposed to a mechanical inspiration.

At the same time, however, it should be acknowledged that the word "verbal" in verbal inspiration is susceptible to a good deal of misunderstanding if combined with the "suggestion of words" and with the kind of explanation frequently given to verbal inspiration.[63] And the idea of dictation or of a whisper is

57. *CD,* I/2, 532.
58. *Ibid.,* p. 534.
59. *Grundlagen,* I, 261.
60. Smart, *The Interpretation of Scripture,* p. 195.
61. *Ibid.,* pp. 195-196.
62. *GD,* I, 387, 408.
63. See Warfield, *Inspiration,* p. 173, n. 9: "It ought to be unnecessary to protest against the habit of representing the advocates of 'verbal inspiration' as teaching that the mode of inspiration was by dictation."

also easily linked to it, so that the authors' activity other than "reception" is wholly excluded.[64] It was thus unavoidable that at a later time men strove for more clarity regarding that "suggestion of words." With all credit to the intention of many not to curtail the "from God" in any way, a lack of clarity in many respects remained, particularly when the contours of the human were so clearly noted in Scripture itself, as well as many differences between the Gospels, a phenomenon which hardly conformed to the idea of divine dictation. True, Preus wrote that dictation "does not indicate the manner in which the impartation of the words of Scripture took place" and that there was no attempt "to explain the *how* of the *suggestio verborum*."[65] But the question is precisely whether this "how" was not implied in all kinds of formulations,[66] and if at any rate it could not awaken wrong ideas later on. It cannot be denied that many figures were used which intended to accentuate the emphasis on "God has spoken," but which nevertheless made it difficult to find a meaningful expression of the true functionality of the human organ. The inspiration seemed lucid because God was called the "real" author. Later, when the human organism is discussed, we encounter varying views concerning instrumentality that at times give the impression that there is an attempt to solve a metaphysical problem as well as explain how it is possible that Scripture is the Word of God and the word of men simultaneously. Thus, a terminology forces itself into the discussion concerning the "union" of the divine and the human factors. When more room for the human factor is called for, the impression is frequently given that we are dealing with a boundary that bears limiting consequences for the room ascribed to the Spirit. In my opinion, it cannot be denied that this idea of "union" can hardly be brought in consonance with the "is" of the confession. It is related to the fact that the Reformation

This remark does not touch the real problem of verbal inspiration and its meaning.

64. *Ibid.*, p. 173. The rejection of dictation by Warfield does not prevent him from saying that "the Spirit's superintendence extends to the choice of words by the human authors (verbal inspiration)," whereby the question arises concerning the character of this choice. It is noteworthy that at a decisive point Warfield speaks of "an influence of the Holy Ghost" with regard to the words to which it applies, "though written by men and bearing indelibly impressed upon them the marks of their human origin."
65. Preus, *The Inspiration of Scripture*, p. 195.
66. *Ibid.*, p. 196. Regarding the Lutheran dogmaticians Preus speaks of "the consistent monergism of their doctrine of inspiration."

quite simply gave testimony to the "is" without falling into theoretical speculation on its "possibility."

We now wish to point out that the nature of the God-breathed character of Scripture cannot be deduced by means of various analogies to the inspiration. It is illuminating to see how Bavinck wrestles with precisely this problem. He starts with the broader meaning of inspiration as *afflatus,* or divine instinct.[67] In his opinion, the inspiration of poets can serve to clarify the God-breathed character of Scripture. He refers to the awareness of great men that their most beautiful thoughts "arose suddenly and unawares in their souls and were surprises even to themselves."[68] With this discussion of the influence of one spirit on the other, it seems for a while as if the God-breathed character of Scripture is a subdivision of general inspiration and its anthropological possibility, theoretically to be elucidated and thus explained as its analogy. But Bavinck adds at once that God-breathed inspiration "may not be identified with the heroic, poetic, religious inspiration."[69] The reference to the analogy with other forms of inspiration apparently serves only to express the "from above," that which cannot immediately be derived from man. But suddenly the boundary of working by analogy is indicated: an aspect entirely its own is evoked. The gift of the God-breathed character of Scripture "is granted only within the circle of revelation."[70] The God-breathed character is not separate from revelation, and for the church Holy Scripture is the revelation, that is, the only instrument "by which the revelation of God in Christ can be known."[71] *Revelation* finds its end in *inspiration* and therefore cannot be explained by means of a general "instrumentality," because it is related to "theophany, prophecy, and miracle," which precede the God-breathed character itself.[72] This relatedness clearly relativizes every human analogy with the God-breathed character of Scripture.

67. *GD,* I, p. 395.
68. *Ibid.*
69. Cf. *Magnalia Dei,* p. 88.
70. *GD,* I, p. 396. In this connection Bavinck speaks of the "truth in the thought of Schleiermacher," regarding the holy circle, in which the writers lived.
71. *Ibid.,* p. 354. Bavinck writes that the God-breathed character of Scripture "is an element *in* the revelation."
72. For a detailed discussion of the *witness*-character, see H. N. Ridderbos, *Authority,* pp. 62-72. "And this witness is, therefore, not only a witness to revelation, but it is itself a part of this revelation" (p. 64).

It is evident from Bavinck's comments that he does not think inspiration by itself makes a writing the Word of God. Scripture is the Word of God because the Holy Spirit witnesses in it of Christ.[73] One may no longer understand the God-breathed character formally, not even by means of a general instrumentality; it must be viewed in connection with the reality of the salvation of which Scripture *testifies*.[74] This led the church to speak of an "identity" that does not change the human word or dissolve it in the divine Word but acknowledges the concrete authorization of the human word because of this relatedness to the Spirit of God. Because of these deep relationships, it is impossible to let the God-breathed character of Scripture fade into a formal concept of inspiration. For that reason alone, extreme caution is called for concerning every inspiration analogy. Starting with a formal concept of inspiration – with the idea of instrumentality – one is no longer able to point to an essential difference between the mechanical and the organic inspiration, because both, albeit in differing degrees, deal with the concept of "instrument." The transition from mechanical to organic inspiration does not in itself offer a prospect for a real understanding of the God-breathed character of Scripture. Such an understanding certainly does not come about when the essential aspect of Bavinck's doctrine of Scripture recedes to the background or is neglected, that is, the witness of the Spirit concerning Christ through the human witness, without which the God-breathed character of Scripture cannot be understood.[75]

The kinship of the God-breathed Scripture with the revelation in Christ (i.e., its content) does not mean that it is not related to the words. It explains rather that everything is at stake with these words; that God-breathed character is a witness which at no time can or may be severed from what is testified to by the words. The mystery of the God-breathed Scripture is not

73. *GD*, I, 414.
74. *Ibid.* Here Bavinck makes the important remark: "Form and content penetrate one another and are not separable."
75. This relationship to witness is strongly underscored by Calvin. See Krusche, p. 170. Thereby the viewpoint is not that of a general instrumentality but the ministry of the self-witness. This is also the focus of H. N. Ridderbos when he speaks of the New Testament word as not existing outside of the human. "For this reason the written word of the New Testament is written and expressed in human language and human writing. It is also an eyewitness report, and as such it remains human, i.e., it is the product of a perception that was not infinite. It is subject to human limitations, its record does not exceed the limits of human memory."

meant to place us before a theoretical problem of how Scripture could possibly and conceivably be both God's Word and man's word, and how they could be "united." It rather places us before the mystery of Christ. The phrase "in the manner of men" has all too frequently been isolated and formalized as an instrumental problem, with the result that discussions about mechanical and organic inspiration often become fruitless, with unappealing charges on both sides. This can only be avoided when "in the manner of men" is understood in terms of the mode of the human witness, which is decisive for Scripture. This should be discussed further, because this formulation frequently evoked the question of whether justice is thus done to Scripture and whether there would not be the danger of Scripture's being understood as merely a witness of men concerning revelation, *their* vision and subjective insight – without power and authority. Does not this make for a separation between human witness and revelation, and does it not place Scripture on the side of man? It would certainly be incorrect at the same time to deny the nature of Scripture as witness in reaction to its humanization (mere human witness). The importance of these questions is shown in the discussion concerning attempts to revise the confessional position of the United Presbyterian Church in the U.S.A. The proposed confession spoke of "the one sufficient revelation of God" in Jesus Christ and of Scripture as "the normative witness to this revelation."[76] In his sharp rejection of this proposal, Edmund P. Clowney saw in this an abandonment of *sola Scriptura* and charged: "The Scriptures are said to be the normative witness to this revelation, but they are not in themselves the Word of God."[77]

We see that here an impure dilemma casts its shadow over the discussion. If the criticism of this proposal would have dealt with questions concerning the meaning of the words "normative witness,"[78] such questions could have clarified the discussion and

76. *The Proposal to Revise the Confessional Position of the United Presbyterian Church in the U.S.A.* (1965), p. 35.
77. E. P. Clowney, *Another Foundation: The Presbyterian Confessional Crisis* (1965), p. 12.
78. We note that the proposed version of 1965 subsequently was revised and as adopted now reads: "The one sufficient revelation of God is Jesus Christ, the Word of God incarnate, to whom the Holy Spirit bears unique and authoritative witness through the Holy Scriptures, which are received and obeyed as the word of God written. The Scriptures are not a witness among others, but the witness without parallel." Thomas M Gregory, who was critical of the original version,

served the Presbyterian Church. But the attention to the deep significance of Scripture as witness is instead weakened by reactionary phrases, and Paul is appealed to against the new confession, which says that "the words of the Scriptures are the words of men."[79] The reactionary nature of this criticism is clearly shown in the statement: "If, as the proposed *Confession* asserts, the Scriptures bear witness to Christ, the Word of God Incarnate, we may ask, What witness does Christ himself bear to the Scriptures?"[80] These questions suggest an antithesis that does not exist. Such questions relativize the nature of Scripture as witness (human witness) from a formal viewpoint of revelation, which casts its shadow over the material self-witness of Scripture.[81] Thus, the discussion is rendered fruitless[82] because it is not focused on the "is" of the confession, which relates the mystery of God's Word to the wholly human witness.

Indeed, when one seeks an analogy for the God-breathed character of Scripture, one should think of prophecy and of the acknowledgment by the apostolate at the same time that the very idea of analogy is here not at all satisfactory: the connection is more close and intensive than is expressed by the idea of analogy. We are not dealing mainly with an accidental analogy, but with a relatedness that illumines the structure of authority and normativity. Thus, there is a deep relationship between the phrase "he who hears you, hears me" (Lk. 10:16) and the authority of Scripture in the analogy between the human word of the apostles and the human writing, the God-breathed Scripture. The mystery of Scripture comes to us in its fullness, not of human views or authority, but with the empowering of the Spirit.[83]

praises the change because of "the greater stress on the Holy Spirit" (*The Presbyterian Outlook* [Nov. 21, 1966], p. 6).

79. Clowney, p. 12.
80. *Ibid.*, p. 14.
81. *Ibid.*, p. 13. Naturally the concept of "instrument" is not denied, but without giving further attention to it, Clowney continues: "Yet Scripture continues to be God's witness."
82. *Ibid.* Clowney writes (and here is where the discussion should take place): "Witness and Scripture are not related in the Bible itself as they are in the Confession of 1967." To this is added that this confession "thinks of witness as a fallible human activity," without further investigating the meaning of "normative" in this confession.
83. In the human apostolic witness lies the dimension of empowering. The apostles are very conscious of this dimension, which comes to expression in the question: "Who is sufficient for these things?" (II Cor. 2:16). Cf. II Cor. 3:5, 6; 4:1; Mt. 3:11; Eph. 4:17; I Cor. 15:9; Acts 9:15, 17.

In Scripture itself attention is emphatically drawn to its nature as witness. We recall Christ's words about Scripture testifying of him (Jn. 5:39; cf. Acts 10:43; Lk. 22:37) and his instruction of the Emmaus travelers in the things concerning himself "in all the scriptures" (Lk. 24:27). This is not only true of the New Testament's echoing the Old Testament's witness concerning Christ, but of the New Testament itself, inseparably linked as it is to the apostolate. When the Comforter testifies of Christ, this testimony includes the charge to witness: "And you also are witnesses, because you have been with me from the beginning" (Jn. 15:27). This witness does not well up from the human heart but from the witness of God, in which it finds its foundation and empowering as a human witness (I Cor. 3:5-8).

Peter mentions the quest of the prophets who prophesied of grace: "They inquired what person or time was indicated by the Spirit of Christ within them when predicting the sufferings of Christ . . ." (I Pet. 1:11). Its manifestation is found in the proclamation through the mouth of those who brought the gospel through the Holy Spirit (I Pet. 1:12). Therefore, the "also" of John 15:27 ("you also are witnesses") does not simply indicate a subsidiary matter, but points to a foundation in the witness of the Spirit. Hence the apostles' witness trusting the Lord, "who bore witness to the word of his grace" (Acts 14:3).[84] The witness of Scripture is inseparably and essentially connected with this deep dimension of the human witness. This is not only seen in the Apocalypse, where the reading aloud and keeping of the word of prophecy is witness of Jesus Christ (Rev. 1:2-3; 22:16), but also for the content of the entire witness of the New Testament. Calling Scripture a human witness, therefore, does not at all mean a separation of Scripture and revelation, but rather an honoring of integral Scripture.[85] The witness is indeed directed to that which is witnessed to.[86] It is not a relativizing of Scripture, but the acknowledgment of its meaning, intention, and

84. Cf. Rev. 19:10; see *TDNT,* IV, 500.
85. Concerning the concept "witness" in Scripture, see Runia, Ch. 2, esp. pp. 25f. He sees it as a "highly appropriate" term which Scripture points to "in a way which reveals its deepest nature" (p. 31), in connection with "the recognition of Jesus Christ as the center of all revelation of salvation" (p. 32). "Even in Reformed Theology this basic idea has not always been sufficiently honored." In this connection Warfield is discussed. His extensive viewpoint regarding the God-breathed character of Scripture deserves further analysis. Cf. J. Rogers, *Scripture in the Westminster Confession* (1967).
86. Barth, *CD,* I/2, 462.

function when it witnesses *of* Christ and therefore as God's Word is distinguished *from* him. Thus, an intelligible distinction can be made between believing in Scripture and believing in the word that Jesus had spoken (Jn. 2:22; cf. Ex. 14:31). One could object to this "subsidiary matter" and read into it a reduction of the living Lord to the level of a book only if the content and the nature of its witness were to be abstracted from Scripture (Acts 15:28). Believing Scripture does not mean staring at a holy and mysterious book, but hearing the witness concerning Christ. The respect for the concrete words is related precisely to this, and the "is" of the confession points to the mystery of the Spirit, who wants to bind men to Christ through these words, through this witness.

This testimony of Scripture through the Holy Spirit shows how important it is not to approach and develop the confession of the God-breathed Scripture by means of arguments concerning form and cause. Precisely those who wish to fully and scripturally honor the "from God" — in contrast to the "mere" human witness — shall never separate the words from their content and their nature as witness. This Scripture finds its origin in the Holy Spirit, who is the spirit of Christ and witnesses of him through the human witness (I Jn. 5:9). It is therefore meaningful and necessary to keep in mind that we do not need in Scripture a revelation of a divine truth (or truths), which we could discuss apart from these words within their nature as witness.[87] Every word about the God-breathed character of Scripture is meaningless if Holy Scripture is not understood as the witness concerning Christ. This indicates that one should never be guided by an antithesis between *words* and the *gospel,* analogous to the antithesis between form and content. The flight from the form of Scripture to its content in various configurations of spiritualism that shun the "dead letter" is a meaningless flight. For the very words are God-breathed and point to the centrality of Scripture. It is only regarding this centrality that it is legitimate to speak of the unity of Holy Scripture. It is a unity of witness and cannot be derived *a priori* and deductively from the revealed character of the entire Scripture. For then the witness concerning Christ, the kinship of the words to Christ, would not have been taken into account as a primary and essential one. This in turn would lead to a view of faith which would be compelled to accept the revelation of Scripture on the basis of its God-breathed quality before being gripped by the message to

87. Bavinck, *GD,* I, 429, 542; Runia, p. 32.

which its words testify. Kuyper has rightly protested against this conception.[88] With such a conception of faith the words themselves are relativized and devalued — though the opposite seems to be the case — because their meaning and intention are misunderstood.

In view of this confession of the God-breathed character of Scripture, one is able to face the questions concerning Scripture that arose in the course of the last centuries. These could be questions arising out of an opposition to the concrete "God has spoken," therewith a misjudging of the meaning of Christ (I Cor. 2:16). But there are also questions arising from the desire to understand the central purpose and intention of Scripture. In the context of these questions the significance of instrumentality can be honored, and it can receive a legitimate place in the discussion when the mystery of Scripture is respected. That which could not illumine mechanical or organic inspiration as a general instrumentality in isolation returns as a truly and completely human witness with its own intention within the biblical God-breathed character. For here it is truly shown that the Word of God did not come to us as a great and isolated miracle but as a miracle and secret of Scripture, of the human witness empowered by the Spirit. And this may lead to reflection on what was so strongly emphasized in the doctrine of instrumentality — that these witnesses were not "lifted out" of their time and milieu, but as living witnesses could interpret in their era what was destined for all times. In the doctrine of Scripture we are to be increasingly concerned with this instrumentality and this centrality of the one witness of Scripture.

It is meaningful to think about the way of the Spirit of Christ and about the mystery that the Word of God does not draw us away from the human but involves us with the human. And thus it becomes intelligible that especially the God-breathed character proves that God's Word — proceeding from his mouth — does not return to him void but that it is heard, understood, and proclaimed in the form of the word of human witnesses.[89] It comes to us in the midst of an overwhelming multiformity of human witnesses, of human questions and answers, of skepticism and trust, of faith and unbelief, of lamentation and jubilation, of tenseness and rest finally granted. The charge to understand in this sense is immense; it encircles the ages. Engaged with this task, one will often be reminded of the words of the psalmist

88. *Princ.*, pp. 564f.
89. Cf. Weber, I, 263f.

in reference to the inexhaustibility of this witness: "I have seen a limit to all perfection, but thy commandment is exceedingly broad" (Ps. 119:96). With these words concerning the "commandment" in mind, one does not fall into a legalistic conception of Scripture, but is more and more freed from it. The church learned to confess within this freedom: "Sacred Scripture *is* the Word of God." This "is" does not bring life to a halt because of an acquired insight; life is rather filled with an ever new responsibility. This "is" is not a postulate of our longing for certainty which cannot withstand the assaults of the human. Rather, it is truly a *confession*[90] that continues to be filled with expectation in listening to the many voices within the one voice in this Scripture. This the church confessed in the midst of the world, and it was not its intention to offer a "proof" of its faith and its legitimacy but to testify and to point to the reliable Word, which in the reading of Scripture had become a lamp and a light "until the morning star rises" (II Pet. 1:19). In this confession the word "truly" is added to the "is" just as deliberately as Paul did, not by way of exaggeration, but of emphasis in every trial. In the context of this confession of the God-breathed Scripture, research into God's Word in its verbal humanity is no threat; instead, it respects the Word of God.[91] Even though this research is surrounded by many dangers, especially by the one great danger of human arbitrariness, we are reminded by analogy of the merchant who found a pearl of great value and sold all that he had in order to buy it (Mt. 13:45-46). Everything in this research is aimed at the goal of purchase in the joy over its discovery. In days of anxiety over many "problems" about Holy Scripture, it is most necessary that this joy not perish in a "problem-orientation." That is the danger when Scripture is not heard, understood, and proclaimed according to the intention of the Spirit (Rom. 8:27). It is written of the Spirit of this Scripture that he "searches everything, even the depth of God" (I Cor. 2:10). This "searching" is rendered with a Greek word that can also be used for our "research" into Scripture (Jn. 5:39; Acts 17:11). This search could bypass the mystery and conclude that no prophet is to arise from Galilee (Jn. 7:52), just as the scribes, with their "it is written," lost their way to him of whom it was written (Mt. 2:5). But there is another possibility through which this research is not without

90. Bavinck, *GD*, I, 407.
91. Weber, I, 257.

expectation and promise. It is not aimed at fathoming the depth of God but at understanding the God-breathed Scripture and thus the mystery of the Spirit inseparably connected with its depth.

CHAPTER SIX

THE GOD-BREATHED CHARACTER AND CONTINUITY

THE PLEA FOR A MORE ORGANIC UNDERSTANDING of the God-breathed character of Scripture cannot stop at a vague and general reference to human "instrumentality." Further reflection is needed on the manner in which *man* functioned in the God-breathed Scripture. In this unavoidable area we touch on a profound consideration. For the part of man is at stake, his real part in the genesis of the God-breathed Scripture. In dogmatics, whenever discussion takes place on the question of whether God's action does not exclude but includes and makes room for man, so that even the word "cooperation" can be used (I Cor. 3:9), one becomes aware that he is dealing with an area of thought surrounded by dangers.

One problem can be characterized as that of synergism, the widespread doctrine in the history of theology that regeneration is effected by a combination of human will and divine grace. It became impossible to withdraw from synergism unless one wished to maintain an unbiblical monergism, which desired to pay tribute to God but lacked clear insight into God's way through the world and through the lives of men. In dealing with the God-breathed Scripture, one is automatically confronted with what is usually called the "continuity"[1] of God's voice with the essential human dimension of the Word of God, which reaches our ears "in the manner of men." This can be understood if one does not initially misunderstand the glory of God and does not wish to interpret the God-breathed character in an abstract supernaturalistic and "miraculous" manner. It is not

1. Berkouwer uses the word *aansluiting,* which means "connection." It is used for being connected to another person by telephone, joining a movement, or being in agreement with another person's views. I have used the word "continuity" to express this intimate interrelationship of God's and man's activity (tr. note).

surprising that all sorts of questions present themselves at this very point in the doctrine of Holy Scripture. They are focused in the question of the way in which God's Word maintains its sovereign and transcendent character in this continuity, so that it does not become dependent on human, temporal, and historical factors with their peculiar relativity.

A consideration of Bavinck's objection to the mechanical theory of inspiration brings this problem into sharp focus. He stated that the mechanical theory placed a one-sided emphasis "on the new," the supernatural element present in inspiration, "which ignored the continuity with the old, the natural element."[2] Here the relation between old and new comes to the fore; it forms the real problem of continuity. This relationship is an essential element in any historical development. Something is presupposed in every continuity which is not without meaning for the new, yet which cannot be explained from the old. We have in mind, for example, the relationship between old and new covenant which concerns both the relationship with the past and the truly new. Thus, it is possible to understand the new covenant (Jer. 31:31f.; Heb. 8:8f.; II Cor. 3:4f.) only when one considers the nature of the continuity and that which is new. In the process of a revolutionary awareness of the absolute nature of the new, the old can sometimes be ignored and forgotten in the transition from old to new. But one can also languidly remain caught in the patterns of the old when confronted with the new, thus pouring new wine into old wineskins, so that the wine is spilled and the skins are destroyed (Mt. 9:14-17).

In order to understand continuity, one must initially look for the unique and surprising character of the "discontinuity" of fulfillment. Bearing in mind the variations in the old-new relationship as it appears in the New Testament,[3] we do not find the element of discontinuity in the God-breathed Scripture. Bavinck describes the continuity with the old (the already present) as the research and thought, the speaking and writing of the biblical authors themselves. Thus, they were authors of their books in the full sense of the word, not with a weakened but a heightened activity through the impulse of the Spirit.[4] What is concretely meant by "continuity" is clear: it is the way of the God-breathed Scripture which takes the living human

2. *GD*, I, 401.
3. Cf. *TDNT*, V, 717. See I Jn. 2:7-8; cf. Jn. 13:34f.
4. *GD*, I, 402f. Cf. pp. 409, 413.

being into service and does not "abstractly, supernaturally" float high above us.[5] Bavinck calls it the "historical and psychological mediation" through which the continuity is expressed. This is parallel to Kuyper's rejection of the notion that Holy Scripture has an "abstractly transcendent" existence.[6] In the God-breathed Scripture there is a continuity with the human by which the Word of God calls the form of the human into being and adopts it. The authority of Scripture is not diminished when one tries to do justice to this activity; rather, one pays respect to Scripture's reality. We are not dealing here with an insignificant element that is pushed aside by the "voice of God," but with an essential form of the Word of God. This is clear from Scripture itself, because man is taken into service and not ignored.[7]

It is often asked whether such a continuity does not imply the limitation of the "divine word," that is, that the Word of God depends on human thoughts and conceptions. Must we perhaps speak of synergism and understand the God-breathed character as a sum of the divine and human, so that in fact we only have to deal *partially* with the divine voice in Scripture? What does this continuity with the old, with the already present, mean? And in what way is the new preserved in this continuity with the old? By ignoring these questions one does not in the least honor the God-breathed Scripture; therefore, there is every reason to consider the relationship between the God-breathed character and continuity.

Understandably, the shadow of dualism often falls over every consideration of continuity, and therefore dualism was spotted as a danger. In what way can one escape this dualism without absorbing the old into the new, or vice versa, causing one or the other to disappear? Here we touch on complex questions that have held the center of the stage in discussions of the doctrine of Scripture. These questions frequently arise when it is emphasized that the authors of the God-breathed Scripture were not "lifted out" of the history of their time.[8] How does the continuity take place with respect to men living in their own times and cultural milieux? How are men who thus had definite historical ideas and conceptions — not lifted out of their time — related to the mystery of the God-breathed Scripture?

No one denies the significance of these questions. They are

5. *Ibid.,* p. 414.
6. *Princ.,* p. 478.
7. *Ibid.,* pp. 511-520.
8. Bavinck, *GD,* I, 402.

especially prominent when the difference between our era and that of the biblical authors becomes increasingly clear, when we recognize a breathtaking broadening of all horizons of knowledge, with all the consequences for thought and action. The question of the meaning of continuity becomes more urgent in that light. Many people have asked whether one should not conclude on the basis of this gaping difference that the gospel and modern life cannot be related and brought into harmony with each other. But, even if this conclusion is decisively rejected, the question concerning continuity becomes more and more important in view of the confession of the reliability of Holy Scripture as the Word of God; in almost every study of Scripture in our time we are confronted with this problem in one form or another. As an example, Ribberbos writes:

> The New Testament does not anticipate the natural development of the human race or of the unfolding of nature; nor does it correct views of the structures and working of the universe which are relative to a particular historical epoch. The New Testament does not correct quotations from the Septuagint by making them agree with the Hebrew text. Nor does it authorize every conceptual definition that Paul derived from his Rabbinical training.[9]

Ridderbos obviously does not place this insight over against the revelatory character of Holy Scripture. He does the opposite — but shows thereby the way to understand this revelatory character according to its "very nature."[10] It should not surprise us that all these problems are usually summarized in our time under the one problem of the *time-bound* character of Holy Scripture. This term evokes varying reactions. On the one hand, this time-bound character is accepted as a matter of course, as an undeniable and evident fact. On the other hand, symptoms can be observed of a certain fearfulness to speak of Scripture in this way. The fear is that, via this time-bound aspect, room is being created for the criticism of Holy Scripture. It thus seems possible to arbitrarily separate within Scripture that which can be accepted as "eternal truth" and that which can merely be considered a "time-bound" expression of that truth.[11]

9. *Authority,* p. 61.
10. *Ibid.*
11. Bultmann is often cited in this connection, especially his description of

In studying the history of the problems of continuity, one must acknowledge that the accentuation of time-relatedness can take on quite different forms and lead to varying results. Yet, in spite of these possibilities, it never became the generally accepted posture to discontinue this concept,[12] because what is intended by it was considered inescapable. The idea of time-boundness has been quite generally accepted, even though various more or less radical applications of this view have appeared. This problem of time-boundness played a large role at the time when historical criticism of Holy Scripture began and persevered in the eighteenth century in the so-called theory of accommodation, of which so much has been heard ever since. Increasingly, the undeniably clear profile of a time-bound Scripture was noted in contrast to a supernaturalistic view of revelation that emphasized particularly the absolute newness and transcendence of Scripture. It was noted that revelation comes to us through concepts determined by the age, implying therefore an element of accommodation that should be accounted for in the understanding of revelation. It is obvious that this term could be comprehended in quite different ways. In a rationalistic frame, for example, it could easily become an aid for sifting the biblical revelation. Thus, the theory of accommodation became generally known as an openly dualistic criticism of the Bible. The supporters of this theory felt that the essence of the Christian faith had to be searched out within the framework of accommodation[13] – in other words, within the framework of the continuity of revelation with the concepts and categories of knowledge from the time of its origin.[14] This necessitated a dissociation of revelation from its realization in time-bound human life and history. For that reason it is important to ask whether the theory of accommodation is essentially related to the problems regarding continuity as they are everywhere discussed today. Do recent expressions differ in quality, or do they merely offer a more precise profile of the old theory of accommodation?

The problem of accommodation is of far-reaching significance because it touches on the problem of the reduction of Scripture to a presupposed kernel. (Later, it was often called the "deduction method" of the liberal theology of the nineteenth century.)

the NT world-view as *mythological,* to which then the exposition of the acts of salvation corresponds.

12. Ridderbos, p. 61.
13. Frör, *Bibl. Hermeneutik,* p. 27.
14. Cf. G. Hornig, *Die Anfänge der hist.-krit. Theologie,* pp. 211-236.

Numerous forms of accommodation in the eighteenth century started with the presupposition that Christ and his apostles had deliberately sought points of connection and accommodation with the world of thought of their day in order to be understood by the people of their time. This was considered the pedagogics of salvation, whereby truth was disclosed and offered in a form intelligible for that time. This concept presupposed that Christ and the apostles knew better themselves but that they chose this path to make the gospel known. However, there is biblical data that does not show such an accommodation at all. This problem surrounding the nature and background of accommodation played a particularly significant role throughout the eighteenth century, occupying the minds of many.

The problems of the doctrine of accommodation come into clear focus in the general distinction between *essential content* and *time-related form,* as well as in the critical question of the criteria used to define and legitimize the dissociation of these two factors. One cannot escape the idea that here a process of distinction has started that is determined by a high degree of arbitrariness, even though there is no observable intention to distinguish arbitrarily. A new insight into reality and its laws had penetrated the area of theology, and the method of historical-critical research began to influence the interpretation of the gospel.[15] The conviction prevailed that revelation was not in the least subjected to reduction, but was rather being interpreted in accordance with its peculiar essence. Regarding this, one could ask whether *every* way of speaking of accommodation or continuity could not be deemed an arbitrary way. Various opponents of accommodation, though they do not use the term in certain ways, do not wish to exclude every problem of continuity. Almost no one is willing to reach a wholly negative conclusion. The reason is that the word "accommodation" was not only used in conjunction with eighteenth-century rationalism, but had already played an important role in earlier times. It was used by seventeenth-century Lutheran dogmaticians in connection with the language and style of the biblical authors, to which the Holy Spirit "accommodated himself."[16] The eighteenth-century Dutch theologian Van Hemert referred to Chrysostom's statement, that "Christ often checked himself for the sake of the weakness of his hearers when he dealt with lofty doctrines and that he usually did not choose such words as were

15. *Ibid.,* p. 232.
16. Preus, *Inspiration,* pp. 62-64.

in accord with his glory but rather those which agreed with the capability of men."[17] Calvin also addressed the concept of accommodation and related it to pedagogical motives in the economy of salvation. We would not know God unless he condescended to us[18] and unless he spoke to us in a human way, in order to be comprehended by us and so be truly near to us.[19] In general, it meant that God spoke to us by way of this accommodation or adjustment "according to the capacity of man," on an "inner human" and "intramundane" level, so that his Word would not fall mysteriously from the clouds but would really reach us. Such tendencies were noted in Scripture itself, such as the wording of John 16:12: "I have yet many things to say to you, but you cannot bear them now" (cf. Jn. 16:4). And there are other statements that obviously imply an "adjustment" in a pedagogical situation or a certain purpose in approaching someone with the Word of God (Heb. 5:13-14; I Cor. 9:20).

Thus, a certain accommodation has always been the subject of theological reflection, and it is incorrect to say that this reflection has nothing to do with the problems raised in the later theory of accommodation. However, in the later theory the problem of the relationship between content and form becomes clear when we recognize how the approach to the gospel via continuity can be determined by rather time-bound criteria. The question in dispute then is whether the pure perspective of the substance of the gospel is still preserved despite the intention to preserve the essential elements. In what way can one speak of accommodation or continuity regarding ideas and conceptions of earlier times so that this time-relatedness does not lead to a dissolution of the gospel? This question returns as a legitimate one in the reflection on the organic, God-breathed character of Scripture. For the latter does not wish to see the human aspect in Scripture as a competitor with God's voice, but wishes to respect the human aspect as an internal necessity of Scripture itself. This also implies an interest in the continuity of the "new" with the "old," a continuity which Bavinck wished to consider.

But first it is necessary to point out the remarkable distinctions between various forms of accommodation that we meet in previous periods as well as in the present reflection on con-

17. Cited in *Verhandelingen raakende den natuurlijken en geopenbaarden godsdienst* (1792), p. 31.
18. See *Inst.*, I, xi, 3; II, xi, 13; II, xvi, 2; I, xvii, 13, etc.
19. See Niesel, *Theology of Calvin*, p. 35.

tinuity. Previously, accommodation was frequently understood as a deliberate coming down to the level of understanding of the hearers, as was believed to be the case with Christ and the apostles.[20] Today, this concept of accommodation, based on the presence of a higher level of knowledge, scarcely plays a role. Instead of speaking of God's accommodating himself, there is more concern today with being accommodated to the biblical authors, namely, to the views and conceptions of the period in which they lived and from which they were not lifted. The pedagogical element in the doctrine of accommodation implies a certain horizon of knowledge, indeed an horizon of Christ himself. This is evident from the New Testament text concerning Christ's not knowing "that day" (Mk. 13:32; Mt. 24:36), in which a limit to the knowledge of "the Son" is emphatically mentioned. Thus, it was pointed out that Christ's utterances concerning the end are expressed in "conceptual themes of the usual contemporary eschatology."[21] At the same time we are not in the least prepared to speak of an error by Christ; something quite different from the previous concept of accommodation is reflected. Christ indeed spoke in such a way that he could be understood, but there is also a limitation that "in principle, at least . . . in no way" could be understood "merely as the history of his pedagogical accommodation."[22] Jesus spoke at times in concepts that were "prescribed by his religious environment."[23] And to Rahner, among others, this conceptual limitation does not mean something puzzling that can hardly be related to his being God. For Christ uses these concepts "to express slowly what he had always already known about himself in the very depth of his being."[24] No one will perceive at once how this knowledge "in the very depth of his being" can be united with his "not knowing." But it is clearly necessary to account for the limitation included in the dictum "truly man." Thus, men sought to overcome the perplexities that were previously felt

20. Kuyper, *Princ.*, p. 430.
21. Rahner, *Theological Investigations*, IV (ET, 1966), 338. See Berkouwer, *The Return of Christ* (ET, 1972), pp. 257-258 and the bibliography indicated there.
22. Rahner, V, 212.
23. *Ibid.*
24. *Ibid.* For Rahner the problem lies in "the very depth." Therein the problem comes freshly to the fore. It is striking that Roman Catholic Christology, which has so often been accused of monophysitism, is so intensely busy with the "true man" on the basis of Mk. 13:32 (in spite of Thomas' interpretation).

concerning this "not knowing," because it was not understood how this was possible in view of the personal union of the divine and human natures of Christ.[25]

This same aspect of limitation comes sharply into focus with respect to the biblical authors. Here we touch on Bavinck's thoughts about the horizon of knowledge of these authors: "The authors of Holy Scripture apparently did not know anything more than their contemporaries concerning all these sciences, such as geology, zoology, physiology, and medicine."[26] Neither was that necessary, Bavinck adds, because they did not offer scientific theories, but spoke in the language of daily experience. Even though a very important aspect is indicated by this "not necessary," it is understandable that some poignant questions could arise with respect to this "time-boundness." However, do not problems of old and new readily crop up within Scripture when Scripture seeks continuity with previous deposits of knowledge, with conceptions and forms which were brought along in the message of Scripture, albeit in a particular context? We constantly return to the question of how one can possibly find nuances and distinguish here between form and content, between the message and its expression. And so we face the fact that the complexities and dangers of such a distinction have led to a rejection of every distinction of this kind. For such a distinction would be unacceptable in view of the authority of the whole Scripture and would lead to a critical dissociation that would not be brought in harmony with obedience to Scripture. This rejection takes its cue from the inspiration of Holy Scripture, with the consequence that every dualism and every method of verification must be overcome, and thus the aspect of time-boundness cannot be of essential significance for the doctrine of the God-breathed Scripture.

However, more and more the idea gains ground that this categorical rejection of every differentiation and every factual reflection on the nature of the authority of Scripture cannot be maintained. This idea concerns itself with the fact that Scripture is not composed of a number of isolated words, theses, and truths expressed, but a centered witness. Dualism can easily

25. It is not true that this "accommodation" theory has just come to the fore in Roman Catholic theology. Already in the 19th century one can encounter this thought, e.g., in Gore, *The Incarnation of the Son of God* (1891), in which one sees a *kenotic accommodation* theory. Cf. McDonald, *Theories of Revelation,* pp. 140f.

26. *GD,* I, 417.

mask itself by adducing the distinction between kernel (center) and periphery. But even when one is aware of this dualism, it cannot be denied that there are other possibilities for discussion concerning the centralization of Holy Scripture.[27] The church has always been more or less conscious of this centralization, mindful of that word of Paul which clearly indicated the center: "For I decided to know nothing among you except Jesus Christ and him crucified" (I Cor. 2:2). As is clear from all his preaching (e.g., I Tim. 1:15; II Tim. 2:8), Paul does not have in mind a quantitative reduction of the gospel according to his own yardstick, a reduction of many truths to the one "truth," leaving other truths in the wings; yet in striking manner we find here expressed a decisive centralization, a concentration (Rom. 15:18).

How shall the God-breathed Scripture ever be understood without focusing on the one concentrated mystery of the Spirit of Christ, who does not speak on his own authority but "will take what is mine and declare it to you" (Jn. 16:12-14; 15:26)? The perspective of this centeredness of Scripture is easily endangered by a leveling process whereby the God-breathed Scripture is primarily approached in isolation concerning the problem of instrumentality. Then the attention for contours and centralization fades. As is frequently indicated, even the firmest confession that the entire Scripture is God's Word does not guarantee that these dangers are no longer a threat. Thus, Kantzenbach writes about Luther that "he is far removed from a doctrine of inspiration that levels all pronouncements in the Bible."[28] There is no room for emphasis and centralization when there is a leveling of the many words of Scripture. The question logically follows (because of the quality of revelation): "Is a distinction between one article and another still possible and justified the moment that the doctrine of inspiration comes into play?"[29] But Luther and Calvin were able to reflect on the centralization not because they were unconvinced of the God-breathed character but because they understood it in its essential relation to the truth of God witnessed to *in* Scripture.

It also becomes possible to honor the idea of instrumentality

27. *Ibid.*, p. 409. Bavinck speaks against atomism and the isolation of words and about a center and a periphery and the circle of thoughts. He points to foolish hermeneutical rules that flow from a view "as if each word and each letter, in itself and isolated, as such was given by God with its own purpose and with its own and thus divine content."
28. F. W. Kantzenbach, "Das theol. Programm der Fundamentalartikel," *Lutherische Monatshefte* (1962), p. 542.
29. *Ibid.*, p. 546.

— now without isolation and formalization — in light of this centralization and intention of Scripture. For if instrumentality is related to this one central witness, then the term "continuity" can legitimately be used in the doctrine of the God-breathed Scripture without falling into dualism. For this is in harmony with the purpose of God-breathed Scripture. One can never have a clear conception of the latter when it is "formally" approached under the category of correctness or conformity with reality; it must be approached in direct relation to the nature and content of Scripture. For the purpose of the God-breathed Scripture is not at all to provide a scientific *gnosis* in order to convey and increase human knowledge and wisdom, but to witness of the salvation of God unto faith. This approach does not mean to separate faith and knowledge. But the knowledge that is the unmistakable aim of Scripture is the knowledge of faith, which does not increase human wisdom, but is life eternal (Jn. 17:3). That is undoubtedly the background of Bavinck's profound remark that the horizon of knowledge of the biblical authors did not need to be broadened with scientific insight so that it could compete with the knowledge of their contemporaries in a strange and surprising way. In this connection, reference is often made today to the need to take note of the goal of Holy Scripture. This need has not been stressed before because of the reality and the nature of Scripture and the idea of goal or purpose which the church has always intuitively taken into account. The fear that this idea of goal (so closely related to the centralization of Scripture) will lead to an arbitrary dualism and to an attack on the authority of Scripture is not only based on a misunderstanding, but also contradicts the seriousness and depth of the biblical message.

Earlier we showed the manner in which Scripture itself witnesses to its intent. Here we wish to reflect numerous questions concerning the relationship between the God-breathed character and continuity in the light of this goal of Scripture. This relation can best be illustrated by mentioning discussions that are inseparably linked with a particular insight into this intent of Scripture. One of the most striking examples is undoubtedly offered by the dispute about the biblical world view.

The origin of the dispute is related to this question: in view of the truth and reliability of Holy Scripture, is it legitimate to believe that numerous conceptions occur in it that fit the world view of an earlier age and not that of a later age? Does not such a notion of a biblical world view call into question the authority of Scripture for all ages? A lively debate took place particularly in the Reformed churches in the Netherlands after the Synod of Assen, which dealt extensively with the direct application of the authority of Scripture. The conviction was defended at that time that, though the Bible does not offer a scientific world view, yet the cosmological presuppositions of the biblical authors clearly demonstrate a contemporaneous view of the structure of the world: for instance, the earth as flat, surrounded by oceans — a geocentric world view held by no one today. It was pointed out that the authority of Scripture is in no way diminished because an ancient world view occurs in it; for it was not the purpose of Scripure to offer revealing information on that level.

Here again we encounter the problem of the relationship between the God-breathed character of Scripture and continuity. In these discussions we find different attributes of Holy Scripture, namely, its *reliability,* its *infallibility,* and its *inerrancy.* The words "infallibility" and "reliability" were not deemed sufficient; it was thought necessary to add "inerrancy."[30] The fact that the Bible contains an "obsolete" world view, and thus an incorrect and erring world view, contradicts the God-breathed character of Scripture, according to this viewpoint, since each "error" is excluded by the God-breathed character. In this view of inerrancy we meet a serious formalization of the concept of erring. The concept of error in the sense of incorrectness is obviously being used on the same level as the concept of erring in the sense of sin and deception. The distinction is left rather vague. As a consequence of this, limited historical perception within a certain cultural and scientific situation is, without further stipulation, put on a par with erring in the sense of lying, the opposite of truth. If erring is formalized in such a way, it cannot later be related to truth in a biblical sense, but it continues to function as a formal structure of exactness and correctness. Thus, we are quite far removed from the serious manner with which erring is dealt in Scripture. For there what is meant is not the result of a limited degree of knowledge, but it is a swerving from the truth and upsetting the faith (II Tim. 2:18).

30. The setting of the "inerrancy" discussion is developed in detail by Warfield, *op. cit.,* pp. 150f. He sees "inerrancy" as implied in reliability and then with regard to "all its parts and in all its elements, down to the least minutiae, in form of expression as well as in substance of teaching" (p. 150). Cf. "entire truthfulness" as "inerrancy" in verbal inspiration (which he does not see as dictation) through which Scripture is protected "from everything inconsistent with a divine authorship" (p. 173) and from whatever conflicts with "a divine book" (p. 151).

The testimony of the Spirit stands opposite *that* erring, and the confession of the God-breathed Scripture could not be maintained with that kind of deception in view. The supposition that limited human knowledge and time-boundness of any kind would cause someone to err and that Holy Scripture would no longer be the lamp for our feet unless every time-bound conception could be corrected, is a denial of the significance of historical development and of searching out as the "unhappy business that God has given to the sons of men to be busy with" (Eccl. 1:13).

It can be recognized that "inerrancy" was emphasized with the intention of warning against a mistrust of the testimony of God and of keeping the church from really erring. But the formalization of inerrancy virtually destroys this intention, because the relationship of the organic, God-breathed character to the organic unity and scope of the total testimony of Scripture is almost totally ignored. It creates numerous insoluble problems in the historical development, so that as a consequence in later years a compromise could no longer be avoided, and various solutions were proposed that made inerrancy a latent dogma without any real function.

The problem of the God-breathed character of Scripture and continuity gained renewed interest in its connection with the authors' level of knowledge in a certain period (Ex. 20:4; Ps. 24:2; II Sam. 22:8; Ps. 136:6; Job 26:5; Ps. 46:3; Ps. 148:4). This does not mean a capitulation to science as an institution opposed to God's Word, with the additional conclusions that Scripture is unreliable and its witness untrustworthy. Rather, it means a greater degree of naturalness in speaking of Scripture, with a view to its nature and purpose. Corrections of various conceptions of the world – its composition and its place in the universe – are not at all needed then to guarantee the full and clear message of Scripure. Formal problems of correctness (inerrancy alongside infallibility) disintegrate with such a naturalness. This is illustrated in Jan Ridderbos' words: "Moreover Scripture bears the marks of the period and of the milieu in which it was written and it shares in part these marks with the culture of the entire Orient, a culture which in many ways was interrelated to that of Israel. This is true for writing, language, style, literary genre, ideas, conceptions, world view (cf. the three-decker universe in Ex. 20:4)."[31] It is possible to be so natural, without a sense of crisis concerning the confession of Scripture, because there is no reason why "a certain time-related conception con-

31. *Geref. Schriftbeschouwing en Organische Opvatting* (1926), pp. 25f.

cerning the composition of the universe" has to be corrected. He who demands that all conceptions occurring in Scripture be precisely correct on the basis of the God-breathed character of Scripture starts with the presupposition that the voice of God can only then be reliable and that the biblical authors cannot be witnesses and instruments of the God-breathed Scripture when they use certain time-bound conceptions in their writings. This notion of "inerrancy" can quickly lead to the idea that the "correctness" of all these conceptions anticipates later scientific discovery: "What a marvelous book that anticipates this triumph of man's ingenuity some four thousand years or more."[32] This anticipation is being adduced then as a sign of the divinity of the Scripture.

However strange they may sound, such ideas should not be ridiculed. The question is rather how such a theory of inspiration is being applied and how some are fascinated by a miraculous "correctness" that forever disregards every problem of time-relatedness. Even though one may hear through it all a note of serious motivation, the conclusion is valid that this earnestness cannot serve as yardstick for the doctrine of Scripture. In the end it will damage reverence for Scripture more than it will further it.

Ramm wrote rightly (cf. Bavinck's opinion concerning the knowledge of the biblical authors) that the Holy Spirit "did not give to the writers the secrets of modern science."[33] Various excessive examples (including even nuclear theories) are in his opinion "a misunderstanding of the nature of inspiration." They do not take into account that Scripture came to us "in terms of the culture in which the writers wrote."[34] This does not imply a dualistic theory of inspiration. For this unmistakable emphasis, as well as the reflection about the nature of faith, corresponds with the intention of Scripture itself. It offers explicit and implicit evidence that it is not a "gnostic" writing but the God-breathed Scripture oriented to the testimony of God's deeds, profitable for teaching, for reproof, for correction, and for training in righteousness (II Tim. 3:16). It is not that Scripture offers us no information but that the nature of this information is unique. It is governed by the *purpose* of God's revelation. The view of inspiration that forms the basis of the misunderstanding

32. E.g., Job 38:35. See B. Ramm, *The Christian View of Science and Scripture* (1963), pp. 162f.
33. *Ibid.*, p. 136.
34. *Ibid.*, p. 96.

of this purpose considers "inerrancy" essential as a parallel characterization of reliability; that is a flight of fancy away from this purpose.

An orientation taking full account of the purpose of Scripture often uses the term the *scopus* of Scripture. This term indicates that the words are related to and tend toward a definite goal (Phil. 3:14). It would be a mistake to consider this a form of dualistic conception of Scripture. The origin of the concept of goal was not in a period when the subjection to the witness of Scripture began to grow lax. The church has always been clearly aware of the need to take account of this "goal" for the understanding of Scripture,[35] and this accounting does not at all imply an escape from the text to the psychological "intent" of the biblical author, for the latter cannot be approached outside the text. It means rather a concentrated attention to the very words, to the Word in the midst of many words, to its intent and purpose. All kinds of misunderstandings are avoided by this attention to the goal, which is an essential theme of interpretation. Christ thwarts the Pharisees' misunderstanding of the Sabbath commandment with a statement that reveals the meaning and intent of the Sabbath in contrast to the Pharisees' imagined goal: "The sabbath was made for man, not man for the sabbath" (Mk. 2:27).

The comprehension of the goal is not a simple matter. But fear of this idea of *scopus* is fruitless, for Scripture disintegrates into many words without the goal, and its God-breathed character is thereby neglected. One must agree that in later times men's eyes were more and more sharpened to observe the goal in the historical development of the understanding of Scripture. This occurred through the disclosure of Scripture's environment and period of origin, of the circumstances and habits of that period, and of the language in which Scripture came to us. That the gospel did not come to us as a timeless or "eternal" truth or idea became increasingly clear. It was seen as a message of salvation received, interpreted, and handed over by men. And the God-breathed character of that Scripture was confessed by the church. It does not seem strange that the question of goal received a more radical significance only in a later period, when the radius of knowledge (both of the Old and New Testaments) was widened. This does not have the consequence, as we already pointed out, that next to Holy Scripture, which "is its own interpreter," a second and equivalent interpreter would appear

35. Regarding Augustine, see Bavinck, *GD,* I, 416.

on the scene, robbing the first in effect of its importance. We would rather say that the discovery of the entrance of the Word of God into the fullness of human life led men to think more and more about the goal of Scripture itself. The goal idea is therefore not the opposite of the God-breathed character of Scripture: it is a part of it, in view of the purpose of the Spirit's voice leading us into all truth. Thus, no one may ignore this question of goal, not even from a fear of threatening the reliability of Scripture. Maintaining a guard against the idea of goal as a method of verification does not accordingly nullify its legitimacy; and neglecting it results in unfruitful exegesis and preaching.

Further reflection shows that frequent objections have been made to terms such as "time-relatedness" and "time-boundness," because they cannot be heard and understood without indicating an extremely relative matter. Is it proper for the limitations of time to enter our discussions concerning the Word of God? For we read that it is *not* bound or fettered (II Tim. 2:9). Paul's statement refers to "the victorious course of the Word of God in preaching that nothing can halt";[36] it seems to resist any attempt to "bind" Holy Scripture. However, Paul's mighty reminder is in no way an authority opposing reflection on the time-boundness of Scripture. For such reflection has nothing to do with denying or minimizing the power of God's Word in this world. One cannot and may not ignore questions arising from the time-relatedness, even though the depth and perspective is discerned in the witness that the word proceeding from the mouth of Yahweh does not return to him empty but shall accomplish that which he purposes (Isa. 55:11), and even though one does not hesitate to speak of the victory of the Word. It hardly seems possible that disagreement would arise concerning this time-boundness of Holy Scripture, for the Word of God is wholly related to the period, the history, and to the fullness of human life.

This time-boundness is already undeniably brought to light through the language of Scripture as it reflects localities and situations of a special period (Hebrew, Aramaic and Greek). It also appears through circumstances and related ideas and conceptions determined by that period. Moreover, these cannot be severed from the language of Scripture. We see that the Word of God was spoken in numerous situations, each having its own color and problems; in the midst of these situations and not beyond them, Scripture sounds as the voice of God. This is

36. C. Bouma, *Komm.*, p. 279.

already evident in the clear aim of various letters of the New Testament. In relation to the understanding of the words of Scripture, speaking of a "creative milieu" does not mean that God's Word finds its origin therein. Rather it enters into numerous situations in such a manner that the period is automatically reflected in the mode of the Word of God. Here one may think of the giving of the Mosaic Law. On a different level, one is reminded of the various kinds of heresy that are opposed in the New Testament. The forms of expression for these antitheses are related to their rejected heresy, as Paul's letters to the Romans, Galatians, and Colossians clearly show. This time-boundness was not generally considered a problem, but these seemingly simple examples may already restrain us from denying this evident time-boundness (as opposed to timelessness) which is related precisely to the depth of the gospel. One does well to keep this in mind, because time-boundness is often readily connected with relativization.

There are various dangers for theology hidden here. For this generalizing runs parallel with a leveling process, because the aim *within* the time-bound situation determines the meaning of the human words. The Word of God does not come to us in generalities, showing no historical outline; if that were the case, it would be able to guarantee continuity through the course of the centuries. Rather, because of the time-bound language, certain words from Scripture cannot be immediately understood in a later period. For example, II Peter 1:4 tells the church that members may "become partakers of the divine nature." This expression strikes us as near heresy if we do not remember that it is a phrase from Scripture. It would remind us of the doctrine of participation, in which this "nature" plays an important role. However, we are not dealing now with the question of how this participation with the divine "nature" was interpreted in a later period. We only wish to point out the language problem that may arise for comprehension when the way of the Word is the way through human life, with all its complicated historical facets.

Moreover, the Word finds its way through periods having their own social structures and "cultural patterns" – customs and concepts relative to the particular period. The Word of God does not remain aloof from this, but is heard in the midst of it. As a result, the time-boundness of certain admonitions and prohibitions is clear to all. Various statements by Paul regarding womanhood and marriage constitute some of the most discussed illustrations of this particular problem of time-boundness. At one time virtually no attention was given to time-boundness in these passages: they were read outside the context of that period and were then applied in other periods in some way, even though the accompanying questions were never resolved. Because of the difference in eras, various insoluble problems formed a barrier. Nevertheless, the attempt was made to understand these passages with immediate and general, but not time-related, clarity in view of the God-breathed character of Scripture. But Paul, in contrast, did not in the least render timeless propositions concerning womanhood. Rather, he wrote various testimonies and prescriptions applicable to particular — and to a certain degree transparent — situations against a background of specific morals and customs of that period. This realization has increasingly penetrated even to areas where there has been no hesitation to affirm Scripture as the Word of God.

We note Paul's statement that the woman must have an "authority" on her head (the veil was a symbol of this) "because of the angels" (I Cor. 11:10), as well as other comments about women that are not at all clear to us initially. The simple pronouncement that God's Word comes to us here will not suffice. One must rather take note of the cultural context and intent of the words within that period precisely *in order* to hear the Word of God. Only in this way will the question of the concrete authority of such words receive its true weight and significance. We also note in this connection Paul's "argument" *from nature* regarding the hairdo of men and women (I Cor. 11:14-15) and other qualifications. For example, Paul says that it is "shameful" for a woman to speak in the congregation of God (I Cor. 14:35) and that some things are "disgraceful" for women (I Cor. 11:5-6). These "arguments" belong to the Scripture of the New Testament, but one cannot draw deductive conclusions from them without giving account of any nuances and time-relatedness. One should also mention Paul's "argument" that man was not made from woman, but woman from man, and that man is now born of woman (I Cor. 11:8-12). It is evident that one cannot make an inch of progress by speaking of the "correctness" of such words in the abstract. One must therefore take into account the fact that "the apostle is aware of other authorities or other proofs next to proof from Scripture to which he appeals when he presents his opinion to his congregations."[37]

The above points continue to be of importance precisely for

37. Michel, *Paulus und seine Bibel* (1929), pp. 159f.; cf. E. E. Ellis, *Paul's Use of the Old Testament* (1957), pp. 28f.

reflection on the God-breathed Scripture, even when one would hold that "proof from Scripture would be sufficient" for Paul himself.[38] The way of God's Word is in the manner of men "in a particular period." It appears clear that numerous and quite varying arguments are used to announce the message precisely for that period and in that situation, and to proclaim God's Word as "truly near." We are dealing here with more than analogies taken from natural life (I Cor. 14:7f.; I Cor. 15:37; Rom. 11:6-24), since God's words themselves cannot be understood in their content and meaning without this time-relatedness. In this way alone can they compose a specific appeal, and anyone who would isolate certain words in order to understand and apply them "timelessly" will encounter peculiar difficulty with such a leveling process. He will, for example, encounter the statement of Paul that it is "well for a man not to touch a woman," forgetting to what extent Paul's words belong to a certain situation (I Cor. 7:1). Besides, we note how Paul himself gives an indication of this situation and time-boundness. He emphatically answers questions which have been sent to him (I Cor. 7:1), and he considers something to be right "in view of the impending distress" (I Cor. 7:26): giving young daughters into marriage is certainly not an evil, but he would spare them the worldly troubles (I Cor. 7:28). Paul is obviously not engaged in lessons in timeless morals. Rather, there is a time-boundness to his admonitions and advice and to his specific polemics for the warding off of concrete dangers.

Deeper themes, in light of which the goal of the argumentation can be understood, form a contrast to the arbitrariness of a confused argumentation. Paul frequently tries to call attention to this, for instance, when he offers further explanations with "I mean" (I Cor. 7:29), showing that the thought that "the appointed time has grown very short" is decisive for all his words. One must also take this into account — in its time-relatedness — when considering the motivation of Paul's "preference" for the unmarried state. Obedience to the Word of God is impossible, even an illusion, if it is not a listening discovery of the *meaning* of the words, of their essential goal. And one is far removed from this obedience if he pleads that we bow down to God's Word without considering any nuances. No one can truly escape the Pauline phrase "I mean." Only nuances and distinctions make the discovery of the meaning possible; and only with effort can one find out what the words of God have to say to us

38. Michel, p. 167.

in human relations and time-relatedness. It is necessary to thus search out the meaning and intent of the words precisely because everything in God-breathed Scripture appears in such an historically human manner (I Cor. 7:25; Eph. 5:32). This search saves us from ignoring much of the Bible as hopelessly irrelevant to us because of the changed cultural situation and the changing picture of our times. In contrast to this apparent irrelevance (even within the confession that the whole Scripture is God's Word), this search for the goal of Scripture, which is concerned with time-related concepts and transient patterns of circumstances, is not dualistic but antidualistic. It cannot be denied that leveling the words of Scripture will never lead to the discovery of the validity of God's Word for all times.

This concept of irrelevance is unmistakably dualistic. It cannot remain covered or hidden by our maintaining the confession that the entire Scripture is the Word of God. Various discussions concerning time-relatedness and inerrancy have begun in our time, and the use of such terms must frequently be defended against the suspicion of relativism. But, with all this defense, there is no reason to neglect a matter-of-fact offensive. A tactical withdrawal or surrender of bulwarks is not at stake, but the depth and inexhaustible richness of Scripture is opposed to the danger of a partially *latent* Scripture, without fruitfulness and power for all time. And just as some goal is inseparably united with all human speaking and writing, Holy Scripture, with its human verbal character, has a central aim. Only in this manner can it be truly read, understood, and proclaimed.

Of course, numerous questions arise from this insight into the time-relatedness of the words of Scripture, the seriousness and weight of which cannot be denied. No one is unaware of the longing for a less "complicated" and more immediately comprehensible Word that would appeal with suprahistorical clarity and without nuances to a childlike faith. Moreover, one must appreciate the fear — no one ought to consider this beneath him — of a relativizing situationism or historicism whereby God's Word fades, not because of its closed nature, but because of a historicization of all human speaking. This would make Scripture subject to a radical "verification."[39] One of the marks of historicization, it is true, is the "relatedness" and therewith the relativity of all that is historical. But this should not blind us to the fact that time-relatedness does not necessarily lead to such rela-

39. A. Richardson, *The Bible in the Age of Science,* where he speaks of a revolution in the thinking of natural scientists and historians.

tivizing, unless one adopts an *a priori* solution concerning the absolute relativity of all that is historical, a conclusion which would exclude the mystery of the God-breathed Scripture. Frequently, time-relatedness has been combined with a relativizing historicism in an attempt to see it as placing a "supratemporal" stamp on Scripture. Time-relatedness, it was pointed out, is not explicitly discussed in Scripture. Thus, the fact that men would think and speak of time-relatedness must be seen as originating in the flow of history, morals, customs, and cultures — and not in Scripture itself. This issued finally in the warning against every denial of the fact that "Scripture is its own interpreter."

It was easy to reach various dangerous conclusions with a "supratemporal" conception of Scripture that honored its vertical dimension but not its horizontal dimension. Some tried, for example, to legitimize slavery with the argument that Paul did not explicitly disqualify slavery as absolutely contradictory to the gospel. Here it is clearly shown how important it is to take the goal of Scripture into account and to reckon thereby with its historical relatedness. For only in this way is it possible to understand that the gospel does not perish in a societal situation, but "keeps its unmistakable significance" for every social relationship,[40] the significance of the centrality of being "in Christ." The reference to background, goal, and intent does not therefore imply a method of subtraction. It desires to understand the Word of God in its "absolute significance."[41] No one will deny the complexity of the problems that have been raised here. These nuances can leave the impression of a dualism; but this cannot be avoided. When biblical affirmations and references to the intrinsic demand of revelation are made, taken from its very heart, differences of opinion may naturally arise concerncerning these affirmations. But it is God's Word itself which again and again arouses this interest, for it penetrates human life in all its forms and situations. For that reason, statements cannot be avoided that may leave a dual impression when this theme is not recognized. Moreover, this is also true for the term "time-relatedness" itself. This is the case, for instance, when Ridderbos speaks of the unassailable divine aspect as well as the relativity of the human aspect in Scripture, rejecting simultaneously both a dualistic process of sifting and a separation of the Word of God and the word of men. These attempts to formulate should not be interpreted as dualism.

40. H. N. Ridderbos, *Paulus* (1966), p. 355.
41. *Ibid.*, p. 348.

For they point to the fact that God's Word is related to human life as the gospel makes its way through the ages.

When the time-relatedness of Holy Scripture is understood, it can be perceived how God's Word is the true and abiding norm. In the history of the church, be it probing or somewhat superficial, something of the nature of biblical normativity has always been understood. Numerous indications of this reflection can be observed. The distinction between the *historical* and the *normative* authority of Scripture, which has become traditional, is one of them. We touch here on a peculiar turn of thought concerning the authority of Scripture. Even the terminology is peculiar, since it contains a clear tautology, namely, a "normative authority" that is distinguished from a different "authority" (an historical one). The question may be interjected whether there is then some authority of Scripture that is not of a normative nature. The question is so obvious that we suspect that this problem was seen from the start. This faulty distinction was used to bring about a certain twist of thought without which the nature of the authority of Scripture could not be understood. The confession of the divine authority of Scripture automatically led to this distinction, according to Bavinck.[42] For the revelation of God has been given in the form of a history, following its course through various periods of time, with the result "that certainly not everything recorded in Scripture should be of normative authority for our faith and life."[43]

Bavinck obviously did not mean to give this arresting clause a dualistic sense. Rather, it is clearly meant in terms of *gradation*. For Bavinck is concerned here with the relatedness of Scripture to salvation history. He notes that "much of what God offered and affirmed no longer immediately concerns us." It referred only to persons in former times. In his opinion, much is written that is not in the least normative for us. This is an important distinction, because it calls to our attention the difference between the Word of God in the formal and material senses and forces us to consider their mutual relation. Bavinck sees the danger of a dualistic usage of this distinction with the acknowledgment that what is normative in God's Word is in a certain manner expressed everywhere in Scripture. But this distinction emphasizes that

42. *GD*, I, 427.
43. *Ibid.*, p. 428.

Scripture cannot and may not be thought of as a book of law. The revelation contained in Scripture is an historical and organic whole. Thus, it must be read and explained. The authority of Scripture is different from that of a law enacted by a legislature. God's Word has historical contours.[44] That implies reflection, listening, attention, insight and gradation with respect to the kind of scriptural authority. One must take into account all data concerning the entrance of God's Word into this world. A reference to the words of Satan in Scripture has often served as an illustration for this vaguely worded distinction between historical and normative authority. But it deals with much more. The distinction is ultimately identical to the problem of the goal or purpose of Scripture. This can and must keep us from an approach to Scripture whereby we think and argue more in a deductive than an inductive manner (the self-witness). For then the Word loses its true function and runs the risk of becoming summarized in a traditional immutability that chokes the application of the rule "Sacred Scripture is *its own* interpreter."

The change in insight and ideas from previous times will not have a destructive effect on the faith of the church when Scripture itself is its true norm and "God has spoken" is its confession. But it is necessary to reflect whether it can be demonstrated that often God's Word has been understood as a leveling of words and as a law (the law of a legislature — Bavinck), which does an injustice to God's Word itself. This question is absolutely mandatory in the confrontation with new questions. In the light of modern biblical research, one becomes more and more convinced of this necessity and is thereby confronted with numerous unsolved problems. These questions did not originate with the formal problem of instrumentality, but with the clear centeredness of the biblical message, its purpose, intent, and witness. For it did not miraculously come into being outside the time of its origin, but it came to us in full and real conversation with that time. We will see later to what extent this problem already occurred in the language of Scripture, and to what extent the very language of a certain period is of pivotal significance for understanding the Word of God. But just as the language in which Scripture was written is not a purely technical and timeless instrument, so the entire Scripture has entered the time and life of man-

44. *Ibid.*, p. 429.

kind to speak to us in that way. The problem of time-relatedness is not a shadow or a threat to the confession concerning Scripture; it exhorts us to caution and patience and to intensive Bible study. More and more the church has seen this not as a frightening complication of faith but as a task implied in God's Word, coming in the form of the temporal words of men. Protest and concern about this new way of reflection stems from the desire to have the Word come in greater "clarity" and greater "simplicity" than is given to us in Scripture itself. In contrast to this illegitimate desire for transcendence, one must be reminded that all this Scripture research of analysis and gradation, of "history of the period" and literary genre, of searching for the goal and for the Word within the many words, is and must be related to the mystery of the God-breathed Scripture. This mystery is not in opposition to all research, but legitimizes it. With this legitimacy in mind, one can understand that many dangers are indeed lurking in this process, with its specific contours in a changed time (and this is true for all times of reflection on Scripture), but that the very heart of all these dangers is the fact that the *message* of Scripture can become a "stumbling block" for us. No technique or hermeneutic but the Spirit alone can save us from that danger. The Spirit of God-breathed Scripture proclaims that which can become a stumbling block to be the wisdom and the power of God; it is the touchstone of all "business that God has given to the sons of men to be busy with" (Eccl. 1:13), whether they become alienated from this mystery of the Spirit or are led by it to a deeper wonder.

The intellectual questions and dizziness should not thereby be belittled. Bavinck wrote about the "difficulties in Scripture that could not be set aside and probably would never be solved," and of "problems with which Scripture confronts us in spite of its inspiration."[45] One must not and cannot wait, he added, "until all objections have been removed and all contradictions have been reconciled." He does not thereby mean to plead for a naive simplicity in contrast to human thought and reflection, but he gives an exhortation against a scientific approach that first demands verification before one is prepared to make a choice and to act in faith. One can only walk the road of biblical research in the way of the Spirit and of the message of Scripture, in truth and purity and in expectation of

45. *Ibid.*, p. 413.

the reliable Word that testifies of Christ and continues to point the way in its human and historical form. It is not the way of logical deduction, of excluding the words, but the way of a continued association with Scripture – Scripture that is *time-related* and has *universal* authority.

CHAPTER SEVEN

THE SERVANT-FORM OF HOLY SCRIPTURE

IF, IN CONFESSING THE GOD-BREATHED CHARACTER of Scripture, we avoid the danger of contrasting the Word of God with the human word, and if therefore the humanness of Scripture is not glossed over or belittled, we can fully appreciate the amount of reflection that has been given to the form of God's Word in human writing. Since the voice of God is not heard outside created reality, and cannot be viewed as merely touching the circle of our reality and leaving it immediately thereafter, the attention given the human word is entirely legitimate and necessary. Without it, justice is not done the voice of God as sacred *writing*. This agrees fully with Scripture's encounter with us in its humanness; the confession "*is* the Word of God" does not rob it of this humanness in any way. God's speaking to us through the words of Scripture does not "deify" these human words. When King Herod made an oration, the people shouted, "The voice of a god and not of man!" (Acts 12:22). Judgment struck Herod because of this deification, with which he apparently was pleased, because "he did not give God the glory" (Acts 12:23). Human voices cannot and may not be lifted at will above their creatureliness to gloss over their human character. The voice of God cannot arbitrarily be disposed of; one may not add to or subtract from it, and one need not protect it against misunderstanding in its sovereignty in the way of God's revelation by accentuating its "divinity." This voice has its own accent and its own sound. The voice of the Lord is so powerful that it breaks the cedars of Lebanon (Ps. 29:5); it is full of majesty (Ps. 29:4); it is the wondrous voice that Israel heard out of the midst of the darkness (Deut. 5:22), the voice of the Almighty (Ezek. 1:28) falling from heaven (Dan. 4:31) like the sound of many waters (Ezek. 43:2). Thinking about God's speaking in and through the words of men should bring to mind the many biblical expressions for the voice of God. It seems as if we pass from the truly spectacular, exalted, and majestic "voice of God" to the ordinary and simple "word of men" of Holy Scripture. It is possible here to forget the glory of God, the sound of many waters, when one is intensely busy with the phenomenon of human writing that is so familiar to us. It is to be found everywhere in the world and seems to lack anything special and spectacular. Here one certainly cannot exclaim: "The voice of God and not of man." Hence the question whether that humanness is not a shadow, a limitation of the high and exalted nature of the voice of God. In this connection we often encounter the phrase "taking into service" of human words. Thus men have spoken of the *servant-form* of Scripture. Not intended to diminish its authority, this expression nonetheless seems to formulate the question in a way that does not first of all remind us of Scripture's authority and exaltedness, but of its form and appearance. The form of a servant immediately evokes concepts of servitude, humility, and subjection; but nothing inferior or disqualifying is meant in any way by this concept. This is evident from the value ascribed to true service in Scripture: service to the Lord (Eph. 6:7), and subjection to one another out of reverence for Christ (Eph. 5:21). This subjection and humility presents the question of what is meant with this servant-form of Holy Scripture, which does not seem to flow immediately from the authority and normativity attributed to Scripture in the confessions.

To understand its purpose somewhat, one should remember that this form was always discussed in relation to the form of another servant pointed to in Scripture, that of Jesus Christ. His coming into the world is specifically related to this service: "The Son of man also came not to be served but to serve" (Mk. 10:45). We see him in the form of a servant in the significant event of the washing of feet (Jn. 13:1-20). When Peter protests against this servitude, Christ makes clear how essential this ministry is in his life. The wonder of this service is related to Christ's being "Lord and Teacher" in a deep and exalted manner; this exaltedness does not nullify the service but is manifested in this humility (Jn. 13:12-14). Special reference should also be made to Philippians 2, where we read that Christ took on the *form* of a servant (Phil. 2:7; cf. Rom. 15:8). This is not at all illusive, but is true reality: he was born in the likeness of men (Phil. 2:7) and was found in human form. He emptied himself and humbled himself to death on a cross in service, surrender, humility, and sacrifice (Phil. 2:8). He did not come in the form of majesty, radiating glory, but in the form of humility and obedience, in the transition from riches to poverty (II Cor. 8:9). Regarding Philippians 2, the church has always reflected on the words of Isaiah concerning the man of sorrows: "He had no form or comeliness that we should look at him, and no beauty that we should desire him" (Isa. 53:2). This external absence of "form or comeliness" is his "form" — forsakenness, surrender, and suffering.

This form of the servant has always been placed in the center of the faith of the church — its preaching and liturgy. It is related to the emptying, the emptiness in the life of Christ, which is not adequately described with the term *occultatio* (concealment).[1] Considering all this, especially the wholly unique form of this servant, we are presented with the question of how an analogy to *this* form of a servant began to be used in speaking of Holy Scripture. This parallel appears to be quite strange at first sight. Is it not a parallel drawn between two heterogeneous "forms," that of Christ and that of Scripture? In spite of this pertinent question, it should be noted that this parallel is frequently used and apparently has a suggestive effect. One motive for the drawing of this parallel was the fact that with the doctrine of Scripture one was dealing with God's Word in the "form" of men's words, while it did not stop being God's Word. Was it not possible and meaningful to see this form of Scripture with its "and-and" quality (Word of God and word of man) in connection with the form of him who was confessed in the church to be "truly God — truly man"? It was always emphasized that the "truly man" did not form a threat to the "truly God." And a certain parallelism seemed all the more self-evident because the form of the servant Jesus Christ did not merely refer to something external but to a specific *mode* of being. Thus, it seemed possible to compare it with the mode of being of God's Word *in* the word of man. The attention is not always primarily directed to the "form of a servant" but to the form or mode of being. Thus, thought is especially given to the relationship between "the divine" and "the human" in Christ and in Scripture.

Since the human form of Christ and Scripture is discussed,

1. See Berkouwer, *The Person of Christ*, pp. 353f.

is not the mystery of Christ therefore closely related to that of Scripture? This consideration led some to speak not merely of the Holy Spirit's "taking into service" the word of man; they thought it was also possible to point to an analogy between incarnation and inscripturation against the general background that the Word became flesh. On the one hand is the thought of Christ as the Word becoming flesh (Jn. 1:14); on the other is the Word of God "becoming Scripture." Since the divine and human factors come into play with Christ as well as with Scripture, could not the God-breathed character of Scripture be illuminated in a significant way by the incarnation and its "union of the two natures"? Was it not possible to behold with the eyes of faith not only the glory of Jesus Christ in the servant form (Jn. 1:14), but also the glory of God's Word coming to us in Holy Scripture? For those who chose this line of reflection, the history of Christological doctrine acquired a certain function. The will of the church neither to separate nor to mix the "truly God" and the "truly man" in Christ led to the well-known formula of Chalcedon: "undivided and unseparated, unmixed and unchanged."

Was it not possible to use this formula for the doctrine of Scripture, which points to the unity of Christ's person? In the discussion of Scripture one thus encounters a terminology which harks back to the Christological struggle, a Nestorian or monophysitic doctrine of Scripture, for example, which indicated a separation between the divine and human or a mixture of both. The term "docetic" in reference to Scripture came into use long ago to indicate a view whereby, while the truly human did not dissolve into a "phantom," yet it did become relativized in its significance. It seemed to fit well and to offer a good criterion for the characterization of Scripture and the defense against all kinds of heresy regarding Scripture. Undeniably, there are elements in these Christological formulas that can be used with good results to point out dangers in the doctrine of Scripture. The characterization "docetic" for a doctrine of Scripture gradually received a function all its own, without further developed parallels between incarnation and inscripturation. There was a desire to ward off the notion that attention for God's Word made attention for man's word superfluous. The warning was directed against a competition syndrome that was often discussed. It was denied that the more one gave honor to the divinity, the more one pushed the humanity to the background. But none of this is a justification for the parallel between incarnation and inscripturation. There are certainly enough reasons to have a closer look at this without initially capitulating to it because of a frequently vague and inarticulate use of this analogy.

Moreover, it is useful to remember that the church did not adopt this parallel in its confessions. It obviously belongs to theological tradition, even though we frequently note in this formulation a strong awareness of the self-evidence of this parallel and of its significance for a right insight into the mystery of Scripture. It appeared to be a useful theme, shedding light on many phenomena in the Christian faith, and opening perspectives on numerous difficult questions.

It is neither possible nor necessary to offer a complete survey of the frequency and variety of usage of this analogy. We simply wish to investigate whether the manner in which this analogy is usually applied offers some help for our thinking about and reverence of Scripture. Looking around in theology, we note that the parallel takes up a good deal of room in the thought of Bavinck and Kuyper. It is explicitly referred to in Bavinck's words: "Christ became flesh, a servant without form or comeliness, the most despised among men . . . and so also the Word, the revelation of God entered creation, in the life and history of men and people in every form of dream and vision, of research and meditation, even as far as the humanly weak and ignoble; the Word became Scripture and as Scripture subjected itself to the fate of all writing."[2] This kind of parallelism of the incarnation of the Word (Jn. 1:14) and of the appearance of God's Word in human writing clearly also has the aspect of the form of a servant with reference to Philippians 2 and Isaiah 53, as Bavinck clearly indicated. Moreover, the focus is especially on the entrance of God's Word into creaturely life. We think of Bavinck's statement about Scripture as the "incarnation" of the Word.[3] To Bavinck, the parallel is not in the least accidental. It is related to his conception of organic revelation, in which he calls organic inspiration "the unfolding and application of the central fact of revelation, the incarnation of the Word."[4] Thus, Holy Scripture is closely related to the salvation of God in Jesus Christ, always confessed by the church. However, it now

2. *GD*, I, 405.
3. *Ibid.*, p. 349.
4. *Ibid.*, p. 405.

receives the function of a *structural* analysis, taking its cue from the mode of the entrance of God's Word into this world in human form. Just as the incarnation of Christ demands that it be searched after to the depths of humiliation and in "all its weakness and revilement,"[5] so the writing of God's Word, the revelation of God, invites us also "to recognize in Scripture that weak and humble aspect, the form of a servant." A certain conclusion to this argument should be noted along with others, namely, that a parallel exists not only in general between incarnation and inscripturation, but also between Christ's sinlessness and the infallibility of Scripture. "Just as the human in Christ, though weak and humble, yet remained free from sin, so also was Scripture conceived without blemish."[6] Finally, a second perspective was added to this parallel, as it was pointed out that resistance to the Spirit was related to resistance to Christ. We need not be amazed that Holy Scripture is being contradicted in the world. "Christ carried a cross, and a servant is not greater than his master. Scripture is the maidservant of Christ. She shares his revilement. She evokes hostility from sinful man."[7]

Several of these themes also played a role with Kuyper, especially revelation's entering into this world. It is not a "transcendent phenomenon standing outside of our human reality," but it enters into our world.[8] In terms of the analogy, Kuyper points out that revelation occurs in two ways in the world: in the world of *being* by means of the incarnation of the *Logos,* and in the world of *consciousness,* because this same *Logos* is inscripturated, so that there is a parallel between incarnation and inscripturation. Just as the Word of God came to us in the cradle of Bethlehem, that is, in the world of our life, so Scripture comes to us in our thoughts and conceptions. Human form becomes the bearer of the divine factor, and that human factor is not first perfected for that purpose but is adopted as it is.[9] Because of all this, revelation has a bridge-building character. God's thoughts take on form and are expressed in human language.[10]

These thoughts of Bavinck and Kuyper presuppose that

5. *Ibid.,* p. 406.
6. *Ibid.*
7. *Ibid.,* p. 411.
8. *Princ.,* p. 478.
9. *Ibid.,* pp. 478-79.
10. Kuyper, *The Work of the Holy Spirit,* pp. 61f.

God's Word is among us in the form of men's words. This thought almost always assumes a central position in the reflection concerning Scripture. Barth calls it the "worldliness" of revelation: "We do not possess the Word of God otherwise than in the mystery of its worldliness," that is, in a form of our human world. The word encounters us "in the garments of creaturely reality" as the reality of fallen man.[11]

However, it is not our aim to pursue this speculation on the mode of revelation. Theology has always been concerned with it in speaking of the "condescension of God" and wishing to indicate the style of God's revelation. A reference to this style does not betray a sense of disappointment; the aim is rather to point to the glory in this humble human form. All this obviously stems from Christology. The form of a servant does not relativize revelation but passes it on and reveals its true riches. The way of Christ, the great servant, runs parallel to the way of the Word – Scripture in the form of a servant.

These and similar thoughts are continually encountered in many diverse nuances and variations. They are clearly not intended to be mere superficial word play, but to illuminate the reality of Scripture and its secret, the mystery of its God-breathed character. It almost seems at times as though this parallel has become an ecumenical "joint opinion," this form of a servant being a matter of course. A closer look, however, reveals an increasing number of questions touching on the legitimacy of whether or not a rationalization is found in this parallelism, concentrated as it is on the union of the divine and human factors – a rationalization not only of the mystery of Holy Scripture but also of the person of Christ. For this union of factors does not at all reach the level of the "personal union" that the church expressed in its confessions. Quite often one gets the impression that with these factors he is busy solving a "problem" and therefore considers the possibility as well as the mode of such a union. Even aside from these problems (Kuyper uses the example of marriage), the question may be posed whether this parallel is possible and meaningful. For with respect to Scripture, such a "personal union" is not at all at stake. This question is so self-evident that it always led to a delineation of the boundaries of this analogy. So Warfield wrote of "only a remote analogy," and for a moment it seems

11. *CD,* I/1, p. 188. Cf. "Were God to speak to us in a non-worldly way, He would not speak to us at all" (p. 192).

that he rejects the entire analogy: "There is no hypostatic union between the divine and human in Scripture; we cannot parallel the 'inscripturation' of the Holy Spirit and the incarnation of the Son of God."[12]

Others have also called attention to the limitations of this analogy. Yet the analogy continued to function, and it appears to have rendered a service in illuminating the truth of Scripture. Thus, even Warfield writes that "in both cases divine and human factors are involved" and "even so distant an analogy" shows that it can be said both regarding Christ and Scripture that "by the conjoint action of human and divine factors, the human factors . . . cannot have fallen into that error, which we say it is human to fall into."[13] Thus, the parallel is especially concentrated on the "sinlessness" of Christ and the "inerrancy" of Scripture.[14] So the analogy, insufficient by itself, does function again in doctrinal conclusions. It is noteworthy in all this that the analogy is first relativized because of the absence of the "personal union," while later the analogy is used as an apologetic with reference to the parallel between sinlessness and inerrancy. Yet these are comprehended on such different levels that they can surely not be used convincingly to clarify the infallibility of Scripture. The fact that this path is nonetheless chosen is related to the problems of establishing union between the divine and human "factors." But certainly no justice is thus done to the verse "the Word became flesh" (Jn. 1:14), nor to the concept of God's Word in human words. A confusing use of analogy occurs here, and it remains necessary to view this apologetic critically, even though the intention is undoubtedly to honor Scripture.

This apologetic theme starts from the result of the "personal union" and concludes that there is no shadow over the incarnation or this inscripturation because of a misunderstanding of the phrase "like unto us in all things." However, the statement about Christ, who has been tempted as we have in

12. *Inspiration,* p. 162. Cf. also J. Packer regarding the analogy: "only a limited one" (*Fundamentalism,* p. 83).
13. *Ibid.,* pp. 162-163.
14. Cf. Packer, p. 83, who says of the evangelical, non-critical doctrine of Scripture that it "corresponds to Christological orthodoxy" in contrast to "Nestorian" biblical criticism which divides the divine and human. This argument from the history of doctrine bears a different character from the indication of a docetic view of Scripture, which functions as a clarifying guideline without claiming a Christological foundation.

every respect, without sinning, is a doxological confession of the glory of this high priest (Heb. 4:15). We find all the blessed comfort implied in his sinlessness during temptation, assuring access to the throne of grace and mercy (Heb. 4:16). No one will deny that this glory is testified to and passed on to us in the human words coming to us as God's Word. However, this relatedness of the apostolic witness is entirely different from the paralleling of the two qualities of sinlessness and inerrancy. In that way, a weaker parallelism takes the place of the relatedness of Scripture to salvation in Christ.[15]

As we have seen, the element of union plays an important role in the parallel between incarnation and inscripturation. Yet it is difficult to understand how such a theme can do justice to the mystery of Scripture and the confession "Sacred Scripture *is* the Word of God." For this confession does not say that Scripture originates from a union of divine and human factors, but points to the mystery of the human words *as* God's Word. The approach of Scripture, which points to men moved by the Spirit (II Pet. 1:21), is quite different from that of a "mysterious" union (as it is often called), which could be paralleled with the personal union. If we follow this theme of union and take the word "union" seriously, we confront the inescapable question of whether the adoration of Holy Scripture is then legitimate. Even though those who employed the analogy rejected this adoration from the start, the question is not thereby proven meaningless. In Christology, adoration was often mentioned in connection with the real personal union, as well as with the church's confession "truly God – truly man." It was also asked whether adoration of Christ's human nature was abstract and dualistic in many respects (concerning human nature in itself),[16] but the question can at least be appreciated in view of certain presuppositions (union as reality).

The adoring words of Thomas (Jn. 20:28) have always been a subject for meditation in view of the concept of "truly God – truly man," and there was no hesitation for an "adoration of Christ." But almost no one drew a similar conclusion from

15. As examples of the use of this analogy, we name among others Emil Brunner, *Revelation and Reason* (ET, 1946), p. 276, with the conclusion of a fallible-imperfect Scripture in its servant-form. See further P. Althaus, "Theologie des Glaubens," *Zeitschrift für Systematische Theologie* (1924), p. 314. Many other examples may be found in the important study of M. Barth, *Conversation with the Bible,* Ch. 5.
16. See *The Person of Christ,* pp. 289f.

this regarding Scripture, and bibliolatry was rejected. This very hesitation — which is correct and legitimate — reveals by hindsight the problematic character of the union whereby Scripture would become divine and human. This is truly something quite different from the "from God," so decisive for the confession of the God-breathed character of Scripture. Markus Barth rightly posed the question of whether the adoration of Scripture should not be considered a consequence of the traditional analogy.[17] This question does not intend to force anyone to certain conclusions, but merely calls for a reflection on the theme of union and the "mysterious" prolongation as a possible result of it. The honoring of Scripture and the praise of the Word (Ps. 56:10), and the trembling at the words of the God of Israel (Ezra 9:3; 10:3) would become remote with this bibliolatry. It is wrong to see in this analogy a true theological thesis of the Reformation which was accidentally not taken into the confessions.

The search for analogies brings with it a movement in the direction of problems concerning union that overshadow Christology as well as the doctrine of Scripture. The "is" of Scripture is of scant significance in the union (of natures or "factors" of the divine and human). Because of the doctrine of Scripture, Christology is gradually pulled into this idea of union in the analogy. It is no longer fully understood that the "personal union" does not fit into such a framework and was not thus understood and confessed by the church. The church did not see a synthesis of the divine and human in this personal union. One who follows this path (even when merely using terms such as "factor") and employs the idea of analogy is bound to come to a Christology that indeed rejects every "mixture" (as a result of union), yet hinders the perspective on the "truly God — truly man." As a result, reflection moves away from the confession of the church because of a theoretical interest in the "possibility" of the union. Those who share the opinion that the analogy — taken seriously — does not offer a real contribution to a true understanding of God-breathed Scripture will fully realize that Scripture cannot be placed on an altar without adversely affecting its meaning, riches, and depth. Scripture was not given to us in the climate of a stupendous miracle, and by speaking with certainty of its *mystery* we aim at something quite different from such a miracle.

17. *Conversation,* p. 156.

This defense does not relativize Scripture but is needed in order not to detach Scripture from its God-breathed character in the dispensation of the spirit of Christ. Confessing the "is" will continue to be meaningful to the church, since it points the right direction for the church's journey through the world under God's Word. The defense against the theme of union does not stem from a distaste for ontology, but from a respect for that which is "ontic" expressed in the "is" as mystery of Scripture.[18] Indeed, we are not dealing with a change or transubstantiation of the human word with this "is"; but it would be a mistake to believe that only in this way would the "is," this identification, be possible and meaningful. We are rather again reminded of the reality and truth of the description of hearing the apostles' word as the word of Christ himself (Lk. 10:16). This identity is filled with the mystery of the Spirit. And this mystery of the God-breathed Scripture is full of authority, urging obedience to this Lord, the Christ of Scripture.

This analysis of the analogy between incarnation and inscripturation is not intended to disqualify every reference to Scripture in the form of a servant. We believe rather that reflection about this aspect of Scripture frequently led to a special interest for the "form" rather than for the "servant." Many parallels, including the apologetic parallels, make this clear. Hence, we do well not only to think about that form — the human word and Scripture — but of Scripture in the form of a servant. Bavinck's description of the form implies that it is impossible even for a moment to isolate the servant from the form, because this very form is aimed at service. He states that Scripture "subjected itself to the fate of all writing,"[19] and he relates this to the engaging of human thoughts and conceptions, of human language and human weakness.[20] The attention to this form is not thereby criticized. This attention is fully legitimate in the realization of the limitations of language, which may result in various questions and problems of translation and interpretation.

This attention for Scripture as a human phenomenon of language has always deeply influenced the view of the form of a servant. This attention need not lead to the notion of

18. H. M. Kuitert, *The Reality of Faith* (ET, 1968), p. 188.
19. *GD*, I, 405.
20. *Ibid.*

an impure and unreliable Scripture, but a special and peculiar aspect of this Scripture was indeed realized — that it came to us to such an extent in human form and thought. Obviously, this form was not limited to the written Word. It can also be considered in relation to the spoken human word and to the question of how this weak human word can be of service to the speaking of God. In reading Scripture we encounter some of the questions aroused in men related to this, objections to becoming bearers of God's Word. Moses does not deem himself "eloquent" (Ex. 4:10), and Isaiah exclaims "Woe is me" because he is a man of unclean lips (Isa. 6:5); Jeremiah claims that he cannot speak because of his youth (Jer. 1:6). But the God of Israel points the way to witnessing in spite of such objections and falterings. He will be with Moses' mouth and teach him what he shall speak (Ex. 4:12; 7:2); he touches Isaiah's mouth with a burning coal from the altar (Isa. 6:6, 7); and Jeremiah's fear is conquered (Jer. 1:8). This divine taking-into-service has an aspect of triumph and sovereignty, yet it does not erase the weakness of the human word nor its limitations. Time and again we note a vivid awareness of God's using weak human "instruments." We remember Paul's words concerning his apostolic ministry: "But we have this treasure in earthen vessels" (II Cor. 4:7).

This text unmistakably indicates a certain tension with regard to preaching with human words. Thinking about Scripture in the form of a servant, Bavinck evidently had this statement of Paul in mind. Though he does not quote this text specifically, he summarizes the speaking of God in human language with this intent: "All this has happened in order to show that the transcendent power, also the power of Scripture, belongs to God and not to us."[21] The words "also the power of Scripture" are added to Paul's reference to the power of God. It obviously refers to the ministry of the human word and human writing. The idea of treasure dominates Paul's entire train of thought when writing of this "treasure in earthen vessels," and his preaching witnesses to it. But however intent he is upon this treasure, he remains aware that it is in earthen vessels. What is the meaning of this discrepancy or disproportionate relationship? It is far from being a word of sad uncertainty or relativity. The remarkable thing is that possessing the treasure in precisely this way is not regarded

21. *Ibid.*

as a regrettable, peripheral phenomenon casting a shadow, but is related to the power of God. It becomes manifest — in view of the treasure in earthen vessels — that the power is not ours but God's. This agrees with Paul's entire preaching: he does not make the ministry of the Word a problem, yet he does not forget the nature of this weak medium, the weakness of man. He is not only aware of being an "instrument" (Acts 9:15), but also to what extent this being an instrument belongs to the sphere of weakness (II Cor. 3:5-6). The treasure is in earthen vessels; that God passes on the treasure and speaks his word in this human way appears to be a mystery. In this connection Bavinck rightly speaks also of the "power of Scripture" and its clarity: it belongs to God and not to us, God revealing himself in the weakness and limitation of human words. It is possible to stop before this human boundary without discovering any perspective in this human word. From Moses to the prophets men have rebelled against this human proclamation of the Word of God. Moses knew the fear of this rebellion: "But behold, they will not believe me or listen to my voice, for they will say 'the Lord did not appear to you'" (Ex. 4:1). The sign of the rod and the serpent, indicating a unique legitimacy, is the answer of Yahweh. And the anger of Yahweh is kindled when Moses still tries to escape from his mission: "Oh, my Lord, send, I pray, some other person" (Ex. 4:13-14). The Word of God, as is evident time and again, does not come in an overbearing manner, excluding every question, reflection, and criticism — even though it is directly addressed to man, making him responsible; but because of this human word it comes in a mode that makes it possible to ask for the name of the one who sent Moses (Ex. 3:13). This ministry is established by the sign that makes it legitimate. Not rational clarification or human verification opened the way: "Say this to the people of Israel, 'I AM has sent me to you'" (Ex. 3:14). The proclamation is a treasure in earthen vessels, and the treasure does not fade and disappear in the fragility of the human instrument. The earthen vessel does not stand in the way of God's voice precisely because the power of God is manifested in it and not because man in his own power has this treasure at his disposal (Ex. 4:14-15).

Thus, the Word of God, Scripture in the form of a servant, is not known to us in the outlines of a supernatural miracle lifted out of time and human weakness, excluding all questions *ipso facto,* but in the human form of word and writing. The human word, even in the written form, must be heard and read, translated and interpreted.

God could have chosen another route, a more direct route to reveal himself to man, as Luther once said. We need not ask what these divine "possibilities" might have been according to Luther, for the reference is merely a preamble to call attention to the inescapable function of the written Word.[22] The "treasure" is a decisive factor of this function, but it may not be forgotten that it came to us in a human mode. Holy Scripture as God's Word traverses a long history with man; it is a part of history and is not submerged in it, neither is it lifted above it, thereby losing the essential relation to it. The Word came to us in specific human languages and precisely in this manner demonstrates its way through the world. What from a postulated view of certainty appears to be a dangerous adventure and risk[23] – the humanness and historicity – is unquestionably the very reality of Scripture. And it is meaningful again to call attention to God's answer to Moses, who because of his weakness deemed the risk of his human witness too great to make it legitimate. This divine answer is decisive for the confession concerning Scripture.

When we reflect on Scripture in the form of a servant, we should recall Bavinck's theme of the "stumbling block" of Scripture, for it plays an important role in relationship to resistance and rebellion, even hostility against Scripture. Though Bavinck discussed this idea in the context of the analogy between incarnation and inscripturation, it is not really related to this analogy. It is not the parallel that is of central importance here, but the relatedness of Scripture's witness to Christ. Bavinck, it should be emphasized, does not use the analogical argument precisely at this point, for his formulation is aimed at "relatedness": "Since it [Holy Scripture] commits to writing the revelation of God in Christ, it must arouse the same resistance as Christ himself."[24] He discusses inspiration in this connection, particularly the Spirit, who does not withdraw from Scripture but still makes it God-breathed, bearing and inspiring the Scripture and "applying its content to the heart and conscience of man in various forms." Thus, it battles

22. Regarding Luther, see K. Löwith, "Die Sprache als vermittler von Mensch und Welt," *Das Problem der Sprache in Theol. und Kirche* (1959), pp. 52f.
23. Cf. *TDNT*, VIII, 181.
24. *GD*, I, 410.

with human consideration, and for that reason "no one need be amazed" at resistance to and attacks on Scripture ("at all times").[25]

As a servant, Scripture is not greater than its master: it shares the revilement of Christ and evokes the hostility of sinful man.[26] Here we are on quite a different level from that of the analogy of incarnation and inscripturation. We may indeed speak of analogy here, but it is determined by the nature of Scripture's witness to Christ. And so it is in complete harmony with the analogy used for living persons in his service. Christ said: "A disciple is not above his teacher, nor a servant above his master" (Mt. 10:24). In Scripture as the "maid-servant" of Christ we encounter the witness concerning him, and for that reason it shares his revilement in the lawsuit concerning *this* testimony. This analogy is not viewed as a miracle in Scripture, arousing amazement because of its mysterious nature, nor the resistance of those who refuse to believe in a "divine" book where precisely the voice of man is heard; but it points to a legitimacy *in* God-breathed Scripture.

In my opinion, Bavinck rightly saw at this very point that the traditional analogy between incarnation and inscripturation was not the center of the discussion concerning Scripture. He indeed uses this analogy, but adds that incarnation and inscripturation do not only run parallel "but are also very intimately related."[27] The way is implicitly opened for a clear insight into the intimate connection between the Spirit of Christ and Scripture, including a perspective on the "stumbling block" of Scripture. This is not a second stumbling block, next to the one mentioned by Paul (I Cor. 1:23), but one inseparably connected with and related to it. For that reason Bavinck can speak of the "ethical significance" of the battle over Scripture carried on through all ages. This struggle is not accidental, but can be explained in relation to Christ himself, who came into the world for "judgment."[28] He did not thereby mean to give a simple solution to the discussion of the problems of Scripture in its human-verbal form, for Bavinck struggled intensely with it. But he did confess the miracle of the

25. *Ibid.*, p. 411.
26. *Ibid.*
27. *Ibid.*, pp. 354 and 397.
28. *Ibid.*, p. 410.

God-breathed character of Scripture, of the Holy Spirit's urging in Scripture's witness for a decision made necessary in the crisis concerning Christ, so that Scripture was not seen as a revelatory phenomenon *in itself*. The emphasis on this writing and this God-breathed Scripture is not a superficial judgment but – in the midst of theological reflection – a warning against darkening the horizon of the "God said" and the mystery of Scripture, a warning also against all dead orthodoxy for not recognizing this secret of Scripture, though it intended to honor it fully.

The secret of God-breathed Scripture is that God's Word can be "near" to man. He has a unique responsibility, rendering impossible any excuse that the Word is "far off," so that one must "bring it from heaven" or from "beyond the sea" (Deut. 30:11-13). This text is the preface to the statement that "the word is very near you; it is in your mouth and in your heart, so that you can do it" (Deut. 30:14). Paul adopted it, and his interpretation refers to "the word of faith which we preach" (Rom. 10:8). Such authoritative words can be written concerning the human act of preaching, and urgent conclusions can be drawn from the fact that one is sent and preaches and hears: faith comes from what is heard (Rom. 10:14-17). The transition from this hearing to the God-breathed Scripture is not odd; it corresponds with the progression of human life and history. But its relation is to the mystery of the Spirit's taking Scripture into its service because of its unique content and intention, referring not to a mysterious occurrence but to the beautiful feet "of those who preach good news" *as* it is written (Rom. 10:15).

Speaking of this Word of God in the form of human words and writings, one must remember the responsibility implied in the nature of this God-breathed Scripture, a responsibility of the church in its preaching. For this is the light of the gospel and therefore also the confession of Scripture as God's Word. At the same time, it is necessary to pay due respect to the critical function of this confession. Bavinck's reference to the hostility against Scripture, to the foolishness of the world's wisdom before God, is meaningful and not arbitrary. Likewise, he writes of the "exalted place" of Scripture,[29] pointing out that, regarding the meaning of Scripture, it is not the hearers

29. *Ibid.,* p. 411.

but the doers of Scripture who are called blessed.[30] He points to the mistaken opinion of "the men of biblical criticism," that the man in the pew knows and feels nothing of the objections raised against Scripture nor of the problems involved in continuing to believe in Scripture.[31] Such a distinction between "science" and "simple faith" would be understandable if we could limit ourselves only to questions raised by biblical scholarship. But, according to Bavinck, the authority of Scripture concerns every Christian, lettered or unlettered, in a continuing struggle "to keep man's thoughts imprisoned under obedience to Christ."[32]

In this way the nature of God-breathed Scripture unfolds itself as the maid-servant of Christ. This deep confession of faith was expressed in the formula "Sacred Scripture is the Word of God." This confession can be attacked by humanizing and despoiling the divinity of Scripture. But one can also be led astray by failing to see God's Word in this form of a servant and even by fearing the problems implied in this complete and true humanness of Scripture. This fear comes from the weakness of some which is expressed in the prayer "lead us not into temptation." But this prayer is not seeking an escape, not even in relation to the attention to Scripture in its verbal form. The stumbling block for the lettered and the unlettered is not that we are called on to "believe in stupendous miracles," but it is found in the witness testifying "of him." Having the choice raised by this stumbling block, it will be possible and legitimate to give concentrated attention not only to the service but also to the form of this service. Then this service will not vanish in speculations that intend to honor God's Word but where it is not truly heard in the "is" – in the human witness. The promise of the complete equipment of the man of God casts a radiant glow over the habit of continually and reverently reading Scripture (II Tim. 3:17). The test of all Bible study and all preaching is whether or not this promise is neglected or forgotten during the sometimes weary journey of research, of needed translation into other languages, with its implied "techniques," and the interpretation of Scripture. So clear and stimulating is the promise that no one should hesitate to continue on this road because

30. *Ibid.*, p. 412.
31. *Ibid.*
32. *Ibid.*

of the many dangers on the horizon. Thus, there is the promise of the Spirit, which is not attacked but reinforced by the admonition to everyone who encounters this *servant-form* of Scripture: "Let anyone who thinks that he stands take heed lest he fall" (I Cor. 10:12).

CHAPTER EIGHT

TRANSLATION AND HISTORICITY

BY CONNECTING THE TWO WORDS "translation" and "historicity," we wish to call attention to the fact that the church recognized that Holy Scripture had to be translated. The historical character of Scripture, its "historicity" as part of the history and life of man, is thereby clearly indicated. The term "historicity" does not imply an historicism that relativizes every consistency and reliability. It does not argue from the historical character of all that determines human life and from the "homogeneousness" of all historical events to a necessary historicization and leveling of truth.[1] We rather call attention to the fact that God's Word truly went into history and participated in it.[2] Bavinck writes, that Holy Scripture has been subjected to "the fate of all human writings." This is not only true regarding the nature of the biblical books written by men, but also because Scripture did not come to us in a supra-historical and supra-human language, able as such to encompass and penetrate all ages and all divergences of language. Scripture came instead in concretely human and localized languages, limited with respect to their intelligibility. This fact gave rise to the immediate necessity of translating God's Word into other languages as it goes out into the world to testify of "the mighty works of God" (Acts 2:11). In that way Scripture could be made accessible to all nations. In our time the term "translation" of Scripture's message is frequently used in a different sense, not simply to denote a problem of

1. The influence of this historicizing and relativizing has become very great in the last few centuries, not only with regard to the doctrine of Scripture, but also regarding the concepts of the church and of dogma (the history of dogma as critic of dogma). Cf. B. Lohse, *A Short History of Christian Doctrine* (ET, 1966), pp. 225f. For a general orientation, see G. Bauer, *Geschichtlichkeit: Wege und Irrwege eines Begriffs* (1963).
2. Cf. Kuitert, *The Reality of Faith*, pp. 151f.

language. It indicates a necessary "translation" of the message of the gospel into an age with different conceptions and ideas, with experiences and an outlook on life different from those prevalent in earlier times. Translation then entails a certain "bridge-building function," or *preaching* with a view toward the intelligibility of the gospel. The use of translation in this sense is not equivalent to, but closely related to, making the gospel relevant, because it aims at intelligibility for the present time. This kind of translation intends to tune the words of Scripture into the channel of our time, in which some ancient concepts are no longer understood. Understandably, a good deal of discussion took place regarding this theme of translation, dealing with the question of how one ought to translate so that the message would not begin to fade; for making the gospel relevant would look more like "accommodation" than true translation. It is possible to translate the gospel in such a way as to remove all stumbling blocks for humans from it; and then Paul's statement that the gospel is not man's gospel is forgotten (Gal. 1:11).

In this chapter, however, we are not thinking first of all of this sense of translating, but of translation as it is normally meant. Like the new sense of translation of the message, though, problems of time and intelligibility – which gave rise to this new meaning of the term "translation" – are also at stake in the old usage of the term. This is all the more reason to ponder the normal sense of translation from one language into another. For this translation is directly related to the fact that God's Word as Scripture came in languages foreign to most people. Translating is therefore needed to break through barriers and conquer distances in order that Scripture may speed on unhindered (Acts 28:31) and triumph (II Thess. 3:1). This problem of translation is already implied, so to speak, in the great commission of Matthew 28:19, the call to proclaim the gospel to "all nations," as well as in the charge to be a witness "to the end of the earth" (Acts 1:8). Every localization and nationalization is thereby broken through in the perspective of universality. The necessity to translate Scripture in view of the divisions of language and speech is self-evident. It is illustrated by the church's interest in the work of Bible translation. However, this does not mean that reflection on "translation" is superfluous; for it reminds us that Scripture is conditioned by its human-verbal form. It clearly shows the characteristics of particular times, peoples, and circumstances.

Complications in the understanding of Scripture are inseparably connected with translation. The word "complication" is not an exaggeration to those who are concerned with actual Scripture. Problems of language and understanding play an important role in all exegesis and reflection. Scripture did not come to us through a supernatural language to be understood only by mysterious and charismatic means. It came through limited human languages and thus assumed a good deal of misunderstanding for those lacking the knowledge of these languages. The experience of Scripture is not like the event of Pentecost, where each heard the proclamation of the mighty deeds of God "in his own language" (Acts 2:6). That event indeed places the universal aspect of salvation in the center and, when the Spirit is poured out on all flesh (Acts 2:17), conquers all distances, particularly the distances of language. But it is impossible to close one's eyes to the historicity of Scripture just because of the mystery of Pentecost, and to be blind to the necessity of letting the written Word go out into the world in other intelligible words in order to conquer the "strangeness."

The universality of Pentecost does not offer a pattern for the *form* of Scripture concerning its accessibility to the world. Rather, it opens the way for the necessity of translation in the horizontality of history. This horizontality does not at all indicate a contravention of the vertical nature of the speaking of God (the "from God"). Rather, horizontality, with its problems of tradition, translation, and the passing on of the gospel message, arises from the importance of this "from God." There is no such thing as a language of revelation that participates so absolutely in revelation that its sanctity, exclusiveness, and perspicuity break through all barriers, thus becoming a vehicle to testify and disclose to the world the salvation of God. A specific structure of God's Word and a certain isolation in the world have been supposed by some, without denying the necessity to translate Scripture: they particularly had the so-called language of Canaan in mind. But it should be noted that Scripture itself does not mention this "language" as an isolated phenomenon. Instead, it opens a wide perspective on salvation when, according to Isaiah's prophecy, "there will be five cities in the land of Egypt which speak the language of Canaan" (Isa. 19:18). This does not indicate an adoption of Israel's language, but that the world will become related to the salvation of Israel's God, breaking the barriers that limited salvation to Israel alone.

The progress of Scripture's testimony in the world of nations shows that its blessings do not occur only in a miraculous way. It happens in the natural human way of language, without any derogation of the sovereignty of the divine witness. It is an "ordinary" way, so to speak, at least if one detaches from this term any triviality and understands Scripture anew in its glorious humanness. In that case, traveling the road of knowledge and research, including the numerous well-known problems of translating God's Word precisely into other languages, becomes unavoidable. One must reject the notion that translation is a simple matter; it is not merely a technique of word-transferring that is rather easily executed with the help of a dictionary. It is the complicated and challenging work of transposing material from one world of thought and language into another. Here the aspect of historicity is well known because of the numerous translations contradicting and correcting each other. But because of Scripture's witness of God's message of salvation to all nations, translation is of a particularly urgent character.

Does not any translation imply an immediate distancing from the original, and does not an element of foreignness and thus relativity remain a part of the communication of God's Word? Nida refers to the despair that some have experienced of pouring old wine into new wineskins. Even though he does not deny the necessity of translation, he adds: "There may well be reason to complain of translating, when one examines closely what happens to a document in the process of being transferred from one language to another."[3] In the actual job of translation, one will soon discover that little is meant by a "literal" translation, even though he may plead for it. We need only note Schwarz's remark concerning God's Word in the world: "No translation is final" or — more poignantly — "Every modern translation is an interpretation of the original work."[4] Questions multiply when, regarding ideas about Bible translation, he distinguishes between the "traditional, the philo-

3. E. A. Nida, *Toward a Science of Translation: With Special Reference to Principles and Procedures Involved in Bible Translating* (1964), p. 1.
4. W. Schwarz, *Principles and Problems of Biblical Translation: Some Reformation Controversies and Their Background* (1955), foreword and p. 1.

logical, and the inspirational view," variations wherein every problem of subjectivity in translation plays a role. According to Nida, the danger in scientific prose is minimal, "but in religious texts it may be rather great."[5] Is interpretation in order only after the (technical) translation, or does it already play an important role *during* translation?[6] Here we treat the problem of translation as a bridge over a fairly large gap, a bridge that is of essential significance for God's Word in the world.

Some have taken this labor of translation as self-evident, reflecting on parallel situations when human literature must reach further than one's own limited language area. But they should ponder the peculiarity of God's Word, that when it is understood and hearers of the Word become doers, it ignites a tremendous human activity. It is moreover an activity making an *understanding* possible for others. Thinking of the way of the Spirit through the world beforehand, we would be inclined to invent a more excellent way whereby the coming of the Word would be exclusively under the care of God. For this only would seem to guarantee a pure and complete penetration of the Word without endangering the Word of God in human hands. These considerations, however, would be a mere postulate that does not agree with reality. Article III of the Belgic Confession speaks of God's care, his particular care whereby he commanded prophets and apostles "for us and for our salvation" to put his revealed Word into writing. But apparently this care does not imply that Scripture in its concrete form entered the world in a pure immutability and in a language clear to all. It entered *history,* so that it shows the contours of historic conditions. This is clearly evident already in the historical situations of the Old Testament. In Nehemiah 8:8, when Ezra opens the book of the law and instructs the Levites, we read: "And they read from the book, from the law of God, clearly; and they gave the sense, so that the people understood the reading." It is generally agreed that the word "clearly" does not refer to speech that was clearly audible, but to a reading by means of *translation.* The returned exiles had become accustomed to the Aramaic language, so that it had become more and more the colloquial language in Pal-

5. Nida, p. 154.
6. *Ibid.,* p. 155, regarding "the role of the translator."

estine.[7] In order to make the words of the Law understandable and acceptable, the Torah, written in Hebrew, was translated and read clearly in that sense. A gap that had slowly widened was bridged, a language barrier broken through. It is possible in an historical situation that God's Word becomes technically inaccessible, so to speak, and is no longer meaningful in the form of that specific language.

Conclusions minimizing the problems inherent in the reality of translating Scripture ought to be avoided. An appeal to the "providence of God" for solving these problems in order to justify a human "idealistic" concept of Scripture is not possible. Besides, starting with such an idealistic concept, we would soon stumble over a great many difficulties because of the well-known fact that we do not possess the original manuscripts of the books of the Bible. This in itself calls for a necessary and intense human activity. This activity implies more than a simple registration, since it requires a choice between various textual recensions in every case. It is not permissible to regard the differences as absolutely unimportant.

Numerous examples illustrate that a difference in text undoubtedly affects the interpretation of a saying in Scripture. One must, for instance, make a choice with respect to Romans 5:1: "Therefore, since we are justified by faith, we have peace with God." There are two possibilities for the original text: the *assertion* that we have peace with God, or an *admonition* to have peace with God. Kümmel, for example, believes that the latter reading is supported by better manuscripts.[8] But since this meaning does not fit with verse 2 (the *gift* of grace), Kümmel investigates the meaning of "peace" in the Pauline corpus with the conclusion that the former reading must be preferred in spite of its support by manuscripts of less significance. Many share this opinion. One realizes in view of this that textual criticism is not simply a technique of comparison in order to establish the text in a technical manner; judgment clearly plays a role, since it takes sentence structure and content into account. Frequently, doctrinal discussion is involved. Various motivations may play a role in this process which appears to be a simple establishment of the text. This indicates that Scripture was not given to us in a form elevated above

7. A. Noordtzij, *Korte Verklaring: Nehemia;* H. H. Grosheide, *Comm. op Ezra en Nehemia,* I, 151.
8. O. Kaiser and W. G. Kümmel, *Exegetical Method* (ET, 1967), pp. 50f.

time but on the human level of historicity; human judgment is thus not wholly excluded from the start. Hence, there is every reason to discuss the phenomenon of textual criticism before we go on to reflect on translation as an indication of historicity.

The distinction between textual criticism and biblical criticism is generally known. Its meaning is that the textual critic does not set himself on a pedestal above God's Word but wishes to search for this very Word in its original form. Though it has bearing on the text of Scripture, the word "criticism" is more carefully used in the sense of a controlling human function in judgment. The acceptance of this "textual criticism" is clearly related to the manner in which Holy Scripture was given to us. Obviously, it was not given to us in such a form that on the subjective human side it was merely possible and permissible to listen, with the exclusion of any "judgment." Concern for a correct text shows clearly that this listening is set in a certain context. Textual criticism would be superfluous, according to Kuyper, "if it had pleased God to leave us perfect autographs."[9] Since this is not the case, we must respect the historical aspects related to it. Kuyper's opinion about why the original handwriting is no longer at our disposal is that "such autographs would soon lead to idolatry, and it apparently pleased God to subject his Holy Scripture to the vicissitudes of time to ward off this evil rather than subject his church to the temptation of idolatry."[10]

Opinions will differ concerning these considerations of divine motivations and providential intentions concerning the loss of the "autographs." But we are interested in the real "fact" of Scripture, which led Kuyper to speak of "the vicissitudes of time." It demands our attention and may not be ignored by a call for listening to the voice of God.[11] In this connection Kuyper speaks of uncertainty that soon arose with respect to the text of the autographs. It is a state of affairs that characterizes the entire revelation, namely, "the complete lack of mechanical, judicial precision." It forces us to exert every

9. *Enc.*, III, 67.
10. *Ibid.*, p. 68.
11. Bavinck discusses the absence of autographs in connection with Scripture's own standard of measurement (no exact knowledge, as in the sciences). "Therefore are the autographs lost; therefore is the text, no matter how slightly, corrupt" (*GD*, I, 416).

effort to "find our way in uncertainty."[12] But he adds immediately that also with respect to the text Scripture falls under the special providence of God, and that the Spirit did not cease to be the "doctor of the church" even during dark times.[13] That a falsification would occur in such a degree that the truth and therefore the future of the church would be at stake was impossible. Scripture was never "forsaken by God." The horizon of providence becomes visible "with the corruption of the text."[14] It runs through the ordinary course of events whereby a mystical factor also played a role in the church, which in the fear of the Lord kept an "unparalleled watch" for the text. Though contingency seemed apparent, it was not left to chance;[15] thus, one may not speak of a "false Bible." But the right and duty to do the minute labor of text criticism is not thereby denied. Even the possibility of *conjecture* must be maintained.[16] A certain "margin"[17] demanding critical research must be allowed even by those who frown on the word "accidents." For "precision is foreign to the totality of revelation." Terms such as "probable" text or "a degree of probability"[18] — rendering the text somewhat uncertain — have no effect on the reliability of Scripture and our certainty under God's "permission," according to Kuyper.[19] The presence of this margin calls for our attention.

This also has bearing on Kuyper's insight into "sacred philology." According to a mechanical conception in the seventeenth century, each product of divine revelation had to bear the mark of God's perfection even in *form*. This idea was contrary to the "rule" of revelation, according to Kuyper.[20] He saw this in connection with the form of a servant without "glory." The ray of revelation "broke into the atmosphere of our sinful-creaturely life." In contrast to a mechanical — in his opinion "anabaptist" view — that which is sinful and fallible had to cling to Scripture.[21] No theory of "perfection" should

12. *Enc.,* III, 68.
13. *Ibid.*
14. *Ibid.,* p. 69.
15. *Ibid.,* p. 70.
16. *Ibid.,* p. 71.
17. *Ibid.,* p. 73.
18. *Ibid.,* p. 77.
19. *Ibid.,* p. 68.
20. *Ibid.,* p. 78. Later men usually spoke of the "style" of revelation.
21. *Ibid.,* p. 79.

be applied to the languages of Scripture. The Spirit is "the teacher of the church" in spite of the vicissitudes of the historical process. The Scripture participates — as "the Word of God in human hands" — in the historical character of human life. Research, analysis, and judgment are needed as they are related to and result from the reality of Scripture.

We now wish to call attention to the problem of the translation of Scripture, for in this connection the same aspect of historicity becomes clearly apparent. We will not deal with the many philological questions at stake in translation but with the necessity of such translation's revealing its historical character. Various problems arise in translations because of the limitations and inadequacies of human language. What is the meaning of these difficult and generally acknowledged problems of translation, related as they are to the proclamation — "from Scripture" — of the gospel to all nations in its verity and reliability?

One translation of the Bible that offers difficult problems is the Septuagint. As a translation of the Old Testament, it was frequently quoted in the New Testament,[22] so that in any reflection on Scripture the problem of authenticity and authorization naturally had to be faced by the church. Passing over some of the problems of Septuagint research, we wish to raise a few self-evident questions regarding the authority of Scripture. When estimating the value of the Septuagint, it was asked whether the fact that this translation was quoted in the New Testament gave it a different character. In examining this problem we clearly touch on the much discussed question of whether the Septuagint received an authoritative character *because* it was quoted in the New Testament, a position which seemed self-explanatory in view of the inspiration of Scripture. Partly because of the juridical character, this would establish the Septuagint as authentic without reservation. If this were considered too hasty a conclusion, how should one then regard the God-breathed Scripture, which also contained parts of the Septuagint? The importance of this problem is illustrated by the solution of the early church, which has been accepted by many — that the Septuagint was an *inspired* translation. This would explain the "unproblematic" quotation of this translation in the New Testament. It would allow the conclusion that

22. Regarding the various ways of citation, see E. E. Ellis, *Paul's Use of the OT* (1957), pp. 11f.

it was inspired and not merely stamped with approval "after the event."

The difference of opinion between Jerome and Augustine is well known. Jerome held that the Hebrew text alone was inspired, whereas Augustine held that the translators of the Septuagint were peculiarly guided by the Holy Spirit. He appealed to the familiar "miracle" of the legend of Aristeas concerning the locked cells of the translators, in which they produced the miraculous result of a uniform translation.[23] Today no one quarrels over this "pseudo-miracle,"[24] but that does not render the problems less important. These problems clearly influenced Jerome in his assumption that the authors of the New Testament used the Septuagint only when this translation did not essentially deviate from the Hebrew text. Because of these problems, we note a concern for continuity and for the God-breathed Scripture. Augustine especially feared the peril of a possible confusion, since people had lived so long with "this Bible" (the Old Testament).[25] Accepting the inspiration of the Septuagint was necessary "in order that the authority of these Scriptures might be commended not as human, but divine, as indeed it was."[26] Concern for humanization plays a role here, and an elimination of all dangers by accepting an inspiration of the translation was its result. This thesis about a translation obviously has the mark of a postulate; the thesis is in fact independent of any analysis of the Septuagint that might determine its conformity to the Hebrew original. The God-breathed character of Scripture thus could be "maintained" (so they thought), and the certainty that truly God's Word was heard "authentically" was left unmolested, but only via this postulate.

Only when the Aristeas legend had long been abandoned was a true comparison, without any postulate, actually made. One began to ponder more freely the Septuagint quotations in the New Testament. Nevertheless, the problem of historicity and of translation continued to have influence, especially with reference to the confession of the God-breathed character of Scripture.

The problem of the quotations of the Septuagint in the

23. See Schwarz, p. 176. See further Polman, *The Word of God According to St. Augustine* (ET, 1961), pp. 184f.
24. Polman, p. 188.
25. *Ibid.*, p. 185.
26. *Ibid.*, p. 186.

New Testament continues to have import and has held the interest of many in our time. We will discuss two examples of Septuagint quotations in the New Testament in order to illustrate this question of legitimacy. A much discussed example is the quotation of Psalm 16 in Peter's sermon on Pentecost in Acts 2. The starting point of this sermon, the raising of Jesus, is related to David's words about him in Psalm 16. Of special importance are the words: "Moreover my flesh will dwell in hope. For thou wilt not abandon my soul to Hades, nor let thy Holy One see corruption. Thou hast made known to me the ways of life" (Acts 2:26-28). The quotation is taken from the Septuagint,[27] and the difference between the Hebrew text and the Septuagint is noteworthy here. The texts differ to such an extent that one might ask whether an appeal to the Old Testament is permissible and meaningful.[28] It is generally held that the poet of Psalm 16 does not deal with raising someone from death but with preservation and protection against death: Yahweh will not give up his soul and his life to Sheol and will not let him see the "pit," but will show him the path of life (Ps. 16:10-11). J. Ridderbos interprets this as a preservation from death, and thus the text receives a different function: "Not giving him over to the realm of death."[29] In Psalm 16 a protected life is set over against the "Pit,"[30] the realm of death, while in the Septuagint the "Pit" has become "corruption."

On etymological grounds, according to Ridderbos, this modification is not justified, and it is not required even by the authority of the New Testament.[31] In Ridderbos' opinion, Peter quoted Psalm 16 according to the Septuagint just as we might quote the King James Version or the Revised Standard Version, without pressing the stamp of approval on each quoted word. The intention of Peter should be noted: he states that David has died and been buried, "and his tomb is with us to this

27. Grosheide, *Komm. Hand.*, p. 76.
28. A similar question can be posed regarding the citation of Amos 9:9, 11, 12 in Acts 15. Cf. E. Haenchen, *The Acts of the Apostles* (1971), p. 448: "the Hebrew text would be useless for James' argument, and would even contradict it." Regarding Hosea 13:14 and I Cor. 15:45f., see Berkouwer, *Return of Christ*, pp. 186-187. The problem is somewhat different in Eph. 4:8 and Ps. 68:19. See H. Schlier, *Der Brief an die Epheser* (1958), p. 190.
29. J. Ridderbos, *De Psalmen* (1955), pp. 124f.
30. N. H. Ridderbos, *De Psalmen* (1962), I, 176.
31. J. Ridderbos, p. 131.

day" (Acts 2:29). By referring to Christ he wants to show that the realm of death does not have the last word, as he stated immediately before the Psalm 16 quotation. Christ broke through the pangs of death, and it was not possible for him to be held by it (Acts 2:24). So "corruption" is the key word in his appeal to the psalm, just as it is the case in Paul's quoting of Psalm 16 in Acts 13:35. Therefore, in these quotations from a conditioned translation we come across a grey area that hermeneutically cannot be made wholly transparent. But Peter is in harmony with Psalm 16 according to the Septuagint (the preservation in death and the pathways of life out of death and through death). It is thus clear what Peter (and Paul) had in mind, and Psalm 16 was quoted for that purpose. Commentators are of the opinion that there is a clear point of contact between the perspective expressed in Acts 2 and in Psalm 16 – Yahweh's power over life, to which death and the perils of death are no ultimate obstacles.[32] Nevertheless, this does not eliminate the grey area that is exposed by the translation of the Septuagint, unless this translation in addition receives the mark of inspiration or of a special divine intervention.

A second example of a modification that does not appear to have an immediate "point of contact" with the Old Testament text is the quotation from Psalm 8 in Hebrews 2:6-8. In relation to the preaching of Jesus' greatness, Psalm 8 is quoted according to the Septuagint. In this quotation we read concerning man: "Thou didst make him *for a little while* lower than the angels" (Heb. 2:7). A good deal of thought was given to the difference between these words from the Septuagint and the Hebrew text, for in Psalm 8:5 (Hebrew) we read: "Yet thou hast made him *little less than God.*" It expresses the high position of man; very little is kept from him. The attribute "little less than God" offers him the privilege of having dominion over the works of God's hands while all things are put under his feet.

However, in the Septuagint this "little less" is rendered by "for a little while," so that the author of Hebrews thinks of a temporary humiliation of Jesus. This temporal meaning comes out in Hebrews 2:9: Even though we do not yet see everything in subjection to man, "we see Jesus, who for a little while

32. Cf. N. H. Ridderbos, *loc. cit.*

was made lower than the angels . . . because of the suffering of death," and now is "crowned with glory." The meaning of Psalm 8 ("a little less than God") is clearly different from that expressed in "for a little while" in this Christological interpretation of Psalm 8.[33] The words "making lower" of Hebrews 2 express a reduction to a lower position from a higher position, making him of less importance.[34] The temporal qualification is lacking in Psalm 8. Here again we encounter an arresting use of Scripture whereby we cannot say that Hebrews 2 goes "along the same lines as the psalmist who composed Psalm 8."[35] A translation is quoted that was at the disposal of this author of Hebrews,[36] which he used to refer to the essential aspect of his message concerning Jesus as Lord.

We call attention to these New Testament quotations from the Septuagint to show how they indicate the aspect of historicity. It is that aspect of the New Testament witness which uses proof from Scripture to convince men with all the more force of the trustworthiness and firmness of the message. A grey area was thereby plainly perceived concerning human and historical data. It may not be eliminated by means of a theory that does no justice to the facts of language and translation. But it emphasizes, of course, the particular importance of this cited problem, which scholars attempted to solve by means of an overarching continuity directly derived from the Holy Spirit. Frequently, attempts have been made to solve the problem in a more complex manner not only with respect to the relationship of the Septuagint to the New Testament, but with regard to the way in which the entire Scripture was used in the New Testament, the way in which the transmission of the message was shaped. We have in mind particularly the much discussed idea of the so-called *sensus plenior* in Roman Catholic theology. This *sensus plenior* is not placed in contrast to the literal sense but indicates a deeper level of meaning in the Old Testament text. In the many discussions concerning the *sensus plenior* it is noteworthy that criticism of this solution is especially directed against an overly strong element of supernaturalism in the use of the *sensus plenior*

33. J. Ridderbos, p. 74.
34. F. W. Grosheide, *Hebreën* (1955).
35. S. Kistemaker, *The Psalm Citations in the Epistle to the Hebrews* (1961), p. 105.
36. *Ibid.*, p. 146; cf. Ellis, p. 143.

for solving various problems encountered in the study of Scripture.[37]

Our intention is not to offer a full treatment of this controversial hermeneutical principle but to emphasize the aspect of an *a priori* sanction implied in it. Questions of historicity are hardly taken seriously, and the interest in the literal meaning of the text is set in the framework of an artificial view. By means of this approach one will understand Roman Catholic criticism, which rejects this solution for the very reason that Scripture ought to be approached as a witness in human words according to its nature, origin, and growth, or, in other words, according to its organic and historic character without any recourse to divine intention hidden in the literal meaning. In view of Old Testament quotations in the New Testament, Fitzmyer, for example, asks whether we "would be forced to admit that the New Testament interpretations are instances of the *sensus plenior* of the Old Testament."[38] In his opinion this solution is not obvious at all, and he points to another important aspect – historical in character and not a mere postulate. In the New Testament we come across a way of Scripture reading quite different from that of our time. "To modern critical scholarship their way of reading the Old Testament often appears quite arbitrary in that it disregards the sense and the content of the original." He goes on to speak of New Testament Scripture proof as "a free, sometimes figurative extension or accommodation of the words to support a position already taken."[39] This historical approach is not intended to relativize inspiration, but it differs a good deal from that of the *sensus plenior*.

We encounter here a cardinal question that may also have consequences for the exegesis of the Old Testament. For if the fuller meaning is discovered in the New Testament, and if the Septuagint renders service to it because of its legitimized quality – though not in the narrow sense of inspiration – one wonders why he could not begin at once and without hesitation with the exegesis of the Old Testament text in the New Testament without worrying too much about the Hebrew text.

37. See R. E. Brown, *The Sensus Plenior in Sacred Scripture* (1955); P. Grelot, *The Bible: Word of God* (1968); B. Vawter, "The Fuller Sense: Some Considerations," *The Catholic Biblical Quarterly* (1964), pp. 85f.
38. J. A. Fitzmyer, "The Use of Explicit OT Quotations in Qumran Literature and in the NT," *NT Studies* (1961), p. 332.
39. *Ibid.;* cf. Ellis, p. 135.

Those who defend the *sensus plenior* obviously do not promote this method, but, in my opinion, it follows from the idea of sanction and legitimacy. Koole, along with a number of Roman Catholic authors, also deals with this problem with an attitude critical of the *sensus plenior*. He states that "one may have a high opinion of the New Testament exegesis of the Old Testament but that this nevertheless may not be regarded as normative for our modern exegesis."[40] Such a complex conception, of course, can only be appreciated if one is aware of the historical process in which Scripture originated. It must be taken into account in the confession of the God-breathed character of Scripture if one does not wish to come into conflict with the reality of Scripture's historical characteristics, for instance, its quotations from the Septuagint. Considerations of the *sensus plenior* frequently appear to have a pronounced dogmatic coloring. It must be asked whether these and those concerning the "interpreting" Septuagint do not ultimately issue from a denial of this historicity, in order to prevent the predominance of this historicity over the God-breathed Scripture.

In acknowledging the problems concerning the acquisition of knowledge of the *sensus plenior*, and especially discovering in it the element of presupposition that overarches the historicity, one will recognize that these questions of the *sensus plenior* and Septuagint quotations lead to a consideration of the use of Scripture in the New Testament in general. This use of Scripture was closely related to translation and transmission and has often been characterized as stemming from a certain apostolic *freedom* — not only in quoting particular texts but also in the linking of various Old Testament passages for a certain *purpose*.

This word "freedom" clearly does not explain everything. But it does indicate that this method of quoting was not as precise as the modern method that we normally use for quotations. This interest in freedom is not found only in our time of historical-critical research and of broad, detailed analyses of the language and background of Scripture and its authors. Calvin already took it into account: he evidently did not worry very much about the different methods of quotation in the New Testament, and he underlined the freedom which the apostles displayed in their quotations. He merely wished to stress that the "main point" was decisive for them. According

40. *De Overname van het OT door de Chr. Kerk* (1938), p. 11.

to him, they did not hesitate to change words, and "Paul," for example, cited Psalm 8 in Hebrews 2 for his own purpose. It seems to Calvin as if the apostle gave another meaning to David's words than David himself intended, because the phrase "for a little while" in Hebrews 2 refers to the period of humiliation.[41] He notes the presence of "allusions," "in terms that must illustrate a *present cause*" as it occurs in Paul. He adds that "the authors were not so precise in their usage of words."[42] This did not in the least imply a devaluation of Scripture, according to Calvin, for in it one listens to the message of Christ. That is the goal of the argumentation and of the proof of Scripture from the Old Testament. In their use of Scripture, the Reformers were so thoroughly convinced of the self-evidence of this central witness that they felt no need to protect this Scripture by means of artificial approaches that might clash with Scripture itself and its undeniable humanity and historicity.

This prevailing aspect of the goal of the message[43] forms the background of this notable freedom that resulted in all kinds of changes, selections, and applications. The question whether this method of quotation was indeed correct and adequate was not raised until later. At any rate, we must start with the idea that we find a unique kind of Scripture proof in the New Testament, alien to our standards of exactness. Ignoring this difference stems merely from the urge to harmonize. But we note at the same time that the background of this large freedom is an unprecedented concentration on the matter, the *content* of the gospel. Koole, in speaking of this usage of Scripture, which to us "is not in the least normative," does not plead for a dualistic theory of inspiration. But he acknowledges the fact that the authors of the New Testament should not be viewed as having the gift of a specific charismatic ability to *exegete*. But they dealt with the Old Testament in terms of their faith with its central categories

41. Calvin, *Commentary on Hebrews* (ET, 1963), p. 22: "But the apostle now seems to use the words in a different sense from that in which David understood them. The phrase 'a little' . . . seems to refer to time."
42. Calvin, *Commentary on Romans* (ET, 1960), p. 61: "We know that, in quoting Scripture, the apostles often used freer language than the original, since they were content if what they quoted applied to their subject, and therefore they were not over-careful in their use of words" (on Rom. 3:4).
43. *Ibid.*, pp. 221f.; Calvin, *Commentary on John* (ET, 1959), I, 138f.; cf. *Inst.*, III, ii, 7.

of promise and fulfillment.[44] They did this in the new situation of the present and of fulfillment. This recalls a principle that we find already in the Old Testament itself with respect to the dynamics of the Word and of the acts of God. It was the experience of Israel that none of Yahweh's promises to the house of Israel remained unfulfilled: "All came to pass" (Josh. 21:45). In the same way the certainty of the promise makes one recall an analogous memory from earlier times: "As the Lord lives who brought up the people of Israel out of the land of Egypt" (Jer. 23:7).[45] We met this "recollection" and "calling to mind" also in the New Testament. It is the knowledge and experience of divine truth and mercy, of his promise from the Old Testament fulfilled.[46]

At a later time, literary-historical research of Scripture examined the background of the time of its origin. Of course, it also faced the proof from Scripture in the New Testament. This obviously caused a renewed reflection on the nature of the God-breathed Scripture. The question was presented of whether or not the confession of the God-breathed Scripture had to lead to certain inevitable conclusions about this proof from Scripture, for instance, that inspiration also implied the absolute normativity of this proof. It was felt that in the New Testament we are not dealing with a scientific study of the Old Testament as it is performed today, and that therefore we should not apply a scientific yardstick. However, the problem cannot be solved by a decision concerning the scientific exactness, since we are dealing with the method of the admittedly unscientific proof from Scripture in the New Testament. In view of the God-breathed character of Scripture, should this method be evaluated as *the* interpretation by the Holy Spirit and the only possible and correct exegesis of the Old Testament? The question refers both to quotations from the

44. Koole, pp. 176f.
45. Cf. Hos. 2:13-15; Ex. 12:24f.; Deut. 16:1-3; Lev. 23:42-43. In all these there is more than an accidental prefiguration and illustration, namely, the future-directed acts of God in the history of Israel. The analogy can gain a place in this circle in the form of "reflection."
46. Calvin, *Commentary on Hebrews,* p. 136. "They [apostles] were not overscrupulous in quoting words provided that they did not misuse Scripture for their convenience. We must always look at the purpose for which quotations are made because they have careful regard for the main object so as not to turn Scripture to a false meaning, but as far as words are concerned, as in other things which are not relevant to the present purpose, they allow themselves some indulgence."

Septuagint and quotations in general; and the weight of this question is evident if one accepts the authority of the entire Scripture in all its parts to be the Word of God.

In this line of thought the attention is sometimes focused on difficulties and changes in a quotation in order to adapt it to the context, or focused on quotations from memory which therefore were sometimes less exact. Historical aspects were also taken into account, for example, the scarcity of books or the fact that a complete Hebrew or Greek Old Testament was not available. As a matter of logic, the investigation was gradually focused on *how* they arrived at such a use of Scripture. Possible influences on the use of Scripture in apostolic times were taken into account in order to incorporate all this fully into an "organic" view of the God-breathed Scripture. Such a view would not exclude these human and historical aspects but would adopt them without denying the God-breathed character. This use of Scripture, as was increasingly emphasized, was not due to a supernatural gift for scientific exegesis.[47] Thus, questions of rabbinical exegesis, for example, were being investigated. The biblical authors were not lifted above their own level of knowledge to a level of later scientific insight.[48] This too was thought to be of significance for hermeneutics and for the interpretation of the Old Testament regarding the knowledge of that time and the availability of the Old Testament text. New Testament interpretation, as was pointed out, did not have a charismatic character and did not issue from a discovery of a "fuller meaning." It was the result of a reflection that in methods and wording was in many respects related to the Jewish use of Scripture. Virtually all scholars agreed with that insight.[49]

47. Kuyper, *Princ.,* p. 450, where he develops his own way of dealing with the fact that NT quotations "are by no means always a literal translation of the original." He asserts that the NT writers "were inspired in a way analogous to the writers whose text they quoted." His conclusion is that it is the Holy Spirit "who, by the apostles, *quotes himself,* and is therefore entirely justified in repeating his original meaning in application to the case for which the quotation is made, in a somewhat modified form, agreeably to the current translation."
48. Bavinck, *GD,* I, 417.
49. Cf. Ellis, pp. 138f., where he indicates that Pauline exegesis employs a great deal of methodology found in rabbinical and other literature. Cf. Kistemaker, p. 95: "dependent upon the tradition of their time"; J. W. Doeve, *Jewish Hermeneutics in the Synoptic Gospels and Acts* (1953), Ch. 4.

Here also the term "time-relatedness" was applied in such a way that it became apparent that deeper questions were at stake than those concerning "relatedness to a certain world view." The biblical authors speak of a present salvation by means of a time-related hermeneutics. This process ran more along generally human lines and less along supernatural lines than was earlier supposed in view of the God-breathed character of Scripture (and the "interpretation" of the Spirit). But this time-relatedness, it should be noted, did not lead to the conclusion that the New Testament use of Scripture should simply be regarded in terms of an invalid use of the Old Testament because of a number of arbitrary customs of the time and norms that cannot claim the respect of later generations. The absence of such a negative conclusion is due to the awareness of a strange and indisputable fact, that this use of Scripture always stems from a central vision of the Old Testament as the book of promise and the New Testament message of salvation as the fulfillment of that promise. This aspect of fulfillment is always at the center of our attention; we have noted it already in Calvin, who was not at all worried about the mode of the New Testament use of Scripture, since the "essence," the message of the present salvation is at stake in these quotations. Through this salvation one sees the promise in retrospect.

In view of the confession of the God-breathed character of Scripture, it is important to investigate this in greater depth. What method is being employed when a "text" from the past is explained and adopted for proclamation? The method does not seem to agree with what we mean by "quotations," since we wish to refer to the *idea* expressed in the quotation and to nothing else. Is it not an anachronistic use of a text to quote it "in view of fulfillment"? Regarding Hebrews 2, Kistemaker states that the author "looks upon the Psalm quotations as a Christian."[50] Michel discusses these quotations "in the light of the Christ event" and from the presupposition of "the fulfillment in Christ."[51] The question here is whether we should regard this method as a trivial *eisegesis* that no longer has meaning for us because it has lost contact with the Old Testament. And if this answer is rejected, the question arises about what might be the meaning of this

50. Kistemaker, p. 90.
51. O. Michel, *Der Brief an die Hebräer* (1936), p. 81.

reading and interpreting "in terms of fulfillment." What is an *interpretation*, a proof from Scripture "which was directed to Jesus Christ, who fulfilled scripture"?[52] What does Goppelt mean in writing of typology: "The result of a typological explanation is first of all a number of statements concerning the New Testament salvation and not concerning the Old Testament"?[53] In the New Testament it is quite remarkable that this "realization" is proclaimed with such courage, surety, and emphasis. The promise and fulfillment of God's Word in the present is becoming manifest (Acts 3:18; Mk. 1:15; Lk. 4:21).[54]

Thus, in view of this unconcern, the question was asked whether this should not be called a completely arbitrary usage of Scripture that manipulates the Old Testament merely to gather material for illustrations or to annex it through a kind of projection arising from one's own conviction of faith.[55] Von Rad emphatically rejected the thought of an arbitrary "reading back into" the Old Testament.[56] In the new presence of salvation one was "led to a completely new interpretation of the Old Testament."[57]

What at first seemed to be anachronistic and in contrast to a genuinely objective understanding of Scripture now received color and depth from the viewpoint of faith. It is noteworthy that we are not dealing with a systematic treatment of the Old Testament; it is an incidental, situated, and fragmentary appeal to certain texts that came to mind in the new situation of salvation in Christ now that Scripture "has been fulfilled in your hearing" (Lk. 4:21). This is something quite different from a trivial retrospective interpretation that has no foundation. It is proper to speak of "retrospect" as a temporal indication without the features of a projection as refined in the New

52. Kistemaker, *loc. cit.*
53. L. Goppelt, *Typos. Die typol. Deutung des AT im Neuen* (1939), p. 242.
54. Cf. *TDNT*, VI, 295f.
55. Cf. Bultmann, "Weissagung und Erfüllung," *Glauben und Verstehen*, II, 163f.: the "impossibility" of this understanding of Scripture.
56. Von Rad, *OT Theology*, II, 331; cf. Th. C. Vriezen, *An Outline of OT Theology* (second edition, ET, 1970), pp. 104f. For the background of the relationship between promise and fulfillment, see Moltmann, *Theology of Hope*, pp. 102, 112, 148, and 152f.
57. Von Rad, II, 329. For an understanding of von Rad's own insight into "typology," it is important to note that he distinguishes his view from the other typology of the 17th century, which in his opinion paid attention to "the data with reference to a salvation-historical progress which it objectified naively" (p. 371).

Testament. Thus we read how the disciples remembered Jesus' words concerning the temple *after* he was raised from the dead. The memory leads to a believing of the words Jesus had spoken in view of a disclosure of meaning in a later situation. An implied meaning that was then partially or wholly hidden is now discovered. This "retrospect" in the New Testament, or memory of the words Jesus had spoken earlier, is closely related to the memory of the meaning of the Old Testament words (cf. Jn. 13:7; Lk. 9:45; Lk. 24:6-8; Jn. 12:16).[58]

This unique perspective is apparently dominant in the use of Scripture in the New Testament.[59] It also proves that the relationship between this use of Scripture and that of the rabbis is a far cry from being described in terms of time-relatedness and dependence. Various "associations" found in the New Testament have the same goal and indicate the same faith that in a later period caused the church to "adopt" the Old Testament into the book of the church.[60]

In the new situation of salvation that had appeared, and in the broad context of fulfillment, "a word might light up based on the word and the work of Jesus."[61] Connections and context are indicated, and words are isolated or quoted in a chain of connections; they are modified and applied in view of one great purpose: to testify of the reality of salvation in Christ. This method is not like that of a modern commentator dealing with the Old Testament; it is obviously also determined by a limited hermeneutics. Starting from that Christological center, attention is focused in retrospect "on an increasing number of texts." In the end predictions of Christ were also found there, "where for us it is difficult to follow the argument."[62]

In reading the Old Testament, Paul is so convinced of this relationship that he believes a veil lies over the minds of Jews when they read the Old Testament. The veil can only

58. Cf. Mt. 17:9. "The resurrection gives new might to this Word [of Jesus]" (*TDNT,* IV, 677).
59. Cf. S. Amsler, *L'ancien Testament dans l'Eglise* (1960), pp. 65f.
60. Cf. von Rad, p. 330.
61. Michel, p. 83.
62. J. L. Koole, *Hermeneutische Oriëntatie,* p. 16. For the scriptural usage of the Qumran community, see F. F. Bruce, *Biblical Exegesis in the Qumran Texts,* p. 66; J. Barr, *Old and New in Interpretation: A Study of the Two Testaments* (1966), p. 145.

be removed when a man turns to Christ. This does not mean that a hermeneutical technique or a hermeneutical gift would automatically be granted through conversion. But because of this veil, the character, intention, and deep meaning of the Old Testament is not perceived. It is remarkable that in the same context in which he refers to the veil Paul gives an exegesis of the Old Testament in which "he shows himself an accomplished haggadist, who constructs his Midrash, his Christian Midrash, according to the same method of interpretation as that followed by the synagogue."[63] The schism between church and synagogue is not found in the technique or the methods of scriptural usage in itself, but in the total and central understanding of the Old Testament as witness to the promise of Israel's God and in the reality of Jesus as Messiah. Because of this new understanding, words and events are combined and associated through a process of selection, modification, and application. The central fact of the proclamation dominates, and the use of Scripture must serve that fact.

Later, this "proof from Scripture" was compared with the use of Scripture developed on a different level of knowledge, with a view to a wider horizon, for example, with respect to the languages of Scripture, the religious-historical background of the Old and New Testaments, the hermeneutics of Qumran, and the difference between the Hebrew Bible and the Septuagint. From that time on it became increasingly evident that the type of approach to the Old Testament used in the New Testament was not at all a supernatural, isolated, and charismatic one. It was determined by the hermeneutics of that time and by the linguistic material at the writers' disposal, that is, Scripture as the Word written by men in their language. Thus, we are dealing with a so-called proof from Scripture that may not be judged and disqualified from the viewpoint of later knowledge. This hermeneutics, in spite of its limitations, is somewhat self-evident in view of the *verbal* form of God's Word. It cannot and should not be approached with the dilemma "truth or error." This dilemma would have to be maintained with formal logic and detailed precision — which no one actually puts into practice. Denying this limit of history does not only mean a misunderstanding of the way of the Spirit in and with Scripture, but is also an intellectualization of the *mystery* of God-breathed Scripture. Certain data of Holy Scripture are

63. Doeve, *op. cit.*, p. 99, in connection with II Cor. 3 and Ex. 34.

being neglected by a harmonizing effort that solves all problems in an "unhistorical" way or escapes with a lame "it is not permitted" when harmonizing is wholly impossible. Those holding this position usually do not reject later scientific research, but they really cannot find a genuine and legitimate place for it.

The aspect of time-relatedness and continuity of the message's clear and central focus can be illustrated by a remarkable passage of Scripture. On the one hand it is filled with the great and inescapable evidence of the gospel, and on the other hand it has aspects that are difficult for us to understand. They are closely related to the historical background of Paul. I am referring to the so-called allegory of Paul in Galatians 4, where it is generally acknowledged that Paul argues in an haggadic manner. In this connection, for instance, he speaks of Sinai as a mountain in Arabia (Gal. 4:25) and thus illustrates the relationship between the son of a free woman and that of a slave. What is the function of the "proof from Scripture" here? It is strange to us that he introduces the words of Abraham concerning Hagar ("cast out the slave and her son") with the statement, "But what does the scripture say?" (Gal. 4:30). He does this in order to bind the message on the hearts of his readers: "We are not children of the slave but of the free woman" (Gal. 4:31). This proof from Scripture is the climax of Paul's proclamation of grace shown throughout Galatians (Gal. 4:29). Even though certain factors that are exegetically time-related play a role in the argument, they do not *conceal* the prospect of that grace but rather *clarify* it. Scripture does not exclude this time-relatedness but makes it possible because it serves the central proclamation of salvation.

The New Testament use of Scripture is not only characterized by the word "freedom,"[64] but also with a "play" of hermeneutics. Of course, this element of play is not thought of in contrast to the seriousness of the message but as a part of it. For plays on words do occur in Scripture and are precisely intended to serve the gravity of the message. The reference to "a mountain in Arabia" and the word play about the veil over Moses' face, with the transition to the veil over the heart (II Cor. 3:12-18), is part of a very serious testimony. With the use of certain arguments within a limited horizon,

64. Men have often spoken of this freedom with regard to the question of whether certain words were always cited "against the context from which the quotations were taken." See Barr, p. 143.

the Old Testament is heard and interpreted in its central relatedness to the message, which is a clear and unavoidable appeal.

Those retaining certain conceptions of inspiration have often objected to such explanations. According to them, the decision regarding "the mountains of Arabia," for example, is as follows: "Belief or unbelief depends on accepting or not accepting the special guidance of the Holy Spirit to which the apostle appeals."[65] This is a purely deductive conception and as such a presupposition: truth is interpreted in terms of exactness without taking into account the true nature of the God-breathed Scripture. Yet it is remarkable that cetrain factors, such as "ways of thought, ways of interpretation, or world view,"[66] are recognized. This recognition hails from the phase of "organic" inspiration that has gained a certain traditional and self-evident fixation. In addition, it is thought that these factors were means in God's hands and that this problem is of "minor importance." As a result, however, time-relatedness loses its real significance in hermeneutics, for it does not become concrete anywhere. This reticence must be seen against the background of a fear of falling into critical dualism, a dualism that can only be overcome with a confession of the God-breathed character of Scripture.

In surveying the history of the interpretation of Scripture, one may soon wonder if there is not a gap between the reading of the Bible in earlier times and the seemingly more complex manner of biblical study in later times. This question has been asked frequently. In answer, we must initially realize that the limited knowledge of the biblical authors (the fact that they were not lifted to a level of knowledge above that of their contemporaries) does not imply that in later times the broader knowledge of God's Word in its human-verbal form would automatically lead to a deeper insight into its meaning, riches, and mystery. A conclusion based on knowledge of the languages (Hebrew, the Septuagint, and the language of the New Testament) and the religious-historical background of Scripture is clearly an intellectual one. It does not do justice first of all to the inescapable fact that precisely those earlier readings of Scripture — though limited in knowledge — frequently led to an understanding of the witness to Christ,

65. S. Greijdanus, *Galaten,* p. 291.
66. S. Greijdanus, *Schriftbeginselen ter Schriftverklaring* (1946), pp. 124f.

which had tremendous power for life and death in proclamation and expectation.

Every age has known differences in the study of Scripture. We read that the Bereans were "more noble than those in Thessalonica, for they received the word with all eagerness, examining the scriptures daily to see if these things were so" (Acts 17:11). To them, reading Scripture was linked to *accepting* the Word. Here the visible distinction has nothing to do with a gradual development of knowledge. Studying Scripture can be viewed apart from accepting it, as a neutral effort that bypasses the mysteries of God's Word. Understanding the meaning in that sense, however, is not equal to the understanding of which Christ speaks (Mt. 22:29; Jn. 5:39). There is a relationship of knowledge between the student and the words, but that relationship does not necessarily include an involvement with the purpose of Scripture. Similarly, knowledge can be broadened with greater access to the meaning of the words through scientific research, while the meaning of Scripture can remain unknown because of the lack of an understanding related to acceptance. We might add that the broadening horizon of knowledge of Scripture could even become an intellectual affair available to only a few. Influenced in the other direction through this impression made by the broadening of knowledge, some may be inclined to get rid of all the "complications" and dangers of alienation inherent in this continued and detailed study.

Nonetheless, it must be realized that the road of Scripture through the world is not one of *human* complications, theorizing, and atomizing. But it is related to the way in which the message of God's Word went out into the world. One may not therefore withdraw from all the questions raised by the universality of God's Word, which all its forms of transmission and translation have raised in wrestling to understand its secrets. One may never move away from the sometimes difficult expressions by means of a spiritualistic or pneumatic explanation (II Pet. 3:16). One may exhaust every aspect of Scripture study in the expectation that limited and inadequate words will not undermine the secret of Scripture. There is thus no reason to complain about the broadening of knowledge when this knowledge is related to words through which God speaks. We think of Luther's deep insight into this relationship when, at an extremely critical and difficult time of transition, he undertook to translate Scripture. It was a translation of the message of Scripture for a proclamation in which all would hear again the original sounds of the gospel. In the context of that daily effort he warns against ignoring the "two languages." This he considers a contempt of God. Since Scripture came to us through the Holy Spirit by means of languages, "let us realize that we shall scarcely be able to maintain the gospel without languages. Languages are the sheaths in which the knife of the Spirit is contained. They are the case in which this jewel is borne."[67] God "had a good reason" to have Scripture written in this way. Luther was deeply aware of the continued disclosure of the meaning of the words in human form. He also kept sight of the dimensions of power and universality of God's Word, as is shown in his illustration of the jewel, food, and drink. According to Luther, if we lose sight of or reject languages, we lose the gospel.

Thus, the church, inspired by all the difficulties and dangers implied in this complex knowledge, never complained about this difficult task; it accepted it and stimulated every study that could serve the gospel. In this perspective the *words* are not considered merely "external" and hence unimportant in contrast to the *spirit* of the gospel, for languages are the "sheaths in which the knife of the Spirit is contained." Without immortalizing Holy Scripture, the church, in reflection and preaching, was continually reminded of the wide horizon of the testimony of Christ: "Heaven and earth will pass away, but my words will not pass away" (Mt. 24:35). Another text speaks of Scripture's meaningful overarching of all transmission: "The grass withers, and the flower falls, but the word of the Lord abides for ever" (I Pet. 1:24-25). This reminder concerning Scripture and its transmission has nothing to do with bibliolatry; it stems from a refusal to think about Scripture and the Holy Spirit in abstract terms. The words are rather viewed from a higher perspective and in the "radiance" of the testimony of the God-breathed Scripture. One may shrink from the danger that this radiance would be submerged in the complexity of exact and detailed research. But this fear will be conquered in the awareness that "for a good reason" God's Word was given to us in a form that called for research.

Regarding the verbal form of God's Word, thought was frequently given to the "risk" of giving to Scripture this "form of a servant." Even though no criticism was implied about

67. Luther, "To the Councilmen of All Cities in Germany, That They Establish and Maintain Christian Schools" (Ebeling, *Luther*, p. 30).

Scripture's obvious historicity and its way through the world, yet this mode of God's Word frequently became a subject of reflection and concern, at least in a theoretical way. But one may not, because of this concern, devise from the beginning a "method" that guarantees the safety of the road of faith. One such method is that of deduction, which seeks to prove as conclusively as possible that Scripture exceeds all time-relatedness. Another is that of induction, which often runs the risk of bogging down in a "canon of interpretation," applying a critical yardstick to God's Word and preventing a true listening to the Spirit's voice to the churches. It is the abiding Word of God alone that tests and accompanies all study of Scripture; it challenges and encourages us to continue on this road, critically weighing all human words about God's Word, with the expectation and certainty shared with the church of all ages that the "jewel" of the gospel will not be lost in a new and still unknown future.

If we admit that a recognition of the historicity of Scripture does not go counter to reverence for it, but rather is *awakened* by that reverence, we automatically meet a number of important questions that are at the center of nearly all modern reflection concerning Scripture. The question that has always been of utmost importance in the total life and tradition of the church is that of *reliability*. Because it is inseparably related to that reliability, new attention has also been given to "perspicuity," the *clarity* of Scripture. A further question was that of Scripture's *sufficiency*, an extremely radical and decisive word, not concerned with a theory about Scripture but with a concentration on God's Word, which does not search for other sources of rest and peace. These terms ("reliability," "clarity," and "sufficiency") received wide coinage during the Reformation and have been discussed under the rubric of "qualities" of Scripture ever since. Reflections about these "qualities" have been of a religious character, as we have discovered in our time: they are related to the certainty about God's Word in Scripture. The terms are closely related to the confession of the God-breathed character of Scripture and its unique authority. This is the test for every concern with Scripture, for growth in knowledge, for the shift in attention from the mechanical to the organic aspect, and for whether we avoid becoming estranged from the perspective and horizon of Israel: "I have seen a limit to all perfection, but thy commandment is exceedingly broad" (Ps. 119:96).

CHAPTER NINE

RELIABILITY

WE HAVE FREQUENTLY COME ACROSS the characterization of Scripture as the Word of God and the word of men. Reliability, of course, was always discussed in direct relationship to this, particularly in view of the truly human aspect of Scripture. We do not merely have in mind the general consideration that error belongs to human nature. We have in mind above all the contrast noted frequently in Scripture between the Word of God and the words of men, between relying on God and relying on man. We think of Paul's statement: "Let God be true though every man be false" (Rom. 3:4). Thus, we may ask if there is a problem lurking in the characterization of Scripture as God's Word and men's words, since all that is human seems to be quite open to error and lies. One need not even be caught up in a fear like that of the poet of Psalm 116 who exclaimed, "All men are liars" (Ps. 116:11, ASV), in order to realize that. Even though we acknowledge that the human has been taken into service in Scripture, does this human aspect not limit and relativize the Word of God? We may well understand that frequently some appear inclined to de-emphasize the human aspect in order to be able to confess the reliability of *God's* Word. Finally, since the human is limited by numerous clear boundaries, and we encounter Scripture in all its time-relatedness, does not the strong affirmation of the church appear to be somewhat strange? The Belgic Confession reads: "believing without any doubt all things contained in them,"[1] and "these Holy Scriptures fully contain the will of God."[2] A "hearty trust" and a "certain knowledge" appear in the catechism;[3] they are related to listen-

1. *BC,* Art. V.
2. *BC,* Art. VII.
3. *HC,* Q. 21.

ing and to obedience. The reliability of Scripture is correlated with trust as surrender, relying on Scripture to banish all doubt and uncertainty. Yahweh is characterized and called upon in the Old Testament as "Trust": "Thou art the confidence [literally: trust] of all the ends of the earth" (Ps. 65:5, ASV).

Salvation is related to this trust: "Blessed is the man who makes the Lord his trust" (Ps. 40:4; cf. 71:5). Throughout the Old Testament this trust is deemed legitimate, because it is said concerning this trust that one shall not be put to shame (Ps. 22:5; Jer. 17:5, 7; Mt. 27:43). Only in a crisis of trust may one hear the dark complaint, "Wilt thou be to me like a deceitful brook, like waters that fail?" (Jer. 15:18). The reliability of God is confessed again and again in Israel in new and surprising experiences, because Yahweh lets none of his words fall to the ground (I Sam. 3:19). This trust in God, it has been pointed out, is much more often referred to in the Old Testament (e.g., Psalms) than in the New Testament, at least in an explicit way. We need not discuss the explanation of this fact, for even though "confidence takes the form of faith,"[4] the intent of this faith (and of hope) clearly is inseparably related to a reliance on the promise. The reliability of God is the unshakable foundation of such a trust; it is a trust encompassing the present and the future, and it embraces one's own life as well as that of others (Phil. 1:6; Eph. 3:12). It may be described as a resting in God's Word "in quietness and in trust" (Isa. 30:15). A reliance upon Yahweh is implied in all this. However, one should not think that he enters into an entirely different sector of trust when considering the reliability of Scripture.

The confession of this reliability does not imply a faith that could be isolated from the trust in God which in Scripture assumes such radical forms. Bavinck writes that our faith in Scripture increases and decreases according to our trust in Christ.[5] He is in fact wrestling with a dualism by which faith in Scripture (in terms of intellectual acceptance) is separated from personal faith. By intuition and later by reflection the church frequently understood the impossibility of that, even though it seemed difficult to clearly formulate the *unity* of faith. As a consequence, reflection on the reliability of Scripture is not a separate theoretical concern. It has a religious

4. *TDNT*, VI, 7.
5. *GD*, I, 569.

background essential and central to faith, just as the hearing of the human prophetic Word was of decisive significance for the whole life of Israel. This reliability has been discussed a great deal in the last centuries, especially in the light of "the phenomena of Scripture,"[6] as Bavinck calls them, and of the knotty problems, objections, and difficulties "even for those who with childlike faith subject themselves to Scripture."[7]

That certain questions arose concerning the reliability of Scripture need not be attributed in itself to a rationalistic approach to Scripture. These questions may not be regarded from the start as a "stronghold" erected against obedience, an "obstacle" against the knowledge of God, or an "argument" against the Word of God (II Cor. 10:4-5). We do not need speculations as a source for this talk about knotty problems and difficulties, for Scripture itself offers them to us.[8] We must thoroughly convince ourselves that no one of the theories of inspiration is true and good which does not agree with the "phenomena" of Scripture.[9] Paul illustrates the obedience to Christ with its radical character of trust by the figure of a defenseless prisoner of war. But this radicality does not imply that we may not think about the nature of the reliability of Scripture. Even though it may seem strange at first to speak of knotty problems and even of "objections" regarding the confession "Holy Scripture is the Word of God," there is every reason to think about Scripture as both God's Word and man's word, particularly with respect to its reliability. For it is not inconceivable to approach Scripture with a concept of "reliability" not derived from Scripture itself, in fact, quite alien to it. Moreover, one should be on guard against operating with a formal concept of reliability in view of the many-sided and inexhaustible variety in Scripture, its laments and songs, its mourning and doubting, its cursings and jubilations. This needed warning, however, does not at all diminish the importance of this question of reliability. It is elementary because the trust of faith is at stake.

First, we must pose the question of whether the reliability of Scripture is simply identical to that reliability of which we frequently speak concerning the record of various historical

6. *Ibid.*, p. 393.
7. *Ibid.*, pp. 412f.
8. *Ibid.*, p. 413.
9. *Ibid.*, p. 393. It is clear here that, according to Bavinck, the "self-witness" of Scripture is not isolated to a few texts regarding inspiration.

events. Frequently, terms such as "exact," "precise," and "accurate" are used for it. If the writing of history is not tendentious, or characterized by one-sided accents, its record is deemed to be reliable and correct, that is, in agreement with what really happened and with what is of importance. Such a modern concept of reliability clearly should not be used as a yardstick for Scripture. I reminded the reader above of Kuyper's view of the "canon," the "style" of revelation. Precision and accuracy are alien to it. Even though the lack of such an accuracy is accepted by nearly everyone as a matter of course, one must be aware of the reasons thereof if he simultaneously wishes to speak of complete "reliability" and complete "correctness." I discussed the way in which reliability and infallibility are at stake with respect to the biblical world view. Now we encounter reliability in connection with the writing of history. Logically, the question was frequently asked whether one could possibly think legitimately of the historical records of Scripture on a par with the scriptural descriptions of nature. For there we find no pretense of an exact "world view."

It is not permissible, however, to apply to historiography the concept that nature is described according to the *appearance* of things, thus undermining the importance of the reliability of Scripture. For speaking of the rising of the sun does not convey false conceptions, but if the biblical authors "write in the area of history according to appearance (and this means at any rate not according to what objectively happened but according to what many believed subjectively in their time), they indeed offer a false representation and their authority and reliability suffers thereby."[10] Bavinck rejects the subjective evasion of history through which history is evaporated in "appearance." He poses the question of reliability because one deals here with the history of God's revelation, told "in order that we may know God in his seeking of and coming to mankind." It is noteworthy that Bavinck, with his protest against evaporation and appearance, is not hindered from giving full attention to the purpose of biblical historiography. He states that it was not done following the rules of modern historical criticism. To apply such a yardstick would mean a denial of the reality of life. In its historiography, Scripture follows "its own direction and purpose." The sacred story is religious history which does not offer "that kind of accuracy which we

10. *Ibid.*, p. 418.

often desire." Thus, the narratives of events and words of Jesus (e.g., those spoken at the Last Supper) are not at all in harmony. We must, moreover, keep in mind that, though everything in Scripture is true, "this truth certainly is not of the same nature in all its parts." For the God-breathed Scripture "brought different kinds of literature into its service to reach its goal," so that further reflection with respect to this "truth" continues to be necessary. Bavinck emphasizes these points at the very end of his discussion of the God-breathed character of Scripture. His last statement is: "The Word of God remains forever." But this conviction does not contradict the immediately preceding argument that strongly emphasized the necessary distinctions and modifications in order that full justice be done to Scripture. It is not by mere chance that at the end of this discussion about the God-breathed Scripture he opens up the possibility of further reflection in an aside: "The dogma of Scripture is not finished at these points and leaves room for much specialized research." Yet he does not feel hampered in his reverence for Scripture and its reliability; it is a book for mankind, ever young and fresh, the language of life.[11]

The discussion of the special nature of biblical historiography is frequently characterized in terms of a specific tendency dominating the description. We must abandon the feeling that the word "tendentious" currently conveys — that it must be judged one-sided and false. By "tendency" we mean the *intent* of the author, who does not wish to write an exact, neutral, and objective story or a theoretical orientation to what happened in the past, but who reckons with God's revealing deeds in his approach and descriptions. This might be referred to as "religious pragmatism" in order to express this purposeful aspect of the story.

In the theory of harmonization, we frequently come across a peculiar theme when the ideal of historiography is being applied. For attention is not focused primarily on the *meaning* of that which is "correctly" described but to uncertainties which might arise regarding other, more central, parts of Scripture.[12] There is a kind of apologetics that somewhat ignores certain details "by themselves," but considers every formal inexactness dangerous because of its consequences. It thus leaves no room

11. *Ibid.*, pp. 418-419.
12. Cf. Koole, *Verhaal en Feit in het OT*, pp. 44-45 in connection with "the tragic struggle" of faith against natural science.

to speak, as Kuyper does, of "innocent inaccuracies."[13] The biblical authors clearly were not motivated by a theory of harmony. Various logical consequences that could be drawn from certain divergences were far from them. However, their historiography was deeply influenced by their awareness of the meaning of history in the religion of Israel. We must therefore think of the encounters of Yahweh with his people in history. Seen from this angle, Bavinck's objection to the transition from nature (its description) to history is more readily understandable. We may add the awareness that the purpose of Scripture is not to orient us concerning the composition of the cosmos in its created parts, nor to inform us scientifically about the "composition of man."[14] The cosmos and man are indeed discussed in various terms, but they are not treated in terms of a revelation concerning composition, but function as a time-bound substratum. Yahweh is creator of heaven and earth, and man is described with all the contours of humanity — the whole man; the purpose of Scripture is directly aimed at the revelation of God *in* this world and *to* man. Opinions may differ about the appropriateness of the title of Cullmann's book, *Salvation in History,* but the message of Scripture is undeniably related to history.

The awareness that God did not reveal himself with a number of profound ideas or timeless truths, but in terms of history and in powerful and saving acts directed to the future, has always prevailed in the church. For that reason the church frequently battled against various forms of idealization and eternalization of revelation, whereby history received at most the role of illustrating that "eternal" truth. As a consequence, concern for the reliability of Scripture was always directed to its description of history. The abandonment of the theory of harmony and of the ideal of exactness, therefore, does not imply disinterestedness in reliability. Thus, its credo is not indifferent to the development of theological thought, which, particularly since the Enlightenment, has been increasingly concerned with the relationships between revelation, faith, and history.

It is no wonder that in our time, with its interest in the kerygma, gospel research has reached a peak. With form-critical and tradition-critical research, attention also was focused on the reliability of the Gospels. This research treats the dif-

13. *Princ.*, p. 457.
14. See Berkouwer, *Man: The Image of God* (ET, 1962), Ch. 6.

ferences between the Gospels, noted in earlier times, and the meaning of these variations. The differentiation did not offer many problems when, at an earlier time, "pluriformity" did not seem to be a shadow over reliability at all. It was rather an indication of the great richness of the witness concerning Jesus: one event was pictured by the various Gospels in its many "aspects" so that one could not speak of a break or contradiction in the testimony. In dealing with the differentiation, there was concern to point to *harmony, unity,* and *pluriformity.*[15] Thus Augustine wrote his "Concerning the Consensus of the Evangelists." Apparently, for Augustine there is scarcely a problem present in this differentiation, because of his faith in the guidance of the Spirit. One is indeed allowed to investigate the causes of these differences, but the authority of the gospel prohibits us from believing that they would pass on lies: "It is not permitted to us to judge that any one of them had lied." The evangelists pass on events in a different way and, for instance, change the order of words; but this does not blemish the truth in any way.[16] Calvin also dealt with the problem, especially concerning the synoptics in his book *Commentary on a Harmony of the Evangelists, Matthew, Mark, and Luke.* He does not deny the differences, but he suggests that they are not arbitrary but guided by God's providence, the Holy Spirit thus submitting an admirable consensus of them in a diverse form of writing.[17] This did not suggest at all the problem of an undermining of reliability. Rather, the variation increases the praise of the Gospels because of their undeniable consensus.[18]

Later, different questions and problems played a role. The providence of God was no longer declared to be the principle of explanation. There was interest in the process of the growth of the gospel, and the Gospels are being compared in their concrete differences in order to find the motivations in *human* considerations that caused the differences. It became increasingly a matter of conviction that various lines connected the Gospels. These lines could be traced by means of comparison.

15. Tatian produced a harmony of the Gospels as early as approx. 175 A.D.
16. A. Bea, *The Study of the Synoptic Gospels* (ET, 1965), pp. 42, 55.
17. *Commentary on a Harmony of the Evangelists* (ET, 1949, Pringle Edition), p. xxxix.
18. Cf. Calvin's introduction to *The Gospel According to John 1-10* (ET, 1959), p. 6: "This Gospel is a key to open the door to the understanding of the others."

We note various attempts to determine the priority of a Gospel (e.g., Mark) by tracing the common and divergent material. Divergences are no longer explained as relatively accidental and arbitrary, nor from a specific purpose of the Holy Spirit (variation as enrichment because of pluriformity). Increasingly, their origin is explained in terms of a conscious choice and composition in view of motivations that can be traced by man. One did not merely note the differences in language and style (which often played a role in the discussion of organic and mechanical inspiration), but also a difference in approach motivated by the evangelist's own concept, frequently referred to as his "theology."[19] It was determined by his own framework and purpose. During earlier days in Reformed theology, men were not accustomed to speak of a "theology" of the biblical authors. A rather sharp distinction was made between the revelation *in* Scripture and the thought *about* Scripture that followed it. This latter then received the name "theology." We will pass over this question of terminology, which is closely related to one's understanding of theology. Here we desire merely to emphasize what is characteristic and deliberate in the compositions of the evangelists.

It was pointed out by many that it was impossible to write a "biography" of Jesus based on the Gospels,[20] not even by adding up the data from the Gospels so that one would complement another. This simple solution of complementarity was increasingly abandoned after it had often served various forms of harmonization, for example, between the synoptic Gospels and the Gospel of John.[21] It merely pointed out that the authors did not intend to give an historical narrative of Jesus' life and work: they did not wish to offer an exact rendering of the facts by way of a "coverage" of Jesus' life. As Ridderbos writes, the evangelists did not intend to give "an historical narrative of Jesus' words and works but a portrayal of Jesus as the Christ." That is the character of our gospel, or, expressed in other terms, not *report* but *witness*.[22] Ridderbos does not mean to construct an absolute contrast between kerygma and that which happened.[23] But the evangelists set out to give a description with a special purpose in mind: to call for

19. H. N. Ridderbos, *K. V. Mattheüs* (1952), I, 14.
20. Kuyper, *Enc.*, III, 158-163.
21. Cf. J. Blinzler, *Johannes und die Synoptiker* (1965), pp. 16f.
22. *Mattheüs*, I, 17.
23. *Ibid.*, p. 19.

faith (Jn. 20:31). The evangelist ordered his material in view of this purpose, which influenced, for example, both the form and content of the speeches of Jesus. Many examples illustrate the lack of exact photographic — historical and precise — records.[24] In view of this undeniably kerygmatic purpose, one must speak of a deliberate process of describing with a structured variety.

In connection with this character of the Gospels, the question was frequently asked whether one could still speak of reliability in the full meaning of the word, since the biblical authors' purpose deeply affects the portrayal. There would have been no problem if an admonition to faith had been added (in the form of a sermon on a text) to an exact description of the sheer facts, events, and words. The situation seems to be much more complex when purpose and application are expressed *in* the description. In the latter case one might ask for the relationship between this "specific purpose" of the evangelists and the reliability of their own gospel story.[25]

In principle, we encounter anew the problem that also plays a role regarding the Old Testament — one's view of the ideal historiography. If absolute preciseness and exactness is seen as the ideal, excluding all interpretive subjectivity, in order to render "facts" as objectively as possible, we must conclude that the Gospels do not coincide with this ideal and therefore are not reliable. According to this view, we can only deal with interpretation and application after the "objective" rendering of facts, without other factors being involved. In other words, only a "value-free" description of history could claim to be genuinely historical. If we are dealing with a penetration of story and interpretation, should we not accept a *creativity* of the evangelists from which "fantasy" could be distinguished only with great difficulty? Is fantasy not the very opposite of reliability? Often the question is presented in a discussion of whether we can be sure of anything with an inexact description, and whether as a consequence every argument falls to the ground. The influence of this question is explainable by the need for certainty that we have noted, even though we observe how various concessions are made, while the legitimacy of these concessions is by no means clear. The fear here ex-

24. Bea, p. 38: not "a stenographer's report, or the accuracy of a photographer or tape recording."
25. *Ibid.*, p. 35.

pressed points especially to the center of the saving events (e.g., the resurrection). It demands an answer to whether interpretation may have shown its influence here also.

One must understand this fear: it may of course be explained as the necessity of some people to lift God's Word above all history and their desire for a closed system of truth. But it may also be caused by a lack of insight into and perception of the harmony of the Gospels as they are constructed and of the reliability of their witness concerning Christ. Even if we are aware of problems posed by the connection between event and interpretation,[26] we may not withdraw into the postulate of an historiography that *separates* story from interpretation for the sake of objectivity.[27] Such a notion will never escape a leveling of the Gospels. In their differentiation, they are reminders of the statement of Paul to the Galatians, before whose eyes Jesus Christ was publicly portrayed as crucified (Gal. 3:1). This statement is free of any vagueness, as he confronts them, so ignorant and beguiled that they do not understand this Christ.

With this admonition we have not offered a solution, but it may urge us to exercise great caution in our standards of reliability. For this portrayal apparently could have kept them from beguilement and could have opened an escape from the suggestion of the magician. It is not a confused portrayal of the Lord that abandoned them to this beguilement "by works of the law" (Gal. 3:2), but the reliable portrayal of the crucified one, which they had not seen in their ignorance even though it was portrayed before their eyes. Paul's amazement begins with the transparency and reliability of preaching. He speaks of apostolic preaching, expressing it not with the category of hearing but of seeing: "before your eyes." It is the story of preaching that is directed to them and appeals to them which they should have and could have trusted. We cite Paul's admonition in order also to point out the unique character of the Gospels; they have a great purpose in mind, and they cannot be criticized more seriously than with the qualification

26. Cullmann, *Salvation in History*, p. 89.
27. *Ibid.*, p. 93. According to Cullmann, interpretation also uses "non-historical elements alongside the historical reports or by investing the accounts of historical events with legendary, mythological, and fabulous elements." There is, however, a "primacy of the event" (p. 136), and myths stand in the service of "the salvation-historical perspective" (p. 139).

that historically they would be unreliable because of their nature.

Noting the peculiar character of the Gospels, we are struck by the fact that every form of criticism concerning their reliability is related to the use of the same inerrancy yardstick of accuracy and exactness that we noted in the attempts at a harmony. This criticism frequently is a reaction to the theory of harmony, in which the yardstick of exactness also plays a decisive role. The critics try to show that reliability cannot be maintained according to that yardstick. In spite of the difference of their themes, this common background of criticism and the theory of harmony makes the solution of the problem absolutely impossible, because it bars the road to the discovery of a reliability in the relationship between narrative and interpretation. However, one may not seek an escape either by severing explanation from fact, or kerygma from history. In the explanation the eye does not wander for a moment from the *events,* so that protest was justly raised against notions of fiction and falsification. For thereby human creativity would render everything unauthentic and far removed from reality.

Of course, various attempts were made to describe the connection between narrative and interpretation. The proof provided by the differences between the Gospels and the purpose of the various evangelists, which became ever clearer, left no escape. The structure of the Gospels is determined by this purpose. Kuyper spoke of the purpose of the Spirit in relation to all the differences in the Gospels, including differences in the words of Jesus himself. The way Kuyper expresses himself is arresting, because he states of the evangelists that they put certain words into the mouth of Jesus. At first this may give one the feeling of fiction or falsification. But this is obviously not Kuyper's intention, for he believes that fiction is excluded precisely because, with the variation, the Spirit meant "to make an impression on the Church which wholly corresponds to what Jesus said."[28]

Note that Kuyper uses the term "impression" in this connection. Apparently he was not at all troubled by the absence of accuracy and exactness precisely *because* of the God-breathed character of Scripture: the reliability of the Gospels was guaranteed by this purpose of the Spirit. This aspect of the God-breathed Scripture is hardly worked out materially by Kuyper

28. *Princ.,* p. 550.

in the area of human motivations. Intensive investigation into these human motivations and purposes came only later. This does not refer to a psychological analysis of the authors, but an analysis and comparison of the Gospels themselves. Time and again reliability became an issue. One will never solve the problem of the Gospels by indiscriminately operating with the concept of "historical reliability," precisely because then one leaves the impression that no further questions need to be answered. As a consequence, all further reflection on this point is subject to suspicion from the start. On the contrary, the right of this research must be maintained, since it immediately flows from the Gospels themselves. These further considerations are caused by clear indications marking differences which far exceed differences in language and style. Attention was given, for instance, to the difference between John and the synoptics. It was asked why John offers no birth narrative (rather than a prologue about the *Logos*), no institution of the Last Supper, no transfiguration on the mount, nothing concerning Gethsemane (which appears in all the synoptics),[29] while he does offer long discourses of Jesus, as well as the high priestly prayer and the foot washing, which do not occur in the other Gospels. Yet one does not get the impression that we are dealing here with a totally different history, without any point of reference to the synoptics, even though, outside the Gospel of John, there are only a few words that in character and emphasis approach Christ's words in John concerning his relationship to the Father (Mt. 11:27).

Moreover, there are notable differences among the synoptics regarding Jesus' encounter with people in his environment, the Beatitudes (cf. Mt. 5:1-12; Lk. 6:20-26), and the parables. There is reason to believe that certain post-Easter situations of the church co-determined the renditions. Frequent use has been made of the concept of a situational application (and change) of Jesus' teaching in order to clarify the arresting differences. But the term "situational" often encountered resistance; for various forms of situation ethics left the impression that God's law depended on, was in fact determined by, a certain situation. However, despite that resistance, it should be noted that the way in which Jesus' words and works were rendered *was* influenced by each peculiar situation. This realization is not due to relativizing but to faith in the living

29. Cf. R. M. Grant, *The Earliest Lives of Jesus* (1961), p. 5.

Christ and the saving event manifest in him, with all its power and grace in every situation and age. To the evangelists, the occurrence of changes apparently did not in the least form a threat to the reliability and authority of their message. This is on a totally different level than that of falsification, which projects a wrong and misleading image. According to Mark and Luke, when Jesus encounters the rich young ruler, he says: "Why do you call me good?" (Mk. 10:18; Lk. 18:19). According to Matthew, Jesus says: "Why do you ask me about what is good?" (Mt. 19:17). This is an often discussed illustration of a latitude implied in the nature and purpose of the Gospels.

One clearly cannot escape these differences with the presupposition of "historical" (i.e., exact) reliability, thus giving no further thought to the differences. In fact, each attempt at harmonization begins with a critical presupposition about the way in which the evangelists most clearly and reliably could have and should have witnessed to Christ's life and work. Harmonization cannot possibly regard this as an innocent concern in view of its purpose (the authority of Scripture). On the contrary, gospel research should be regarded as perfectly legitimate, even in its analysis of composition and purpose. The analysis shows that it is not determined by a flight from history. What *happened* is decisive for all evangelists. One might say that their tendency is clearly anti-docetic, even in John, who witnesses to the Word who became flesh (Jn. 1:14).

Thus, various emphases on witness, truth, and reliability are clearly evident (Jn. 19:35; 21:24). But these are not in opposition to a freedom in composing and expressing the mystery of Christ; their purpose is rather to point in their testimony to that great light. The light that shines in the proclamation of cross and resurrection is central, and the creed of the church has always been aimed at that testimony as a reliable witness. For the aim of the portrayal was not to mislead and to deceive; it was not even a "pious fraud," for it was wholly focused on the great mystery. This explains why the church through the ages was scarcely troubled by the differences pointed out long before, and by the inexact, non-notarial portrayal. A problem was created only as a result of attempts at harmonization and the criticism that followed. Either the inexactness was considered dangerous for inspiration, or the Gospels were thought to be merely a conglomerate of contradictions. But through a recognition of the true nature of the Gospels, the way is opened to hear and understand the one testimony.

The witness of the apostles is concerned with history: its nature is not eternalizing or abstract. This is especially evident from the importance given to the "eyewitnesses" (Lk. 1:2; II Pet. 1:16).[30] This does not mean that only the eyewitnesses were in communion with Christ, as distinguished from those who were not his "contemporaries" (cf. Jn. 20:29). Via the eyewitnesses the testimony issues into the tradition, in the word of preaching, so that "faith comes from what is heard" (Rom. 10:17). Reliability and certainty go along with it, since it is written that salvation "was declared at first by the Lord, and it was attested to us by those who heard him" (Heb. 2:3).[31] In this process of transition the attested reality of salvation goes counter to all vagueness and any flight from reality. Throughout the New Testament, a passionate resistance can be noted at this point, because everything is at stake, just as all preaching and faith are in vain if Christ has not been raised (I Cor. 15:14, 17). The testimony of preaching would be false, since it would not be backed by the truth (I Cor. 15:15). The idea is sharply condemned throughout the New Testament that the message of salvation could be a creation or a projection of men, a fabrication of the human spirit. The limit of all subjectivity and all variety in the portrayal of the mystery of Christ is the reliability of that which is passed on, which was seen, heard, and understood. It is remarkable that, in this defense, a word is often used that has become particularly relevant for our time — *myth*.

The word "myth" occurs in the pastoral letters and in II Peter. We are instructed to have nothing to do "with godless and silly myths" (I Tim. 4:7), and not to wander into myths (II Tim. 4:4) that do not agree with sound doctrine. In so doing we would no longer heed the truth, as is the case in Jewish myths (Titus 1:14). According to II Peter, to be an eyewitness of Christ's majesty is the opposite of "cleverly devised myths" (II Pet. 1:16). It is hardly possible to get a clear and exact picture of these "myths," but that which diminishes the truth of salvation is clearly being rejected, and we must recognize it within the area of fabrications of the human

30. *TDNT,* V, 373f. See also p. 348 concerning "the full historicity and totality of the event of revelation."
31. Cf. Heb. 6:16. For further examples, see *TDNT,* I, 601f.

spirit.[32] The above-mentioned sharp contrasts make this quite clear: along with the warning against godless myths in I Timothy we also read of the saying which is sure and worthy of full acceptance, "that Christ Jesus came into the world to save sinners" (I Tim. 1:15). And along with the rejection of myths we are called upon to remember that Jesus Christ is risen from the dead (II Tim. 2:8). We are not dealing with the contrast between the Greek words *logos* (word) and *mythos* (word), because myths are also expressed in words (*logoi*).[33] The content of the words is decisive. But clearly the reality of salvation is at stake here, whereby myth stands over against the truth (*alētheia*) of the history of Jesus Christ and of the appearance of the grace of God (Titus 2:11). Decisive is the purity and health of the words, as opposed to unreliability and falsehood (cf. Eph. 4:29; 5:6).[34] Thus, the concrete words are distinguished from myth or fable, and the question of the *reliability* of the words is of primary and decisive significance in this contrast.

It might be asked whether, in all the discussions about the so-called demythologizing that take their cue from the "mythical" formulations of the New Testament, the decisive die has not been already cast in the New Testament opposition to myth. Is not "a divine fact with all the weight of historical reality" placed over against myth in the above text?[35] However, we must keep in mind that Bultmann does not mean the same thing by "myth" as what is called idle, godless, silly myth in the New Testament. Therefore, we "cannot directly take up a position against Bultmann's theological concern with demythologizing by means of a text such as II Peter 1:16."[36] By "myth," Bultmann does not mean those myths that are rejected as fabrications and are opposed to the truth as *mythoi*. He means rather an *imagery* connected with a mythical world view. This world view is characterized by the presence of three levels — heaven, earth, and the underworld — so that earth is

32. Cf. *TDNT*, IV, 762.
33. J. Barr, *The Semantics of Biblical Language* (1961), pp. 221f. Barr argues against Stählin (in Kittel), because the latter sets *logos* and *mythos* over against each other. Barr points to the cancerous *logos* (II Tim. 2:17). In my opinion, Barr does Stählin an injustice, because the nature and the content of the *logoi* are not denied by Stählin and because for him the *mythoi* stand in contrast to the words of faith (I Tim. 4:6).
34. Cf. *TDNT*, VII, 97.
35. *TDNT*, IV, 786.
36. K. H. Schelkle, *Die Petrusbriefe* (1961), p. 198.

considered to be the "scene of the supernatural activity of God."[37] It is this "world view" which, according to him, forms the background of the New Testament portrayal of the saving events. In Bultmann, this "world view" has broader implications than the discussions of a biblical world view mentioned above; there the cosmological aspect was discussed in a much more isolated manner. Bultmann connects it with all the imagery of the saving events, for example, the categories of God's sending his son to earth, his resurrection, ascension, and return: "All this is the language of mythology." To modern man this entire world view does not deserve belief.[38] "What meaning, for instance, can we attach to such phrases in the creed as 'descended into hell' or 'ascended into heaven'? We no longer believe in the three-storied universe which the creeds take for granted."[39]

It is not Bultmann's intention to apply a method of quantitative reduction in order to peel the myth from the New Testament. Rather, he wishes to interpret myth.[40] This is only possible by recognizing a *meaning* in it, in order to distinguish it from "fabrications." The purpose of myth is not really *cosmological* but *anthropological,* that is, it expresses something about man.[41] Man is limited and finite; he is not in control of himself but dependent on the powers that surround him. To Bultmann, myth is thus something quite different from the *mythoi* rejected in the New Testament as human fables. "Demythologizing," therefore, means the attempt to *understand* the

37. "NT and Mythology," *Kerygma and Myth,* I (ET, 1961), p. 1.
38. *Ibid.,* p. 3. Cf. Bultmann, *Jesus Christ and Mythology* (ET, 1958), pp. 14f. Cf. the modern world-view for which "the cause-and-effect nexus is fundamental" (p. 15), and "the intervention of God." The appeal of J. A. T. Robinson in *Honest to God* is closely related, namely, in the rejection of the miraculous and supernatural. Cf. Bultmann: "No one who is old enough to think for himself supposes that God lives in a local heaven" (*Kerygma and Myth,* I, 4). Regarding the incarnation as *non*-miraculous, see Jaspers and Bultmann, *Myth and Christianity* (ET, 1958), pp. 68f. Cf. Bultmann's reply to Robinson in *The Honest to God Debate* (1963), pp. 134f., regarding supernaturalism (p. 135), with Bultmann's question to Robinson about the paradoxical identity of "a historical event with the eschatological event" (p. 137).
39. *Kerygma and Myth,* I, 4.
40. *Jesus Christ and Mythology,* p. 35: demythologizing "takes the modern world-view as the criterion." Cf. the antithesis between mythological and natural-scientific as "two ways of thinking" (p. 38).
41. *Myth and Christianity,* p. 61, n. 1: "The myth expresses man's knowledge of the ground and limits of his being."

myth. Even though Bultmann strongly emphasizes that he does not aim at elimination but at interpretation, the very word "demythologizing," and its parallels "dehistoricizing" and "de-eschatologizing" do suggest a shift in interpretation. This is particularly the case when Bultmann describes the saving event in connection with the mythical world view. Because of the explicitness of this description, the question is naturally raised concerning its trustworthiness. Indeed, the myth rejected in the New Testament may not be lightly identified with Bultmann's concept of myth. But the resistance in the New Testament against these myths is closely related to that which, according to Bultmann, belongs to the mythical imagery of the New Testament. Seen in this light, it is understandable that criticism of Bultmann frequently was directed at this connection between the biblical world view and the saving event.

Brunner charged Bultmann with "mixing the question of world view with the question of myth," even though "fundamentally different problems" are at stake here. The question of historical revelation can be argued entirely apart from the question of which world view is adopted.[42] Kümmel also believes that Bultmann "extends the idea of myth." Kümmel agrees that at times a mythological *language* is used in the New Testament, for example, in Philippians 2 (emptied, humbled, exalted). But this does not mean that a saving event can no longer be discussed in terms of an act of God *in time*.[43] "But the core of the kerygma of the New Testament is affected when this temporal saving event is brushed aside." This saving event is described in a form that cannot be separated from its content, namely, "that of historical reality."[44] All stress is given to the witnesses of this reality; it is an important decision whether or not this witness is accepted.[45] But it cannot be denied that the witnesses had in mind a real event in time. The emphasis on eyewitnesses makes sense only in this way. They did not merely proclaim certain "truths" expressed in the categories and images of their time (time-relatedness), but they testified to a reality in terms of seeing and hearing, and of touching with the hands – reality aimed at faith, fellowship, and joy (I Jn. 1:1-4).

42. *The Christian Doctrine of Creation and Redemption* (*Dogmatics,* II) [ET, 1952], 263f.
43. "Mythos im NT," *Theol. Zeitschr.* (1950), p. 332.
44. *Ibid.*, p. 336.
45. *Ibid.*

Bultmann applies the term "mythical" to something "other-worldly" and divine that appears to be something "this-worldly."[46] According to him, the decision with respect to the conceptions and thought patterns of the New Testament falls into that area. At stake here is the large question of whether or not Bultmann calls "mythical imagery" that which according to the gospel is the real message. This apparently is a central question in any discussion of Bultmann's program;[47] for he acknowledges that his view of the mythical imagery of the kerygma cannot be applied everywhere in the New Testament. He notes that the resurrection of Christ is often used in the New Testament as a miraculous proof, for example, the stories about the empty grave and the appearances. This tendency can even be noted where Paul "tries to prove" the miracle of the resurrection by adducing a list of eyewitnesses (I Cor. 15:3-8).[48] Bultmann calls this "a fatal argumentation."[49] The way in which Paul speaks of Christ's resurrection (and the eye-witnesses) in I Corinthians 15 makes it clear to him that this indeed belongs to the immediate and real content of the kerygma in connection with a faith that bears fruit, and not with a preaching that simply is false (I Cor. 15:14f.). Thus, the case of Bultmann's program is focused on the problems of "mythical imagery and saving event in view of the question of the *essence* of the message and its true *skandalon*." According to Bultmann, the world view is so closely related to the New Testament that it simply necessitates an unmythical interpretation. With Paul Schütz he feels that mythical religion will die out because of modern technical and medical encroachments.[50]

A program of demythologizing is therefore unavoidable if the real intention of the gospel is to be understood and to be made intelligible.[51] Bultmann's remark that the use of radio and the electric light could not be brought into harmony with a New Testament belief in the world of spirit and miracles[52] led Barth to speak of "the quite humorless tradition of Mar-

46. *Kerygma and Myth,* I, 11.
47. For many variations of the concept "myth," see J. L. McKenzie, *Myths and Realities: Studies in Biblical Theology* (1963).
48. *Kerygma and Myth,* I, 39.
49. *Theology of the NT,* I (ET, 1951), 305: "The resurrection cannot — in spite of I Cor. 15:3-8 — be demonstrated or made plausible as an objectively ascertainable fact on the basis of which one could believe."
50. *Kerygma and Myth,* I, 5.
51. *Ibid.*
52. *CD,* III/2 (ET, 1960), p. 447: "Who can read this without a shudder?"

burg." He wondered whether truth could be discussed in such a way, as if indeed Christianity had the task to accept or reject world views![53] With Brunner, Barth is obviously not impressed with the connection of world view with the description of the saving event. For, in his opinion, we are not dealing here with mythical imagery but with a witness to the reality of salvation described as a coming and going, a descent and an ascension. The conviction stands, so Barth concludes: "We must still accept the resurrection of Jesus, and His subsequent appearances to His disciples, as genuine history in its own particular time."[54]

Thus, the *content* of the kerygma is continually at stake in the struggle over demythologizing, and hence also the kerygma's reliability. The fundamental question is whether the world view can be innocently reduced to a problem of cosmic composition or whether the entire New Testament is so determined by the ancient world view, with its implications, that one cannot be separated from the other and only an interpretation along the lines of Bultmann's program will do. Is it true that the biblical world view is presupposed into the very heart of the gospel and of the creed resulting from it? This is Bultmann's judgment. He does not regard the world view in terms of a pattern of concepts whose nature is time-related and incidental; rather, it plays a role in the total description of the saving event. At this point the great significance of the question of reliability comes into view, for here the apostolic testimony witnesses to God's great salvation, so that we are convinced of the fact that, for example, this "coming" belongs to the message worthy of full acceptance (I Tim. 1:15).

Why was not the church convinced long ago, one might ask, that in view of a changed world view its creed had become untenable because it referred innocently to Christ's birth, resurrection, ascension, and return? The reason this did not happen is that it did not refer to heaven, for example, as if it had an adequate "perception" of heaven. That the biblical conception of heaven also functions as a boundary was never quite forgotten.[55] The church thus continued to use biblical categories, such as "from above" (Jn. 3:31), "to heaven," and "whence he shall come," not because it fully understands what they meant,

53. *Kergyma and Myth,* I, 3f.
54. *CD,* III/2, 443.
55. See Berkouwer, *The Return of Christ,* p. 213.

but because it felt bound to follow the apostolic witness interpreting the mystery of Christ in those terms.

Even the Old Testament shows that God cannot be "localized" with the help of the concept of "heaven" in the same way in which places are indicated by boundaries on earth, so that terms such as "inside" and "outside" are applicable. Solomon exclaims: "But will God indeed dwell on the earth? Behold, heaven and the highest heaven cannot contain thee" (I Kgs. 8:27; cf. Deut. 10:14). And Jeremiah passes on the word of Yahweh: "Do I not fill heaven and earth?" (Jer. 23:24). It is incorrect to conclude that the New Testament witnesses would be unaware of this in their expressions about "heaven" (Heb. 4:14; 7:26; Eph. 4:10). At times, indeed, more has been asserted and defined in various theological considerations than the Bible warrants, for example, the subtle discussions concerning the Lord's Supper and the phrase "sitting at the right hand." However, the meaning of the apostolic witness is not molested by these foreboding dangers. In looking at attempts to substitute and translate these phrases, one can appreciate Barth's irony concerning the need for demythologizing on behalf of modern man. Next to Paul, Bultmann appeals particularly to John as a crown witness of the fact that the process of demythologizing began already in the New Testament itself.[56] But it is remarkable how even the Gospel of John contains "dimensional" expressions of this kind as a matter of course. We read in the Epistle to the Colossians of the things that are "above," where Christ is seated at the right hand of God (Col. 3:1f.; cf. Phil. 3:20). But John likewise uses the term "from above" to indicate the mystery of Christ's coming (Jn. 3:13, 31; 6:32f.). This includes the warning not to disqualify dimensional terms, such as the ones that serve as signs. Nor should they be regarded as stumbling blocks for modern man.

Thielicke said that the ancient world view "left open the door for the idea of transcendence." Therefore, it is precisely fitting "to express the otherness of God and his intervention in salvation history."[57] He obviously has in mind a contrast with the closed world view of the natural scientist, which is emphatically charged by Bultmann with being an obvious denial of the mythical imagery of the New Testament. The

56. *Jesus Christ and Mythology*, p. 32. "Mythology has been transposed into history" (p. 34).
57. "The Restatement of NT Mythology," *Kerygma and Myth*, I, 169.

issue is not so much the question whether God acts in history; Bultmann also maintains this emphatically. To him, the real contrast is between God's hidden eschatological acts in Jesus of Nazareth and the miraculous, supernatural phenomena of which he speaks again and again. However, these conceptions are not clear in themselves, even though they have deeply influenced theological discussion. Bultmann sees them only in view of the fact that we, because of our world view, can no longer follow the imagery. He expresses agreement with the general distinction between *sign* and *miracle*. The sign does not vanish when the miracle is discarded, because the sign is related to God's hidden acts.[58] Bultmann points out that the miracle always has the force of proof. It seems overwhelming that a decision between faith and unbelief becomes superfluous while the sign is aimed at precisely that decision.

Now the New Testament clearly does not contain the kind of miracle that frees one from the calling to believe; signs in the New Testament are intended for belief and do not function as "proofs" that exclude faith.[59] They were nowhere used by themselves as external evidence, without meaning or relationship, so that, like a "show miracle," they would stun the audience. But, though they do not have the function of a rational proof,[60] the very unique significance of the "signs" shows that one may not lightly operate with a contrast between hiddenness (sign) and visibility (miracle), thus leaving the impression via mythical imagery that the problem of miracle — in the kerygma — has been solved. For it is possible to interpret "miracle" in such a way that essential features of "sign" are included, and the opposition against miracle also affects the sign, that is, through strong presupposition concerning a "supernatural" world view with its "miraculous" conceptions.

The boundary between sign and miracle seems to lie between that which is conceivable and that which is not. This in turn is determined by a presupposition concerning the modern world view. In modern New Testament theology — that is, among a good number of those not accepting Bultmann's view — miracles are being discussed on a level quite different from the one above. The attention is focused on the way the saving events are described in the New Testament, with all its varia-

58. *Faith and Understanding*, I (ET, 1969), 252f.
59. See Berkouwer, *The Providence of God*, p. 215.
60. Pannenberg, *Jesus — God and Man*, pp. 98f.

tions. Just as in systematic theology, the question is being considered whether in the course of history the boundaries of what seems to be "unbelievable" can shift because of the acquisition of new knowledge (Lk. 5:26).[61] But consideration is especially given to the meaning and function of the miracle stories in the New Testament in connection with the composition of the gospel of the living Lord and his power over all things.[62]

Bultmann's research in the Gospels indeed is also closely related to "form-historical" considerations, but questions concerning the modern world view and the problems of conceivability are a part of these considerations of method. At this very point, both the view of miracles and the perspective that belongs essentially to the kerygma are determined by a presupposition. The nature of the kerygma is no longer determined by the nature of the Gospels themselves and by the uniqueness of their composition, but by this conceivability.[63] At this point in the discussion we note how frequently views appear that are closely related to this "world view." According to Bultmann, Barth's simple questions should be considered an escape from the problems. But Conzelmann likewise voices them, in that he relativizes the relevancy of the "world view." Speaking of the heart of the message, he says that we are not at all concerned with "a lesson about world views" but with a perspective of revelation that "for the present day mode of thought" is just as "significant as for all previous and for all future times, not more and not less."[64] The proclamation of the gospel, which made the witnesses go out into the world, is not determined by problems of height (or depth) but of cross and resurrection, of humiliation and exaltation, and by the hiddenness of Christ's new reign.[65]

The time between resurrection and ascension has been described as having "a veil of mysteriousness" to indicate the lack of any accurate description offered by a chronicle. This does not deal with the mysteriousness of a proving miracle but with the concrete perspective of the exaltation. It is not

61. See Berkouwer, *Providence*, pp. 194f.
62. Cf. C. F. D. Moule, *Miracles* (1965), pp. 235f., especially regarding the vocabulary and classification of the "miracle-stories."
63. H. M. Kuitert, *The Reality of Faith*, pp. 165f.
64. Conzelmann, "Ontmythologisering," *Theologie voor niet-theologen*, II (1965), 96.
65. Cf. Barth, *CD*, III/2, 454.

a cosmological "conception" gradually becoming obsolete that determines the message of the witnesses, but it is this reality of exaltation, reconciliation, and salvation aimed at the future. If one wishes to speak of the "cloud" in terms of a cosmic "horizon" (Acts 1:9),[66] this must be the horizon of perspective, service, joy, and expectation at the same time.[67] It is inseparably related to that other horizon of Christ's return. This horizon does not disappear in a time in which the universe becomes less and less "conceivable" to our mind with all the new discoveries and horizons. We must rather say that this horizon was and is fundamental to the creed of the church. Just as with the term "from above" in early Christian language, it cannot become a "myth." The horizon is not that of a stunning "miracle"; it is the new horizon in which the sign of the kingdom of God in the Messiah Jesus continues to be of decisive and essential significance throughout the entire kerygma because of what occurred once for all. So Weber was not wrong in describing Christ as the *end* of myths.[68] He referred to a groping and searching for another "higher" world and to the "traffic" between that world and ours as a searching "in the beyond," as if true and real insight had to come "from above" in a mysterious and odd way. In that way one could no longer look around him (in our world) in order to hear, to understand, and to find. The end of this restless and nervous search is in Christ. One need no longer descend into the abyss or to climb into heaven, because all this has become near in the word of preaching (Deut. 30:11f.; Rom. 10:6-7; cf. Jn. 14:8f.). In view of that word, perspectives are opened of a new heaven and a new earth.

The unique significance of Christ's coming, of his cross and resurrection, is proclaimed as good tidings through various means. This witness comes to us in the context of the entire Scripture — as human Scripture inbreathed by God — and as such calls attention to its human and time-related aspects, its motivations and background subservient to the Spirit. Thus, when in due course the genuinely verbal witness of Scripture was taken seriously, the impression might be given that a rift appeared in the continuity of the church with respect to the

66. *TDNT,* IV, 909: "with a chaste safeguarding of the mystery."
67. See in detail Moltmann, *Theology of Hope,* pp. 195f. regarding "vocation," "promise," "mission" and against all reduction, which is impossible because of this horizon.
68. *Grundlagen,* I, 381.

reliability of Scripture. It should not amaze us that several shifts in the emphasis of the church indeed at times give that impression. And even if one is of the opinion that the continuity of the church's creed was not broken by it, nonetheless the meaning of this shift may not be made relative. Even when a position regarding "demythologizing" has been taken, and the continuity of the preaching of the crucified and truly risen Lord has been discovered, a number of questions still require answers. For the content of the church's faith is not the result of intellectual and logical distinctions and reductions, as in all traditionalism and confessionalism; but it is only understood, on a deeper level, in the openness to the witness of Scripture as the canon of the church. The verbal witness continues to challenge and stimulate us to ponder every detail and context.

In view of this challenge, a rigid immutability and immobility of the church would be unthinkable: that would mean a decisive *devaluation* of the biblical witness on the church's journey into the future. With such an unchanging rigidity the meaning of all genuine Bible study would become an illusion. On the contrary, today various processes are at work, the background and consequence of which are very difficult to analyze — more difficult than in the time when the reliability of Scripture was clearly and rationally defined. New questions continually arise with the discovery of the variety in Scripture, such as the literary styles, the time-relatedness, and the particular goal of a genuinely human "passing on" of the message of salvation in the service of the Spirit. However, the conviction becomes continually stronger that we do not face a choice between reliability and unreliability, as if we could no longer rely on the witness of God's Word. At the same time we see that we cannot use the argument of reliability without an understanding of *how* the Spirit wishes to guide us to salvation and joy through the use of the real Scripture. The continuity of the church's creed is found not in a presupposition, separate from the reading of Scripture, but *through* reading it and by taking seriously its witness in all its human aspects. Since Scripture cannot be understood in an abstract way, but only in terms of a witness concerning Christ and his salvation (God-breathed), we should bring to mind the anti-individualistic statement of Paul: to comprehend "with all the saints" what is the breadth and length and height and depth, and to know the love of Christ which surpasses knowledge (Eph. 3:18-19).

It is incorrect—in view of the Holy Spirit's influence—to regard individualism as an ineradicable evil. But who in the church is not aware of the perennial danger of one's subjectively gaining a conviction and yet losing the perspective of the true reliability of God's Word? With its dimension of salvation, this "with all the saints" would not have to do with a "dialectic" between the individual and the community; but a reminder of the mystery of the church is included in it. It exercises a true discipline in all our reflections and leads us on to the ecclesiastical aspect of the doctrine of Scripture. This aspect neither extinguishes individuality nor leaves the last verdict to the "authority" of the church. For the church itself can be church only when it listens attentively. However, we are warned of error and confusion, of short-sightedness and stubbornness, and of distrust of the God-breathed Scripture. And we are called to the ministry of the gospel. If Scripture is truly what the church confessed it to be in its creed, we should continually be reminded of the prayer during all reading of Scripture: "Come, Creator Spirit!"

Along these lines of growing trust, it becomes increasingly clear that meaningful thought and speech concerning faith in Scripture and the reliability of Scripture is not possible without our being simultaneously confronted with "the heart of the matter," of which Scripture testifies—its witness. The message of Scripture alone, convincing and overwhelming as it is through the power of the Spirit, clearly can lead us quietly to trust this reliability. Questions concerning the nature of this reliability arose automatically when problems about the reliability of Scripture multiplied, particularly in historical-critical research, and the attention was increasingly focused not on decisions based on presuppositions but on concrete problems raised by Scripture's own specific form. Even the simple fact that questions were posed in a variety of fields could easily give the impression that the message was greatly relativized. It is quite important to discover that this impression rests on a misunderstanding, because Scripture itself shows us clearly that a yardstick of reliability may not be applied which is not in agreement with the purpose of Scripture. The effect of shock caused by a number of new questions and problems in connection with reliability is related to an earlier use of such a yardstick. Such varying questions were not and could not be posed at that time, since they were thought to belong to a forbidden area in view of the God-breathed character of Scripture.

The same problem that we discussed in connection with the infallibility of Scripture appears here. Any new aspect of infallibility appeared to be a relativization, and frequently the question was asked if one could continue to speak honestly and truthfully about infallibility. This question may conceal a desire for a clear and easy-to-use concept of infallibility and reliability as well as a concern over the gradual slipping away of certainty. On the other hand, with the influence of the new biblical research, there was a frequent plea to drop the term "infallibility," saying in effect that it would give rise to the misunderstanding of a mechanical, inflexible "inerrancy"—an accuracy of all matters discussed in Scripture. It seems as though some spoke of infallibility out of two sides of their mouth; hence the plea to drop the term. Adopting this suggestion, in my opinion, would contradict the confession of the God-breathed character of Scripture. For it would in turn leave a similar and wrong impression that, because of various concessions, we would be forced into a transition from the reliability of Scripture to its "unreliability." In that case a break would appear in the continuity of the church's belief in Scripture through the ages.

The notion that *today* it would be difficult, if not impossible, for us truly to hear the voice of God in the biblical witness, would mean a capitulation. It would also mean a crisis of tremendous dimensions in the church: the uprooting effect of this crisis would be greater than all the questions that frequently confront us concerning the human nature of Scripture. Of course, no human exorcism can ward off a crisis of this kind. We are reminded that belief in Scripture truly is faith. This faith is not empty and abstract. Only in relationship to the reliable witness of Scripture itself is faith able to stand. Therefore, it is never without works. But the fact that in our time the confession of the infallibility of Scripture is maintained as meaningful and legitimate, and is not dropped because it might lead to "misunderstanding," is only due to a respect for this God-breathed infallibility. It is not added to reliability as a miraculous novelty, but coincides with it. The church expresses with this confession that it honors the Holy Spirit, who in his witness to the truth does not lead us into error but into the pathways of truth (II Jn. 4). The Spirit, with this special concern,[69] has not failed and will not fail in this mystery of God-breathed Scripture. Because of this testimony we are guided by him on the way, and on this side of the horizon of the future we are led to the full truth (Jn. 16:13). To this reliability of the biblical witness corresponds an unlimited trust that in our interaction with Scripture by faith we shall not be put to shame but confirmed.

Other aspects are naturally included in this confession of the reliability of Scripture. When we confess this reliability, the Word of God, the cause of our trust, implies that we have understood and will more and more understand something of what the Spirit says to the church (Rev. 2:7). Faith does not mean a "sacrifice of the intellect" in terms of a forced and rigid subjection. For that is the opposite of the obedience of faith, and it will not awaken us to understand afresh the things of the Spirit (Rom. 8:5). Closely related to the confession of Scripture, therefore, is the confession of its *clarity*. We are naturally aware that here we also encounter many questions that seem to render this clarity doubtful in view of the variety of interpretations during all periods of the history of the church. But precisely because of the confessed reliability of Scripture we have every reason not to withdraw from questions concerning clarity; for these are absolutely significant within the horizon of true reliability. Therefore, we must deal with the *perspicuity* (or clarity) of Scripture.

69. *BC,* Art. III.

CHAPTER TEN

CLARITY

IN CONNECTION WITH THE AUTHORITY of Scripture and its interpretation, in Chapter Four I offered a lengthy exposition of the well-known rule of the Reformation: "Sacred Scripture is its own interpreter." In the sixteenth century it was obviously used in a polemical way in opposition to the Roman Catholic view of church and tradition; but this does not in any way diminish its positive significance. It implies far-reaching consequences for the reading and correct understanding of Scripture, for it points to this activity, to the witness of Scripture and to a self-interpretation. It includes an urgent warning far beyond the controversies of the sixteenth century. It is directed against reading and understanding Scripture with the help of various presuppositions and within a certain frame of thought, because as a result of such presuppositions Scripture is scarcely able to speak in its own words. Closely related to this emphatic admonition for a continued listening to the biblical witness itself is the Reformation conviction that it is "its *own* interpreter." It was expressed in the confession concerning the perspicuity, or clarity, of Holy Scripture. Here we encounter a confession which, through the history of Bible reading, was besieged by many fundamental questions. The church always has been concerned with these in an intensive and very concrete way.

One may ask first of all whether the confession concerning the clarity of Scripture leaves any room for the need of interpretation. Is not all interpretation rendered superfluous because of the perspicuity of Scripture? In speaking of an interpreter and of interpretation, we automatically think of a certain strangeness and distance, such as a language barrier, that must be bridged and conquered through the penetrating function of an interpreter. Does the idea of interpretation have any meaning with respect to something deemed to be clear in itself? And when Scripture is named as its own interpreter, does this not imply that there is no more need for our interpretation?

We are so accustomed to the need for exegesis of Scripture and so impressed with this intense and laborious work that we are hardly able to take the above questions seriously. We immediately think of the story from Acts 8, where the eunuch replies to Philip's question of whether he understands what he reads in Scripture: "How can I, unless someone guides me?" (Acts 8:31). It is Philip who enters the relationship between the eunuch and Scripture (Isaiah), bridging the "gap" by means of the proclamation of Jesus (Acts 8:35). The statement "its *own* interpreter" apparently does not exclude or make superfluous human mediation, an exegesis, and an interpretation. At the same time this seems to imply a certain lack of perspicuity and clarity which the explanation must dispel. These questions concerning the clarity of Scripture, of course, were not unknown at the time of the Reformation. We must realize that Luther and Calvin themselves were intensely occupied with the interpretation of Scripture throughout their lives, so that the statement that Scripture is clear and interprets itself with clarity does not stop all arguments, that is, if one does not wish to close his eyes to pertinent questions concerning this clarity.

An attempt has often been made to solve this problem by referring to the "objective" clarity of Scripture, so that every incomplete understanding and insight of Scripture is said to be due to the blinding of human eyes that could not observe the true light shining from it. Thus, the subjective side is wholly blamed for this failure, and a misinterpretation can in no way be an argument against the utter clarity of Scripture. This blindness of the eyes clearly presents an important question. Scripture itself frequently deals with it. Paul speaks of the god of this world blinding the minds of the unbelievers "to keep them from seeing the light of the gospel of the glory of Christ, who is the likeness of God" (II Cor. 4:4). The light shines in all directions, but blind eyes cannot observe it. There is only one road open to sight, the one experienced by the Israelite and reflected in his prayer about the law: "Open my eyes, that I may behold wondrous things out of thy law" (Ps. 119:18; cf. 42:16; Jn. 9:39-41). Is perhaps "objective" clarity the unchallenged opposite of hearing but not understanding

(Mk. 4:12) by means of a sharp separation between clarity and blindness?

In considering this seemingly simple solution, which fully maintains perspicuity as an objective "quality" of Scripture without any restrictions, we will soon discover that not all questions are answered by it. It may be pointed out first of all that an incomplete understanding or a total misunderstanding of Scripture cannot simply be explained by blindness. Certain obstacles to understanding may also be related to Scripture's concrete form of human language conditioned by history; a barrier and distance is implied in this language form as a matter of course. A breakthrough and bridge was sought by means of translation. Speaking, for instance, of the clarity of the Hebrew Old Testament as an "objective" quality would be speaking of the clarity of Scripture in rather abstract terms, with no reference to insight. This fact has nothing to do with blindness, neither is it solved by an "uncovering" of the eyes, but only by translating Scripture into a language clear to all. Moreover, Scripture that comes to us in this way is tied to historical situations and circumstances in so many ways that not every word we read is immediately clear in itself. The interpretation of Scripture is thus not simply a problem of objective opening of blind eyes but of an explanation of the meaning and relationship of Scripture that came to us in history. Therefore, it will not surprise us that many questions have been raised in the course of history about the perspicuity of Scripture. When the church considered all the problems of understanding, the conclusion was frequently drawn that all ecclesiastical and confessional disunity was thereby explained. Was not the Bible evidently a book without easy access and — apart from the question of translation — without clarity? Was it not therefore necessary to cast some light on Scripture, unillumined as it is in many respects? Concerning the confession of perspicuity, one can state without exaggeration that in practical life many would feel more at home with the statement in II Peter 3:16 about Paul's letters: "There are some things in them hard to understand. . . ."[1] Some wondered whether this confession of clarity was indeed a true confession. A certain

1. Cf. Calvin, *The Epistle of Paul the Apostle to the Hebrews and the First and Second Epistles of St. Peter* (ET, 1963), p. 367: "There is sometimes obscurity, which the unlearned take as an occasion to wander off to their own destruction."

degree of perspicuity seemed to be the *result* of interpretation rather than a previously determined "quality" of Scripture. They wondered whether the Reformation had perhaps gone too far in emphatically calling attention to the perspicuity of Scripture. Perhaps there are certain elements of polemical reaction in this conviction because of the opposition to the Roman Catholic tradition.

The statement that God dwells in inaccessible light (I Tim. 6:16) has never been applied by analogy to Scripture; yet the church has frequently been aware of a certain "inaccessibility." At any rate, the need for explanation was deeply felt. The clarity of Scripture evidently does not in any way have the character of simplicity, as is the case with a startling newspaper report that reveals a certain state of affairs without the need of further "interpretation." The news that a war has broken out somewhere in the world does not in itself call for interpretation, even though the report must be seen in the context of historical facts whose bearing on it cannot at once be assessed by all. A news report speaks to us because of its immediate accessibility. The perspicuity of Scripture differs from a direct and accessible report of this kind in many ways. We must, therefore, further explain what we mean by the perspicuity of Holy Scripture. One might indeed ask if this needed explanation of clarity does not tamper with and relativize the confession itself in all its evident clarity. But this question does not discharge us from the task of further reflection. It is all the more urgent in view of the many apparent shifts in understanding that we have seen above, for example, a changed and deepened insight into the languages in which Scripture came to us, or the insight into the contemporaneous world of Israel and the New Testament. These shifts remind us that in earlier days the self-evidence of Scripture had often led to convictions and positions shared by almost no one today. In view of this, is it still possible and permissible to discuss the perspicuity of Scripture in this naive way? Is it totally divorced from that process of disclosure that has found respect both in the church and in all exegesis? Is it possible to speak of the evident perspicuity of Scripture in terms of a quality separate from all the fruitful efforts of the church to understand Scripture? It was in fact felt from the very start that the word "clarity" did not say everything, that all questions were not solved, to which the extensive discussions about it attest. Moreover, this confession has been interpreted in quite different ways.

According to Bavinck, perspicuity has been "misunderstood and misrepresented by both Protestants and Roman Catholics."[2] Various attempts at clarification of the doctrine of clarity in further detail and depth have been offered. Bavinck says that clarity does not mean that scientific exegesis would be unnecessary; nor does it mean that in the doctrine of salvation Scripture is intelligible to everyone without distinction.

The Reformation doctrine of clarity is usually characterized as part of the controversy with Rome, characterized by the statement that Rome does not begin with the clarity of Scripture but with its obscurity.[3] However, this characterization must be modified. Bavinck adds that it may not be overlooked that, according to Rome, the Bible is "not an opportune literature for laymen." This indicates that Scripture is not regarded as a completely obscure and inaccessible book, written, so to speak, in secret language and hence without meaning for the church. Instead, Rome is convinced that an understanding of Scripture is possible — a clear understanding. But Rome is at the same time deeply impressed by the dangers involved in reading the Bible. Their desire is to protect Scripture against all arbitrary and individualistic exegesis. Thus, we are dealing with Rome's concern regarding free reading of the Bible, even though the issue is usually described as the "obscurity" of Scripture.

Today a new view is breaking through, and at times this new insight has led to a more critical judgment of the church's previous attitude, the intent of which was to protect Scripture from arbitrariness. There is general agreement concerning the dangers involved in any contact with Scripture. Various admonitions are clearly found in Scripture itself against a high-handed interpretation and a distortion of Scripture (II Pet. 3). The Reformers also were aware of these dangers but did not choose a legalistic approach in reaction to them; they rather made every effort to overcome them. Their attention was wholly focused on true interpretation in contrast to any high-handedness or arbitrariness. Although it cannot be said that Reformation thought always reached the point of full clarity concerning the relationship between personal reading of Scripture and

2. *GD,* I, 447.
3. *Ibid.,* pp. 420, 422, 466.

the interpretation of Scripture by the church, the principle of the ruling function of Scripture in the church became the point of departure, so that every isolation of Scripture was excluded. Respect for Scripture as the Word of God, as a lamp for the feet and a light on everyone's path, was a decisive element, rather than opposition to ecclesiastical interpretation. This was also the case in the ancient church within the range of possibilities of that time, and it was not jeopardized because of the abuse of Scripture. This insight becomes increasingly evident. The appeals to Haggai 2:12 (asking the priests to decide these questions of law) and to Matthew 23:1-3 (the scribes sit on Moses' seat) lose their isolating effect with respect to Scripture. With the encyclicals of several popes laying the groundwork, a new approach has been chosen. This cannot only be explained by the awareness that the church has come of age but also from an awareness of the power of the Word's priority and sovereignty. So a prospect is opened again of following the example of the Bereans, who fully accepted the Word, "examining the scriptures daily to see if these things were so" (Acts 17:11). Apparently they functioned here differently from what can be frequently observed in history, and this development ought to be welcomed as it opens up numerous prospects for the future. When fearful reactions disappear, the way is opened for a renewed functioning of an unfettered gospel (II Tim. 2:9).

Seen against this background, the Reformation confession concerning the clarity of Scripture can be appreciated for what it was. In their controversy with Rome, the Reformers repeatedly emphasized that the message of salvation really came through; this was the purpose of Scripture. To them it implied an "accessibility" that was not in the terms of a theoretical construction. Their confession was born of a concrete reading and understanding of Scripture. They were therefore not at all concerned with exhibiting a limitless trust in the subjectivity of an individual deemed to be competent to undertake the risk of interpreting Scripture. They continually cautioned against individualism and the dangers of arbitrariness, and they reminded their readers of the phrase "with all the saints" (Eph. 3:18). But they were deeply convinced at the same time that the message of Scripture could not be isolated from God's Word as the sword of the Spirit (Eph. 6:17). According to Calvin, we may not withhold the Bible from the "Christian people," because that withholding would rob them of necessary armor in their struggle.[4] The light of Scripture had become an indisputable reality, with a good number of new and surprising discoveries. Men saw the relationship between this light of Scripture and the command of God with regard to the prophetic writings "made known to all nations . . . to bring about the obedience of faith" (Rom. 16:26).

The Greek verb *gnōrizein* means "to make known," to bring forth from hiding to full accessibility.[5] This was the decisive view of the Reformers in their confession concerning the clarity of Scripture. It was born of the reading of Scripture itself and was not based on a theory of presupposed "qualities" of Scripture. The clarity and the "efficacy" of Scripture were inseparably related to each other. Scripture was seen in direct relationship to the revelation of the mystery (Rom. 16:25). Therefore, people meditated about Scripture in terms of those words of Scripture in which the Word of the living and speaking God was called a light and a lamp (Ps. 119:105; cf. 19:9; Prov. 6:23), a light in a dark place (II Pet. 1:19). People thought about God's Word exclusively in terms of this emanating light, as well as of the intention of the Word, so that the veil over their hearts was lifted by the Word. This does not mean that this light stands in an immediate and direct correspondence to the correct insight and knowledge; but it does mean that in contrast to the secret things, which belong to God, the things that are *revealed* "belong to us and to our children for ever" (Deut. 29:29). Even though blinded eyes could not see the light, men were not prevented from speaking of perspicuity and self-evidence. For these words expressed an accessibility in addition to "sight," a bringing to light of the truth (II Cor. 4:2) and of imperishable life through "the light of the gospel" (II Cor. 4:4). Within the framework of this "light of the gospel of the glory of Christ," the Reformers spoke seriously and with unusual emphasis of the perspicuity of Holy Scripture. They were not preoccupied with a purely anthropological or epistemological theory, but with a "confession" of faith that praised the Word in its clarity and power.

But is it truly possible, one might ask, to follow the road to the perspicuity of Holy Scripture by means of categories such as lamp and light, revelation and unveiling? Do we not

4. *The Epistles of Paul the Apostle to the Galatians, Ephesians, Philippians and Colossians* (ET, 1965), p. 221.
5. *TDNT*, I, 718.

run the risk of a theory that does not apply in the practice of reading Scripture? Are not numerous specific difficulties for understanding a clear argument against a theory of this kind? The Reformers did not understand the confession of perspicuity by means of a preconceived theory, as is clearly shown in their thought about Scripture. They were very well aware of numerous "difficulties" that could be used as arguments against clarity, problems inherent in the fact that God's Word comes to us in the form of language. In this connection we come across a more detailed and arresting terminology, which leaves the impression that the confession of perspicuity was not as clear as the words seemed to suggest. Because of these problems, some spoke of a clarity that was not absolute but relative.[6] Moreover, in this more detailed description of perspicuity the attention was focused on a special aspect of the problem, those parts of Scripture necessary for salvation: "the things that are necessary to be believed for salvation."[7]

According to Bavinck, the central truth of salvation "is set forth in a form so simple and intelligible" that someone in search of salvation will come to know the truth through his own reading and investigation.[8] The heart of Scripture shines light forth to all sides. Perspicuity is surrounded by some restrictions, but Bavinck maintains that the message of Scripture is clearly recognizable in spite of the obstacles to understanding. First of all, this recognition is not gained by circumvention of the Scripture given to us in human language. It is not inaccessible and beyond our reach, nor is it a "book of secrets" or riddles with a strangeness that keeps us from understanding.[9]

Since Scripture is in the form of language, it does contain a certain degree of accessibility. But the confession of perspicuity obviously cannot be described in terms of the general accessibility that it has in common with other literature. Accessibility of this kind, one might point out, is an attribute of all written words and need not become the subject of an emphatic confession. As Rossouw firmly stated, the Reformation doctrine of perspicuity did not aim at the clarity of the words as such, but at the message, the content of Scripture.

6. Cf. C. H. Ratschow, *Luth. Dogmatik zwischen Reformation und Aufklärung,* I (1964), 23f.; Weber, *Grundlagen,* I, 311.
7. Quenstedt (cited in *Grundlagen,* I, 310).
8. *GD,* I, 447.
9. Weber, I, 310.

A religious clarity was confessed concerning the good news for sinners. It is not until post-Reformation theology that a shift occurred: for the idea of perspicuity is then applied to the *words* of Scripture, particularly in their semantic function. In this manner Scripture is isolated from its context of salvation, and perspicuity is no longer religious clarity in the midst of our sinful darkness. It is a theoretical and verbal perspicuity that the natural mind can appreciate and perceive in a general framework of knowledge.[10] Moreover, a distinction is made between the hidden *issue* and the clear *words* concerning this issue. However, this does not solve the tension, for one is still forced to acknowledge that Scripture (as a verbal phenomenon) cannot be called clear in all respects. This hidden tension makes itself felt in the obstacles to understanding, and as a result, perspicuity is shifted to dogmatic truth and related to the doctrine of the church.[11] However, genuine perspicuity is the intrinsic intelligibility for the believing sinner; verification of Scripture takes place in the heart. One can only speak of perspicuity in a confession of faith.

But it is not Rossouw's purpose to deny that perspicuity is that of the whole of Holy Scripture; he does not let go of the words of Scripture. We are not dealing with the message by circumventing the words of Scripture, since this very message comes to us through words: "However, the message does not become speech in any other way than in and through humanly constructed language which is in the text itself."[12] There is then a perspicuity of Scripture without spiritualism.[13] The Reformation was not dealing with the words by themselves, but with the message in Scripture of which the words spoke. This clarity of the message *presupposes* the accessibility of the words, but that accessibility was not the subject of the real purpose of the confession. According to the Reformers, the force behind this connection of message and words was the power of the Spirit. For that reason the confession of perspicuity is not a statement in general concerning the human language of Scripture, but a confession concerning the perspicuity of the gospel *in* Scripture. Ascribing to perspicuity the nature of a confession clearly does not imply a reference to the

10. H. W. Rossouw, *Klaarheid en Interpretasie* (1963), p. 333.
11. *Ibid.*, p. 337.
12. *Ibid.*, p. 251.
13. *Ibid.*, p. 253.

area of subjectivity. For it is this very perspicuity that is the object of witness and confession born of a "perceiving" by faith.[14]

Luther's considerations of the clarity of Scripture make it particularly clear that the Reformers were not concerned with a confession concerning the clarity of Scripture merely as a phenomenon of language, apart from its message. In his well-known conflict with Erasmus he offers a lengthy discussion concerning clarity. Erasmus had stressed the many "problems" in Scripture: we ought not to penetrate too deeply into Scripture, since much will only be understood later (e.g., what it teaches about free will). According to Erasmus, Luther is too cocksure – pretending too much with his "assertions." Scripture is obscure in many places, and certain statements about the *liberum arbitrium* apparently find a counter argument in other texts.[15] As a result of all these obscurities, one is bound to follow the office of the church.

What is Luther's reaction to this viewpoint? He starts with the acknowledgment that there are obscure places in Scripture but that these are not the result of the majesty of the message, but of the lack of clarity of the words.[16] The fact that some proverbs in Scripture are still obscure to us does not hinder us from asking what mystery is still hidden in Scripture now that the seals are opened (Rev. 6:1) and the stone is lifted from the grave. Now that the message has come to daylight, what does it matter that one of its signs is still obscure when many other signs are standing in the light?[17] The same message is "published quite openly to the whole world, which in the Scriptures is sometimes expressed in plain words, and sometimes lies as yet hidden in obscure words."[18] With Luther the words "public" and "daylight" are of decisive importance throughout. The great mystery is no longer hidden, and the

14. The Westminster Confession of Faith, Ch. I, states that "those things which are necessary to be known, believed, and observed, for salvation, are so clearly propounded and opened in some place of Scripture or other," that all can come to a "sufficient understanding of them." Cf. J. B. Rogers, *Scripture in the Westminster Confession*, pp. 369f.
15. See E. Gordon Rupp, Philip S. Watson, *Luther and Erasmus: Free Will and Salvation* (1969), pp. 38-41.
16. *Ibid.*, p. 110. It is striking that in the later Lutheran theology significant shifts occur in the relationship of message and words. Cf. Ratschow, pp. 125f.
17. Rupp, p. 110.
18. *Ibid.*, p. 111.

source of light shines forth in the market place.[19] Remarkably, Luther speaks of a double clarity, both externally in Scripture and internally in the heart.[20] The internal clarity is decisively significant for the right knowledge of faith, but the external clarity does not evaporate because of the problem of internal clarity. Internal clarity is only possible through the Spirit, without whom no one understands anything of Scripture. But this does not turn Scripture into a secret document. Luther refers to Luke 21:15, which deals with a wisdom "which none of your adversaries will be able to withstand or contradict." The enemies also must know it, and Luther is able to speak of the sure fact that Scripture is a light clearer than sunlight;[21] the clarity of the message in Scripture is that brilliant. It stands in immediate relationship to saving faith, and difficulties with some words do not affect the clarity. The stone is lifted from the grave.[22]

Luther is clearly not concerned with an isolated statement about the languages of Scripture. At stake is the message of Scripture coming to us through these languages. It is Luther's perspective on Scripture's testifying of Christ that explains the cocksureness and certainty that aroused Erasmus' irritation: "Take Christ out of the Scriptures, and what will you find left in them?"[23] Luther is aware of the importance of words and therefore of philological research; but, he points out, at the same time that the Spirit speaks through these words, true knowledge of the message *in* these words does not follow automatically from grammatical understanding.[24] Indeed, Luther discusses with Erasmus on the level of exegesis, but he is at no time concerned with a discussion that leaves the message in the words outside of consideration. Thus, the question is warranted whether Luther is really concerned with the clarity of Scripture. According to Beisser, it is striking "that the clarity of Scripture is hardly discussed as a matter in itself."[25]

19. *Ibid.*
20. See F. Beisser, *Claritas Scripturae bei Luther* (1966), pp. 85f.
21. H. Ostergaard-Nielsen, *Scriptura Sacra et viva vox* (1957), pp. 116-117.
22. R. Herrmann, *Von der Klarheit der Heiligen Schrift* (1958), pp. 22f. This points to allegorical elements in Luther's later exposition of Scripture, especially a papal statement of 1524 in which the sealing of the stone on Jesus' grave is used as an image of Scripture that is not rightly understood.
23. Rupp, p. 110.
24. Beisser, pp. 62, 85.
25. *Ibid.*, p. 79.

The answer to this question is that Luther does not avoid discussing the words because of his interest in the message, and yet he is not able and willing to isolate the clarity of Scripture from the content of these words. To him the *servum arbitrium* in Scripture is clear. What Scripture *says* is all-important to him, that is, the word of Christ, God's saving Word. Salvation is public and calls for a decision. As we noted above, this does not mean, according to Luther, that the unbeliever does not understand a word of Scripture. The blindness of the unbelievers does not imply a total obscurity and incomprehensibility of the words; yet it is only by faith that the message of Scripture is truly understood.[26] This message, seen as a declaration and a proclamation of salvation, is the decisive aspect of Luther's concern with clarity. It is the dominating factor in his understanding of the message, that is, in his faith. But this does not result in Luther's exalting an inner experience as the norm for a doctrine of Scripture. The Word is a power persevering through the Spirit as the word of Christ: "I have done nothing; the word acted and carried out everything – I let the word have its way."[27] But the important question that has been asked is whether Luther had too optimistic an opinion of this clarity. Does not his conviction reflect tradition too much, even though it is focused on Christ and the open grave? Later problems go beyond those of Luther, as has been frequently pointed out. There are many questions posed by the complete and genuine humanity of Scripture; the possibility of such complications as well as of a better understanding should not be denied. Complications and insights arise because of the verbal and historical language form of Scripture, precisely in view of the Reformation maxim "Scripture alone." Thus, attention to Scripture and its clarity remains fluid. The principle of Scripture itself forces us continually to give renewed and close attention to the words of Scripture so that we are kept from going beyond that which is written as well as from an uncritical traditionalism. Research in Scripture, therefore, is never left behind as a closed affair. This must always be kept in mind if we are not to deny the principles of the Reformation regarding perspicuity. It is possible to uphold the confession of the perspicuity of Scripture

26. *Ibid.*, pp. 81-87.
27. Cf. H. von Campenhausen, "Reformatorisches Selbstbewusztsein und Geschichtsbewusztsein bei Luther," *Tradition und Leben* (1960), p. 337.

in word and deed only when one is fully prepared to respect this research.

One ought to remember that a Reformation challenge was implied in Luther's reference to the clarity of Scripture. He himself did not withdraw from it. It may be said that his central interpretation was of cardinal importance for the understanding of the interrelationship of Scripture and salvation in Christ, in spite of the awareness that new exegetical reflection was not rendered superfluous in the least. Some may fear that the clarity of Scripture may slip from our hands because of a continual detailed exegesis of Scripture. But those who disqualify this research should know that the way is thus opened to uncontrolled arbitrariness, to "subjective interpretation" cited in the warning of II Peter 1:20, and to an appeal to Scripture that wholly disregards the dynamic of God's Word as sword of the Spirit. Not only the appeal of so-called spiritualism (note Luther's struggle with "the enthusiasts")[28] but also the calls for simple clarity suffer from a lack of respect for the *words* of Scripture. Luther did not abandon the languages or conscientious Bible study after his recognition and discovery of the central message of Scripture. This is a warning against every approach to Scripture which in the end tries to oppose the spirit to the letter. This realization enables us to regard the confession of clarity as "a deep evangelical truth" with and in spite of certain complications and modifications.[29] Rational clarity, about which one may intellectually argue, is not at stake here, but the clarity of the church in its relation to the message of Christ.

In light of the above, we must have a closer look at the so-called proof from Scripture as it is concretely related to the confession concerning the clarity of Scripture. For with a proof from Scripture one does not wish to circumvent or surpass Scripture; but the way is opened to a convinced and convincing insight as this clarity is presupposed in each "proof from Scripture." A frequent objection to the term "proof from Scripture" is that the concept of "proof" is out of order with respect to Scripture and its witness. Faith, it is pointed out, is not and cannot be a matter of logical arguments and conclusions furnishing proof comprehensible to the human mind. It is a matter of choice and trust. Frequently, the cue is taken

28. Cf. R. Prenter, *Spiritus Creator*, pp. 247f.
29. Herrmann, p. 19.

from the meaning and functions of "conclusions" in science, the force of logical evidence being noted especially, since it convinces everyone who is intellectually sound. One thinks of certain axioms and the theses derived from them. Is that kind of proof ever possible in dogmatic reflection or in unscientific study of Scripture? Does not the heart of a gospel that does not tolerate syllogisms exclude it? Is not this proof the very opposite of the revealing and surprising character of revelation, of that which is not revealed to the wise and understanding but to children (Mt. 11:25)? This is a formidable problem indeed. For that which appears to be proof from Scripture is frequently caused by dealing with Scripture in an axiomatic way, whereby a number of "conclusions" are drawn that are formally analogous to proofs in other sciences.

In spite of these frequent objections to the term "proof from Scripture" and the numerous speculative aberrations connected with it, the term continued to be used. The primary reason for this is that people did not think of a process of thought from axioms to theses based on the truth of those axioms; rather, they were concerned with the truth — the witness of Scripture. Many of these "proofs from Scripture" stem from a deep awareness of the unity and coherence of Scripture, in contrast to the notion that Scripture could only be approached in an irrational and charismatic way. Seeing in this light the purpose of Scripture proof is to find a foundation in God's witness for the church's thought and utterances. Thus, a barrier is thrown up against all arbitrariness. Also the notion prevailed that in the gospel we are not merely dealing with truths whose subjective correlate is a "sacrifice of the intellect," a blind acceptance of what "happened" to be revealed. Nor was a rational transparence seen as its opposite, but rather the illuminating character of the message — both in dogmatics and in the confession's Scripture proof — with its interrelations, depths, and perspectives. This is a light that does not blind but opens eyes to the joy of the gospel's mystery. Attention was called to the fact that the church is not merely dealing with perspicuity but also with perception and discovery, seeing and understanding, an accepting and trusting of the one central testimony that radiates light in all directions. There is every reason to ponder the nature of Scripture proof because of its use in the realization that Scripture cannot be broken (Jn. 10:35). Its central and inner coherence must always be given close attention.

Aside from the particular "proof from Scripture," the word "proof" occurs in the history of church and theology especially in relation to the "proofs" for the existence of God. This refers to human reason in connection with a certain "accessibility" of God in creation. According to the First Vatican Council, God can be known with certainty from the things of creation through a natural light of reason.[30] Much discussion has been devoted to this demonstrability of God, and most of these proofs took the shape of a causal argumentation. Through reason, conclusions were drawn from what the eyes see, that is, created reality. A seeing based on legitimate conclusions was especially emphasized here in terms of perception. The word "evidence" was frequently used, and reason functioned as a link in the chain (together with created things). A process of thought was shown that led to a knowledge implying a certain "seeing."[31] However, this "proof" is now subject to fundamental change in Roman Catholic dogmatics and apologetics. It is related to a different evaluation of the "isolated" reason and is especially concerned with the relation between seeing and the link of reason. But with Scripture proof we clearly have to do with a totally different kind of proof,[32] since it deals with the meaning and correlation of Scripture and with the bearing and perspective of the biblical witness. It does not at all concern a verification by reason that at least theoretically has its basis outside revelation. It is rather focused on the given and accepted Word in the proof from Scripture.

Caution must be observed in all thought concerning Scripture proof, and not every use of the word "proof" should be brought under one denominator. The way this word is used in the Revised Standard Version of the New Testament is a clear indication of this. For there it is often used in a sense quite different from that which is normally believed to be logical or mathematical proof. So we read in Romans 5:8 that God shows his love: what is meant here is a manifestation, a bringing to light of the reality of salvation. Indeed, we are dealing here with something that can be "seen"; yet it has

30. See Denzinger, *The Sources of Catholic Dogma* (ET, 1957), section 1785. For details, see Berkouwer, *General Revelation* (ET, 1955), Ch. 4.
31. The appeal to Rom. 1:20 for a "natural theology" is full of problems. See *General Revelation,* Ch. 10, especially regarding Article II of the Belgic Confession.
32. Regarding the problems of the proofs for the existence of God (in their isolation and abstraction), cf. Moltmann, *Theology of Hope,* pp. 271f.

nothing to do with a logical syllogism based on isolated thought. It is a "manifestation" in the reality of divine action.[33] Its analogy is found in the reality discovered by faith, through its convincing power.

But the verb "to prove" is used in a manner that appeals to human thought, conclusions, and argumentations. So we read that Paul confounded the Jews in Damascus "by proving that Jesus was the Christ" (Acts 9:22). But at the same time we read of Paul's *proclaiming* that Jesus was the Son of God (Acts 9:20). This confounding proof apparently could scarcely be resisted in view of his testimony from the Old Testament. It shows Paul's strong conviction concerning his proclaimed truth, whose nature was not arbitrary or irrational yet had a divine priority and sovereignty. Paul seeks to convince by means of a certain reasonableness; he makes a meaningful appeal to insight and to capitulation. Many "arguments" are used that would exclude every aspect of passivity: salvation is not blanketed in a haze of mysticism but is preached with concrete and clear outlines and with humanly coherent words. It is noteworthy that persuasion by means of words plays an important role in all apostolic proclamation.

Clearly there is room for "therefores" and "so thats" in conclusions and counter arguments within the realm of the gospel (II Tim. 3:16). In the New Testament we indeed encounter warnings against controversy and disputes about words that produce envy (I Tim. 6:4) and against contradictions of what is falsely called knowledge (I Tim 6:20). But this protest against "wrangling" concerns those who are depraved in mind and bereft of the truth. Sound words have the very opposite function, and they are adopted as they argue against error (I Tim. 6:3). The result is an emphatic reference, a desire to convince, and an urging on in the direction of truth. The mystery is not thereby surrendered, for we are dealing with a clarity and a unique evidence that irresistibly radiates light and on which the proclamation of the Word is focused. There is the kind of proof that does not render choice and decision superfluous, and that must be seen against the background of wide and deep connections, of a perspective and correlation in God's salvation manifesting itself in history.[34] This "proof" is not surrendered to the illusion of pure argument. Thus, Paul's

33. See II Cor. 7:11; Rom. 9:22; Heb. 6:17; II Cor. 8:24; Jas. 3:13; Heb. 11:1.
34. *TDNT*, II, 474f.

challenging message on the Areopagus issues in a call to conversion (Acts 17:30f.).

This proof and this evidence enter into a discussion with the heart whereby the contradiction may increase in strength because of the very clarity of the proof. So a denial of the evidence of this manifest salvation is possible. Christ's saving deed may be interpreted in terms of demonic possession (Mt. 12:24), the fire of the Spirit in terms of drunkenness (Acts 2:15), the proclamation in terms of madness (Acts 26:24). On our way to salvation we do not encounter an irrational event that demands slavish subjection, but a mystery that has been brought to light. And as mystery it calls for being convinced in the liberty of faith (Jer. 20:7) and for a radical surrender that coincides with insight. Thus, proof from Scripture has always received room in the Christian church in connection with proclamation and teaching,[35] and with the insight and perspective that it offers. It has functioned in relation to the unity of history and interpretation, illustrating their meaning as part of the proclamation.[36] Analogous to it is the fact that the comprehending of God's ways with Israel and the gentiles issues in a doxology praising God's decrees and ways, which are inscrutable and unsearchable.[37] But the proclamation of salvation does not automatically fragment into isolated and unrelated facts and truths. Anselm's question "Why did God become man?" should not automatically be rejected as rationalism. For we read everywhere of the coherence, centrality, and depth of God's actions.[38]

In all these correlations we deal with the relationship *in* Christ as the true light of the world. Regarding our question, Scripture proof appears to have nothing to do with a number of logical conclusions derived from presupposed theses or truths. The nature of Scripture itself forbids it, and the history of theology shows the enormous dangers of such deductions. Yet

35. In this teaching there is no hint of a rational system. Cf. Jn. 17:16f. concerning the *doing* of God's will and the knowing that the teaching is of God. *TDNT,* II, 163f.
36. Cf. C. Michalson, *The Rationality of Faith: An Historical Critique of the Theological Reason* (1963), pp. 146f.
37. See Berkouwer, *Divine Election* (ET, 1960), Ch. 3.
38. Think, for example, of the New Testament "must" in connection with Christ's suffering and death. Cf. Berkouwer, *Sin,* pp. 399f. Note also the word of Hebrews 2:10 concerning what Christ "should," namely, suffer with a purpose. This is not an instance of rationality that eliminates the stumbling block, but, in contrast, it is an irrational happening.

men have always been captivated by the perspective of the correlation, unity, and coherence of the biblical witness as well as with the riches and fullness of meaning implied in it. A number of groping formulations indicate this problem of coherence, as Scripture itself repeatedly refers to it. The Westminster Confession (I, 6) deals with "consequences": "The whole counsel of God, concerning all things necessary for his own glory, man's salvation, faith, and life, is either expressly set down in Scripture or *by good and necessary consequence may be deduced* from Scripture" (italics mine). The terms "consequence" and "deduced" leave the impression that a logical system of truth was being constructed with the use of a number of "axioms" as building blocks.

Here we encounter a problem that has repeatedly occupied the church: the "Scripture proof" in the confession. The confessions do not offer a technical "repetition from Scripture" in a literal sense. Rather, they draw lines and show inner relationships. Many dangers are implied in such lines and combinations, and biblicists of all kinds preferred to limit themselves to what the Westminster Confession calls "expressly set down in Scripture," avoiding the "consequences." They wished to keep within the sharp limits of that which was regarded as explicit biblical testimony, preferably remaining within its very terminology. In fact, Scripture itself becomes a system of truth with such a biblicism; not a single truth needs to be added. However, the legitimacy of seeking to understand the unity and coherence of the message of salvation should be recognized. This attempt to understand is in contrast to a "sacrifice of the intellect," whereby the "object" — as an irrational, incoherent, and contingent datum — is placed over against a "subject" who must blindly accept this datum without true human affinity and digestion and without the "amen" of faith. What course this human activity of listening, searching, and affirming takes is indeed a critical question. This may be deemed a question of the rightness of any "consequence" concerning the one message of Scripture. The Westminster Confession does not explain further what it means by "good and necessary consequence." It may intend to warn against speculation and against "erroneous deductions"[39] (only the good and necessary consequence); but the phrase "expressly set down in Scripture" is not like stagnant water but

39. Rogers, *op. cit.*, p. 335.

like a current taking up faith, trust, acceptance, and affirmation in its stream of the penetrating perception of truth. It may also imply the refusal to surrender to foreign authorities and frames of reference by standing on scriptural grounds for every "consequence."[40]

Of course, the problem is not solved with the words "good" and "necessary"; its inevitability is merely indicated. It is the unity and coherence that is inevitable, the interrelation of all aspects and facets of which we repeatedly find telling examples in the biblical witness (I Cor. 15:13f.; Rom. 6:1). At the same time one should never be blind to the dangers of "consequences." In a sense, the struggle over these consequences and implications forms the background of all confessional divisions. An appeal has often been made to "evident" consequences of this kind — almost as a direct expression of the perspicuity of Scripture — while these consequences were rejected by others as mere speculation. A clear warning is implied in Scripture's own indication of the illegitimacy of certain implications, for example, the warning that the words of traditional law do no justice to God's law itself but rather render the words powerless and teach "as doctrines the precepts of man" (Mt. 15:1-9; Mk. 7:7-8).

Perspicuity cannot be discussed meaningfully and fruitfully if one does not ponder this perception in the midst of all its dangers. Precisely because the gift of Scripture does not exclude the human activities of research and understanding but rather calls for them, the church may not retreat outside the danger zone. It must continually be aware of the dangers. In the struggle for the perspicuity of Scripture, for what is truly implied in it and what follows from it, we should not think exclusively of the sharp contrast between sight and blindness referred to in Paul's statement concerning the unbelievers who are kept "from seeing the light of the gospel of the glory of Christ" (II Cor. 4:4; cf. Jn. 9:39-41). There are other variations of seeing, for example, among those who would not want to accuse each other of blindness (because of the god of this age), even being aware of their unity with the same Lord and with each other. In view of this unity, one is often tempted to relativize the variations and to deem them irrelevant. But the history of the church frequently shows that the divergences take root in deeper levels of human life and may

40. *Ibid.*, p. 343.

thus lead to important frustrations to the unity of the church.

It is indeed one of the most moving and difficult aspects of the confession of Scripture's clarity that it does not automatically lead to a total uniformity of perception, disposing of any problems. We are confronted with important differences and forked roads that often lead to far-reaching consequences for the life of the church, and all parties normally appeal to Scripture and its perspicuity. The heretics did not disregard the authority of Scripture but made an appeal to it and to its clear witness[41] with the subjective conviction of seeing the truth in the words of Scripture. It is incorrect to explain every heretical appeal to Scripture psychologically in terms of a deliberate, pure construction of a particular insight that calls in the aid of Scripture as hindsight in order to give individual ideas the aura of legitimacy in the church. Rather, it is striking to discover truly inalienable aspects of the gospel in these appeals to Scripture. The great problem of heresy is related to various degrees of isolation, with the lack of modification in their appeal to Scripture, and in the selectivity of this appeal, whereby numerous motivations often play a subconscious role. As a result, some have been unreceptive to corrections regarding essential aspects of the gospel because, being subjectively convinced, they prefer to read and understand Scripture selectively.

Taking his cue from methodical doubt, Descartes pointed to the one undoubted truth of "I think, therefore I am." On the basis of this solid certainty he would accept as "truth" that which would force itself upon us as being "clear and distinct," as clear as this self-consciousness itself. Thus, clarity and evidence contained the decisive viewpoint for him. It made him the father of Western rationalism. But a different problem is encountered regarding the perspicuity of Scripture: it is not that of the clarity of human reason, but that of the inner coherence of the words of Scripture, growing with all its pluriformity through history. This especially made possible all varieties of projection on the screen of Scripture, which are believed by those who project to be derived from perspicuity. He who recognizes that not only others but also he himself is subject to these dangers of projection — conditioned as he

41. As one example from many, we remember Arius' appeal to Deut. 6:4 ("The Lord our God is one!"), and to Prov. 8:22 ("The Lord created me"). See Berkouwer, *The Person of Christ,* p. 61.

is by history, psychology, and tradition — may at times long for a position far above the problems of subjective projection in the neighborhood of unchallenged clarity.

This longing obviously is not fulfilled, and such a posture is offered to no one. The heart of the matter is that we cannot be redeemed from the anxiety of divergences by means of a preconceived technique. For with respect to perspicuity and perception, we are always pointed to God's Word alone, and to the inner coherence and structure with a focus indicated by itself. This does not break the deadlock at all, for it does not offer a prefabricated "therapy." This is not possible, but on the road to pure perception an exhortation is heard to openness, to silence and listening, to receptive attention, research, respect, and expectation, to faith and prayer.

One should not mourn the fact that this is the only accessible road. For God himself chose to go this way with man, since his Word has "the form of a servant" in human language. No one may escape, therefore, with the excuse of the "poly-interpretability" of Scripture as the main reason (if not the only one) for all tensions and divergent appeals to Scripture throughout the history of the church. But responsibility is the very opposite of such an excuse. It is aimed both at a perspective — in light of the central perspicuity — and at a way through the divisions of the church. With respect to the hope for the future of the church, we hear both pessimistic and optimistic words. The fatal division of minds concerning the understanding of Scripture becomes more and more sharp, according to many people. This is often attributed to scientific study of Scripture. As a result, one is thought to withdraw from the common task when doing research in the Scripture; this isolation may at times result in the arbitrariness of private understanding.

However, optimistic voices are also heard in our time not only confessing perspicuity "in general" but also calling surprised attention to the fact that converging lines in the understanding of Scripture become visible. These are seen in the light of the clarity of Scripture, exposing the danger of private interpretation with the concrete words of Scripture. It cannot be denied, moreover, that converging lines may be noted alongside diverging lines in the fascinating process of continued biblical research. From the viewpoint of church-going confessionalism, it is rather difficult to note these genuinely converging lines; for soon enough they are irresponsibly surrounded by suspicion. Contrary to such suspicion, we should expect to see an eager longing for this convergence in terms of a scriptural faith. This eagerness does not relativize or slur over the truth. Problems of interpretation will always constitute a potential danger, and an "irenic" attitude will not serve the unity around this perspicuous mystery. But one should never neglect attention to the slightest symptom of convergence that may, in the midst of confessional struggle, break through the confusion at some places. This negligence would be tempting to those who wish to avoid the dangers of this irenic attitude and wish to follow an intuitive resistance.

It is not a legitimate realism to close one's eyes to convergences, for that is but a denial of the clear and unshackled Word in the power of the Spirit. The notion that all times are filled with divergences and that they will not be removed in the future is a kind of ecclesiastical fatalism that can only be measured with the worldly yardstick. This course of thought does not coincide with Paul's amazement concerning the divisions in light of him who is not divided (I Cor. 1:12-13). In fact, the confession of perspicuity has been abandoned by such fatalism and Scripture surrendered to arbitrariness and subjectivity. If God's Word truly comes to us in Scripture, in the witness to Christ, then *seeing* is of utmost importance, as well as the common recognition of the voice of the shepherd and not the stranger. No confession concerning Scripture is more disturbing to the church than the confession of its perspicuity.

In reflecting on the clarity of Scripture and its meaning for human perception, insight, and understanding, one automatically touches on a question that is always relevant in the history of the church — whether Scripture must be "literally" understood. This word is charged with emotionalism in various discussions, both when a "literal" understanding is demanded and when it is criticized. There is on the one hand a desire to warn against a spiritualization or an evaporation of the words of Scripture, and on the other hand a desire to warn against a "literalism" that is labeled a slavish dependence on the letter with no perspective on the deep meaning and the real intention *in* the words. It is important to take a closer look at this last criticism, not dismissing it beforehand as needing no further explanation.

We should remember that resistance to the "letter" was attributed particularly to spiritualism — not without justice —

while the Reformers were fighting it tooth and nail. One must therefore determine what sort of problem he encounters by criticizing a so-called literalism. It should be noted first of all that the problem cannot be resolved by an appeal to Paul's statement that the letter kills but the Spirit gives life (II Cor. 3:6). This statement is often severed from its important context in the third chapter of II Corinthians. The fact is often ignored that Paul is speaking of the very active deadly function of the letter, in contrast to the similarly active life-giving function of the Spirit (II Kgs. 5:7; I Sam. 2:6; Gal. 3:21). In Paul's thought, letter and Spirit are not opposed to each other as isolated phenomena in the way that "externals" are depreciatively opposed to eternal truth. The opposition of letter and Spirit is not a blank check for spiritual interpretation; it can only be understood in certain correlative connections. Paul never disqualifies the written text itself;[42] he rather pays due respect to the meaning of the Word that externally comes to us in written form. This is evident in his statements concerning preaching and the God-breathed Scripture. The fact that Spirit and letter occur in opposition to each other in Paul's writings (e.g., Rom. 7:6; 2:29) is related to the misunderstanding of the nature and meaning of the external letter of the law. The dispensation of death "carved in letters on stone" is accompanied by glory (II Cor. 3:7), and the Spirit stands in opposition to the letter when it is severed from its intention and deep meaning, thus receiving a separate function opposed to the purpose of God.[43]

The opposition of externals to internals, as noted in spiritualism, is of an entirely different order, and it becomes clear that there is no reason to speak in a simplistically depreciating way of the letter in order to avoid spiritualism.[44] According to the Revelation to John, he who hears the words of the prophecy and keeps "what is written therein" is called blessed (Rev. 1:3). That which is written is therefore of decisive importance for us on our journey into the future: nothing may

42. Regarding the misuse of II Cor. 3:6 see Ebeling, *Luther,* pp. 100f.
43. Therefore, one cannot say with R. M. Grant (regarding II Cor. 3:6) that the Spirit "destroys the tyranny of words" and makes possible an interpretation that is "intuitive rather than based on words" (*The Letter and the Spirit* [1957], p. 51).
44. Often an appeal is made to the word of Christ about the Spirit that gives life versus the flesh which is of no avail (Jn. 6:63). One should notice that Christ names the *words* which he had spoken "spirit and life" (Jn. 6:63). Cf. Jn. 6:68: "words of eternal life." Cf. *TDNT,* I, 768.

be added and nothing taken away from the *words* written in the book of prophecy (Rev. 22:18, 19). In view of this, the question of the literal understanding of Scripture gains new significance. An uncritical use of the term "literal" does not offer a correct perspective on the real situation. One must begin with the necessity of a literal understanding in order to be wholly concerned with grasping the written text; and it would be incorrect to see this characterization of literal understanding as subtle word play. Without giving the words of Scripture full attention, it is wholly impossible to confess the perspicuity of Scripture.

This statement does not, of course, solve the problems raised in the history of the church concerning this literal understanding. But they can be approached without the use of reactionary antitheses not founded in biblical thinking. Moreover, the attention to the words of Scripture clearly does not in the least warrant a simplistic exegesis that glories in a literal understanding of everything. For these questions must be posed: what does an understanding of the words entail, and where are they meant to lead us? The problem of the letter frequently became a matter of interest in connection with the interpretation of the Apocalypse. No mere reverence for the letter is involved in the plea from various corners for a "literal" understanding of this book of the Bible; for the apocalyptic predictions are understood to be an exact and detailed "report" of the "history of the end." This kind of interpretation of the literal text calls for a naive and simple reading of what is written.

The identification of the literal text ("it is written") with an exact "description" of an occurrence in a particular place, correct in every detail, is the presupposed starting point of this view. The story is supposed to have the style of a chronicle in, for example, the description of the final battle and the assembling of the armies at Armageddon (Rev. 16:16). This approach is offered with an appeal to the perspicuity of Scripture as the only possible and literal one. The peculiar imagery and figures of speech of apocalypticism, taken particularly from the Old Testament, are scarcely taken into account. This ignores the fact that these words can only be understood if all components and backgrounds of the written text are fully taken into consideration.[45]

45. Often those doing the so-called literalistic exegesis are convinced that

All this is closely related to the confession of the clarity of Scripture. The example of the Apocalypse in particular may help to convince us that we cannot discuss perspicuity naively via an isolated consideration of the words, but only after careful study. Consideration of Scripture (as words), therefore, must take into account the specific literary form in which the words appear and the great variety of ways in which Scripture speaks to us.[46] One may appeal to the perspicuity of Scripture to ignore this variety and reduce all the stories of Scripture to one denominator, but this offers no contribution to a clear understanding.

One cannot operate with this concept of clarity, for example, by judging a story by the yardstick of whether it conveys a strong impression of realism. There are stories in Scripture that portray "reality" in a lively manner for a particular purpose, though it need not be an historical account. Attention is often called to parables and stories such as the one about the Pharisee and the publican (Lk. 18:10). The problem of reality does not trouble us in this story because this kind of colorful characterization is not at all strange or unthinkable. But the realistic impression of the story (or parable) does not imply that it is historically true. One might speak of a certain "self-evidence" in an Old Testament fable, for example, Jotham's fable in Judges 9:8 ("The trees once went forth to anoint a king over them"). The purposeful application of the fable is readily seen (Jgs. 9:16f.): the story has a clear structure, and its moral is only possible in this way. Here we see a poetic clothing of a certain idea in the garb of reality. The same is true of Jehoash's message to Amaziah: "A thistle on Lebanon sent to a cedar on Lebanon, saying, 'Give your daughter to my son for a wife'; and a wild beast of Lebanon passed and trampled down the thistle" (II Kgs. 14:9f.). There is no speck of vagueness in it; thus, there can be no difference of opinion concerning this matter (the fable), but we learn from it in order that we not be led by a first impression of "realism,"

there is no other way to discover meaning in the prophecies of the future in Revelation. Cf. H. H. Rowley, *The Relevance of Apocalyptic* (1955), Ch. 4, on "the enduring message of apocalyptic" (pp. 150f.).

46. Bavinck, *GD,* I, 419, where Bavinck speaks of the God-breathed Scripture as making serviceable to itself "all genre of literature" (prose, history, prophecy, fable, and parable), so that the truth "in each case has a different character."

called forth in the story through its imagery. The taking into account of the literary style of the story is thereby implied.

This is all quite important for the question of what it is that is "clearly" conveyed in Scripture. The understanding of the letter does not mean the "spiritualization" of the letter. This very problem is significant for the understanding of numerous passages of Scripture, resulting in a great many more differences of opinion. For the parables and fables (which are clear to all) are not merely clever pedagogical devices; they are bound to the message of Scripture concerning man's relationship to God. In our time these questions have become more and more relevant, particularly with respect to the problems of "origin" in the first three chapters of Genesis.

It is not within the scope of this study to elaborate on the question of the creation and man's fall from God's hand in guilt and alienation. But I do wish to note the very important aspect of the clarity and self-evidence of Scripture concerning creation and the fall. For this subject triggers various important questions that are quite meaningful to a discussion of the perspicuity of Scripture. We may start with the fact that for a long time virtually no real problems were raised concerning the clarity of the stories of Genesis, even though various questions about their meaning had been raised in earlier times. For they were regarded as a clear and detailed description of history, namely, of the beginning, creation, the fall and expulsion from paradise, as well as the shining prospect of promised salvation. In its considerations, the Christian church took it for granted that here also we are dealing with a part of God-breathed Scripture, with divine revelation concerning that which happened to be unknown territory, unreachable by other routes of knowledge. In this respect a parallel was seen with eschatological predictions, since these are revelations concerning a future inaccessible to us.

With respect to our knowledge concerning the future, people became more and more convinced of the specific character of apocalyptic visions and predictions. The term "apocalyptic literary style" came into use, having its own criteria for interpretation. It could not be identified with historiography in the ordinary sense of the word. With respect to protology (the first things), a good deal of thought was also given to literary style and its importance, but other motifs came into play alongside it, each scholar having his own emphasis. Its reason was the awareness that in this life the final fulfillment of the eschatological promise could not be "verified." One could only move forward into the future in expectation of its fulfillment. At the same time protology became the subject of thought, not in the sense of a positive verification, but nonetheless concerning the content of these Genesis stories about the world and man. There was also consideration of the findings of science, which were put forth with an increasing degree of certainty as a result of research. More and more people became concerned with various prophecies of science, particularly with the natural sciences, biology and geology; and the question of whether these results could be "reconciled" with biblical faith was raised.

The starting point of these thoughts is that any imagery or "clothing" is related to fiction and fantasy, to a dehistoricization in terms of a spiritualization of reality — the reality of guilt in which God intervenes with saving grace. The reality of salvation does not correspond with the "nothing" but with the reality of guilt. This guilt is not and cannot be clarified by means of an explanation. Those who demand a clear human understanding and "intelligibility" ask for more than God's revelation can and will give. Genesis describes the radical dissociation of creation and guilt, the break, the rebellion, the autonomy, the dark and enigmatic beginning. The discussion of the self-evidence, therefore, is focused on the nature of the description of this reality through human mediation. Greater interest and respect have been asked for this human mediation by giving organic inspiration its due. It is not related to an antithesis between real and unreal, but it is in response to the way of the Word, which we should fully acknowledge and account for regarding the self-evidence.

We can call attention to the nature of revelation adopting the human-historical aspect by referring to the polemics of Israel. Especially with regard to Genesis 1, clear polemical features are noteworthy, particularly aimed at mythical theogonies and cosmogonies and at every deification of creatures. This shows how the thinking of Israel concerning the creation by God took shape in confrontation with all kinds of myths, theories, and views of life. With this confrontation a perspective was opened to the incomparable nature of Yahweh. By giving these polemical elements their due, we are brought to a level different from that of a supernatural and mechanical concept of revelation. For God's revelation does not exclude human thought and historical confrontation, but it adopts them and brings their unique relevance to light in those contours. The fear of giving full account of this human aspect — the polemics and the different kind of imagery — is related to earlier theories concerning Israel's total dependence on pagan myths and ways of thought. But the very polemics, together with all the imagery related to it, spells a radical independence and antithesis. It shows to what degree a new perspective is found for the Creator under the breath of the Spirit, a perspective which is beyond doubt. The inspired nature does not come to light in complete isolation but in the content and intention of revelation. Human mediation and consideration are not thereby eliminated; on the contrary, the human elements of reflection (such as polemics) receive real significance and much more attention than had they been influenced by the fear of spiritualization and evaporation. In view of the clarity of the matter, the conquest of this fear will create the possibility — amid all the dangers of arbitrariness — of considering self-evidence with a greater degree of openness, so that an "intuitive" insight will no longer dominate the perspicuity.

The aspect of self-evidence should, of course, be broadly treated in a study of creation in systematic theology. We are merely concerned to indicate that the questioning of traditional exegesis need not be caused by a rationalistic and faithless approach to Scripture. Moreover, in the traditional exegesis not everything was clear "at first sight." This is shown by the distinction made between the anthropomorphic features of the story and other more "literal" features. The story itself in Genesis 1-3 does not lead to this distinction nor to the interpretation of the serpent as an instrument of Satan. It raises the question whether due credit has been given to the composition of the entire story. For the anthropomorphic features cannot possibly be isolated from the total description. They are inseparably linked to the description of God's dealing with man as such. The question is truly warranted whether such a distinction is really made in view of the self-evidence of the story, or if no dogmatic and complicated factors are mingled with anthropomorphism. The exclusive right of the traditional exegesis is not bolstered in the least in this way, for frequently the story is characterized in terms of a "primitive story." This makes the distinction between "real" and "unreal" extremely difficult, particularly if one wishes to fathom the intent of the author. Thus, there is all the more reason to exercise caution while discussing Genesis. One must above all be on guard for a false dilemma of *reality* or *fiction* when choosing between the traditional exegesis or a different one.

The question has often been asked whether hesitation concerning the traditional interpretation would have arisen had not "outside" factors played an important role alongside exegetical factors. Indeed, scientific research as an "occasion" did play a role. But it cannot be stated that this occasion and the exegesis are in clear conflict with each other. In reality, we rather see a certain interdependence at work. Problems concerning occasion have a stimulating effect on exegesis (critical self-examination), while, on the other hand, exegesis calls for a renewed attention to the problem facing us because of the occasion. In the direction of crediting and respecting the "occasion" (also by the church), a closer examination of the relation between Bible and science automatically begins. Each occasion of examination points out how one is inclined to regard the conflict between the two as unreal. However, this does not reflect a new form of concordism but is an examination of the nature of Scripture and of organic inspiration, which is demonstrably important for crediting the occasion. This results in a contempt for dualism, for the ghost of "a double truth."

More and more one begins to sense the frightful dilemma caused by various unexpected disclosures of knowledge, which Schleiermacher once formulated as follows: "Shall the knot of history be thus loosed: Christianity with barbarism and learning with unbelief?"[47] No one will deny the danger of that dark dilemma. Schleiermacher's motivation to let the message of the gospel speak even to "its cultured despisers" deserves appreciation.[48] It is readily understood that the perspicuity of Scripture played a decisive role in all this. In history we see how the relationship between church and science has been frustrated by the imperialistic and positivistic tendencies of science on the one hand, and on the other hand by hesitations of the church to take seriously new and gradually unavoidable insights and "occasions" that may lead to correction.

The question of whether and how these frustrations can

47. Cf. K. Barth, *Protestant Thought: From Rousseau to Ritschl* (ET, 1959), p. 321. Cf. Berkouwer, *The Second Vatican Council,* p. 87 and the epilogue, pp. 249f.

48. From the subtitle of F. Schleiermacher, *On Religion: Speeches to its Cultured Despisers* (ET, 1958). Whether Schleiermacher himself made an essential contribution to overcoming the dilemma is naturally itself a question.

possibly be undermined is very important. The only possibility open is to give a clear form to the rejection of dualism. But, as we are all aware, this very task is quite difficult and challenging. We are more than ever impressed by the need to not relativize perspicuity but to appreciate it in its focusing light and power. It is not sufficient to deal with this confession by simply declaring perspicuity a static, objective, and unchangeable fact, so that all unorthodox insight can be termed blindness. We rather see how perspicuity is related concretely to the way of God's Word – in human words – throughout history. If one fully accounts for this, a negative approach to the problems of science that confront us today is no longer possible. The fact that the problems of occasion and of possibilities for correction are recognized does not indicate that clarity is thus made a problem. Rather, we are increasingly confronted concretely with the clarity that challenges us to a right and pure understanding. In that pursuit we find ourselves, so to speak, at a fork in the road. It is possible to make an intellectual game of the relationship between faith and science, and bow in unbelieving subjection to the dictatorship of science without critically examining its presuppositions, which can have a bearing on the results. In view of the dangers of this first path, interest may be awakened for the second. However, the second path is even more difficult to pass. In our time the church is confronted on all sides by many varied questions concerning science, not merely by those about the beginning. We thus come back to the central question of the lamp and the light, a question that has always been at the heart of the church's confession of perspicuity. In the complex problems of life and science the feeling might arise that a perspicuity that is directly applicable is slipping away from us. No one is prepared to fix the commandment by means of a casuistry clear to all, not even those who refuse to have perspicuity perish in the absolute norm of a "situation." In all of Christian life we are confronted with the relationship between perspicuity and human insight.

The very confession of perspicuity, inseparably bound to the message of Scripture in the Reformation confession, automatically forced a concentration of thought on the gospel. This concentration was not always maintained in the post-Reformation period. But a new course was opened which, in view of the cause of the gospel, could keep the church from perishing in the historicity of a limited horizon. Thus, it can be said that, following this course of concentrated thought, Scripture may gradually become clearer. This would not be due to an attempt to make it subjectively relevant but due to the recognition of the function of perspicuity in history.

It is indeed possible that when confronted by new problems, one will be troubled by the question of whether this perspicuity will not eventually slip away from us. However, this is related to an earlier and frequently held idea of perspicuity, that God's Word — as a lamp and a light — would answer all old and new questions from whatever direction they might come. Even though this idea was already conquered in principle during the Reformation, perspicuity apparently became blurred in later times because of it. It became a less effective and less applicable argument than was the case in earlier times. This temptation and the feeling of crisis that goes with it can only be withstood and conquered if perspicuity is rightly understood in each specific case, that is, in the reading of Scripture itself, which may lead us to recover the right perspective. In order to conquer subjectivism, one must be prepared not to absolutize his own insight but to be led and corrected by God's Word as it addresses us with its own peculiar structure in history.

The numerous interpretations of the words of Scripture do not indicate that its nature is antinomian and broken. They indicate rather the perpetual danger of being influenced by one's own presuppositions and frames of reference, enabling one to escape from the thrust of God's Word, the light of Scripture. In the struggle of the church, it becomes increasingly clear that the confessed perspicuity is not a mere notation of a "quality" of Scripture in the manner in which we attribute certain qualities to other things, after which we can relax. This confession of the church will only be meaningful if it includes an insight into the power of the *Spirit's* way through the world and to men's hearts as the great witness through the Word (divine and human) in its historical form. This occurs with such strong and prevailing force that it is not possible for man to relax. We are being challenged by ever-increasing responsibility in the face of new questions and tasks.

When men are filled by the Spirit of Pentecost, they do not relax but become devoted to prayers (Acts 2:42). The testimony of God-breathed Scripture likewise places us in a world that has not been given over to chaos but to the blessing of divine promise. Therein lies the stimulating aspect of perspicuity. This confession has some of the features of pressing on when one has not yet obtained the goal (Phil. 3:12). It is not aimless, for it is aimed at the willingness to surrender all resistance to the voice of God, and it sends into the world men who by faith have come of age, having received the ability to perform every difficult task. With the mention of the phrase "come of age," we are brought to a transition from the confession of Scripture's *clarity* to that of its *sufficiency*. The joining of both elements – varied though their historical aspects may be – also offers a perspective on the unity of the church. This is bound to be so, for this clarity and sufficiency are related to the voice of the shepherd. An element of amazement is always included in the confession of clarity, an amazement that troubled Paul when he considered the divisions of the Corinthian church in spite of the gospel of its one and only Lord: "Is Christ divided?" (I Cor. 1:13). It is a revealing and stirring fact that Paul does not take this "reality" for granted, that is, the gap in insight, the divergence, the schism, and the heresy. Rather, he observes in amazement this disunity against the background of the message. Only if this feeling of apostolic amazement is to some extent shared by those who are faced by new responsibilities will it be possible to continue to confess the perspicuity of Scripture with conviction, since it contains both a promise and a task.

CHAPTER ELEVEN

SUFFICIENCY

IN THE HISTORY OF THE CHURCH, the Reformation confession of sufficiency, like the confession of Scripture's clarity, acquired a markedly polemical form. In Protestant circles, as soon as the term "sufficiency" is used, thoughts turn immediately to the controversy between Rome and the Reformation concerning "Scripture and tradition." However, as was also true of perspicuity, the confession is not exhausted in or lost by polemics. When *sola Scriptura* (Scripture alone) became the center of the controversy, it had a positive and affirmative content which also functioned fully in polemics. The sufficiency of Scripture expressed in *sola* is closely related to its perspicuity. For the confession concerning sufficiency is concerned with the light of Scripture, which was confessed to be sufficient for life's journey.

When this confession took on the form of "Scripture and tradition" in the sixteenth century, the Reformers did not in the least mean to say that Scripture was of no value to Rome. As they saw it, however, the teaching and practice of the Roman Catholic Church did not seem to consider Scripture "sufficient." It could be demonstrated, so the Reformers thought, that certain "truths" and "values" had been adopted that appeared to have no essential relationship to the gospel of Scripture. However, Rome underscored with assurance its conformity with the gospel. Thus, a dispute arose concerning legitimacy and verification by means of the appeal to the gospel. The way in which it was considered possible to demonstrate this continuity became an acute question: Had that which was "entrusted" (I Tim. 6:20) to the church been preserved in the course of the centuries? Thus we face the problem of "tradition," which played a role not only during the time of the Reformation but throughout nearly all phases of the church's existence. It became a central question whether the deposit of faith had been handed over from generation to generation in a pure and undefiled manner.

Various problems of analysis and verification are naturally implied in such a question. It should be noted that the need for continuity itself was not a matter of dispute between the various churches. The "preservation," so important during the First Vatican Council, is not in the least a concern peculiar to the Roman Catholic Church. Every church is concerned with it if it indeed wants to be the church; that is why each controversy on this point is of such a decisive nature. Furthermore, it is a complex question, since the church is not and cannot be an exact replica of the church of the New Testament. It entered history and was naturally influenced by its own life through history in numerous new situations. Tradition plays a decisive role in this development. The gospel, heard and accepted, is not being carried along as a rigid and erratic block, just as the people of Israel — certainly from a desire for continuity — took the bones of Joseph with them from Egypt (Gen. 50:25f.; Ex. 13:19; Josh. 24:32). It is a living thing with its own dynamic. Hence the continued and frequently complex reflection both in the Eastern and Western church concerning the essence and meaning of the gospel, as well as the manner in which this deposit must be handed over.

The church never lived from an external "repetition of doctrine." For the doctrine — the "teaching" — was understood to be a power in every new situation, challenge, and confrontation. For that reason it had to be preserved by the church without taking anything away from it or adding to it (Rev. 22:18-19). Hence, an important function was attributed to this process of preserving and handing over in the history of the church. One must be on guard, therefore, not to approach the problem of "biblical tradition" in a reactionary manner, as if to claim that the gospel would be present in different periods and cultures without human mediation and without "tradition."

With their emphasis on *sola Scriptura* regarding the sufficiency of Scripture, the Reformers were often upbraided for thinking unhistorically. It was said that their view of the life of the church was much too abrupt, too contingent, and too vertical, while the tradition and process of "handing over" itself was being slighted. However, it is clear and generally admitted that such a characterization is all too simplistic and does not do justice to the real situation. The Reformers did not close the doors to the past by glorifying the present in which the church lived. Rather, they devoted a good deal of attention to continuity with the ancient church and its councils. Nor can it be said that Rome canonized, without critical examination, every concept that came up through the course of the centuries. Thus, the characterization of the conflict as vertical (Reformation) versus horizontal (Rome) represents an unhistorical and incorrect dilemma; the problem was clearly much more complex. For "tradition," and therefore also the desired continuity, was emphasized in both cases. The idea of any arbitrary addition is not originally implied in tradition; rather, it implies the awareness of the importance of that which is and must be handed over through the ages. In fact, the difference is not found in tradition as such but in the "manner of tradition" and all that is historically connected with it – in other words, in the legality and purity of tradition and its specific formulations.

The term "sufficiency" acquires its significance in that situation, for it is quite radical when seriously uttered. One does well to ponder this radicalness expressed in the term *sola*. For we become aware that we are not concerned with a subjective preference or selection in which not all aspects of sufficiency are being given their due but only one particular aspect is gazed at, the heart being slow and the mind limited. In relation to the real and radical sufficiency, various texts and situations in the New Testament come to mind. When Philip asks Christ, "Lord, show us the Father, and we shall be satisfied" (Jn. 14:8), he is asking from a notion that what he has received and experienced in his present communion with Christ is insufficient, however valuable that may be. The answer to this question opens up a perspective of the complete sufficiency of Christ himself: "He who has seen me has seen the Father" (Jn. 14:9).[1]

The revelation of Christ is not marked by insufficiency; it needs no "addition" in order to become sufficient. It is rather a sufficiency drawing faith and trust to itself as its subjective correlate. Though it is often disparaged, one may rest in what has been granted him with a satisfaction of which the New Testament speaks. Psalm 23 also speaks of this contentedness. We "lack nothing" in the presence of the shepherd (Ps. 23:1), and we are called upon to live from the gifts granted us in the present: "Be content with what you have; for he has said,

1. See *TDNT*, I, 466.

'I will never fail you nor forsake you'" (Heb. 13:5; cf. I Tim. 6:8). This sufficiency does not bar life in the future, for it is precisely a sufficiency "on the way," in view of the future. It does not mean an escape to a vertical *eschaton,* but it means that new perspectives are continually opened up by it. Hence, it is not placed in contrast to the restlessness of the "not yet" and the "pressing on" (Phil. 3:12; cf. Heb. 12:14) so characteristic of the entire Christian life. For this continued activity and this longing are fed by and issue from a definitive sufficiency. It enables one to face the future with good courage: in all kinds of tense situations Paul must be mindful of what is "sufficient" for him – the grace of his Lord (II Cor. 12:9).

We are on this terrain when we begin to think about the sufficiency of Scripture, that is, if the struggle during the Reformation concerning this sufficiency is regarded as more than a theological game about a number of "sources," and if we do not lose sight of the meaning of this sufficiency for the Christian life. We are concerned with a religious confession when dealing with sufficiency, as we were with perspicuity. The passion of those involved in the struggle proves this. According to their testimony, no "supplement" to this Word and this Scripture was needed. In fact, Rome was reproached for deeming this Word insufficient. In the Reformers' opinion, this was clearly indicated in various doctrines and institutions, "human traditions" of Rome that implied insufficiency. This was the background for *sola Scriptura.* The sharp criticism of the Reformers was closely related to their deep central concern for the gospel. From the Catholic viewpoint, as is well known, this *sola* was regarded as quite one-sided. In Rome's opinion, it was not merely accidental that not only the *sola Scriptura* was uttered but also accompanied by *sola fide* (faith alone), *sola gratia* (grace alone), and *solo Christo* (Christ alone). Of course, it is quite difficult to level the charge of "one-sidedness" at *sola gratia* and *solo Christo* in view of the gospel, for in Scripture itself we are clearly confronted with this *sola* (I Tim. 2:5; Acts 4:12). Nevertheless, it was thought that the frequency of this "alone" indicated an exclusiveness that hid the perspective of the fullness and multifaceted nature of salvation, which had entered our human reality.

Indeed, it cannot be denied that the *sola* of the Reformation is exclusive and radical. The purpose of the *sola fide* and *sola gratia* was to exclude the meritoriousness of good works, while the *solo Christo* excluded any other "mediator"; and the coordination with tradition was finally rejected with the *sola Scriptura*. This struggle was not aimed at positing an ultimate contrast between faith and works or between Scripture and tradition, in which there would be no place in the church for good works or for tradition, and no place would be assigned to human function and "mediations" in God's dealing with man in the history of salvation. However, because of the specific nature of the gospel, the urgency of a specially accented *sola* was realized. Since a number of relativizing "contiguous beliefs" were observed, it was thought to be unavoidable to speak of insufficiency with regard to Scripture. Herewith we reach the conflict that was waged over Scripture and tradition in the sixteenth century.

The decisive question that the Reformers considered and answered in the affirmative was as follows: Had not tradition in the Roman Catholic Church become an independent and in fact a normative authority, valid in itself, through a gradual historical process? The Reformers wished to protest against that independence and its range of influence. The sentiment was not that of an antihistorical revolt but that of a desire for preservation and continuity. A protest against tradition was not at stake, according to Bavinck, but a means was developed by which the entire tradition could be tested. Bavinck says that tradition should be given its due, insofar as it was deemed to "flow forth from Scripture."[2]

It is not immediately clear how this statement should be interpreted in specific cases. But the intention was obvious: to combat the possibility that tradition would acquire a supplementing function as a second and equivalent source of revelation alongside Scripture. The struggle concerning this tradition does not date from the much discussed decree on tradition by the Council of Trent in 1546. It had already become quite bitter in the criticisms of many traditions of the church, as various Reformation confessions clearly show. Many traditions were viewed as noxious parasites on the gospel. Time and again these traditions were compared with Jewish traditions that were sharply rejected in the gospel as "precepts of men" (Mt. 15:9; Col. 2:8) and as a veiling of the real Torah of Israel through man-made regulations, so that the essential and "weightier" matters of the law were lost (Mt. 23:23). The dangerous process of supplantation was being attacked with a sharp pro-

2. *GD*, I, 454, 464.

test against the "authors of the traditions" opposed to the "divine mandate,"[3] and against traditions that were forced on the church to ensnare man's conscience. One is reminded of Peter's admonition not to put a yoke on the neck of the disciples (Acts 15:10).

Why, it was asked, is it forbidden so frequently in Scripture to make human regulations and heed them (I Tim. 4:1f.)?[4] They concern traditions that are not in conformity with the gospel according to its "clear testimonies."[5] The question of conscience frequently mentioned in this criticism is not a matter of chance. The explanation is that during the Reformation the struggle over tradition was not thought to be a formal problem dealing with intellectual knowledge but one with a central religious dimension. Everything was focused on the preaching of salvation and on the freedom granted through it. It is in this connection that the sufficiency of Scripture is mentioned repeatedly, for the sun in Christ had risen and life was placed in the brightness of midday – the decisive testimony of God at the last hour. The full emphasis on the sufficiency of this light may be characterized by Calvin's statement that this perfection of Christ's doctrine must be *sufficient* for us: since all the treasures of knowledge are found in him, we need no new doctrine, and all "additions" have therefore become meaningless.[6]

It is in this eschatological perspective of "the last hour" that the Reformers found the fundamental principle for their polemic.[7] This does not imply a simple repetition without new responsibilities for new times, since the churches of the Reformation themselves would be confronted with this process of "tradition." But it did mean the radical rejection of *addition*.[8]

The confession *sola Scriptura* has often been criticized for being an isolating and one-sided statement. In choosing one

3. The Augsburg Confession in J. T. Müller, *Bek. Schr. der Ev. Luth. Kirche*, p. 66.
4. *Ibid.*, p. 67.
5. *Ibid.*, p. 66.
6. *Inst.*, IV, viii, 7.
7. *Ibid.* Calvin points to Heb. 1:1, 2 with its "of old" and "in these last days." Cf. Calvin's commentary on Heb. 1:1 concerning to "go beyond Christ" as *evil* and as "the transgression of this limit" (Torrance edition, p. 6).
8. Cf. The First Helvetic Confession (1536), Art. I. For subsequent periods, see The French Confession of Faith (1559), Art. V; The Belgic Confession (1561), Art. VII; The Westminster Confession of Faith (1647), Ch. I, vi.

source instead of two, this objection should not be superficially ignored. One must also be concerned with the problem of tradition. Otherwise, one would fail to realize that the church, in its relationship to God's Word, has always been informed by traditions. We never deal with a blank sheet of paper. Certain traditions — not as additions but interpretations — may even become attached to the life of the church in the course of time to the extent that practically they have the features of additions and are therefore out of reach of the critical and sovereign Word of God. The mere confession of the *sola Scriptura* does not safeguard in the least from the dangers of such additions. We become aware of this at once when we consider the confessional divisions. For an appeal to Scripture's clarity and sufficiency is continually made, but the situation of separation is not radically changed and startling tendencies toward confessional unification do not appear. One may of course consider himself an exception by discovering corrupt additions made by others in order to find a clear solution to the ecumenical problem. However, there is every reason to warn against such a premature and reassuring solution. It must rather be noted that a deeper and continued consideration and critical testing must flow forth directly from the *sola Scriptura* itself.

The Reformation viewpoint will not be understood if it functions only in a polemic with Rome. The *sola Scriptura* did indeed function in the history of the controversy concerning Scripture and tradition in the Roman Catholic Church. However, this must be understood in a wider context, embracing the polemic against all additions that influence the life of the church, even where the *sola Scriptura* is not an issue at all. It is not easy, therefore, to confess the sufficiency of Scripture: it is not a self-evident, handy chapter in systematic theology, but it is the dominating tone for the entire chorus of the church. Sufficiency may never be isolated, as if it has to do only with a formal problem of epistemology and is thus of a "technical" nature. It is a confession implying the responsibility to keep an open perspective on the message of Scripture. It is as clear as daylight that the Reformers did not separate this calling from the *sola Scriptura:* with a deep conviction and an urgent pastoral admonition they witnessed to *sola Scriptura,* having this sufficiency in mind. The function of that confession never was to find an answer to the question of where Christian "truth" could be found, for it deals with the one testimony to the truth unto salvation, with its exclusive, concrete, and normative significance. The confession of "Scripture alone" does not begin with the "alone" as a general principle, but with Scripture. For the meaning and weight of the "alone" can be perceived only along that route. Only in this way is it possible to suppress the inclination to a one-sided reaction and to a personally biased preference.

It should be recognized that the phrase *sola Scriptura* was not coined by the Reformers; it occurs already in the literature of the Middle Ages in various connections.[9] It all depends on the context in which the words are used. The function of the *sola Scriptura* in the Reformation was to focus attention on God's Word as a principle of interpretation over against human arbitrariness. At the same time, this clarifies the fact that there was no intention of shaking off all traditions, nor of returning to the source, with the idea that the source contained water of the purest kind. A general preference of this kind for what is "ancient" and "original" is often found in humanism and in the Renaissance, with their calls for a return to the "sources" and to "the classics"; but different and deeper motifs impelled the Reformers.[10]

The phrase *sola Scriptura* expressed a certain way of reading Scripture, implying a continual turning toward the gospel as the saving message of Scripture. The Reformers were aware of being confronted with the original and canonical gospel, not because it was ancient as such, but because of this concrete and qualitative "originality." They did not propose a general (isolating) principle to be applied to faith, to grace, to Christ, and to Scripture respectively, but they confessed a perspective in which this unique past was preserved. In this light it may be said that the term *sola Scriptura* represented "the struggle for the genuine tradition."[11] A statement of this kind must always be further clarified because of the numerous complicated problems concerning the term "tradition." But the idea is not to overtrump the many traditions in an attempt to simplistically protect oneself against the objection of antitraditionalism. For

9. H. A. Oberman, *The Harvest of Medieval Theology* (1963), pp. 389f.; Ebeling, *The Word of God and Tradition,* p. 127: "The formula as such is not peculiar to the Reformers." In many contexts the words are used especially in the polemical rejection of papal power and authority without attaining the depth of the Reformation thesis.
10. Cf. Weber, *Grundlagen,* I, 304f.
11. Ebeling, p. 109.

to the Reformers continuity was a matter of deepest concern, a continuity historically expressed in the terms *paradosis* (tradition) and *paralampanein* (to receive). The emphasis on the critical function of the gospel in relation to human traditions is explained in the light of this continuity. Through traditions that entered the life of the church, the gospel could be molded to conform to human considerations, and men would no longer be able to perceive to what extent the gospel is "not according to man" (Gal. 1:11). In the light of this issue of the Reformation, the artificial and nearly self-evident harmony between the gospel and the empirical factuality of the church was broken through.[12]

In this way the *sola Scriptura* first became a thesis and then received a polemical and hermeneutical function in the actual life of the church. The Reformers were deeply bound to remain faithful to the pattern of the New Testament. For in it there is a radical boundary (an emphatic *sola*) that could not be transgressed. The idea was not to condemn the past of the church but to claim that belief in a self-evident continuity ought to be placed on the touchstone of the gospel. They desired to stand in the light of tradition themselves; this is evident from Calvin's high regard for the doctrinal decisions of the early councils. But the critical function of the Word of Scripture was respected *within* this context, not only theoretically but practically, with a clear freedom regarding the ancient church and the manner in which it had spoken of salvation in Christ.

On the basis of *sola Scriptura* it remains true that the church stands under the authority of the Word, and only thus will it truly remain the church. Warnings are continually heard against the arbitrariness of insight that develops within the church, which may result in the gospel's no longer being understood. For this reason alone it was impossible for the Reformers, on the basis of the so-called formal insufficiency of Scripture, to seize upon the authority of the church to render Scripture functional. The Reformers' conviction must be seen against the background of the critical closure of the canonical gospel to which they pointed. It is striking that Rome and the Reformation disagreed concerning the canon but not concerning the acceptance of the canon of Scripture itself, in spite of Rome's view that the fixation of the canon was based on the

12. Cf. E. Schlink, "On the Problem of Tradition," *The Coming Christ and the Coming Church* (ET, 1968), pp. 239f.

authority of the church. It is difficult to deny that the acceptance of the normative canon presupposes as its subjective correlate a submission to Scripture as God's Word. There is good reason to ask whether the idea of the canon does not naturally imply a recognition of the sufficiency of Scripture in view of the factual recognition of the canon, and, moreover, whether the concept of tradition as "addition" is thereby not excluded. Indeed, reflection about the canon in Roman Catholic theology did contribute to the devaluation of the two-source theory. For the recognition of the canon itself implied a process of sifting aimed at preserving the "purity of the gospel" against numerous traditions arising in the church. As a result, everything in the later interpretative tradition is related to the canon of Scripture — Scripture itself. Viewed from this angle, the entire focus is on the functionality of the canon within the church, and the authority (just as with the fixation of the canon) acquires a decisive function for the *interpretation* of Scripture.

According to the Reformation confession of Scripture, such a solution was not possible. The growth of the canon implied an historical development, and it was considered impossible to refer to an absolutely clear and assuring criterion of canonicity that countered the Catholic reference to the authority of the church. This became particularly apparent when the exact boundaries of the canon were being considered. Yet the conviction prevailed that believers were bound to this canon as the witness concerning Christ in the midst of the historical aspects of God's Word in the world. This subjection to the canon did not imply an attempt to offer a system of "watertight" security but an insight of faith historically expressed in the recognition of true apostolic authority. And thus it received its function in the journey of the church. No matter how much *sola Scriptura* concerned *Scriptura,* it did not formalize faith and submission to Scripture; because of the essence of Scripture, they remained centered on the *message* of the gospel.

In the reflection on continuity as the true tradition, a conformity with the exclusiveness required by the gospel itself was sought in the *sola Scriptura.* This is not an exclusiveness by which "others" are excluded by a high-handed procedure of isolation. It is a unique exclusiveness, deriving its structure from the broadness and universality of the gospel. For the gospel is aimed at the world and does not exclude family, race, or nation, but allows salvation to go forth to all peoples. The centrality of this relationship is certified throughout the New

Testament in a radical rejection of and defense against any attempt to overshadow, undermine, or replace true salvation. We hear the biblical protest against a different gospel (Gal. 1:8), a different Jesus (II Cor. 11:4),[13] a different spirit (II Cor. 11:4), or a different doctrine (I Tim. 1:3).

This battle is waged in view of the absolute character of the proclaimed salvation in its blessing and freeing character.[14] This gospel is opposed to any insufficiency that might demand something different or something more. The need for tradition arises because of the gospel's redemptive importance as the ages expand from generation to generation until the return of the Lord (I Tim. 6:14, 20). With this tradition we are confronted with the horizontal dimension of salvation in history. In history, tradition takes the form of an urgent reference to the past, to that which saved "from the beginning." Hearing and sight are related to that which was "from the beginning" (I Jn. 1:1). The old commandment, which was from the beginning (I Jn. 2:7; II Jn. 5:6), does not exclude the new commandment, which is a sign of light, of the departure of darkness (I Jn. 2:8). The "from the beginning" is determined by the knowledge of him who is from the beginning (I Jn. 2:13). One must abide in that which was heard from the beginning (I Jn. 2:28), in the message from the beginning (I Jn. 3:11). A unique continuity is therein assured in terms of an abiding in love, a token of the reception of the Spirit (I Jn. 4:14, 16) and the doctrine of Christ.[15] For the sake of his life, one may not "go ahead" (II Jn. 9), since this saving beginning is full of promise through its absolute sufficiency.

The past is not thereby romanticized. We hear a hymn about the light that already shines (I Jn. 2:8) and about the grace that has appeared (II Jn. 9). This "going ahead" is perhaps a slogan of the Gnostics, but that kind of progression "is subjected to his most severe condemnation."[16] The link to the teaching of Christ is needed, for everything is focused on the fact that one now "has" the Father and the Son. Herewith

13. Cf. D. W. Oostendorp, *Another Jesus: A Gospel of Jewish-Christian Superiority in II Corinthians* (1967).
14. Cf. the pointing to *sound words* (II Tim. 1:13) in connection with faith and love and the parallel to the guarding (by the Holy Spirit) of the truth which has been entrusted (1:14). Cf. I Tim. 1:10-11; I Tim. 6:3; Titus 1:9, 13; 2:1, 2, 8.
15. On abiding, see Isa. 40:8; Dan. 6:26; I Cor. 13:13. Cf. *TDNT*, IV, 574f.
16. R. Schnackenburg, *Die Johannesbriefe* (1965), p. 280. Cf. Gal. 5:25.

the boundary line is indicated, that is, the radical *sola*; this boundary calls for the responsibility and care for the tradition that is filled with God's salvation. The above words show to what extent this exclusiveness has a positive meaning. Moreover, it may never be formalized by means of a traditionalism. This is clearly paralleled by the Old Testament admonition not to leave the "ancient paths" (Jer. 6:16). Such statements about continuity are numerous in Scripture. At first sight they appear to be extremely "conservative" and they could be summarized with the one call to keep what you have (Rev. 3:8; Jude 3). Words such as these would have a deep influence later on all kinds of historical conservatism, in which "the old" imperceptibly begins to prevail over "the new." When that is the case, the living link to the new withers away,[17] and it is no longer clear that the continuity of the teaching of Christ can only be preserved in faith, hope, and love. Hence, a sufficiency, a "being content" appears derived from the fact that the latter things (the present) are linked to the former things, yet the meaning of the former things is being neglected and ignored. The unique value of that which is preserved is in danger of vanishing in various forms of traditionalism and conservatism through a formal principle. In this way the power and blessing of true tradition have trickled away, and a timeless repristination is left, with no perspective of the past nor of the virtues of the gospel for all times.

The concepts of preservation, tradition, and "from the beginning" (cf. Jn. 8:44) are no guarantee in themselves that later generations will be blessed.[18] It is possible to pursue a continuity that is simply a protest against all "going ahead" and a stubborn adherence to rigid formulas.[19] Men accused Stephen because he said of Jesus that he "will destroy this place, and will change the customs which Moses delivered to us" (Acts 6:14). It is possible for one to preserve the "human tradition" (Col. 2:8), and yet with all his preserving find

17. The guarding of what has been entrusted (I Tim. 6:20) is according to the depth of the gospel related to the "I have guarded" (Jesus) in Jn. 17:12 and to the divine keeping (Jn. 17:11). See *TDNT,* VIII, 164: "The genuineness of continuity is established not by the transmitted teaching as such but by the One who is Himself its content."
18. Cf. H. N. Ridderbos, *Authority,* pp. 19f.; *TDNT,* IV, 11f. The content of that which is transmitted is decisive.
19. Cf. Kuyper, *Conservatisme en Orthodoxie: Valse en Ware Behoudzucht* (1870), p. 15.

himself against Christ, in whom the "whole fulness of deity dwells bodily" (Col. 2:9). Absolute sufficiency is found in him "in whom are hid all the treasures of wisdom and knowledge" (Col. 2:3), in such a measure that Paul reacts by "abounding in thanksgiving" (Col. 2:7). In the midst of all traditions, therefore, a *critical* authority is posited, to examine what has been handed over in view of the future. Neither the old nor the new is the deciding factor on the basis of its inherent quality as old or new (II Cor. 5:17; Gal. 6:15; Heb. 8:13).

A blessed preservation is only possible because of the radical newness of that which is preserved with its evangelical sufficiency. Tradition, with its horizontal dimensions, receives its deep meaning from the vertical dimension of salvation, which entered history and in history evokes and preserves continuity through human witness and "tradition."[20] This tradition is not rigid or conservative, for the tradition is maintained in a frame of reference that excludes any petrifaction (Col. 2:6).[21] It is maintained in the radical transition from the slavery of sin to freedom and the slavery of righteousness (Rom. 6:17-18). It is thus possible for the tradition to function in such a frame of reference. It proves how far removed we are from the cliché and from a languid reliance on the past, without a perspective of the future. Tradition must be seen in the framework of continuity from generation to generation through a sincere faith (II Tim. 1:5), and for that reason it is taught to others (II Tim. 2:2; II Thess. 2:13-15). Maintaining *this* tradition coincides with the preservation (II Thess. 2:16; I Cor. 15:1-2), the glorifying, and the speeding on of the Word of the Lord (II Thess. 3:1).

Against the background of this gracious continuity the *sola Scriptura* must be understood as a reference to the critical, prophetic-apostolic witness of Scripture, for it must be linked to this tradition in order that the freedom of the newness of life that includes all perspectives may not be lost. It means

20. The question of horizontal and vertical is much discussed regarding Paul's relationship to the Jerusalem church, especially his "independence" (Gal. 1:15-17; Rom. 15:20-21, with a citation from Isa. 52:15). This independence, cf. Gal. 1:12, 16 (the revelation of Christ), does not break the continuity of tradition (the gospel), but is related to the specific place of Paul as an apostle to the gentiles and to his authority not derived from men. Cf. his later visit to Peter (Gal. 1:18). Cf. Ridderbos, *Authority,* p. 21; Barth, *CD,* IV/3/1 (ET, 1961), 197f.

21. Note the eschatological orientation in I Tim. 6:14 and II Tim. 1:12.

submission to the critical norm in confrontation with the gospel, which itself constitutes the tradition. For that reason it may not be endangered by anything or anyone. In explaining the critical function of the "over against," Paul's opposition to Peter in Antioch is particularly instructive. Paul opposes Peter to his face because Peter is clearly wrong (Gal. 2:11). This conflict was frequently featured in the discussion of the decisive issue of authority and this critical "over against." Luther particularly dealt extensively with it in his commentary on Galatians. The conflict is not only significant for the discussion concerning the infallibility of the Pope. It is deeply significant also for an understanding of the nature of authority itself, for Paul defends here "the greatest and cardinal article of Christian doctrine." He is concerned with more than the "dignity and glory of all apostles and angels."[22] The conflict points to the gospel as the critical, authoritative norm over all persons and every status, which is always present with its examining and sifting activity. It can never be derived from men or from any "succession" that would guarantee and legitimize as such the pure tradition in a formal, temporal way.

It is impossible to distinguish here between *doctrine* and *life*; such a distinction would indicate that one could err in practice, while his doctrine would be beyond examination in an abiding continuity. Paul had entered the arena at this decisive point because the issue was "that they were not straightforward about the truth of the gospel" (Gal. 2:14). Even if full attention is given to Peter's considerations, according to the story of Galatians 2:12-13, and their practical consequences, it cannot be denied that here a critical decision was made at a crucial point in the church's history and in direct relationship to the essence of the gospel. It is an illustration of the *a priori* that may never vanish in the church.[23]

The Reformation *sola Scriptura* was not meant to be separatistic and isolating. It called for the battle for true tradition and implied an hermeneutical appeal of the first order for the life of the entire church. This specifically meant that many questions were raised — some within the Reformation itself — that were related to the function of this principle. But the

22. Luther, *Ausführl. Erklärung der Epistel an die Galaten* (1856), p. 153.
23. *BC,* Art. VII points to this critical aspect in affirming that the "truth of God . . . is above all," including "the great multitude, or antiquity, or succession of times or persons, or councils, decrees, or statutes."

power of this principle was not broken by the tensions it evoked, since its purpose was to show the church that it needed to turn toward the gospel of Scripture itself again and again in the midst of all human traditions. In the sixteenth century, reference was made repeatedly to the New Testament criticism of Jewish tradition. A profound problem was thus put on the agenda because of the specific analogy: the Jewish legalistic interpretation of Torah. The Catholic Church considered this not merely a formal but also a material criticism. But this does not take away from the fact that the general testing of tradition has a value all its own and is somewhat self-evident precisely because it is dealing with critical authority.

The Reformers did not wish to endanger the principle of tradition; rather, they wished to protect it. Hence its function remains, not only in the face of dangerous "traditions" of others or oneself, but also against dangers of interpretations (one's own and others) that might be condensed to "additions" in the course of time. The *sola Scriptura,* therefore, will only have significance when it is not used in terms of a theoretical axiom for polemics, but when it takes on visible and concrete forms, showing to what extent the entire church is prepared to take every objection captive to obey Christ (II Cor. 10:5). Without this preparedness every polemic loses its power.

In the transition from the confession of Scripture's perspicuity to that of its sufficiency, I used the phrase "come of age" in passing. In using this term, I do not mean to enter the discussion concerning the concept of "maturity" with respect to modern man's relationship to God, as has been discussed for some years now in connection with Bonhoeffer's thought. By using the word "maturity" I wish to point to the meaning of God's Word placing man in the world and there showing him the way. God's Word does not bring man to a standstill in his thinking and acting, but it activates and stimulates him and fills him with a new responsibility. The very fact that the witness of God comes to us through the mouth of human witnesses already points in this direction. It is not sufficient to speak of a solitary work of God resulting from his exalted majesty. For we can speak without any reluctance of "fellow workers" for God (I Cor. 3:9). Yet this very word "coworker" led to the knowledge and experience that this could not be used as a plea for various forms of "synergism," by which the work of God and the activities of man were frequently divided in history. We are not interested here in a simple "application" of salvation, a "result" not essentially belonging to salvation, but in the Christian life itself – the faith which is lived by persons who are on the way. The confession of the sufficiency of Scripture – leaving every polemic beyond the horizon – is of decisive significance for that life.

With respect to that well-known phrase "all Scripture is inspired" (God-breathed) in II Timothy 3:16, so significant for the doctrine of inspiration, one may not forget its important context – the great *purpose* for which Scripture was given. For a great activity is evoked by the concept of the *usefulness* of Scripture, its purpose as it is aimed, through writing, at human life in the midst of the world: "Profitable for teaching, for reproof, for correction, and for training in righteousness." Everything is subsumed under the one goal of Scripture: "that the man of God may be complete, equipped for every good work" (II Tim. 3:17; 2:21; cf. Titus 3:1; I Pet. 3:15; Eph. 4:12). It is this equipment in the inspired Scripture that links the sufficiency of Christ to the Christian life. It causes us to speak of an ability, a maturity, and an independence. It is not superfluous to discuss this further, because here a perspective is clearly opened for life in the world. It is the perspective of the sufficient Scripture that enables man for this life, this equipment, this service, this completeness. The aim of Scripture concerns a situation that is the complete opposite of all passivity, since it is filled with concrete activity.

In times when human life is in the midst of change and complications because of new questions and problems, the believer is often caught in the grip of a fear that this Scripture – from ancient times – is no longer sufficient to show the way in the here and now and to enable men for all good work. He is impressed by the distance between God's Word and everyday life, when the cares of his heart are many and consolations do not cheer his soul (Ps. 94:19). At most, one would be willing to speak of a certain sufficiency of Scripture in connection with the inner devotional life, which has hardly anything to do with the ability to do every good work in the midst of life. For this life inexorably pulls us with it, and hence there is only room left for a "private cult" in the inner life and in subjectivity.[24] However, in the light of the

24. Moltmann, *Theology of Hope*, p. 312, concerning spirituality "beyond the relationships that have been reduced to materialist terms" and "escapism" (p. 315).

New Testament this is no more than an isolated and pale concept of sufficiency. It can hardly be harmonized with the biblical perspective on the Spirit, who will lead into all truth (Jn. 16:13), and on the God-breathed Scripture, which is aimed at all of life of the "man of God," and by which he is marked. This process of isolation into a "religious" province leaves no room for the specific purpose of Scripture, nor for "reproof," nor for "righteousness," and certainly not for the broad and all-encompassing "every good work," done with completeness. Even when giving full attention to the God-breathed Scripture, one runs the risk of overlooking the aim of this Scripture, which appears in the "every good work" of II Timothy 3:17 (cf. Rom. 15:4; I Pet. 1:10; Rom. 4:24; I Cor. 9:10; I Cor. 10:11).

It is obviously meaningless to play off the "function" against the "essence" of Scripture and thereby to isolate function from the impulse and breath of the Spirit in this concrete testimony. When we reject this dilemma, Scripture fulfills the worth of being sufficient to its aim and function. In reference to clarity, we pointed out its features as function for the new responsibility of understanding and obedience. This clarity is essentially related to sufficiency. The imagery of the guide (Jn. 16:13) for difficult roads, and of the light (II Pet. 1:19; Prov. 4:18) in a dark place, expresses their inner relationship. All those allusions to the Christian life are focused on the way that is open before us, in accordance with the well-known Old Testament image of the lamp for our feet and the light on our path (Ps. 119:105). The ability to walk on that way is so clearly shown that we are not justified, because of a fear of perfectionism, to weaken the serious call of Scripture or, on the other hand, to transpose it into insufficient mediocrity. The man of God[25] is not addressed in terms of such a mediocrity, which makes excuses legitimate and possible. The inescapable fact is that he is classified high and not low. He is placed under the arch of a wonderful mercy, and an appeal is made not to his powerlessness but to his power; he is thus placed on a road that opens up high perspectives. The confession of sin does not contradict this high qualification. It is related to it, and every "not yet" is not a self-evident condition but a recognized insufficiency in the light of the *sufficient* Word of God.

That "way" is discussed variously, sometimes with a further elaboration, other times as simply the well-known way (Acts

25. Cf. Berkouwer, *Man: the Image of God,* Ch. 10.

9:2; 19:9,23; 22:5; 24:15). It has been pointed out that this absolute usage (*the* way) in the New Testament is rather limited and that other expressions offer a further qualification (Acts 18:24-25).[26] Indeed, we are not dealing with an undetermined way; but the Christian life can be characterized simply in terms of a way full of blessing, calling, responsibility and perspective in the light of Christ, who is "the Way" (Jn. 14:6). The way is characterized by its beginning and its direction. We read of "the scriptures" that lead "in the way of the Lord" and from which one is accurately taught the "things concerning Jesus" (Acts 18:24-25). Here we meet the Christian life as pictured with its power and maturity — its having come of age. It is the way of "every good work" (II Tim. 3:17), of "lacking in nothing" (Jas. 1:4), the way on which the victory over evil is won (I Jn. 2:13-14). There is no misunderstanding about the nature of this victory; its background is the forgiveness of sins (I Jn. 2:12), and thus we read the assurance: "Because you are strong, and the word of God abides in you, and you have overcome the evil one" (I Jn. 2:14). It is also the way of knowing the truth (I Jn. 2:21) and of the anointing by the Holy One (I Jn. 2:20). Indeed, we do not read in that verse that "you know all things," but that "you all know."[27] But somewhat further the unction is mentioned again, which renders learning superfluous, "as his anointing teaches you about everything" (I Jn. 2:27; cf. Jn. 14:26; 16:13). From John — but not only from him — we hear the sounds of a radical newness of life, of the totality of this new beginning, all within the many-sided framework of the Word (I Jn. 2:14), of the Spirit (I Jn. 3:24), of commandment (I Jn. 3:23), of promise (I Jn. 2:25), and of hearing the testimony (I Jn. 5:10f.).

Here and elsewhere we cannot escape the thought of a deep and all-embracing sufficiency that forces itself upon us as the sufficiency of the revelation of testimony. It is sufficient in the sense that one is not left in the dark for a moment, for it always shows the way in a full perspective. One would not do justice to the confession of the sufficiency of Scripture by trying to avoid the force of this sufficiency. This would only be possible if one considered it exclusively within the framework of controversy and polemics that sought to defend the "sufficiency." Whatever this apologetic might be, and however it

26. *TDNT,* V, 42.
27. Cf. Schnackenburg, p. 135.

may be needed in view of the essence of the Reformation, the depth of this confession would not have been fathomed if no consideration were given to the radical test included in this confession, the test of the Christian life in its newness in Christ through the Spirit. Just as the confession of the clarity of Scripture does not at all have an exclusively controversial character, but points to a radical testing of our comprehension, so the sufficiency of Scripture confronts us with compelling and inescapable questions. They are inescapable particularly for those who wish to revere God-breathed Scripture, with all its "many and varied uses."[28] Calvin uses the same word ("reverence")[29] that was used at Trent.

The consequence of this reverence is that the "usefulness" is sought in the "right use of Scripture." This "use" of Scripture has been hotly debated, particularly when the question was considered whether Scripture was also truly God's Word "before and apart from its use" or whether it became God's Word only "by its use." A good deal of confusion frequently entered this controversy, and the parties did not always correctly understand and fairly judge each other's position.[30] This question can never be decided if the indwelling of a "mystical supernatural ability"[31] within Scripture is placed over against a Scripture that *becomes* God's Word "through its use." Naturally, there were objections to this inherent "supernatural power," for in that case it would almost lead to the idea of a "transubstantiation" of human words. But also in the case of the letters *becoming* God's Word, a sort of transubstantiation would take place, occurring in "its use." If one understands the significance of God's Word in the human words of Scripture, he will quickly reject this dilemma as completely fruitless. For it is incorrect and offers no true perspective on the God-breathed Scripture.[32]

The debate about the question "before and apart from its use" or "in its use" is meaningful only insofar as it deals with the interest in the priority and sovereignty of the Scripture that confronts us with its witness. It does not and cannot

28. Calvin's commentary on II Tim. 3:16 (Torrance ed.), p. 330.
29. *Ibid.*
30. Cf. Preus, *Inspiration,* pp. 175f. See Berkouwer, *Sin,* pp. 215f.
31. Cf. the critique of Kuyper, *Hedendaagse Schriftkritiek,* p. 55. For the "inherent" in Quenstedt, cf. Weber, *Grundlagen,* I, 315; Bavinck, *GD,* IV, 437, 440 versus a magic, impersonal power that lay in the Word.
32. Cf. Preus, pp. 177-178.

derive its authority from the fact that *we* use it, not even when we use Scripture in faith. For because of its nature and origin the witness of Scripture evokes its use as real testimony. The message of the God-breathed Scripture, which comes "from beyond us" and is meant "for us," becomes clear precisely through the correct use of Scripture while hearing and understanding it. While all subjectivism[33] regarding Scripture is being rejected, it must also be taken into account that Scripture can be known only together with its purpose – implying both its use and application. Only in this way is Scripture known and understood, and only thus does it become the guide to perfection. For Paul did not describe Scripture in terms of an abstract object outside reality, but in terms of the purpose of this writing.[34] In this way it is the critical, testing, guiding, and revealing Word of God that poses the most central and profound question concerning "the way."[35]

In the light of this clear and urgent witness concerning inspired Scripture, it will finally be possible to discuss the question of why Scripture is often considered insufficient to really show the way toward a complete equipment, a true apologetic, and a true polemic (II Tim. 3:16-17) by virtue of Scripture's comfort, endurance, and hope (Rom. 15:4). This idea of insufficiency is awakened when one is impressed by the complexity of life, which at times seems to be frail and confused, to proceed from questions to questions (in contrast to Ps. 84:7). This notion of insufficiency was often felt in earlier times, particularly in connection with problems and uncertainties concerning the inner life. Compensation for this insufficiency was sought in many directions.[36] Even when the God-breathed char-

33. It is self-evident that one must be careful in his judgment concerning all kinds of expressions about Scripture and faith. We remember the word of Calvin which – unkindly – can be interpreted as subjectivism (*Inst.*, III, ii, 6): "As for its certainty, so long as your mind is at war with itself, the Word will be of doubtful and weak authority, or rather of none." One can only understand this correlative speaking of Calvin in the light of the whole of III, ii, 6: "Therefore, take away the Word and no faith will then remain" (Battles ed., I, 549). The formulation, however, is striking.
34. See Barth, *CD*, I/2, 737 concerning "a necessary function inseparable from the existence and therefore from the explanation of Scripture" and concerning the "use of Scripture" with Scripture as subject. Cf. "the unconditional sovereignty of the Word" (p. 739).
35. Cf. Calvin on II Tim. 3:16: "This is indeed the chief part of our knowledge – faith in Christ" (Torrance ed.), p. 331.
36. Preus, p. 176.

acter of Scripture is confessed, this notion may undermine the Christian life: gradually the confession of Scripture is no more than a latent dogma that no longer functions. In that case the high qualifications of the Christian life according to the New Testament are no longer understood. They are considered distant and unreal words that indeed deal with the way yet do not show and open the way in reality. The more complex life became in later times the more this notion of insufficiency grew, evoking new and unsuspected questions and problems, for which clear answers were vainly sought in Scripture. Such a situation can be compared to Jesus' conversation with Thomas. Christ's statement that the disciples know about the way is countered by Thomas' answer: "Lord, we do not know where you are going; how can we know the way?" (Jn. 14:4-5). The distance between knowing and not knowing, between the promised sufficiency and the notion of insufficiency, may lead to a distrust and a loss of the joyful trust in the sufficient light and the reliable guide.

But this notion of insufficiency stems not only from the complexities of life which, because of their confusing disarray, make a discovery of the way difficult (Jn. 11:16); it also stems from the expectations one has concerning Scripture. It is quite conceivable that approaching Scripture with a certain hope and a particular view leads to a disappointing experience, the experience of its insufficiency. It happens when a person believes that Scripture is able to give specific answers to all questions that may arise at any time. Holy Scripture is then considered revelation in terms of a general disclosure of knowledge and a point of reference for much that would otherwise be hidden from us. In that view revelation is *apokalypsis,* that is, taking away the "veil" from all human questions. The encouraging Bible statement about the lamp and the light was often understood in that way (Ps. 119:105). As a result of this prior expectation, Scripture was often used for specific situations and problems, and its interpretation was thus naturally influenced by particular periods and backgrounds. The nature of Scripture was at least partially judged from the viewpoint of general questions and answers (revelation), with an emphasis on questions. As a result, Scripture was ultimately measured by the degree to which satisfactory answers were provided to men's particular questions; accordingly, the answers seemed more and more artificial. Scripture was deemed sufficient and satisfying to the person who believed that nearly all his questions could be answered in it. But a crisis could arise for one who was increasingly plagued by hesitation or doubt because of a frustrated expectation that had been founded on a particular view of Scripture.

It is important to note that eyes were slowly opened to the fact that Scripture itself offered no grounds for an approach with such expectations. It is not intended to offer a general timeless satisfaction or enrichment of man's deep desire for knowledge, nor a general satisfaction of human curiosity. Thus, a feeling of "disappointment" because of the "insufficiency" of Scripture must be subjected to the discipline of Scripture itself. It is evident that Scripture could be *over-questioned*.[37] The origin of the eventual feeling of crisis concerning sufficiency — via the untenable and often artificial nature of various answers — is an approach to Scripture that contradicted (usually unwittingly) the fact that Scripture "is its own interpreter."

There is indeed a clear correlation in the gospel between seeking and finding, praying and receiving, knocking and being opened to (Mt. 7:8); but this does not make Scripture a source of revelatory answers to arbitrary questions. One is far removed from the gospel when he is caught in the net of such general questions. One must be reminded anew that Jesus thanked the Father for hiding "these things" in his good pleasure from the wise and understanding but revealing them to children (Mt. 11:25-26). This is not the proclamation of a crusade against knowledge and wisdom, but it is decisive for the correct understanding of revelation. We find this kind of understanding in Paul, for he learned to know the crucified Christ and to realize that the wisdom of the wise perishes and the understanding of the knowledgeable is annulled: "Where is the wise man? Where the scribe? Where is the debater of this age?" (I Cor. 1:20; cf. I Cor. 3:19f.). These words derive their meaning from the revelation of the mystery, since God can be known only through the "foolishness of preaching" (I Cor. 1:21), "the foolishness of God" that is wiser than men (I Cor. 1:25). This clearly means a radical penetration of the general question-and-answer approach and of the acquisition of knowledge and

37. Bavinck, *GD,* I, 416f. According to Bavinck, if Scripture made a *choice* between scientific systems, it would not be a book for humanity (p. 417). For Bavinck there was no dualism in this or in his characterization of Scripture as "religious," namely, "the Word of God for salvation" because "precisely therein" was Scripture a word for "family and society, for science and art."

wisdom. Each consideration of revelation, as well of the unveiling, is tested by means of that "foolishness."

The background of the disappointment concerning insufficiency is the denial of the depths of the revelation; it can thus become a "stumbling block." Something is lacking in the crucified Christ for Jews, who demand signs, and for Greeks, who seek wisdom (I Cor. 11:22). This denial[38] must lead to an insensitivity to the glorious aspects of the New Testament as it concerns the way that is opened through the revelation of the mystery (II Cor. 7:4; Eph. 1:19; 2:7; 3:20). The Christian church, battling for true knowledge and true wisdom according to Scripture, became increasingly aware of the error of this misunderstanding (the priority of questions), although it did not always escape the danger of forcing from Scripture all kinds of "answers" that often appear arbitrary, incidental, and inorganic. The very discovery of the purpose of God-breathed Scripture led to the deepening realization that respect for the concreteness of revelation did not mean a devaluation or a relativizing of the message. It rather brought to light the unique relevance of the revelation, that the witness of Scripture is inseparably connected with it. Paul writes of the mystery that was hidden for centuries but now is revealed. In that connection he writes of a command of God to proclaim this mystery to all nations through the prophetic writings (Rom. 16:25-26; cf. Rom. 1:1-2). Revelation and the veil can only be understood when all the attention is focused on this unique reality of the mystery and not on a network of general knowledge (question-answer; hiddenness-being revealed).[39] The knowledge it implies, the knowing of the truth, the received unction, and the perfect equipment do not form a theoretical and intellectual "illumination" that can be isolated, but are related to the great mystery and are structured by it (I Cor. 3:18).[40] Consequently, this *possible* way — the way of Scripture — is being discussed in full assurance regarding a radical sufficiency.

Not all questions, problems, and cares are taken away on this journey; it is not the way of "sight." The great witness of this mystery describes many cares on this road (II Cor. 4:7-

38. *TDNT,* VII, 519f.
39. Cf. the important views of Karl Rahner, "The Concept of Mystery in Catholic Theology," *Theological Investigations,* IV, 36f.
40. Cf. *TDNT,* VII, 521.

15), of a seeing through a mirror into riddles, of an imperfect knowledge, and of a decisive "not yet" (I Cor. 13:12). But on this road the equipment is given, and walking this road is the real purpose of God-breathed Scripture. As a divine gift—of Christ's Spirit—it is sufficient; and in this way it must be respected and accepted with gratitude and faith. This road and this sufficiency cannot be discussed meaningfully through the approach of a theoretical pro and con that seeks to test Scripture by our questions, to see whether it is truly sufficient and satisfying. God's salvation is more than an answer to human questions and more than the complement to a felt intellectual hiatus. It rather evokes absent questions and those pushed into the subconscious; it opens a way on which the believer is being trained to righteousness, to recognition of heresy, to the dangers of darkness and all demonic powers. Scripture is sufficient in the midst of unsolved questions. It is sufficient precisely for this way as its comforting blessing penetrates to the very depths of temptation on the way of perseverance (Rom. 15:4).[41]

On this way and in view of Christ and his great witness in the world, our "knowledge" is indeed knowing "all"[42]—but it is not knowing "much." Because of all this, glorying in knowledge is excluded. Hence, no barricade is erected on the road to human research, as if to consider that meaningless and superfluous. Various attempts have been made to show that a "Christian science"[43] can be meaningful. In it we note a justified rejection of those who view this science against the background of a two-source theory, which adds revelatory knowledge to "natural" knowledge. This is all too simplistic a characterization. For a "Christian science" was launched particularly in times when science was hailed as the ultimate answer to explain the world and life. A defense was sought in the attempt to solve the relationship between Scripture and science in a dualistic and mechanical way. However, through this approach both turned out to be competing factors, and when a synthesis of a two-fold knowledge did not appear to be tenable, one could easily turn away from science and isolate his religion

41. Cf. *TDNT*, V, 789 concerning "God's proper work." The God-breathed Scripture is the Scripture of the Holy Spirit.
42. See Phil. 4:13; Eph. 1:19; 3:20; Col. 1:11.
43. Berkouwer again uses the word "science" to mean systematic study. Such study is carried on in every academic discipline and not only in the natural sciences (tr. note).

as a last escape. However, the concreteness of revelation clearly excludes this fearful and worried approach. Nowhere in the New Testament do we meet a dialectic of creation and reconciliation or a dualism that leads to a disinterest in the works of God's hands. We rather note the wide horizon of a "summing up" of all things in Christ in the fullness of time (Eph. 1:10) and of a groaning of all creation (Rom. 8:19, 22).

The very writings that are filled with the concreteness of the revelation of the mystery (Romans and Ephesians) do not lead our attention away from the world. Hence, the hope of an ultimate harmony does not legitimize a concordism with respect to Scripture and science. For the concreteness of the revelation would be dissolved into a system that would not do justice to the central purpose of Scripture, and in the end the stage would be set for the complaint that Scripture is insufficient. On the contrary, we see how the man of God is placed in this world with his own freedom and responsibility in Christ. On this journey we need not get lost in a doctrine of double truth or a dualism that consumes the inner man. One can easily be robbed of conquest over this temptation because of the alluring process of science, whose analysis and induction increasingly manifest its evident power. This process indeed has breath-taking dimensions, and more persons outside the scientific realm than inside may become aware, now more than ever, that here a degree of sufficiency is attained that can overpower all of human life to such a degree that the perspective and hope of the mystery (the revelation) may lose all its relevance.

In earlier times the reality and the relevance of the mystery were often attacked in view of certain unscientific presuppositions. These presuppositions may still be heard in our time. Yet we note a shift, in fact a sharpening, in the direction of the sufficiency of science. I do not mean that science proclaims to have solved the mystery of human life, but that apart from this sufficiency no other way is shown, unless it be an isolated "religion" or a "private cult" quite apart from that which man can truly know. Revelation is clearly being reduced to the opposite of all universality. To avoid this issue means nothing but a crisis of the faith, knowledge, and wisdom to which we are called precisely by the proclamation of the gospel. In a conflict of this kind one ought not to grasp the last straw of a deeper "quantitative" knowledge, which might be derived from the source of Scripture and might thereupon be fused harmonically into the results of science. One must rather be aware that the "conflict" between faith and science, which is so real for so many people, can never be solved in this way. For it would be a solution in which the perspective on man's freedom and maturity is lost. Because of the foolishness and weakness of God in the world, man is called into this world and for this world. In view of the revelation of the mystery, one cannot escape this calling; it spurs him on, even though this calling is the very occasion for many questions concerning specific problems of science and concerning the understanding of the sufficient Word. This Word speaks of promise and expectation in the face of seeming irrelevance and insufficiency.

The last chapter of Moltmann's book concerning hope deals with the "church of the Exodus."[44] He does not characterize therewith a congregation that avoids the world or wishes to leave it. Rather, with the use of this term "exodus," he calls us to adopt a critical attitude of concern in this world. For, with the increasing materialism and technology, all questions seem to be soluble through reason and technology. This concern is the opposite of the escape into a "private cult" and of an individual and isolated religion in the midst of a world that is void of any "value" and "neutral concerning religion."[45] Such an escape is the reverse of the call to face the future by faith and to put the question of meaning on the agenda once more against the "horizon of the expectation of the kingdom of God."[46] The calling springs forth from the central promise of God's Word as the word of the crucified and risen Lord. It calls a person away from lethargy and dullness to righteousness. Exodus does not mean "fleeing the world";[47] it means expectation and service. The church has always been confronted with this expectation and service when it realized that it must give full attention to this world because of the *eschaton*.

The suggestion that the Word of God is insufficient and unsatisfactory increasingly leads to a disturbance of the relationship between Scripture and the church, and to a deep alienation, though this is not always explicitly and nakedly so. Hence, during the same period in which the dangers of "over-

44. *Theology of Hope,* Ch. 5.
45. *Ibid.,* pp. 305f., 315f.
46. *Ibid.,* pp. 325f.
47. *Ibid.,* p. 331.

asking" Scripture are recognized, the problems of another insufficiency arise, leaving little room for the "future of Scripture,"[48] as Moltmann calls it. He means the Word of God in the dimension of promise and not as a "closed circle." One does well to recall that in the very book of the Bible in which Scripture is extensively discussed and its interpretation is protected against arbitrariness (II Pet. 1:20-21; 3:16), one finds a vivid expectation of a new heaven and a new earth in which righteousness dwells (II Pet. 3:13). This may ward off the danger of regarding the penetrating judgment of Scripture as a powerless word that is unable to solve "problems." The idea of the insufficiency of Scripture (except in the "realm" of religion) often arose after a misunderstanding of the *pro rege* with its hermeneutical consequences. Those who considered Scripture significant for the inner life alone had to admit that the world and human life could not be penetrated on a broad and deep scale "with Scripture." Thus, the perspectives of the New Testament and its manifold testimony of the mystery and of God-breathed Scripture were blurred, and it seemed as though the written word of the Comforter was robbed of its sounding board.

It also appeared as if the emphatic testimony of the New Testament to "the man of God" was too high a qualification, which could not be brought into practice because Scripture was no longer viewed and understood in a truly "functional" manner. This function of Scripture seemed to vanish when man was no longer able to add an isolated plus to knowledge as an immediate solution to all baffling problems, and when it seemed possible to choose his own way of life with some success. We have often referred to the close inner relationship between the clarity and the sufficiency of Scripture. Speaking in terms of the present cultural situation, the crisis concerning the sufficiency of Scripture is deeper than that concerning its perspicuity. For different forms of scientific research rendered an unmistakable service with respect to its clarity, even apart from the question of whether this increased accessibility was felt to be a blessing. But regarding the sufficiency of Scripture, the problems of research seem to become superfluous. The concentrated witness of inspired Scripture indeed pretends to bring to light the contours of the gospel for all times, but through alienation from the gospel these contours are no longer felt to be decisive and sufficient. It is absolutely clear that these

48. *Ibid.*, p. 283.

contours did become a problem not only for the world but also in a particularly decisive way for the church. We will recognize the seriousness of the problem when we recall that a claim of the congregation is tested in view of the sufficiency of these contours. They are the contours of the kingdom in which power is perfected in weakness, in which the disciple is no more than his master, and in which service and proclamation are inseparably related.

The concentration of the witness of the Spirit does not imply the poverty of the church, an embarrassment that may be excused. It implies a calling of mature people come of age. The God-breathed Scripture has become the subject of much discussion and dispute. Because of its unique importance, there is no reason to belittle the meaning of that dispute; for the mystery of Scripture is the mystery of the Spirit. But the meaning of that dispute comes to light only when the God-breathed Scripture is really understood and obeyed. Its purpose and sufficiency are described clearly enough, so that this goal and this reality should not be blurred. For the process of blurring means that the Spirit is extinguished (I Thess. 5:19). In a letter that must be "read to all the brethren" (I Thess. 5:27), we are warned of that danger with an admonition underscoring the seriousness of Scripture *because* of its message. This concrete admonition has nothing to do with an adulation of the letter, nor is it a symptom of rigidity. It stems from respect for the Spirit, and in this way it is related to the hope of the coming of the Lord (I Thess. 5:23).

CHAPTER TWELVE

HOLY SCRIPTURE AND PREACHING

IT IS NOT OUR PURPOSE to deal extensively with particular aspects of the preaching of the gospel in this chapter. But the question of the relationship between Scripture and preaching is not a superfluous one. For in dealing with it we touch on an essential aspect of the reflection concerning Scripture as God's Word: that Word, the message of Scripture, enters history in search of the entire world. It enters the wide context of time and space that embraces all generations. We are charged in the presence of Christ to go to "all nations," making them his disciples (Mt. 28:19); the witness must penetrate "to the end of the earth" (Acts 1:8). When we think of this expansive power of the gospel, our attention is not drawn first of all to a written book but to the proclamation of salvation as it has appeared through messengers. The progress of the gospel becomes visible in earthly human relationships through missionary journeys intended to reach specific human lives with the message of salvation. In speaking of his journeys, Paul clarifies their meaning: to bring the preaching of the gospel of Christ to completion (Rom. 15:19-20) in different areas of service.

New perspectives are seen again and again, and Paul is impelled on his journeys by the desire to be fully in the holy ministry of the gospel (Rom. 15:16), and to come in the fullness of the blessing of Christ (Rom. 15:29). The only explanation for this missionary activity is the unique charge and thereby the knowledge of the unique importance of that which is proclaimed. Living people must be reached in their daily lives. It means a far-reaching "interference" in their life as a direct expression of the concern with which God visits man (Lk. 1:78). Paul speaks of necessity: "For necessity is laid upon me. Woe to me if I do not preach the gospel!" (I Cor. 9:16). It is an irresistible and meaningful task to preach the gospel (I

Cor. 9:18). Hence the passion and restlessness with which it is preached unceasingly, a proclamation that cannot be silenced. It is the very opposite of passivity or fatalism. It is not done with cool objectivity but with apostolic ardor, with the awareness that everything must be done to avoid a *skandalon* that is not the stumbling block of the gospel itself (II Cor. 6:3). But no single question or problem is dodged on that road. Therefore, it may take the form of argument and refutation, accusation and appeal, and of a correct answer to every individual (Col. 4:6). There is no single situation, moral or intellectual, and no single milieu that in an *a priori* manner renders an "answer" impossible or an occasion untouched by this confrontation. The proclamation is universal; it writes off no prodigal son, either at home or abroad. It does not shrink back because of closed doors, but it seeks man in his thoughts and feelings, his culture and milieu, his possessions and acquisitions, his religiosity or his "atheism."

We face here the original apostolic awareness of an unheard of and new relevance of proclamation. Many discussions — even meaningful discussions — were held in later times concerning the relevance of preaching. In those cases thought was given to the "mode of preaching," specifically the language of preaching, as it occurs in changed situations and reflection seeks to clarify what the purpose of this "interference" of preaching is. This reflection on the relevance of preaching does not in the least imply a devaluation of God's Word or an attempt to make the gospel fit certain times. This reflection may stem from the anxiety that the gospel may pass the soul of man as an empty rumor and an ancient story. Then it would no longer be understood in its arresting and absolute newness and its relevance for the present moment of every day. This relevance is expressed with the challenge to "behold": "Behold, now is the acceptable time; behold, now is the day of salvation" (II Cor. 6:2).

In view of the gospel, this relevance clearly does not imply eye-catching close-ups of current events or a lively orientation of things that are long-known by the hearers because of modern means of communication. It is rather a relevance founded in the gospel itself, which does not only seek man in a timeless sector of his life — his intellect or feeling — but seeks to reach him in his total and concrete existence. It is not sufficient to refer here to preaching in its "objective" reality, with which any kind of subjectivity must correspond. God's Word does not address man in an abstract isolation but in his real life. As is clear throughout the New Testament, this Word acquires its own color and purpose. Every sermon reflects the period in which it is preached not because the structure of the sermon is dictated by that period but because the whole man is confronted with salvation. The relevance of preaching and the reflection on all its aspects is based on something quite different from modern methods of application. It is based on the triumphant knowledge of the meaning and bearing of this message. Paul expressed this with enthusiasm when he said that Christ always leads us "in triumph" and through us spreads the "fragrance of the knowledge of him" (II Cor. 2:14). Authentic preaching presupposes this kind of expansion, universality, and perspective.

The inner relationship between the unchangeable gospel and relevance implies our being on guard for and our recognition of all resistance. It is based on the fact that the gospel is not "according to man" (Gal. 1:11), and hence takes on the form of a contradicting protest. In every age it implies a being troubled (I Kgs. 18:17f.; Amos 5; 7:10) that affects man as a blessing in his "independence," "autonomy," and resistance — to be radically and forever involved in this new message. As it "interferes" authoritatively with the lives of others, preaching can be irritating and absurd. It is possible and bearable only because of its absolutely unique motivations, whose source must become clear in word and deed if the proclamation is not to perish in frustration and resistance (II Cor. 2:17). These motivations are focused in the redemptive mandate in the face of all opposition (II Tim. 4:2; Acts 24:25), which does not allow for rest simply *because* of the proclaimed rest. Thus, one will understand that, because of the hardness of the house of Israel, Ezekiel's forehead is made "like adamant harder than flint," so that he need not fear (Ezek. 3:7-9). The universal responsibility of the proclamation for all time is justified and founded in certainty concerning the "appointed time," which happened "once for all" (Heb. 9:26; Rom. 5:6f.). Without this appointed time, every interference with the lives of others sinks to the level of meaningless pretense, a meddling that justifiably arouses resistance and is not accepted.

The trial of all preaching may be formulated with the question of whether this importance is seen and acknowledged. Is this mystery meaningful for all times? According to the New Testament, there is no doubt about this meaningfulness. We already saw this when dealing with the aspects of tradition: the message of salvation must be preserved and passed on from generation to generation. These expressions stem from a unique norm that can only be expressed by means of identifying words concerning the messengers of Christ: "We beseech you on behalf of Christ, be reconciled to God" (II Cor. 5:20). It is the perspective of the message entrusted to Paul and the gift of the mystery of reconciliation, as God in Christ was reconciling the world to himself (II Cor. 5:19; 4:1). We refer continually to the humanity of this testimony in which God's Word manifests itself: in the human words we hear the Word as witness of God (I Cor. 2:1), the gospel of God (Rom. 1:1; II Cor. 11:7; I Thess. 2:2,8). The humanity of these words may not be considered separately, in opposition to God's speaking (II Thess. 1:10; Rom. 2:16; II Cor. 4:3). The speech of the apostles is speaking in Christ "as commissioned by God, in the sight of God" (II Cor. 2:17). Its aim is faith, capitulation, acceptance, and trust, and from that direction human speech acquires its power, function, and meaning.

The deep motivation for this human service is expressed by Paul in a series of well-known rhetorical questions: to call upon and to believe, to believe and to hear, to hear and to preach, to preach and to be sent (Rom. 10:14-15). Preaching with authority is central in this context: "Faith comes from what is heard" (Rom. 10:17). Paul is not dealing here with an unqualified "revelation," for he cites Isaiah's expression concerning the bringer of good tidings (Isa. 52:7). There we also see the sense of universality breaking through all barriers: "Their voice has gone out to all the earth" (Rom. 10:18). For that reflects the perspective of Isaiah: "And all the ends of the earth shall see the salvation of our God" (Isa. 52:10). It is the function of the human word of proclamation to break through the barrier of silence. Thus we hear the emphatic admonition: "Preach the word" (II Tim. 4:2).

When we take this authority and norm of apostolic proclamation into account for our thought concerning the relationship between Scripture and preaching, we are faced with a number of important questions. They are all related to the transition from the biblical witness ("today" and "once for all," the "appointed time of God's favor") to history and hence to preservation and continuity, which come to the fore because of the testimony to the gospel's content. This continuity of salvation for the world and for all generations does not appear under the signature of self-evidence and automation. It is related to preaching in its power. Significantly, nowhere in Scripture are human words regarded as a powerless sign or symbol, so that their effect is felt only in the area of human subjectivity and activity. On the contrary, we continually come across expressions which refer us to the Word's coming with power. We read that by the Word of the Lord the heavens were made and that God "spoke, and it came to be" (Ps. 33:6,9). However, we also sense something of this same powerful event when he speaks through human words. It has not escaped notice that when speaking of the cross, Paul describes the word of the cross in terms of the power of God and not in terms of a word that by itself is powerless (I Cor. 1:18). The gospel is the power of God unto salvation (Rom. 1:16) and a sword of the Spirit (Eph. 6:17). The proclaimed Word is at work (I Thess. 2:13), and preachers are co-workers with God (I Cor. 3:9; II Cor. 6:1).

According to Paul, the preaching of the gospel is going out not only in word, but also in power and in the Holy Spirit and with full conviction (I Thess. 1:5). According to Isaiah, it is a word that does not return empty but accomplishes that which God purposes and prospers in the things for which he sent it (Isa. 55:11). Clearly, this view of the power of God's Word (Jer. 23:28-29)[1] has nothing to do with a rhetorical and overpowering word magic that brings life under its spell through words. Isolated words are not the subject of discussion. Paul both knew and rejected the temptation to consider human words in themselves as filled with power, even though they might be words of human wisdom (I Cor. 2:1,4). He reminds his readers emphatically that the kingdom of God does not consist in talk but in power (I Cor. 4:20). However, this definition of the kingdom (formulated as a sharp polemic) does not undermine the word of preaching. Later discussions concerning the "relationship" between Word and Spirit, sometimes emphasizing the Word, other times the Spirit, are foreign to Paul's thought. All magic and all attempts to isolate and categorize are far from his mind. He sees the Word going out into all the world (Rom. 10:18), but it does not break loose from on high as a power that strikes and has an "automatic" effect.

1. See *TDNT,* IV, 91f. The connection between word and power is not exclusively Pauline. See Jas. 1:18, 21; I Pet. 1:23; II Cor. 6:7.

Rather, it requires prayers that the Word of the Lord may speed on and triumph (II Thess. 3:1; Rom. 15:30).

Against the background of the fervor of this preaching, its liveliness and its penetrating character of personal involvement, we seem to be confronted by Scripture in a totally different atmosphere: the fixation of the words in a written form, seemingly petrified in inscripturation and hence existing "by themselves." Indeed, these words may be accepted, read from, and preached, but already then it is the human activity at work that appears to bring the fixed words to life. Here we face a significant problem that we encountered to a certain extent with the suggestive contrast between letter and spirit. However, it now calls our attention to the relationship between Holy Scripture and preaching.

Our thoughts frequently lead us to a kind of phenomenological comparison between the written and spoken word of preaching. It is pointed out that the essence of the Word is found in its being spoken: spoken expression dominates among persons who know each other very well and have communicated for years, while the written word is missing or functions only as a substitute (II Cor. 13:10). Likewise, according to Ebeling, "to the essence of the Word belongs its oral character, that is, its character of an event in personal relationship."[2] The great mistake of orthodoxy, according to him, was that it made no "distinctions" by identifying Scripture with the Word of God. It discussed Scripture as God's Word "apart from the proclamation of it," though the importance of the "living voice" for preaching was realized. This emphasis was understandable, says Ebeling, because of the need to refer to the written Word as norm over against human traditions. But the tension "between the character of the *verbum Dei* as spoken word and the character of writtenness" was taken too lightly. He feels that there is "a startling divergence" between this view and that of the Reformation.[3]

However, we are not concerned here with an analysis of this post-Reformation orthodoxy. We too proceed from the idea that Scripture may not be isolated from preaching, for this would be in contradiction to the entire life and responsibility of the church, and it would imprison believers in isolation and individualism. Yet it is important to give close

2. *Word and Faith,* p. 313, n. 1.
3. *Ibid.,* p. 312, n. 1.

attention to the relationship between the written and the spoken Word. That relationship becomes interesting precisely when we start with the "secondary," substituting function of Scripture and reflect on it. Often mentioned in this connection is Luther's statement emphasizing the priority of the oral tradition in the gospel. He points out that the apostles preached before they wrote. That was their real apostolic work: "That it was necessary to write books is in itself a great breach and decline from the Spirit; it was caused by necessity and not by the proper nature of the New Testament."[4] However, this emphasis on the priority or the "primacy" of the spoken Word does not prevent Luther from paying close attention to the written Word.[5] This is related to his insight into the meaning of the proclamation: he speaks of a necessity and of special circumstances; there is reason to come to a literary fixation so that the gospel does not perish in the confusion of heresies.[6] However, through preaching the message of the gospel is expressed in living form. It is possible to live with Scripture only when the message of Scripture is understood and is not considered "a metaphysical document,"[7] but a living instrument serving God for the proclamation of the message of salvation. Luther's view leaves no room for a devaluation of the written text, and it includes an appeal not to reduce the written text to mere letters in an unspiritual way. Hence his reference to the preceding oral activity of preaching.[8] Only in the light of this can the written fixation be rightly understood.

It is true that this "preceding" element of the oral proclamation was also emphasized at a later date. It plays an important role in various Roman Catholic views of tradition, making room for the function of the "unwritten" tradition. The way in which this "preceding" aspect is used and what conclusions are drawn are of decisive importance. It was frequently used as an argument against the norm of the apostolic witness. In that case the argument of the priority of the spoken word resulted in a devaluation of the written Word,[9]

4. *Ibid.* Cf. Ebeling, *Luther,* p. 132. Cf. also Luther's remark that Christ did not write his teaching, but spoke it; and gave no command to write, but to preach.
5. Kooiman, *Luther and the Bible,* p. 205.
6. *Ibid.,* p. 203.
7. *Ibid.,* p. 206.
8. *Ibid.,* p. 203.
9. Cf. Bavinck, *GD,* I, 437-439.

and it could be used as a concentration on the Spirit as opposed to the letter in a spiritualistic sense. This conflicts with Luther's idea. Above all, though, it breaks the bond between Scripture and gospel that has become visible in history for the ministry of the good news. One must be on guard for any superficial phenomenology because of that very bond.

There is indeed a difference between the written and spoken Word. However, this difference is not one between impersonal and personal. A person is able to reject the living proclamation just as easily as the written Word (Rom. 10:16). In Scripture, both appear together without noticeable tension (Lk. 24:25,27; Mt. 22:29; Jn. 2:22). The problems begin to arise when Scripture is lifted out of its context and approached as an item "by itself," as letters. In that case the living Word is seen as the opposite of the frozen, rigid Word. A dualism of this kind is at bottom not only unbiblical but also unnatural. In practice no one notices such a dualism: witness the enormous interest in all "written words." For that reason the secondary, substituting function of the written Word may never be placed in opposition to preaching, for it is related to the living message both in origin and in aim.

The fixation of the written Word means the preservation of what is important. This historicity, shared by all human life, is not removed from the mystery of the gospel to such an extent that Scripture cannot be made into an instrument of the exalted witness of Christ. In history (the tradition from generation to generation) the Word has taken on this form of a servant in order that its power be retained and that the subject of the gospel may be heard in all ages. The written Word is never discussed in Scripture itself as an abstraction, but it always appears in a clear and appealing context. In the introduction to the Revelation to John, a beatitude is linked to the reading aloud, the hearing, and the keeping of the words of the prophecy, "what is written therein; for the time is near" (Rev. 1:3). The written text finds its place in the life of the church and is taken up into it; it does not stand in opposition to it as something rigid and frozen. It is therefore of eschatological importance. It need not be spiritualized or robbed of its "letters," but it must be heard and understood. We notice this relationship throughout the New Testament.

There is no isolated reflection on the difference between the written and the spoken Word, for one is always immediately referred to the meaning of Scripture. For instance, the reading of a letter from one of the apostles fills the heart with joy (Acts 15:30-31). There is a writing, reading, and understanding (I Cor. 1:12-14) in the light of God's grace. Paul wrote that one must read his letter in order to "perceive my insight into the mystery of Christ" (Eph. 3:4). It is indeed possible, by objectively comparing the written and the spoken words, to sense a tension between that which is rigidly fixed and that which is living and personal. However, in the sphere of faith and of meaning, of purpose and context, this tension disappears. Thus, it can be understood that the eunuch begins to listen to the proclamation of Jesus (Acts 8:28f.) by first reading Scripture and then hearing Philip, who again begins with Scripture. Likewise, the hearts of the walkers to Emmaus burned within them when Christ *spoke* to them on the way, beginning with Moses and all the prophets (Lk. 24:27,32). Unsolvable problems arise only outside this evangelical context. They are overcome because of the form of Scripture, which truly is the form of a servant.[10]

The question concerning the nature of the relationship between the written Word of God and preaching was repeatedly raised in the church. The question deals with preservation and continuity, with purity and the legitimacy of preaching, and with its conformity to the gospel. In order to get the problem into clear focus, it is best to ask whether we may perhaps speak of an identification such as Paul ascribed to the Thessalonians. For he thanks God that they received *his* word "not as the word of men but as what it really is, the word of God" (I Thess. 2:13). There is no hint here of a "problem." The Thessalonians recognized and accepted the real nature of the message brought to them, and Paul's gratitude in turn shows that this was the very intent of *his* word. This reference to the recognition of *God's* Word in human preaching is of primary and ultimate importance for the reflection on all preaching. Should the adverb "really" (I Thess. 2:13) be used without qualifications? One is often referred in this connection to a phrase from the Second Helvetic Confession, where this question appears to be answered in the affirmative at first sight with this statement: "The preaching of the Word of God is the Word of God."[11] We note the word "is" here. In a further

10. See I Thess. 5:27; Col. 4:16; Mk. 2:25; 13:14; I Tim. 4:13; II Thess. 2:15.
11. A. C. Cochrane, ed., *Reformed Confessions of the 16th Century* (1966), p. 225.

explanation it is said that "the very Word of God" is proclaimed through "preachers lawfully called."[12]

These formulations, of course, lead to further reflection about that legitimate calling. But what is the meaning of the word "is" within that legitimate calling? It certainly does not reflect a boundless trust in men,[13] but it most assuredly implies a trust in God's Word in relation to preaching. This preaching is not "useless," and it does not depend on "inward illumination." The will of God is mentioned with a reference to the missionary command of Mark 16:15: "Preach the gospel to the whole creation." It appears as though there is a direct continuity between the apostles and all preaching of later times, an unbroken manifestation of the "reading" of I Thessalonians 2:13. However, it would be incorrect to view this confession of 1566 and the entire Reformation from the viewpoint of a problemless "is," leaving no room for questions concerning self-evident authority. The Reformers always realized that this "is" could not and should not be discussed without further modifications, for all human preaching was preaching of the gospel and hence could not be understood without the relationship to the apostolic witness. This does not mean that because of this further modification concerning the "is" preaching necessarily would lose all authority, since this relationship is a critical and testing one.

The Reformation emphasis on preaching stemmed precisely from the conviction that the authority for preaching was inseparably related to the apostolic norm and to submission to the gospel. Even the words of the Second Helvetic Confession may not be separated from this context of the Reformation. The burning problem in this connection was not the "weakness" of the preacher, for Scripture itself clearly shows that the power of God's witness, which sounds forth into the world as the true and reliable witness, is not hindered by this weakness. The real problem was that of an authority that must be bound to the gospel if it is to be the true authority for the church. That explains the sense of the unique responsibility of preaching and the care to fulfill this task in conformity to the gospel. However, it is striking that this deep

12. *Ibid.* The wording is reminiscent of I Thess. 2:13.
13. *Ibid.* "The Word itself which is preached is to be regarded, not the minister that preaches; for even if he be evil and a sinner, nevertheless the Word of God remains still true and good."

sense of responsibility (the critical norm) did not lead merely to some hesitant words about the seriousness and authority of preaching. According to the Reformation view of preaching, the proclamation does not become a merely human opinion or message that appears to be somewhat "acceptable." The word "is" was not chosen accidentally and points in a different direction.

Nowhere is the authority of preaching expressed in stronger terms than in Lord's Day 31 of the Heidelberg Catechism. There we read that the kingdom of heaven is opened and shut with the proclamation of the gospel.[14] And sure words are added which approach the certainty of the word "is": "according to which witness of the gospel will be the judgment of God, both in this life and in that which is to come."[15] This usage of a "key" shows that we are not dealing with a weakening of the "is" and of authority. This use of the key of the kingdom of heaven clearly is not considered to be in contradiction to a text that exclusively refers to the Lord: "Who opens and no one shall shut, who shuts and no one opens" (Rev. 3:7; 1:18). Rather, against this very background of exclusiveness an open door was seen: "I have set before you an open door, which no one is able to shut; I know that you have but little power and yet you have kept my word and have not denied my name" (Rev. 3:8). Christ's exclusiveness is not announced in terms of a transcendent mystery that is wholly foreign and alien to the life of the church. The emphasis is rather on the church, not as a self-evident entity but in relation to the keeping of his word and the loyalty to his name (I Cor. 16:9; II Cor. 2:12). Of course, there is a danger that one may desire to take possession of the opened door and quickly to identify preaching with the voice of the Lord. This is the great and ominous misunderstanding with respect to all preaching, that the "is" of the confession and the authority of preaching is loosened from its context of the test and responsibility. It must always be remembered that strong statements like those in Lord's Day 31 find their exclusive legitimacy only in conformity to the apostolic witness.

It is absolutely clear that reflection on the relationship between Scripture and preaching is no secondary and trivial matter. Rather, it is inseparably related to scriptural faith

14. *HC,* Q. 83.
15. *HC,* Q. 84.

itself. Since it is impossible to separate form and content, the inner connection between Scripture and preaching clearly is found in the relevance of the *message* of God-breathed Scripture, which has the form of an appeal: "that you may believe" (Jn. 20:31). Here alone perspective on the continuity and actuality of the proclamation is found. The confession of the God-breathed character of Scripture belongs within the domain of the Spirit if it is a real confession. For the Spirit witnesses to Jesus Christ, convincing the world of sin, righteousness and judgment (Jn. 16:7-11). When this focus and aim of the preaching of Scripture becomes blurred, preaching becomes unbelievable in every aspect. Every rhetoric, emphasis, and accommodation becomes as ridiculous as form without content (I Cor. 15:14), for it is not related to the Spirit, who glorifies Christ (Jn. 16:14). For the Spirit's witness is focused on him to such an extent that we read the remarkable statement that he will not speak on his own authority, but "he will take what is mine and declare it to you" (Jn. 16:13-14). A preaching that has lost this context should no longer be discussed in terms of the God-breathed Scripture, for it is radically misunderstood at the least. The relevance of preaching is structured by the relevance of this Scripture.

Already in the New Testament we read of a perverted preaching that is in conflict with the relevance of Scripture and of the witness of the Spirit. The humanity of the preacher may be determined by motivations contradicting the message itself. At times Paul sharply and emphatically warns against preaching that seeks gain from God's Word, and he notes that "many" do this.[16] These apparent "motivations" have absolutely nothing in common with the message of salvation. This does not mean that for Paul preaching is personalized to such an extent that the proclamation becomes dependent on the person and his intentions. In Philippians 1, he writes about the motivations of preachers, motivations that are impure and stem from hostility to Paul. He deals with preaching out of envy and rivalry (Phil. 1:15), out of partisanship and insincerity (Phil. 1:17), or in pretense (Phil. 1:18); nevertheless, he states that Christ is proclaimed and in that he rejoices. It is quite difficult for us to see the background of these controversies clearly, but it is evident that Paul, without bitterness or reproach, focuses his attention here on the proclaimed con-

16. See II Cor. 2:17; I Tim. 3:8; cf. I Pet. 5:2; Acts 18:9f.

tent of the message, on the objectivity of the proclamation that refers to Christ and his salvation.

However, there is another kind of preaching in which the gospel itself is at stake and whereby a different gospel comes forward as a threat to salvation and the way of Christ (Phil. 3:2f.).[17] This preaching is judged according to its content, for it blurs the gospel message and can no longer be approached in terms of motivations alone. Here arises the great presupposition that the gospel must maintain its relevance for all times, the undisputed conviction of faith of the church for a long time. The point of departure was the New Testament calling to proclaim this gospel to the ends of the earth and to the end of the age (Mt. 28:19-20), the gospel of him who is the same yesterday, today and forever (Heb. 13:8). The program and the structure of all preaching appeared to be founded in the word "same." There were times in which aspects of the surprising and overwhelming newness of the message of salvation were blurred, and the proclamation appeared to become quite trivial — unable to awaken the deep resonance of salvation in the heart of man.

At the same time, however, the realization of the universal significance of the proclamation itself was not challenged. It was deemed "self-evident" that the content of preaching was that "same" Christ and his salvation for the "same" man in his distress and guilt and with his old and new questions. However, in our time this conviction is continually challenged by the pressure of many facts and questions from all quarters. This may be due to a doubt concerning the tradition of preaching in the church (its truly penetrating actuality and comprehensibility). It is striking that the analysis of our time plays an increasingly dominant role because of the realization that preaching becomes more and more incongruous with the numerous problems troubling man today. The question here posed is much deeper than appears from naive considerations of relevance, for it touches both on Scripture and on preaching.

One facet of the problem is the emphatic question of whether it ought to be considered legitimate to concentrate preaching on the concerns of personal "salvation." The problem is sometimes expressed in this way: Is that question still

17. Cf. K. Barth, *The Epistle to the Philippians* (ET, 1962), pp. 30f. concerning questions of prestige and concerning Pauline "superiority" in his "wholly objective concentration of interest" (p. 32).

our question in the same way and to the same extent that it was Luther's? To Luther it was a central and existential question because of his concrete struggle of faith. His question, as well as the answer, which actually annulled that question, was focused on a gracious God and was expressed in the confession of justification, the article of faith with which the church stands or falls. However, have not other questions, problems, and needs of today taken the place of this concentrated attention on the person – questions and needs that persistently knock at our door?

These considerations are governed by diverse factors. In the first place, we note a sharp reaction against a so-called salvation-individualism, paralleled by the realization that we are no longer troubled by Luther's question as the "ultimate question." Today the quest for forgiveness of sins and personal salvation is no longer in the foreground; other experiences force upon us the question whether human existence is still possible and meaningful. These experiences have to do with daily needs and dangers, and with moral questions in a cold, technical reality that is becoming more and more hostile. How are we able to live from God's goodness when we must experience the reality of God while in the power of a cold reality, coerced by inescapable relationships and fate's shadows, making an existence of human dignity impossible? If this is indeed the decisive question for us, then it is the same question that Luther faced in a different form: "a gracious God in spite of the experience of his wrath."[18] Thus, Luther's question is not totally pushed aside; it is acknowledged to be "a meaningful, perhaps even an unavoidable question," though its shape is different.[19]

This aspect of the problem of the continuity of preaching touches on an analysis of our age that leads to a hierarchy of questions, in which Luther's central question of justification and forgiveness has lost some of its pivotal features in a modification of form. Although some contemporary problems facing our "planet" are featured in the analysis of our age,[20] it is remarkable that many of our modern experiences are not char-

18. E. Leppin, "Luthers Frage nach dem gnädigen Gott–heute," *Z.Th.K.* (1964), p. 102.
19. *Ibid.*, p. 93.
20. G. Gloege, "Die Grundfrage der Reformation – heute," *Ker. und Dogma* (1966), p. 3.

acteristic of our time alone. We must recognize that various experiences and temptations were faced by man in every age in relation to the "hiddenness" of God. The most telling example is Israel's being pressed by "powers," so that life was taken captive and bound in distress, encompassing both the individual and the community. Perhaps the most penetrating experience was the long exile, seen in direct relationship to the wrath of God (Ps. 42:4,10-11; 43:2; 74; 88:15f.).

Even though one may have a keen eye for changes in history, he will be hard put to demonstrate that shifts in the hierarchy of questions are the unavoidable result of the specific characteristics of this age. One could fail to recognize the needs and temptations of an earlier period and overestimate the specific characteristics of our time. The continuity of inhumanity's manifestations in recognizable forms can be forgotten, while it cannot be explained at the same time (for example, anti-Semitism with its unfathomable aspects) from "the future that has already begun." Even for that reason one must be extremely careful to compare "questions," being on guard against the idea of a break in the continuity of human questions. The real problem of continuity and thus also of the meaning of preaching, seen in the light of the importance of Scripture, is not found in the absolute uniqueness of modern questions. It must be found in what is often called "salvation-individualism," which quite naturally may take on the form of salvation-egotism. This question, put to the preacher, is a rather penetrating one. For individualism and religious egotism undeniably have often influenced the structure of scriptural faith and preaching. The inevitable result of the development of human life was a turning away from the individualization of salvation, as some have noted. "Has not the individualistic question about personal salvation almost completely left us all?"[21] And does not all traditional preaching run the risk of becoming a voice crying in the wilderness?

It is not possible here to give a survey of all aspects of the discussion concerning salvation-individualism. Yet we must consider it for a moment, for it touches on the heart of all scriptural faith (a Scripture that is focused) and of all preaching. The background of this rather general protest is found in the fact that here we deal with a particular kind of soteriology. Man as believer is being isolated here in terms of a

21. D. Bonhoeffer, *Letters and Papers from Prison* (ET, 1967), p. 144.

"mathematical point," believing himself to be of utmost importance. It is an anthropocentric creed concentrated on the individual and his ego to such an extent that he becomes a lonely – albeit saved – individual. Ethical questions, his neighbor, life, and the world become secondary to him because of a secret opposition between "the other world" and "this world." One can find in the history of the church guilty individuals who were involved in this kind of perversion of the Christian faith. This individualism has often been connected with Protestantism, though an exception was noted in Luther's case. For to Luther justification did not merely have a forensic and declaratory nature, but it coincided with regeneration and sanctification. On the other hand, forensic justification was of foremost importance to the other Reformers and was considered by itself, even though sanctification had to follow it.[22]

There can, of course, be no doubt about the illegitimacy of salvation-individualism and salvation-egotism. It takes the form of man's seeking his own well-being in faith and of a concentration on his own happiness and ego, outside "the others." Thus, his view of salvation is so exclusively focused on the individual himself that it takes on the form of a "self-understanding" that is individualistic and merciless. This salvation-egotism is an arresting phenomenon, for it no longer manifests the contours of salvation itself in any respect. In fact, it is the very opposite of salvation because of the image "turned toward oneself," an image that is the opposite of divine love and mercy, which appears "for the salvation of all men" (Titus 2:11). Salvation-egotism has nothing in common with this "epiphany." A sermon not challenging this danger zone in a penetrating way certainly would not be based on Scripture. It would leave man completely in the dark concerning salvation. However, it would be a great mistake for the question of salvation itself to be pushed to the periphery in a protest to this salvation-individualism and salvation-egotism that seeks escape in the hierarchy of questions. For a time such an escape may appear to be an obvious solution, for it calls the believer away from problems of self-analysis and self-concentration to the wide horizon of life and the world. On the other hand, it must be realized that calling a person away from individualization, egotism, and isolation without perspectives

22. U. Meyer, "Zu Herkunft und Überwindung des protestantischen Individualismus," *Evang. Theol.* (1964), pp. 267f.

is possible only through a new understanding of salvation itself. Even though this too may take on the form of personal and individual life in view of the gospel, it is meaningless to play the game of a dialectic between interest in salvation and interest in service. The gospel of salvation itself goes beyond this tension and can only be truly understood and accepted as such.

The accusation of salvation-egotism, sometimes laid at the feet of preaching, cannot be based on the interest in salvation — even with its personal aspects. Every defensive protest bounces off the fact that the issue of salvation (in preaching) is placed before us in clear contours in the gospel itself. Someone motivated by salvation-egotism always (but unjustly) felt secure on this terrain, building up around himself bulwarks of the biblical witness. Hence, this problem cannot be conquered by a counter-reaction that blurs the evangelical clarity of the fact that salvation is "for us." The great presupposition of the gospel is found in the power of salvation, whereby the individual aspects of salvation can be and are preserved without the individual's becoming isolated, a fruitlessness that is the very opposite of salvation. Meyer has written of "the conquest of individualism by the motif of ministry."[23] But the depth of this conquest can be fathomed only when the question of personal salvation is taken into full account, yet in relation to the divine answer. Only in that context does this protest against salvation-egotism remind one of Paul's passionate "by no means!" (Rom. 6:2), which is far removed from any compensation or addition to salvation through "morality" or "good works." Rather, this exclamation makes us understand what salvation is.[24]

The solution is too simplistic and even wrong of meeting a preaching of salvation-individualism by shifting the attention from salvation to service. This kind of apologetic preaching is all too easy; one may not seek to escape the charge to preach the gospel. The gospel does not exclude the personal aspect of salvation, for that too is a part of the meaning, content, and reality of salvation. A conquest over salvation-egotism is found only in the gospel itself. By realizing this fact more and

23. *Ibid.*, p. 272.
24. *HC*, A. 64 reflects something of Paul's "by no means!" when speaking of justification: "It is impossible that those who are implanted into Christ by true faith should not bring forth fruits of righteousness."

more in the light of Scripture, we will begin to understand something of the continuity of scriptural faith and of preaching in history, which finds its norm in Scripture. The expression "the same" in Hebrews 13:8 acquires anew its meaning and actuality not in a reduction of all ages, experiences, world views, needs, and powers to the same level, but in a promise and perspective offered *in the midst* of all these. Thus, it becomes increasingly questionable whether "Luther's question" should indeed be considered alien to our modern times and thereby shifted to the periphery of interest.[25] It may well be that the hierarchy of questions — with its potential for shifting — is radically pierced in the light of this religious concentration. Then it will be understood to what extent this question of justification and forgiveness (the answer) is of decisive significance for new temptations that man may experience in his inner and outer life. The Reformers considered justification "the article whereby the church stands or falls." That did not merely concern an isolated chapter in the hierarchy of "articles," but it concerned a radical view of the epiphany of salvation — the cross and resurrection of the Lord. When this view is blurred either by a salvation-egotism or by reactions against it, salvation is misunderstood. The task of preaching is and remains to testify of this salvation and to contradict any caricature of it.

It is not an arbitrary matter to discuss these things under the heading of *doctrine* of Scripture; for it is part of the nature and function of God-breathed Scripture. Bavinck's statement that inspiration is "an abiding quality" of Scripture[26] indicates no bibliolatry. It does not refer to a "mysterious" event but to the Spirit and Scripture. Here we are treating a perspective that is not locked in the past, but one in which the future is embraced and disclosed through the Spirit, who "prepares the coming of Christ" in this way.[27] For that reason,

25. Barth, *CD,* IV/1, p. 530, expresses sharp reaction against the thought that modern man — compared with man in the 16th century — is "much more radically concerned about God Himself and as such." This represents a total misunderstanding of the radicalness of the question about a gracious God in the 16th century, namely, "to ask concerning God with this reality compared with which there is no other." That implies, according to Barth, not knowing what justification signifies, that it is not an arbitrary, sin-underestimating "tolerance," but *righteousness,* in which he is righteous. Cf. Rom. 3:26: "that he himself is righteous" (p. 532).
26. *GD,* I, 357.
27. *Ibid.*

true scriptural faith and preaching are inseparably related within the tradition and the continuity that are and will be founded in the Holy Spirit alone. Thus, the *meaning* of scriptural faith is to be understood not as a "form" of faith that can be isolated, but as the written word of the Paraclete, whose witness concerning Jesus Christ conquers all distrust. In that case we may think anew of the promise that pierces through to us in human words and of the biblical phrase "that you may believe." "The promise is a correlate to faith."[28]

Come, Creator Spirit!

28. Müller, *Die Bekenntn. schr. der Ev. Luth. Kirche* (1928), p. 142.

CHAPTER THIRTEEN

FAITH AND CRITICISM

IN LOOKING BACK ON THE ABOVE CHAPTERS, one is naturally inclined to attempt to summarize, or even compress into one formula, all considerations and all that has been said or intended concerning Scripture and its authority. Is it perhaps possible to offer a synthesis of all reflection on Scripture that may serve as a usable principle, as a kind of "method" whereby old and new problems may be solved and conquered? This is a natural inclination, for it indicates a desire to turn from the many considerations, questions, discussions, and divergences to the one way that is needful and immediately related to the true authority of God's Word for our lives. This desire is particularly pertinent in a time when it is felt that the questions outnumber the answers. Impressed by the many questions, one is inadvertently reminded of the "sum" that the "mind" of the preacher had sought but not found (Eccl. 7:27-28). One should ponder whether or not such a synthesis or "sum" is offered us as a matter of course in view of the authority of God's Word itself – in the obedience of a childlike faith.

To regard this as a cheap solution and to return to the "problem" slightly irritated is an absolutely irresponsible attitude. For we must be fully convinced that true scriptural faith is inseparably related to childlike faith and trust if we have indeed understood something of the Reformation confession concerning the testimony of the Spirit. The child is principally and overpoweringly involved in entering the kingdom of God according to the gospel (Mk. 10:15), and one has all but lost a real scriptural faith if he does not immediately relate it to the call to become "as a child." In this connection we recall Bavinck's statement that nowhere is so great an agreement found as that concerning the doctrine of Scripture.[1] He refers to a statement by Calvin concerning the experience of all believers. This agreement amid so many questions (fully discussed by Bavinck) is the result of a link with Scripture and its message that can be adequately described as obedience. This hope of "receiving" as a child, in the light of Christ's emphatic word "truly" (Mk. 10:15), should not tempt anyone to relativize or push aside the meaning of the searching reflection on Scripture over the centuries by means of a simplistic interpretation of this "childlikeness," that is, an attempt to outgrow the sonship. Someone who is inclined in that direction, either in theory or in practice, has his own limited idea of "being a child," interpreting this, without any further thought, as a form of naiveté that can scarcely be distinguished from immaturity. He overlooks the fact that childlikeness can be discussed in other connections — for example, in speaking, feeling, and reasoning as a child, which later can be given up (I Cor. 13:11) — while at the same time this sonship of God and receiving the kingdom as a child is not relativized.

To consider the phrase "as a child" a form of naiveté whereby serious questions and reflections are out of the picture is wholly untenable. When one reads the Bible completely and seeks to understand it, it inevitably becomes necessary to show what is meant by a childlike faith and trust. And all reading of Scripture through the centuries was undeniably related in various ways to that reflection on the specific meaning of childlike trust. This is not an isolated reflection that goes beyond this stage of a "child," for thought is focused on Scripture and its authority. Bavinck, in speaking of a childlike submission to Scripture, does not have the attitude of one who walks with closed eyes. He searches Scripture, even though there is much left in Scripture that arouses doubt, though there are and will be questions and struggles for a correct understanding of Scripture, objections and knotty problems that ought not be disguised or hidden from view. He knows that Christians throughout the centuries acknowledged Scripture to be God's Word, and thus one does not need to wait until all questions are answered and all difficulties solved.[2] Just such a childlike faith searches Scripture and in that search touches on many questions concerning Scripture.

1. *GD,* I, 561, 372.
2. *Ibid.,* pp. 412-413.

Thus, it is fully correct with respect to scriptural problems to be mindful of the one sum of childlike obedience. Precisely this obedience has been the subject of much thought in the light of the opened Bible. Questions and problems that disturb the silence and quiet of a childlike faith were always related to this search of Scripture. *A priori* answers cannot be found by means of a special method or a hermeneutical technique whereby all scriptural questions could possibly be solved by excluding them on the basis of a childlike faith. In essence, that would be a spiritualistic solution found outside the context of the words of Scripture. When the words are being devaluated, one runs the risk, despite his own intention, of undermining the authority of Scripture. The Word of God as a lamp to our feet and a light upon our path can only be accepted, acknowledged, and confessed by walking as Israel walked (Ps. 119), step by step, in continual amazement at that light in the midst of dangers and obstacles.

No single theory can convince us that we must venture out with this light and not be put to shame. A denial of this because of the dangers of an experience-theology would lead to but a shadow of trusting faith, for the latter is confirmed by the light on the way. We think of the meeting between Philip and Nathanael. Philip's witness concerning the newly discovered Messiah is a strange and unbelievable story in the ears of Nathanael. Around the declared mystery he builds his objections, which take the form of a counter-argument: "Can anything good come out of Nazareth?" (Jn. 1:46). There is no possibility for Philip, via theory or proof, to take the power of skepticism from that question and give an answer that goes beyond the given testimony. Only one possibility is left, the urgent call, "Come and see!"[3] Nathanael must go the way on which the mystery triumphs over all objections, as it is discovered, seen, and confessed with his joyful confession (Jn. 1:49). Here we are not dealing with a subjectification of authority, which might only become reality through acknowledgment. But we are referred to the fact that the unique authority can only be acknowledged and experienced on the way; it is not acknowledged on the grounds of a preceding consideration, and the way then followed as a conclusion. This acknowledgment cannot fall in one way or another into the hands of men or

3. R. Bultmann, *The Gospel of John* (ET, 1971), p. 104: "No attempt is made to give a rational defense."

into the grip of human reasoning. This is underscored by the Reformation confession concerning the Holy Spirit. It is the authority of God's Word itself that alone leads to an acceptance in the depth of the heart. The continuity of faith and trust is found here, not in human authority. Indeed, God's witness always comes to us in human form, but scriptural faith does not have its foundation in human trustworthiness. Through this Reformation confession the human witness is not devaluated in any respect (Lk. 24:25).

The acknowledgment that God's Word comes in human words can be compared to the experience of the Samaritans who believed in Jesus "because of the woman's testimony" (Jn. 4:39). When they met the Lord himself, however, they believed "because of his word," saying to the woman: "It is no longer because of your words that we believe, for we have heard for ourselves, and we know that this is indeed the Savior of the world" (Jn. 4:41-42). This is not to imply that Scripture's human witness is without value, as if it were possible to speak of an "eternal" or "false" witness in contrast to the security of the witness of the Lord himself. The word of the apostles came with an appeal to faith (Jn. 17:20; 20:29), but the mystery of the apostolic calling implies more than an appeal to trust men. In the end, faith is not founded on human reliability but on the explicit authority of God himself, the deep foundation of all apostolic authority. This authority does not exclude experience and man is freely a part of it; but *in* the experience the authority is acknowledged and confessed.[4] Scriptural faith is part of this acknowledgment and is manifested in submission and the obedience of faith. All reflection concerning this point is focused on questions concerning the relationship between *faith* and *criticism*.

We discussed at length Scripture's authority in relation to the interpretation of Scripture as it is determined and channeled by that authority. In reflecting on faith and criticism, we should keep in mind that the authority of God's Word is not being enforced like an arbitrary external authority. Rather, its purpose is in the way of the Spirit, which leads man to obedience and draws him in his full existence to the gospel and its good news. Wherever this authority becomes manifest we see a wooing and conquering authority at work. It may express itself in an apostolic authority that does not wish to

4. *GD*, I, 491f.

lord it over others (II Cor. 1:24) but is nevertheless a true evangelical authority, as is shown by the phrase, "we work with you for your joy." It is not an irresistible authority at work outside the sphere of all human activity and reaction. For it evokes that reaction when the thoughts of many hearts are revealed (Lk. 2:35). God's Word is not intended to have man in its grasp automatically (Mk. 4:26-27), so that man is reduced to passivity.

Nowhere is this portrayed more clearly than in the parable of the sower: that is, many diverse possibilities are present in connection with the seed of the Word. We read of a satanic aspect, whereby the seed is taken from the field, and of the rocky ground, and, when tribulation or persecution arises, of the choked and fruitless seed; on the other hand, we read of the good earth accepting seed and bearing fruit (Mk. 4:14-20). The Word of God does not switch off human reactions; it rather confronts the hearers with a choice and the necessity of a decision. Its authority does not have the features of an external authority, which in fact does not allow an encounter with any insight, understanding, or response. Scripture's authority does not demand blind obedience, because it is not blind itself. Even Paul, in speaking about submission to the authorities, does not speak in terms of blind submission. The "authorities" of Romans 13 are found in the context of ministers and servants of God, at work "for your good" (Rom. 13:4-6). Never does it have the features of a dark dictatorship that enforces its will in a despotic manner, with no concern for man's way of life under this dictatorship. Indeed, to the man who submits himself, God's Word is a far superior power.

A number of analogies come to mind to express the radical submission as a "happening." We read of a capitulation, of being persuaded by a superior power, and of becoming a servant. However, all these terms express the very opposite of slavish submission. It is rather a subjection that spells redemption. It is not a general kind of obedience that can be approached in a neutral or phenomenological fashion, but a subjection to Christ whereby he is never out of view. Thus, scriptural faith is not a blind faith, if one agrees with the Reformation perception of a direct relationship between this faith and the testimony of the Holy Spirit, in which acceptance occurs with joy and willingness. For the testimony of the Spirit is appealing and convincing, and all human testimony reflects this wherever Scripture is proclaimed. In every discussion about and from

Scripture, the challenge of "take up and read" and "come and see" is clearly found.

It would be quite wrong to think that this mode of the authority of God's Word would not issue in real obedience. But it would also be wrong to say that the Christian faith finds its very climax in blind obedience. This notion occurs when faith – even scriptural faith – is considered a "sacrifice of the intellect," an abandoning of human thought in the encounter with the revelation of God. This idea often prevailed in discussions of faith that reacted against rationalistic criticisms of Scripture. The desire was to counteract the opinons of a haughty and autonomous reason by putting in its place the "nevertheless" of faith as blind obedience.[5] Faith is then considered an irrational event that cannot be searched out in any respect and in which one subjects himself to the authority of God. This faith will easily reveal the features of the statement, "I believe because it is absurd," or "I believe because it is impossible." In those expressions the sacrifice of the intellect acquires the aura of the miraculous. Blind submission is seen as the ultimate God-honoring obedience.[6] However, that conception of faith is nothing but a caricature of the Christian faith, because that is not the way God deals with man; the Spirit, as the Spirit of Christ and of the God-breathed Scripture, does not blind man but opens his eyes and calls him to discipleship. Man in turn becomes a witness of what he has heard, seen, and tasted of the Word of life, "so that you may have fellowship with us" and "that our joy may be complete" (I Jn. 1:3-4). Faith in terms of a sacrifice of the intellect is a perversion of the Christian faith and of obedience.[7]

A concept of faith as a sacrifice of the intellect would never have received any agreement if it had not had a semblance of similarity to the obedience of the Christian faith. This analogy is seen particularly in the essential category of submission to God's Word because of its authority ("God has

5. It is, by the nature of the case, not possible to appeal to the "Blessed are those who have not seen and yet believe" of Jn. 20:29, because the "not seen" in Christ's statement to Thomas lies on a wholly different level than that of blind faith.

6. Something is intended which is quite different from the feigning of obedience of which we read several times in Scripture. See II Sam. 22:45; Ps. 18:44.

7. Concerning the sacrifice of the intellect, see, for example, G. Vahanian, *The Death of God* (1964), p. 221, regarding Bultmann. Cf. Bavinck, *GD*, I, 585-586, 562, 590.

spoken"). However, considering this obedience a sacrifice of the intellect is a dangerous view of faith; for faith would then be called to a decision without inner conviction regarding the object and content of the faith to which man is called. Inadvertently, this faith adopts the form of an achievement as a deed of blind submission; it will not be able to resist any temptation or sustain any struggle of the soul. It is a faith that "accepts." However, the acceptance is severed from the content of the message of salvation: it has no inner affinity with this message, and its reaction is resistance against any theology of experience. There is agreement, but there is no biblical trust, even though there is reference to the authority of God, which must be accepted unconditionally. Something of "nominalism" is always found in the sacrifice of the intellect. The inner response is not emphasized, but the bowing under the words of God as such is emphasized, as if such words were indeed spoken to us.[8] This willful sacrifice always led notably to an intellectual depletion of faith. This is something quite different from what Calvin said in his well-known definition (even though he speaks of knowledge): "Now we possess a right definition of faith if we call it a firm and certain knowledge of God's benevolence toward us."[9]

Faith can become depersonalized and empty, contrary to the entire witness of Scripture, in which no such abstraction is found. It is also contrary to the nature of God's message through concrete and meaningful words. Scriptural faith, therefore, cannot be characterized as a faith "on command" (Titus 1:3)[10] because of the authoritative fact that "God has spoken"; but it is a trusting surrender to God's Word in obedience. The attack against the concept of a sacrifice of the intellect does not imply a weakening of the confession of divine authority, nor a relativizing of obedience in scriptural faith (Rom. 6:16; I Pet. 1:14). However, this obedience is by no means blind, and human activity is not at all excluded. It is much more implied in the hearing of and the obedience to the Word (Deut. 6:4-5; 11:13f.). One is persuaded through the reality of the proclaimed content of the gospel so that he is not led to a

8. Concerning reason and authority, see H. A. Oberman, *The Harvest of Medieval Theology*, pp. 51f., 68f.
9. *Inst.*, III, ii, 7.
10. See the context of the "command" in Titus 1:3. Cf. Bavinck, *GD*, I, p. 586.

sacrifice of the intellect but to renewal of his thought (Rom. 12:2), born in the freedom of faith and issuing in gratitude and adoration.

We are dealing here with a faith that is not subject to rational yardsticks and needs no approval of rational verification and yet cannot be separated from insight. In scriptural faith a submission becomes manifest, which can be compared to some strange experiences referred to in the Gospels, for example, Peter's reactions to the word of Jesus not in terms of resistance but trust in the midst of doubt: "But at your word I will let down the nets" (Lk. 5:5). It is the faith of the centurion's trusting the effect of Christ's command even from a distance, a faith not even found in Israel (Mt. 8:9-10). The features of submission are clearly noticeable, and sharp imagery may be used to illustrate this humble obedience. However, all blindness is absent from this faith and it does not rest in a conviction concerning a formal authority that can and must be believed no matter what words are spoken. In contrast to the blindness of a faith of mere assent stands the believer's being convinced and persuaded, a freedom and adoration. This faith is no less full of *certainty*.

If the certainty of faith is possible only because it is based on God's Word as it comes to us in human words, and if, according to the Reformation confession, it is not the result of rational considerations, the question may still arise how it is possible that we are confronted by "questions of Scripture" and that "scriptural problems" are so often discussed. In view of scriptural faith (i.e., faith, trust, and obedience), can problems ever arise when obedience and listening are intimately related to each other? Does not this faith and obedience imply a clear and radical break with criticism and problems, as expressed in Solomon's prayer for an understanding mind, a prayer that was pleasing in the eyes of the Lord (I Kgs. 3:9-10)? These problems obviously have no other source than a crisis in this understanding mind. Are we not faced here with an inner and absolute antithesis between obedience and criticism? In view of the fact that "God has spoken," are we able to think of any other correlate than the one of which Paul testifies to Agrippa, that of not being disobedient to the heavenly vision (Acts 26:19)? In what way must we deal with the testing and sifting activity that apparently always accompanies the word "criticism"?

To find an answer we must first of all give up the idea

that listening to God's Word will ever occur in complete passivity, that is, a receptive attention that excludes all activity. We may start with the notion that in many ways Scripture itself speaks of the active attention of believers. It is expressed in human consideration and research, with no hint of a sacrifice of the intellect born of a surprise attack. In many ways believers are called on to test and to try: they are not only admonished to *do* God's will but also to *acknowledge* his will (Rom. 12:2), and furthermore to "approve what is excellent" (Phil. 1:10). That does not happen when believers have closed their eyes but when their love abounds "with knowledge and all discernment" (Phil. 1:9; Prov. 1:7).[11] This is so important because it is related to believers' purity and blamelessness, anticipating the day of Christ and working to the glory of God (Phil. 1:10-11). A great activity is visible in the congregation. Truth has not attacked it by surprise, excluding any activity, but the call is heard for a training "by practice to distinguish good from evil" (Heb. 5:14; cf. Lk. 12:56).

This research and this acknowledgment are not superfluous, for the calling to this comes precisely when love abounds (Eph. 5:9-11). This is the activity of the "children of light"; it is noteworthy that they must try to learn what is pleasing to the Lord, to arrive at the right deed and have no part in the unfruitful works of darkness. When the grace of God has appeared (Titus 2:11), eyes must be opened wide from then on. Believers must test all things (I Thess. 5:21); they must even test the spirits to see whether they are of God (I Jn. 4:1). Here there is no overpowering force at work that of itself replaces all other spirits. A testing is required now that the revelation of the Spirit has come in the midst of our ordinary reality, taking on the earthly and human form. Hence, there is no room for passivity, but we are rather challenged to intensive activity and clear insight and distinction. Here the man of God (I Tim. 6:11) is shown in his place, since God seeks to have fellowship with him in this way.

It may be asked, however, whether this activity does not clearly point to a dissociation from the norm of "God has spoken" and an association with assertions and pretensions by other voices of "spirits." Should we not say then that believers may and should have a critical function with respect to human writings and thoughts, but that with respect to Scripture they

11. *TDNT*, I, 187f.

may only be engaged in the activity of listening with an attentive heart because of the normative "is"? This brings us to questions and discussions of biblical criticism.

Biblical criticism took on many forms during the last centuries, including many excessive forms. Hence, there often was little inclination to study the various nuances of the word "criticism"; but attention was given especially to the presuppositions of biblical criticism. It was pointed out that many results of biblical criticism were not based on a simple listening to what the text of Scripture said, but on presupposed theories by which Scripture was read and explained. However, it is not easy to give a clear description of what "simple listening" might mean; and what is meant thereby is clearly important in connection with the practice of reading Scripture. The idea is not that one can approach Scripture as if it were a "blank sheet," with no particular interest in what the result of his biblical research might be. A "simplicity"[12] of this kind is not only unreal; it also threatens a true understanding of Scripture. An encounter with Scripture — within the church — is never an absolutely new situation, without a past or memories. But we are called precisely in that situation to a "readiness" to hear God's Word on its own terms and to understand the point it is making. True simplicity excludes "prejudice," that is, the placing of an opinion or decision ahead of the reading (I Tim. 5:21; Jas. 2:1-9),[13] so that one already knows his decision before God's Word is truly heard. A particular frame of reference has been established, and man, in fact, rules God's Word and judges it consciously or unconsciously, shaping ideas according to his "pre-judgment" (II Pet. 3:16). This prejudice is judged by God's Word, which itself discerns the thoughts and intentions of the heart (Heb. 4:12; Jn. 12:48).

In all analysis of "criticism," a radical view of this *kritikos* of God's Word must be preserved, whereby a sharp distinction is made between criticism *of* the word and *by* the Word. The question naturally arises whether any human criticism is in order in the light of this distinction. In popular language, the

12. Cf. Barth, *CD,* I/2, 469: "There is a notion that complete impartiality is the most fitting and indeed the normal disposition for true exegesis, because it guarantees a complete absence of prejudice. For a short time, around 1910, this idea threatened to achieve almost canonical status in Protestant theology. But now we can quite calmly describe it as merely comical."
13. Kittel, *TDNT,* III, 953 on "preconceived opinion."

word "critic" usually implies a process of sifting, separating the good from the bad, the true from the untrue; hence it is a judgment that always is partly a condemnation, for example, in the expression "criticizing the church." Even though the term "positive criticism" or a "criticism in love" is used in this connection, this criticism is clearly a testing and sifting by means of a norm that is above the church. Of course, with this concept of criticism a problem naturally arises regarding the confession "Holy Scripture *is* the Word of God." For such criticism is not possible or conceivable, at least if it is not to damage this "is." It is not possible to exalt oneself above God's speaking, nor to criticize it. It appears that God's Word can only have one subjective correlative, namely, faith. That the problem of criticism was often discarded without further discussion must be seen against this background. Is it not sufficient, in view of this "is," to remember Christ's admonition to Thomas in his temptation and doubt: "Do not be faithless, but believing" (Jn. 20:27)? The church may be exhorted to ask in faith, with no doubting, "for he who doubts is like a wave of the sea that is driven and tossed by the wind" (Jas. 1:6; cf. Mk. 11:23-24; Mt. 21:21; Rom. 4:20-21).

The biblical charge to believe the reliable Word of God implies something radical and total, and this radicalness is both challenging and promising in spite of all temptations and the tensions that result from ambiguities.[14] When God speaks, we are not dealing merely with a margin of reliability alongside another margin of unreliability, so that criticism may have a free hand in it. That kind of criticism belongs to the area of the contradiction that was resisted by Paul: "But who are you, a man, to answer back to God?" (Rom. 9:20; cf. Heb. 12:3; Lk. 2:34; Phil. 2:14; Rom. 10:21). Is this reply not clear and sufficient and does it not exclude any shading of meaning? Indeed, there is a certain critique of contradiction that can only be characterized as an obstacle to the knowledge of God (II Cor. 10:5), and this obstacle must be destroyed and overcome by obedience. Without further argument we are called away from this kind of opposition by means of apostolic weapons of warfare with divine power (II Cor. 10:4), because the contradiction is aimed at the unanswerable Word. Again and again in Scripture we hear warnings against this criticism of men who do not want to submit themselves either to hear

14. *GD,* I, 389.

or listen, against the criticism of the "natural" man, who "does not receive the gifts of the Spirit of God, for they are folly to him, and he is not able to understand them because they are spiritually discerned" (I Cor. 2:14). In view of the gospel, a stop is put to every prejudice – conscious or unconscious – for it falls outside the dimensions of salvation, which cannot be measured with the yardstick of any prejudice. For "no eye has seen, nor ear heard, nor the heart of man conceived" it (I Cor. 2:9), and the message is not "man's gospel" (Gal. 1:11).

Therefore, it is quite evident that the gospel is unanswerable, and for that reason Kuyper noted something "objectionable" in the biblical criticism of his day. Yet the word "criticism" can be used with a somewhat different meaning. The word became familiar even to those who, thinking of Scripture, confessed it to be God's Word addressed to us, and did not wish to belittle its authority. This is true of "textual criticism," a term that is generally used for the study that deals with the text of Scripture. It does not cause much concern, for it is regarded not as a desire to stand above God's Word but as a serious attempt to come to the original text. But along with this usage there are other shades of meaning. For instance, Bavinck does not just reject historical criticism without further arguments, but he makes the following modifications: "Historical criticism of Scripture is only resisted by the congregation to the extent that it attacks the divinity of Scripture and thus undermines the witness of the friendship of God, the hope of glory and the certainty of salvation."[15]

With the words "to the extent," Bavinck leaves open the possibility of an historical criticism that need not arouse resistance in the church. It is quite evident from Bavinck's total teaching on Scripture that he does not wish to introduce an element of doubt alongside the obedience to Scripture, so that this obedience might be relativized.[16] Nevertheless, he writes of a degeneration of historical criticism into a "hypercriticism" that destroys its object. It appears that here (just as with Kuyper) we touch on a distinction between a correct usage and a misuse of a certain critical approach or method. Even from the viewpoint of clarity, it is necessary and meaningful to ask whether such a distinction is legitimate. Here we approach the aspect of the scientific study of Scripture.

15. *Ibid.*, p. 567.
16. *Ibid.*, p. 389.

This is indeed an important aspect of the entire doctrine of Scripture, for it is inseparably related to the way God speaks to us in his Word – in the form of a witness through human words. God's Word does not break through or undo this human aspect; it comes to us in such a way that it can become the "object" of human research. The Word does not come to us by way of a supernatural evidence that makes every human activity superfluous and even dangerous. Indeed, the imagery of rain and snow from heaven can be used to indicate that the word of Yahweh brings forth fruit and does not return to him empty (Isa. 55:10-11). However, this does not mean that God's Word takes us by surprise and that we may only speak of the "event" of the Word, unrelated to any activity from our side. Frequently, too little attention is paid to the possibility and legitimacy of biblical research. A supernaturalistic view of revelation would consider any human "research" puzzling and inconceivable. It *is* conceivable, however, that one concern himself with the questions of whether and where God reveals himself, followed by recognition and discovery (Gen. 28:16). There is the example of the discovery Elijah made after the wind, earthquake, and fire, through a still small voice: "And when Elijah heard it, he wrapped his face in his mantle" (I Kgs. 19:31f.). In that instance, all that is possible is the tense listening at the entrance to the cave, and when God's voice is heard, there is only room for an *answer*. The same is true of the young Samuel, who gradually began to distinguish and understand, answering God's call: "Speak, Lord, for thy servant hears" (I Sam. 3:9-10). However, these instances themselves warrant the question whether the voice of God requires an immediate and direct answer. Is it still possible to speak of "research"? Almost everywhere, the church answered this question in the affirmative without a doubt: research is legitimate. Therefore, the question whether or not human opinion implies a critical function of man becomes quite significant.

It has always been recognized that in principle this research can only be considered legitimate and meaningful with respect to the human form of God's Word (Acts 17:11; Jn. 5:39-40). We note again the danger of thinking in terms of a competition between the "divine" and "human" aspects of Scripture, a dilemma that easily leads to an emphasis on the divine to the depreciation of the human, which is a misunderstanding of the God-breathed character of Scripture. As a result, God's voice "in the manner of men" is de-emphasized, so that there is scarcely room remaining for real research. However, in the light of the God-breathed Scripture, there is no sanction against human analysis of this Scripture. Eyes and ears may be opened wide in scrutiny of the written text when it concerns this witness of the Spirit. This has always been realized in practice, simply because God's Word comes in the form of language. Through the ages many believers feared that something would be taken away from God's speaking by the consideration of human questions and problems. However, in the course of history researchers faced real biblical questions without opening themselves to the charge that these questions were born of a desire to "criticize." The notion that such questions and problems could arise only from the subjective side of "seeing the truth" seemed incorrect; for not all questions disappeared naturally when a person had a simple and childlike faith. Thus, in later times the real human aspect of Scripture was illumined with increasing clarity.

Research is therefore warranted as both legitimate and necessary, but it should be done with eyes open to the dangers implied in every analysis. This is not a concession scholars have to make to an argument that Scripture is placed on a pedestal and came to us in categories and forms other than human ones. For the message of salvation, as the mystery of the Spirit, truly reaches us in human channels; so it falls within the circle of comprehensible language. If this is not taken into account, not even methodologically, in order to give greater honor to the voice of God, the essence of the Holy Spirit is denied. Research does not relativize authority or attribute greater value to criticism than to faith. Scripture is respected as the work of the Spirit, which, as the witness of Christ, says all that must be said through human writings, not partially but truly and reliably, in contrast to all prejudice, thereby preserving the great "stumbling block." The word is very near us in this central and all-encompassing way (Deut. 30:14; Rom. 19:8) and remains the judge of all our considerations.

There is another question often raised in close connection with analysis, criticism, and research. Does not the student of Scripture inevitably alienate himself from the listening congregation because of his attitude and approach? Is not the way of research much more complex than the less reflective approach usually prevalent in the church, whereby it derives strength from God's Word for life's battle? Often this question is directly related to the question whether research should be kept from the congregation in order not to disturb it with complex problems. This gives the impression that research might lead to correction of long-standing traditional ideas that through the years have been linked to the certainty of faith in Jesus Christ and are not to be separated from it, according to the feeling of many.

It should be emphatically noted that a criterion of this kind may never be used. The Bible itself is at stake, and a kind of "division of property" practically leads to the idea of a double truth, unacceptable to one who confesses the unity of Scripture. Moreover, a division of this kind is practically impossible because of the modern means of communication and the popularization of much research. Furthermore, it attacks the heart of the calling and the possibility of listening to God's Word in communion, and thus inevitably leads to a thorough-going crisis of scriptural faith. The confession of Scripture deprives us of a choice between science and faith; in addition, such a choice is unrealistic. One who chooses in principle for the supremacy of science over faith inevitably considers the congregation totally dependent on (biblical) scholarship.[17] One who chooses for faith over science inevitably withdraws himself from all deeper study of the Bible, its problems, translations and commentaries – so important for preaching and for the understanding of God's Word. However, rejecting this dualism need not mean that there is no possibility of scholarship's rendering a service, that is, with the degree of "dependence" implied in all service. The church is indeed served by much research. This does not deny that God's Word has led believers with its central clarity and accessibility and has comforted them on their way through the centuries. And, to be sure, science is not able to disclose the secret of the Spirit in Scripture. For that very reason it is absolutely wrong to place the scientific approach to Scripture over against a "naive" way of understanding Scripture, which would hardly claim to be a true understanding of it. A comparison of this kind naturally leads to pride, since it presupposes that the "real" message can only be discovered through the spectacles of science, particularly the science of the last few centuries. This view leads to painful frustrations and confuses the congregation, since it denies the mystery of Scripture.

In this connection, however, there is a real problem that

17. Kuyper, *Princ.*, pp. 327f., where he speaks against this idea.

is not related to an overvaluing of science but to the manner in which God's Word became accessible in history through human words. There is a distinct difference between scientific analysis and a more superficial reading of Scripture that asks less questions. It would create no problems if Scripture could be reduced to a number of central truths that could be known and understood by all. However, if such a reduction is shown to be a misunderstanding of Scripture — with its multiplicity of meaningful words — we can understand that continued biblical research may have meaning for the church. Just as with education, which helps to show the way to growth and insight, research can fulfill a corrective function, as the history of the church often indicates. Such "corrections" need not be indicative of a proud understanding of Scripture and a contempt for "simplicity."[18] Service and dependence are related, so that no one needs to be put to shame, and no one may glory in himself. But the important question is whether the way of analysis — with its large amount of detail — may not result in an interruption of true listening to the voice of God. It was pointed out by Smend that the way of listening was not closed by critical analysis. He expressed it as follows: "Criticism made an end to naiveté, but not forever; there is rather a post-critical period during which Scripture is again read naively."[19] His terminology ("naiveté") is not quite clear, and it appears as though we are dealing with different periods that follow each other. But the intent of Smend's words should have our full attention. For this claim is closely related to the call of the mystery of Scripture. We are not called to be captured in the net of analysis, discoveries, and details, forgetting that making words accessible simply means to pave the way for the understanding of God's Word through human words.[20]

The methodological attention to the words of Scripture (implying a research into all relationships without spiritualism) is no obstacle to the way of listening. It must rather be said that close attention to its meaning may result in the protection of the Bible reader against all arbitrariness, whereby the words of Scripture are violated through prejudices. Attention to goal

18. *Ibid.*, pp. 329-340. In addition to acknowledging the spiritual growth of the church without the help of theological science, Kuyper warns: "From clearer consciousness to go back to mystic darkness is obscurantism."
19. R. Smend, "Nachkritische Schriftauslegung," *Parrhesia* (1966), p. 218.
20. Cf. Barth, *The Epistle to the Romans,* p. 6.

and tendencies, to literary style and interpretation,[21] may sharpen the eyesight and so may become meaningful for the understanding of the specific contours of the message. A dike is thus erected against preconceived notions and postulates. Hence, every analysis and method is a responsible activity. But they may and must be accompanied by critical warnings; for the words themselves are at stake, resisting any human violence (II Pet. 3:16), words with the unique purpose to bless life with the power and the majesty of the Spirit.

In this way it is possible to resist and overcome the danger of losing "everything" in the analysis of Scripture and of letting it evaporate into thin air because of corrections felt to be necessary. No one studying Scripture will underestimate this danger. Is it not possible in the church to begin with research that respects the Spirit and end with the sad acknowledgment that nonetheless God's Word returns to us empty? Experiences of this kind are not negligible exceptions; they are manifested in the feeling of emptiness, alienation, and a loss of openness. This alienation is often accompanied by the acknowledgment that the road taken was unavoidable and necessary for the sake of truth, denying the possibility of return to a simple, direct, and childlike faith. Experiences of this kind are deeply rooted in what is called the scientific area of historicism, a relativizing process that undermines "everything."[22] It was no longer possible to discover a foothold in God's Word with its human form, a foothold that previously offered security in times of temptation and dizziness.

A situation might arise that can be characterized in the words with which Troeltsch was praised: "He was honest enough to limit himself to postulates after losing his Christian-theological convictions and to await the fulfillment of these postulates from the God of history. Moreover, he was courageous enough to persevere to his death in the painful situation of a man with empty hands, unable to do more than postulate."[23] Choosing the example of Troeltsch was not accidental, for it

21. Cf. *CD,* IV/2, p. 479.

22. Ebeling, *Word and Faith,* p. 22: "The question of the critical historical method is far from being a formal, technical problem of methodology: it is a question which, from the historical and the factual point of view, touches on the deepest foundations and the most difficult interconnections of theological thinking and of the church situation."

23. W. Bodenstein, *Neige des Historismus: E. Troeltschs Entwicklungsgang* (1959), p. 209.

was he who struggled throughout his life with historicism and relativism in his fight against supernaturalism. This is a form of truthfulness that brings the crisis to light, and it is of decisive importance to ask if this threat is necessarily implied in the fact that Scripture came to us in human words, in the "form of a servant."[24]

The person who respects the nature of Scripture has no other alternative than to answer this question in the negative. An affirmative answer has always led to an escape into spiritualism and sectarianism by persons who no longer think they need pastoral care with the new problems of these new times. However, it is important to understand that this escape does not entail a return to the safe home of simplicity and security after a dangerous period of wandering. For the dangers of prejudice, which acquire large proportions in any method, cannot be localized in the light of this written Word, for they are present in all reading of Scripture. Scripture itself shows these dangers in an unmistakable manner, even though it does not deal with modern scientific problems. It is possible to read Scripture in a frame of reference whereby a method — though unscientific — or a prejudice deprives human understanding of the mystery of Scripture. It is possible to read and use Scripture out of context and coherence, to isolate and atomize it, and to abandon it to arbitrariness and literalistic exegesis. It is possible to malign Scripture without realizing its dimensions, thus losing all contact with the focused command of God's witnessing to the mystery which was kept secret for long ages but is now disclosed (Rom. 16:25-26). It is possible to discover "Bethlehem" in Scripture without going the way to Bethlehem (Mt. 2:4f.), to search the Scripture without coming to Christ (Jn. 5:39f.), and to read Scripture and yet err by not knowing it (Mt. 22:29, 31). The words may be accessible, yet knowledge of the secret is not thereby guaranteed. Paul's words can be heard as the words of a madman (Acts 26:24). Therefore, dangers do not lurk exclusively in the area of science but in all reading of Scripture.

In view of Scripture's character, it is possible and permissible to regard the scientific approach not merely as a right but also as a duty. For the mystery of the God-breathed Scripture came to us in no other way than through accessible words. In the fulfillment of this duty, we may be victimized by preju-

24. Ebeling, p. 19.

dice even here, since it can creep into every method. A method may degenerate into hyper-criticism, clearly showing with what presuppositions Scripture is approached. If this is true, the method, not science in general, must be condemned. A plea must be made for increased rather than less scientific earnestness and resolution.[25] Only in this way may we guard against arbitrariness whereby an apparently open approach perishes in prejudice during this process of analysis. The struggle over the authority of Scripture does not originate in the dilemma of whether Scripture is or is not scientific, but centers in the *method* of science — its earnestness, openness, and its boundaries.

A certain unreasonableness can creep into a method at the very point where it begins to bear fruit in new aspects. Then the text is lorded over by methodology and can be put on the rack of that method. Not the test of reason but the test of Scripture itself will determine where transgressions have taken place and where, in the light of Scripture, the true "reason" implied in the accessibility of the words is found. So Paul does not counter Festus' interpretation with the statement that he does not and is not able to understand anything, but by characterizing his own words as "the sober truth" (Acts 26:25). Herewith the gospel is not at all rationalized, for it merely implies the refusal to capitulate to unreasonableness. No appeal is made here to blind obedience, for we are dealing with an appeal surrounded by prayer and spoken in the certainty manifested by clear words, related to those things that did not happen in a corner (Acts 26:29,26). Hence, the testing of every approach and every method is meaningful and necessary. Thereby it is not possible to encompass both the boundaries and the overstepping of them in a system by means of a "dogmatic" key that works outside of the specific words of Scripture. With its confession the church did not use an *a priori* or key of this kind, but gave testimony to God's Word in this Scripture. When the arresting fact that God's Word challenges us to

25. Cf. Barth, *Romans,* p. 8: "The critical historical needs to be more critical." Cf. his statement regarding criticism as "the measuring of words and phrases by the standard of that about which the documents are speaking — unless indeed the whole be nonsense. When documents contain answers to questions, the answers must be brought into relation with the questions which are presupposed, and not with some other questions. And, moreover, proper concentration of exegesis presses behind the many questions to the one cardinal question by which all are embraced."

research is understood and honored, the church will be kept from prejudice, from dogmatic exegesis and traditionalism, from the dictatorship of a method, and from neutrality. For the Scripture of the Spirit interprets to the church the great mystery and keeps the church "dependent" in a very particular way, so that its listening will never become a matter of the past.

Since the church is protected against this danger, we are also able to walk this way without fear. The fear cannot be overcome by human considerations; the very time when it seems to be suppressed it reappears in view of a new potential for anxiety. The problem of fear is not found in newly raised questions that cannot be immediately answered, but on a deeper level. The fear is that the foundation can no longer support the superstructure, so that "entrance into heaven" threatens to become a problem. For many persons feel that that facet of scriptural faith — believing "as a child" — appears to be in danger. No human agent and no single theory can halt this fear. If it is more than an apologetic game, there is only one way in which it may be conquered: through the Spirit himself, who opens the way through these questions, so that we do not lose sight of Christ, to whom all Scripture testifies. The fellowship of the church itself is not the most profound guarantee and authority able to take away fear, but the weapons of warfare against fear are manifest in the church: "So if there is any encouragement in Christ..." (Phil. 2:1).

The church of Christ would obviously not have kept this deepest mystery of Scripture if it had felt itself in the position of the disciples in the storm on the lake, when they asked the Lord: "Do you not care if we perish?" (Mk. 4:38; cf. Mt. 8:25; Lk. 8:24). His answer reveals his concern in terms of a counter-question: "Why are you afraid?" and "Have you no faith?" Moreover, these questions are accompanied by his word of authority over the sea. The memory of this situation points out the disproportion between much human concern and the reality of Christ. This fear is often the result of a situation that is no longer clear, so that one is deeply impressed by the dangers. With respect to scriptural faith, these dangers are particularly evident today in terms of a blurring of Scripture and in terms of many "counter-authorities," whether they come from the side of natural science or biblical science. In this situation it would be irresponsible for the church to neglect its pastoral care of answering questions to the extent that the questions are real questions. This pastoral care may not be described in terms of "protecting" the mystery of Scripture. We are not called to this kind of protection (it is taken care of), but pastoral care is meaningful and necessary when attention is focused in word and deed on the *message* of Scripture. For only by proclaiming this message does the meaning of Scripture become clear, as it is intended to lead us and to be a light unto us.

It may seem like a roundabout way to go from the message of Scripture to its unique authority. In reality, it is the true and only way to obedience. This way resists a relativism whereby the deepest intentions of the Spirit are no longer understood precisely in and with Scripture. In that case new questions will no longer appear to be like the wild power of the storm abruptly rebuked by Christ (Mk. 4:39), but will be questions that force us to continue to listen with ever-renewed attention in the spirit of the Israelite, who knew the commandments and asked precisely for that reason: "Hide not thy commandments from me" (Ps. 119:19). Peter's deed "at thy word" was a strange deed, yet it meant not a "blind" trust (in spite of all real questions and because of the temptation), for it was done in view of the Lord. Apart from this way, it will not be proven or made clear to anyone that this way of trust is and remains accessible. To consider this the "poverty" of faith would mean a denial of the miracle and the way of the Spirit, whereby he truly conquers precisely through human words and conquers in such a way that new witnesses are found again and again. In this way Scripture encompasses the ages. The way is marked by the mystery of Scripture, its inescapable goal, centrality, and simplicity. In this way the Spirit conquers the dangers of an objectivism that misunderstands the Spirit and of a subjectivism that loses perspective on the reality of Christ, and hence is not ready for the kingdom of God with all its dimensions to the ends of the earth.

These dangers are overcome in the relationship between the heart and Scripture. In spite of all differences, this road for the church is the same as that of the walkers to Emmaus. After they had recognized the stranger and encountered the living Lord just prior to the dispensation of the Spirit, they came to themselves and said to each other: "Did not our hearts burn within us while he talked to us on the road, while he opened to us the scriptures?" (Lk. 24:32).

INDEX OF PRINCIPAL SUBJECTS

INDEX OF PERSONS

INDEX OF SCRIPTURES